OBJECTIONS

Forms of Abstraction, Vol. 1

Sven Lütticken

Sternberg Press

CONTENTS

ACKNOWLEDGMENTS

Objections: Forms of Abstraction, Vol. 1 is the result of a personal, unfunded research project—or rather, a research strand—that developed gradually, morphing and mutating along the way. My 2008 essays “Living with Abstraction” (*Texte zur Kunst*) and “Attending to Abstract Things” (*New Left Review*), which were the basis of chapters in my 2009 book *Idols of the Market*, contain inklings of what would become the *Forms of Abstraction* project, as does the *2010 e-flux journal* article series “Art and Thingness.”

More than ten years later, “Performing Preformations: Elements for a Historical Formalism” (*e-flux journal*, no. 110, June 2020) presented a condensation of this first volume (partly overlapping with the introduction). In the intervening period, much of my work fed into *Objections* to a greater or lesser extent. The various chapters are based on these texts in particular:

Chapter one was originally written for *Curatorial Things*, edited by Beatrice von Bismarck and Benjamin Meyer-Krahmer (Sternberg Press, 2019). Chapter two goes back all the way to 2003, to an exhibition project by Krijn de Koning at the Musée des Moulages in Lyon; the accompanying book never materialized, but my text was later published in the journal *Kunstlicht* (nos. 2/3, 2004) and reworked for the catalogue/brochure for the exhibition “The Imaginary Museum” at Kunstverein München (2012). A first version of the third chapter was published in *New Left Review* as “The Coming Exception” (no. 99, May/June 2016). A first step toward chapter four, “Concrete Abstraction—Our Common World,” appeared in *Open!* online (2015) and in a more fully resolved form in Gean Moreno’s volume *In the Mind but Not from There: Real Abstraction and Contemporary Art* (Verso, 2019). Chapter five first saw the light of day as a two-part article in *e-flux journal* (no. 94, October 2018; and no. 96, January 2019), while the final chapter got its trial run in *Grey Room* (no. 59, Spring 2015).

I thank the editors of the various publications—including Susan Watkins, Rob Lucas, and Emma Fajgenbaum at *New Left Review* and Kaye Nielsen, Mariana Silva, and Ayham Ghraowi at *e-flux journal.* In the course of this project, a number of invitations for lectures and seminars also allowed me to try out ideas: Iman Issa invited me to Ashkan Alwan, and Holly Arden and Campbell Grant hosted me at the University of Queensland Art Museum.

While I was juggling my teaching and my freelance projects to maintain a precarious hold on intellectual autonomy, the development of this project benefited greatly from a variety of collaboration and exchanges, not least with my students—even if time for sustained writing was often hard to come by. Particular gratitude is due to Eric de Bruyn for his attentive reading of parts of this manuscript and his ongoing feedback, to Ana Teixeira Pinto for keeping me informed and on my toes, and to the artistic interlocutors whose practices have shaped my thinking (many of which are discussed, usually all too briefly, on this book's pages).

At Sternberg Press, Caroline Schneider and Tatjana Günthner saw this book through under difficult conditions—and with a difficult author to boot! Sarah Stephenson, Zoë Harris, and Rogier Delfos were instrumental in making it all come together.

Lastly, I'm happily indebted to Yen Noh, for making life so much more than survival.

Introduction

> "Form fractures whatever enters into its fold."
> —Paul Chan, "Odysseus as Artist," 2017[1]

Works of visual art tend to be concrete things, yet they have invisible and often checkered histories. Their sensuous presence comes with barely visible strings attached. This became obvious in the case of the Scheringa Museum of Realist Art, a private institution dedicated to modern and contemporary "realist" painting founded by Dirk Scheringa, owner of DSB Bank, a Dutch bank specializing in subprime loans. In 2009, when DSB went into bankruptcy, a creditor (the slightly more reputable ABN AMRO Bank) had the collection repossessed, leaving behind empty white cubes and orphaned wall texts and labels. Following the closure, supporters of the museum and their children covered the walls with graffiti. One by a twelve-year-old girl asked: "Where is the realism?" Another, spanning a corner, was particularly pointed—"This is realism"—suggesting, perhaps unwittingly, that real "realism" is an artwork dealing with the abstractions of today's financial capitalism.[2]

Scheringa's collection had attempted to stand in contrast to this, arguing that "realist" tableaus provided a firm hold on the real world, just as seventeenth-century Dutch art had done. His bank, however, was entangling consumers in financial constructions that provided them with material assets of a phantasmagoric nature, ready to disappear as suddenly as Scheringa's paintings. Still lifes of peeled lemons seem inadequate in this situation, as they melt into thin air. Proponents of "realist painting" usually pit it against what is seen as a regime of abstraction in institutionally sanctioned art, encompassing not only modernist abstract painting but also the even airier ideations of conceptual art. This is, consequently, a fight over form, but the Scheringa affair indicates that visual form needs to be seen in conjunction with formal registers that are less immediately accessible to the senses.

Never a neutral descriptor for a clearly defined phenomenon, the notion of form has always been an unstable signifier that has been paired off with concepts such as *content*, *matter*, or *structure*—creating dichotomies that haunted modernist and anti-modernist criticism and theory alike. With traditional iconographies being eroded by the storm of history, modernism often revolved around the problematic relation of form and content; Theodor W. Adorno's *Aesthetic Theory* analyzed form as a "sedimentation of content" in a far from effortless and remainderless process.[3]

If the form/content dialectic came to the fore in modern art theory and criticism, the pairing of form and matter had been a mainstay of Western thinking since Aristotelian hylomorphism, which analyzed substance in terms of matter (*hylos*) that is imprinted with form (*morphe*). And was there not a peculiar return to hylomorphism in modern formalism? Yve-Alain Bois, for one, has claimed that the modernist conception of form is, ultimately, "an Aristotelian one, where form is an a priori UFO that lands on raw matter."[4] And beyond rarefied modernist aesthetics, is capitalist technoscience not marked by what one could call an operational hylomorphism, in which designed forms do indeed remake matter and humans and social relations? Paul Chan has analyzed the templates of social media platforms such as

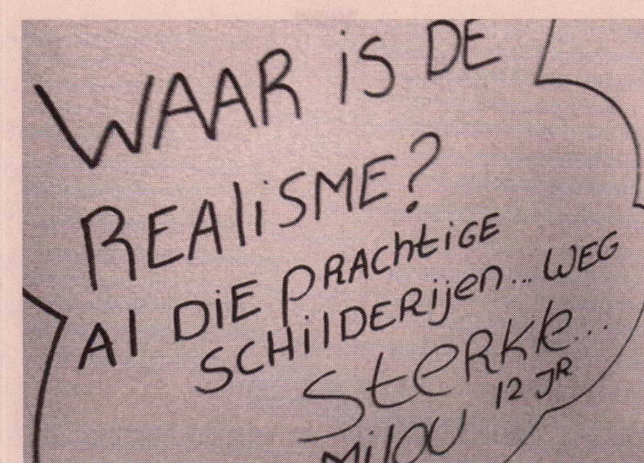

Graffiti written on a wall of the Scheringa Museum of Realist Art, Spanbroek, 2009

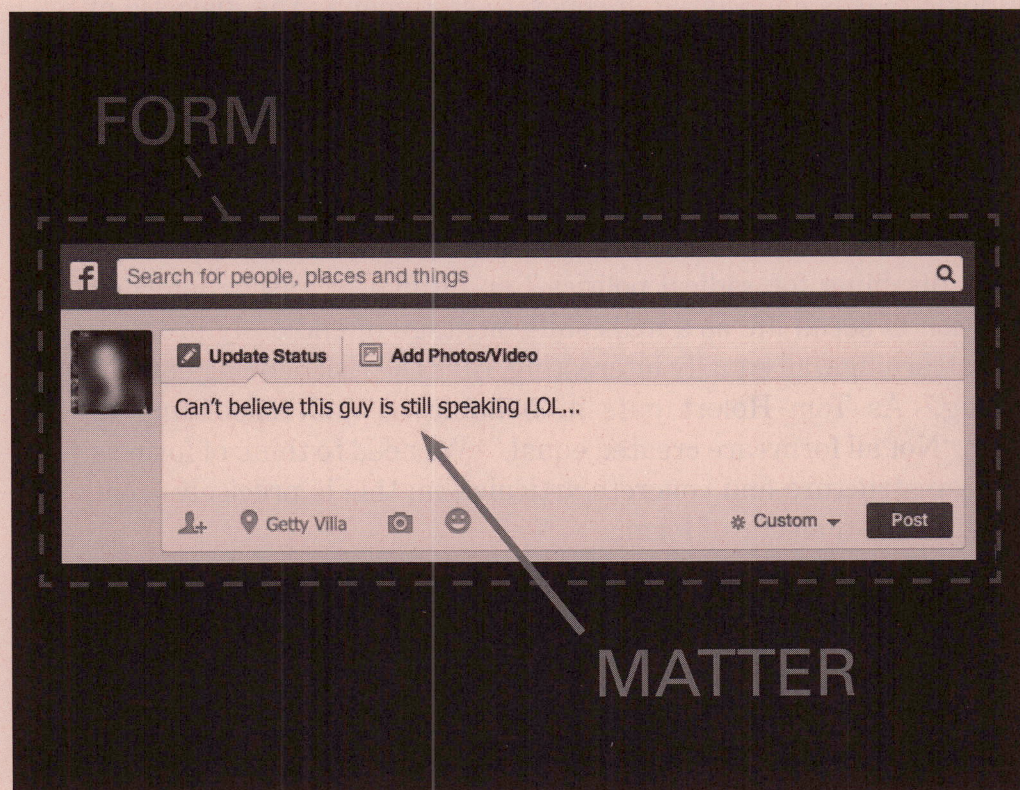

"This is a form," illustration in Paul Chan, "Our Data, Our Selves," 2019

Facebook, Twitter, and Instagram in hylomorphic terms, noting that "a form is something we fill out with what matters in our lives. And the principal substance that motivates and underwrites this operation is every bit as valuable, vital, and immaterial as what was once called the soul. Today, we call this substance data."[5]

The notion of form became such a master signifier of modern aesthetic theory precisely because it tantalizingly oscillates between the concrete and the abstract, the ideal and the real, the a priori and the post-factum, the immaterial and the sensate. Some formalists idealized specific compositional forms and colors in abstract art; a different breed, closer to Saussure, sought to identify the deep structural logic that is enunciated in concrete statements: the dialectic of langue and parole.[6] Meanwhile, Marxists analyzed capitalism as an economic system that shapes social forms. Caroline Levine's recent plea for a neo-formalist art theory that rejects the (Marxist and structuralist) privileging of "deep structures" in favor of emphasizing the patterns of lived experience strikes me as veering too far in the opposite direction. While I agree that "too strong an emphasis on deep structures is disabling for radical politics," an ultimately rather informal conception of social life as a makeshift montage of endlessly proliferating patternings, all equally interesting, runs the risk of being equally disabling.[7] As Tom Holert puts it, building on and responding to Levine: "Not all forms are created equal."[8] We need to think of form as both deep structure and concrete articulation; this is precisely what constitutes the dialectic of form.

Overall, modernity has been marked by the progressive becoming-concrete of the abstract, the productive operationalization of the abstract. However, this often results in a lack of sensuous concretion, a failure of form: the commodity may sit right before our eyes, but its *value* is not apparent to our senses. The object is pseudo-concrete.[9] And are these senses not themselves conditioned and shaped by economic and other historical factors? This is what Marx articulated when he argued that commodities have both a natural form and a value-form:

> In order for a thing to possess *commodity-form*, it must possess a *twofold form*, the form of a use-value and the form of value. The *form of use-value* is the form of the commodity's *body* itself, iron, linen, etc., its tangible, sensible form of existence. This is the *natural form* (*Naturalform*) of the commodity. As opposed to this the *value-form* (*Wertform*) of the commodity is its *social form*.[10]

Marx emphasizes that form is relational, though specific forms may be fetishistic condensations of the very relations that constitute them: "The money-form is merely the reflection thrown upon a single commodity by the relations between all other commodities."[11] And is the fundamental relation in capitalist modernity not that between subject and object, between worker or consumer and commodity? Today, the deep structure of the value-form has remade the natural form through the medium of design. This reshaping of the material world very much includes the subject—which is wearing a fitness tracker, has all but merged with its iPhone, and is optimizing its performance chemically. Meanwhile, as we self-objectify, corporations may be the real acting subjects of contemporary capitalism.

This book is the first of a two-part work, *Forms of Abstraction*, that engages with subject and object as the fundamental dual relation of capitalist modernity. The two parts that constitute this study—*Objections* and *Personafications*—represent different lines of inquiry rather than entirely separate topics. The first volume focuses on the position and production of objects and on forms of objectification more generally, and the second addresses modes of subjectivation and subjectification. Through these two volumes, I seek to concretize recent and ongoing mutations in the subject-object relation—that binary pair whose longevity, instability, and mutability are the results of the operational abstractions of capitalist modernity. How do the value-form and other real abstractions inform processes of individuation and socialization; how do they produce social assemblages and breakdowns? By raising and addressing such questions, I aim to contribute to the elaboration of a historical formalism that would be a component, or complement, of historical materialism.[12]

In the Scheringa case, the fate of the figurative representations in traditional mediums was profoundly shaped by the capitalist value-form, but also by juridical parameters (allowing the subprime loan market to grow) and technological factors (making it easy for consumers to apply for loans online or for credit institutions to trade subprime assets). The end result is a society of creditors and debtors, in which some may vicariously enjoy the aesthetic profits of their own peonage by visiting a display of "recognizable," "humane" art—providing viewers with a sense of mastery-through-harmony, which may actually be illusory and fragile.

Subject, Object, Tableau

For certain theorists, the *thing* has come to stand for what upsets and problematizes the "ordered ranks of objecthood,"[13] as described by W. J. T. Mitchell. Little surprise, then, that "thing theory" has met with significant success in art; after all, what artwork does not at least aspire to this? On the other hand, one might choose to emphasize that this alterity or non-identity is always latent in the object, as Vilém Flusser has done with recourse to etymology: "An object is what gets in the way, a problem thrown in your path like a projectile (coming as it does from the Latin *obiectum*, Greek *problema*). The world is objective, substantial, problematic, as long as it obstructs."[14] This sense of the object as an obstacle or obstruction, as a problematic thing, is the one I'm interested in. This is where the object, or ex-object, meets the subject, or ex-subject, or sub-subject. What about the human being as *thingified* obstruction—à la Melville's Bartleby, or indeed in the humanity of the slave as "screaming object"?[15] And what about the object as having no clearly defined existence, as always being subject to performance, to being re-performed, existing in transit?

Reflecting contemporary theoretical challenges to the modern subject/object division, the art collective Slavs and Tatars states: "We've witnessed the limits of a world perceived through the bug-eyes of René Descartes and thought through his alpha-male perspective of *cogito ergo sum*, where the subject and object are split. In this view, the subject is separate from the world: the former thinking, the latter unthinking and unconscious. Which is why the exploitation of the environment for human interests has been so easy: when it comes to Mother Nature, apparently, 'no' means 'yes' and all abuse is consensual."[16] Here, then, Descartes takes the rap for various real and/or perceived evils of modernity. By contrast, Bruno Latour has claimed that it was Western Reinaissance *painting* that "invented [...] *a pair whose two members are* equally bizarre, not to say exotic, a pairing that has not been observed in any other civilization: the object *for* this subject, the subject *for* this object."[17] To illustrate his point, Latour commissioned an artist to create a graphic of the subject/object pairing in which a master designer sets up the overall *dispositif* by putting a single, autonomous eye in front of a painting on which he arranges a Dutch still life by freeze-framing objects and arranging them for the gaze.[18]

Latour treats the picture plane as a window. When discussing objects, he refers to those represented by the painting, but never the easel painting itself as artifact or formal device. The easel painting or tableau is the exemplary form taken by Western art since the early modern period. Still lifes were a paradigmatic early form of easel painting produced for bourgeois buyers who could use their artistic property to mirror or mold and modulate their subjectivity. The tableau is both object and representation, both picture and image—though for Latour, to reiterate the point, it only seems to be the latter.

Etymologically and historically, the *tableau* is primarily an object, a "table," a material substrate for painting. It consists of wood or a stretcher on canvas. But a medium does not coincide with its material substrate, and the tableau is also the visual superstructure on top of this base; or rather, the set of conventions that organizes the medium's materiality.[19] In English, the term in fact never refers to the painting as a material object but only to the kind of scenes, of artfully staged figurative groups, that one associates with Western painting since the Renaissance: scenes that also can be staged with living people, as *tableaux vivants*. The tableau vivant is the tableau-scene without the tableau-object, the dreamlike image without the material picture, depicted by people in frozen motion.

Concerning physical pictures, Georg Simmel noted in a 1902 essay that the *picture frame* serves as a kind of buffer zone that sets the painting as object apart from the surrounding world: "For as a natural existence, each thing is a mere transitional point for continuously flowing energies and materials, comprehensible only from what has preceded it, significant only as an element of the entire natural process."[20] Simmel argued that the picture frame helps to turn the painting—the tableau—into a self-sufficient entity that needs no outside. The frame articulates and strengthens the painting's autarky: "It excludes all that surrounds it, and thus also the viewer as well, from the work of art, and thereby helps to place it at that distance from which alone it is aesthetically enjoyable."[21] Thus, the painting's seeming autonomy only binds it closer to the viewer. Set apart from the mundane mess of reality, the picture becomes a prop for the seemingly self-determining subject. Demanding an investment of subjectivity, or an opening up and emptying out of the viewer's (reader's, listener's) everyday person, the tableau becomes the site of human self-actualization.

In his essay, Simmel also draws an instructive contrast between the picture and a piece of furniture, arguing that the work of art is "like an island in the world that waits until one approaches it and which one can as well pass by and overlook. In the case of the piece of furniture, we make contact with it constantly, it intervenes in our life and thus has no right to exist for itself."[22] Of course, much art since the 1960s has worked precisely to undermine this distinction between a painting and a table or chair. The frame has been removed, and works of art have become seemingly "arbitrary objects."[23] However, this abandonment of the classic picture frame has meant an increasing reliance on, as well as a critical examination of, different types of frames: the gallery space, the institution, the art market, and art discourse.

Willem de Rooij's installation of one of Jacob van Ruisdael's paintings of Bentheim Castle in the castle itself (in a space that actually postdates Ruisdael's work, having been built in the 1750s) centers on a seventeenth-century tableau with a simple wood frame, but the whole installation also reframes this work. For one thing, the technology that is often hidden away is made visible by De Rooij's completely transparent display case: the alarm system and equipment for controlling the humidity, temperature, and light. The secondary frame—the display case—draws attention to itself and to the primary frame. De Rooij's installation exacerbates the painting's *Doppelcharacter* as image and picture, as landscape and object. In this act of reframing, the tableau-object itself becomes an image—the image of a physical picture. De Rooij's installation is a trap for the gaze: we are encouraged to pay attention not just to the tableau-image but also to the tableau-object. As physical pictures, all paintings belong to the domain of still life, that is to say, to the world of portable property.

Throughout the early modern period and well into the nineteenth century, still life was considered a lowly genre by academic theorists (especially in France) intent on safeguarding the position of history painting. However, art historian Victor Stoichita has argued that it was this very marginality that allowed still life to become a test space for artistic reflection on the medium of painting.[24] With its trompe l'oeil effects, early modern still life served as an artistic practice that claimed a certain degree of autonomy from the dominant regime of representation. However, such gestures were likely to be interpreted as divertissements for connoisseurs, and were thus neutralized as virtuoso exercises paying homage to refined (or quirky) tastes. The entire theoretical and discursive framework for art had to change in order for such gestures to be interpreted along the lines of Stoichita's analysis.

Modern aesthetic theory and practice since the decades around 1800 involved a problematization of the representational logic of the tableau. The aesthetic revolution toppled the hierarchy of genres, and the lowly still life became a privileged site for experimentation. By the second half of the nineteenth century, the critic Eugène Fromentin asserted that there are "great laws in little objects."[25] Cubism would make heavy use of still-life subjects, morphing newspapers and guitars into a quasi sign language and turning still-life painting into modern painting sui generis. Marcel Duchamp, originally manifesting himself in the context of Cubism, moved from the meticulously painted *Broyeuse de chocolat* (1913) to the readymades: objects selected rather than painted, integrated into the Duchampian network of obscure references and puns, yet also visual objects, object-images, precisely by dint of being selected and recontextualized. His 1917 urinal *Fountain* becomes the "Madonna of the Bathroom" or the "Buddha of the Bathroom," as Duchamp and his allies referred to the reframed object.[26] With the still life leaping into three dimensions, art effected an "objectual turn," which, in turn, bred performative practices.

As the stuff of still life par excellence, flowers are visual objects even before being painted. As per Bergson's philosophy, here matter already seems to be image. De Rooij has made a number of flower pieces, some together with Jeroen de Rijke, consisting of vases filled with artfully arranged real flowers. De Rijke / De Rooij's *Bouquet II* (2003) is combined with an illustrated text that has been presented in various ways; as wall text, as a brochure, or as an online text accessed via QR code. Written in a factual style and illustrated with press images, the text discusses four women—including a Miss Turkey who grew up in the Netherlands—whose lives reflect the relation between Europe and the Muslim world in various ways.[27] The bouquet is always made by a florist, within the parameters set by the artists. Associated with Holland but originally from Turkey, tulips must always be part of the mix, and the colors reflect Miss Turkey's dress when she was crowned Miss World—which, of course, is not immediately apparent from the bouquet itself. The relations between this piece's pieces are thus precarious and problematical; *Bouquet II* happens in the interstices between its parts.

An arrangement of flowers is, generally, meant to be pure visual plenitude. With *Bouquet II*, the image-object is placed in the context of a complex network of other images and narratives. The bouquet's presence is offset by a semiotic supplement. There is no synthesis; one can relate the work's various components to each other, but there is always a gap between the fragrant visual object and the images and texts. Form, here, is not conceived as fetishized and substantial, but as relational and processual. Such art is aesthetic practice that goes beyond the staging of a fixed subject/object opposition à la Latour's meta–still life. From the tulip mania of the seventeenth century to the current corporate push for patenting living organisms, plants have always been subjected to capitalist accumulation, and the flowers in De Rooij's bouquets are the product of centuries of (horti)culture.

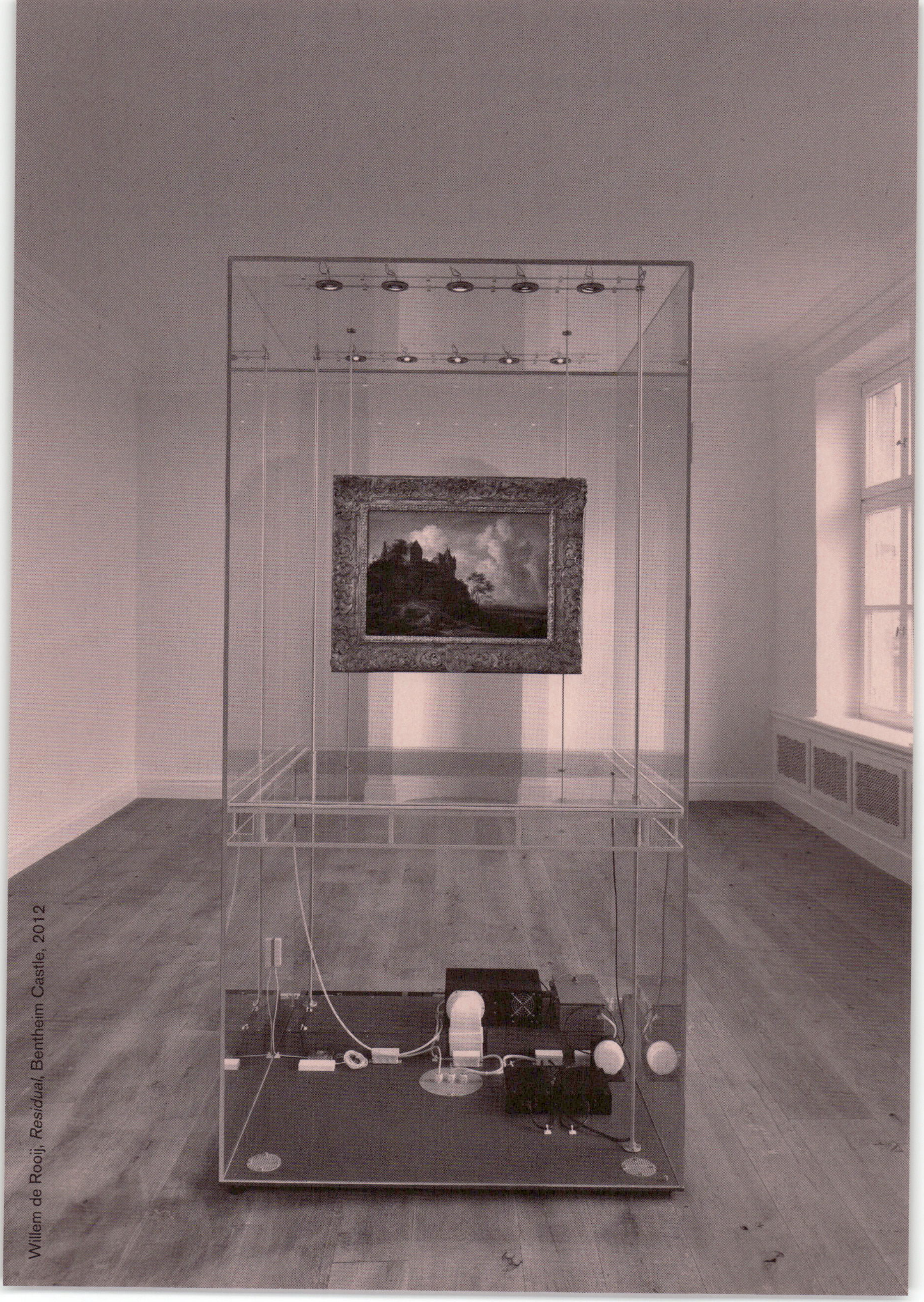

Willem de Rooij, *Residual*, Bentheim Castle, 2012

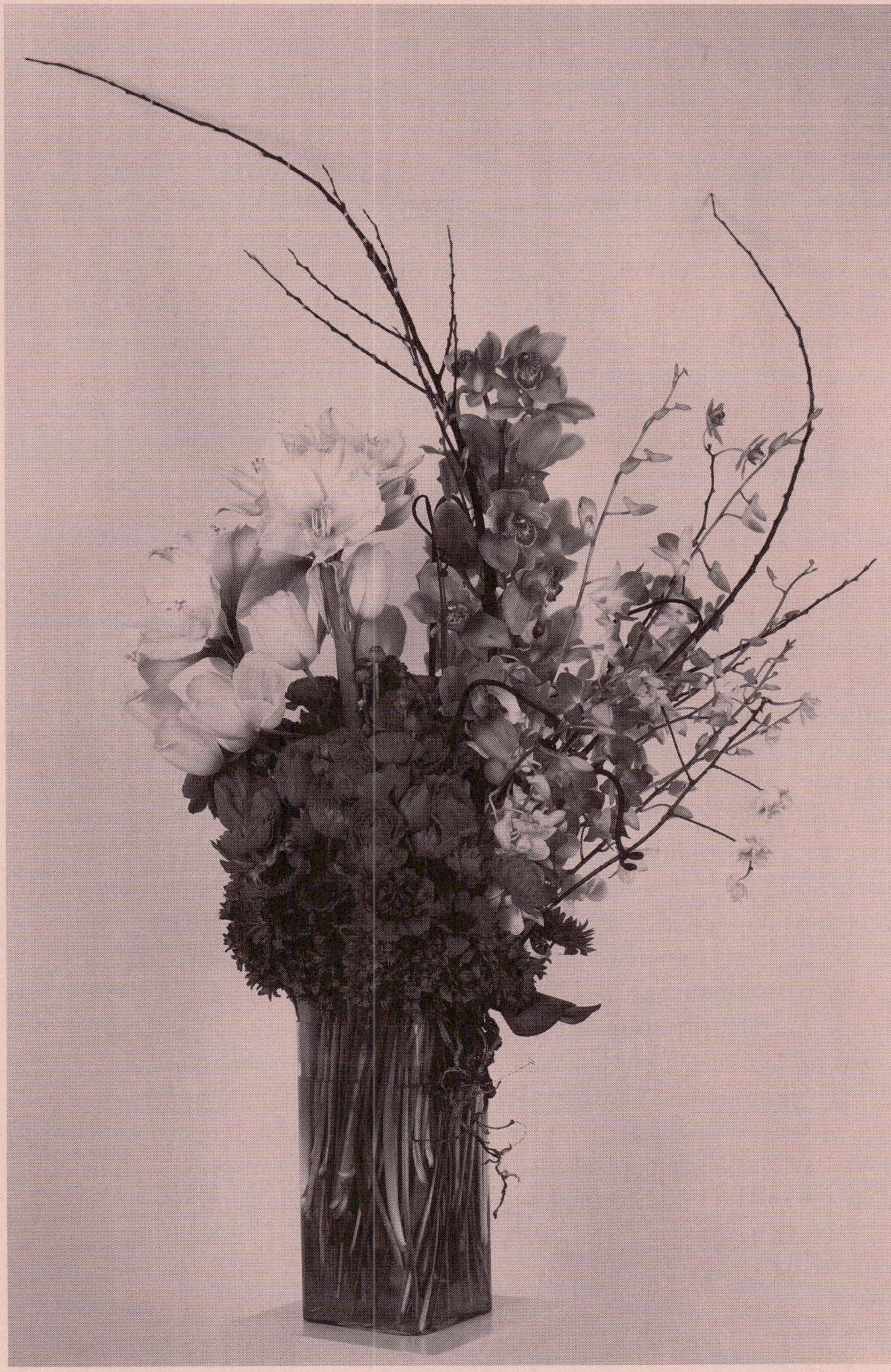

De Rijke / De Rooij, *Bouquet II*, 2003

As subjectivized objects, as floral fetishes, the flowers in *Bouquet II* and De Rooij's other pieces are mirage-like aesthetic apparitions (*Erscheinungen*) that depend on ongoing maintenance work. Before any specific realization, the editioned artwork exists as a kind of Platonic legal entity: it takes the form of a certificate of authenticity.[28] It is this that legitimizes the maintenance work by florists hired to "perform" the piece during exhibitions, to create its actual—mutable—form. Meanwhile, the online circulation of photos, descriptions, and reviews also adds value; it is part of the ongoing performance of the piece.

The Flattening

I'm interested neither in shoring up rigid dichotomies nor in flattening distinctions. How could I be, if the point of departure is aesthetic? Ever since idealist aesthetics, the artwork has functioned as a volatile subject-object. Aesthetic experience offered the alienated modern subject a glimpse of reconciliation, with the artwork suggesting a world in sync with the subject's deepest desires. On the other hand, aesthetic practice has also offered ways to think and act through modernity's antinomies—producing distantiating encounters with obscure artifacts and selves, rather than rosy reconciliation. If, in Melanie Gilligan and Marina Vishmidt's words, "in the history of the avant-garde and in much contemporary art, identification with objects has been an important aesthetic and political move for artists," this kind of overidentification or collapse of subjectivity into objecthood is predicated precisely on the reality of a split between the two.[29]

Thinkers such as Michel Serres, Isabelle Stengers, and Latour have attacked the modern subject/object divide through notions such as that of the aforementioned thing, which refuses to play the part of object to the triumphant subject—or the *quasi-object*, which has subjective traits. This labor of differentiation results in a certain flattening, especially with Latour, as "the humblest accessories henceforth play a role, as if there were no more distinction between the main characters and the extras."[30] Latour has created a seemingly welcoming and generous but ultimately hermetic universe of networks and actors. This universe is made up of endlessly multiplying and proliferating forms of agency, but there is no place for critique even in the face of cataclysm; no room for "the kind of inquiry that reveals the structure of antagonism generating these affairs, in the hopes of destroying them and generating a different configuration."[31]

Taking cues from Serres and Stengers, Latour has been something of a hype man for concepts that promise to extract us from the folly that was modernity. Keen on demonstrating the fallacies of the moderns, with their subject-object and culture-nature dichotomies, and on showing that "we" have never actually been modern because we are all hybrids, Latour dehistoricizes even as he appears to historicize.[32] He ends up with a home-cooked ontology of hybridity in which difference is curiously abstract and equalized. In Andreas Malm's words, Latour's definition of agency as "the ability to make a difference" is so general as to obviate the need for a true politicization of responsibility for climate change, for instance.[33] Contestation and critique (particularly of the Marxist kind) have always been Latour's real enemies; rather than engaging in the conflicts of history, it is much nicer to imagine vague "parliaments of things" that never go beyond ivory-tower pipe dreams.

As Joshua Clover notes, when Latour lists all of the human and nonhuman actors making up a network, these are "enumerated with an insistent leveling of its contents where what matters is that all these actors stand in ratio with each other, mute equivalents. It is as if exchange value had taken up a side hustle as a theorist."[34] Such valid critiques notwithstanding, Latour's problematization of agency is not entirely devoid of interest. In the register of aesthetics, it comes as no surprise that artworks can have agency that goes beyond (and sometimes against) an author's subjective intention. On a larger scale, the limits of intention and control have become all too clear, owing to the weaponization of human agency in modernity. Post-Promethean humans can feel (and be) helpless in the face of social, technological, and ecological processes they have set in motion.[35] Under the circumstances, it may indeed be expedient to consider the differences that nonhuman agents make, or to theorize the planet as a quasi-subject—Gaia. Those who refuse any suggestion of equivalence between different agents and their impact on the Anthropocene—or Capitalocene—can still find much critical use-value in Latour (see chapter six).

The law of diminishing returns kicks in with Graham Harman's object-oriented ontology. Radicalizing or caricaturing Latour's rejection of subject/object dualism, Harman concocts an ontology in which everything is object, from cars to corporations to fairytales. One of a number of "speculative realists" who oppose the "Kantian reduction" of philosophy to epistemology, Harman argues that modern philosophy sees the object as too superficial and/or too fundamental. The object is variously being "undermined" by those who see it as a surface effect, and "over-mined" by those who regard it as being inaccessible to human cognition—the Kantian *Ding an sich*, or thing-in-itself. Performing a daring "ontological turn," Harman and his gang brand most philosophy since Kant as merely "correlationist" in its epistemological filtering of reality through the human mind.[36] However, to attack Kant in a purely philosophical register, in the name of ontology, is extremely limited and limiting. The central chapters of this volume will engage with Alfred Sohn-Rethel's analysis of Kantian "thought-forms" as idealist versions of the value-form; the *thought abstraction* was merely a mystifying reflection of the operational *real abstraction* of exchange, which has remade the world in its own image.[37]

If we move from tragedy to farce, a similar critique can be leveled at Harman. The latter defines objects not in relation to any shared reality with human perception and life (as "sensual objects" that "exist only for another object that encounters them") but by being "autonomous in two separate directions: emerging as something over and above their pieces, while also partly withholding themselves from relations with other entities."[38] These conceptual objects are strangely like fetishized, auratic artworks—except that they don't share any white-cube space with other artworks, let alone humans. This takes us beyond the world so frequently photographed by Louise Lawler, in her pictures showing artworks (often cropped) in dialogue with each other. Lawler's practice is grounded in a tentative yet stubborn hope that this dialogue may be about something more than mere exchange value, even when the works are seen in an auction house or in storage. In today's freeports—those tax-exempt zones where artworks and other valuables are stored by the 0.1%—storage rather than public display becomes the natural condition of artworks. Noting that Harman speaks of the object as "a dark crystal veiled in a private vacuum," Stefan Heidenreich observes that packaged works of art seem to be the perfect realization of Harmanian objecthood, as "Harman's metaphysical conception of objecthood bears a striking resemblance to the requirements for things to be stored in a freeport," leading him to conclude that "the freeport represents the ideal environment for object-oriented works of art."[39]

Today's new ontology is regressive in that it negates the historical turn of thought after Kant. Both idealists such as Schelling and Hegel and a materialist such as Marx *historicized the ontic.* In the case of Marx, this became a full-blown attack on philosophy as a self-contained academic discipline, which is perhaps still too close to home and too close to the bone for certain academics.[40] In both German idealism and Marxism, the much-maligned duality of subject and

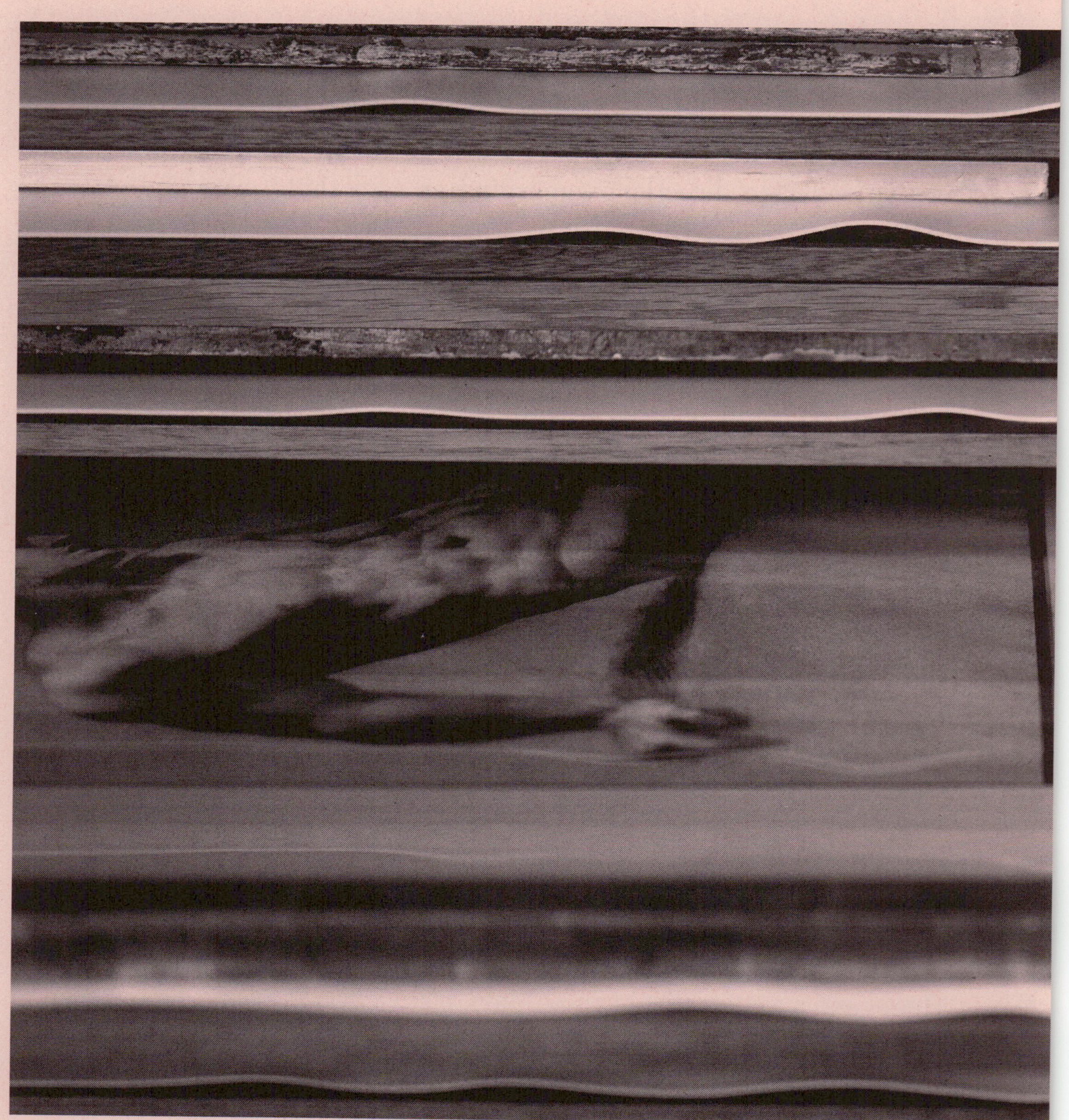

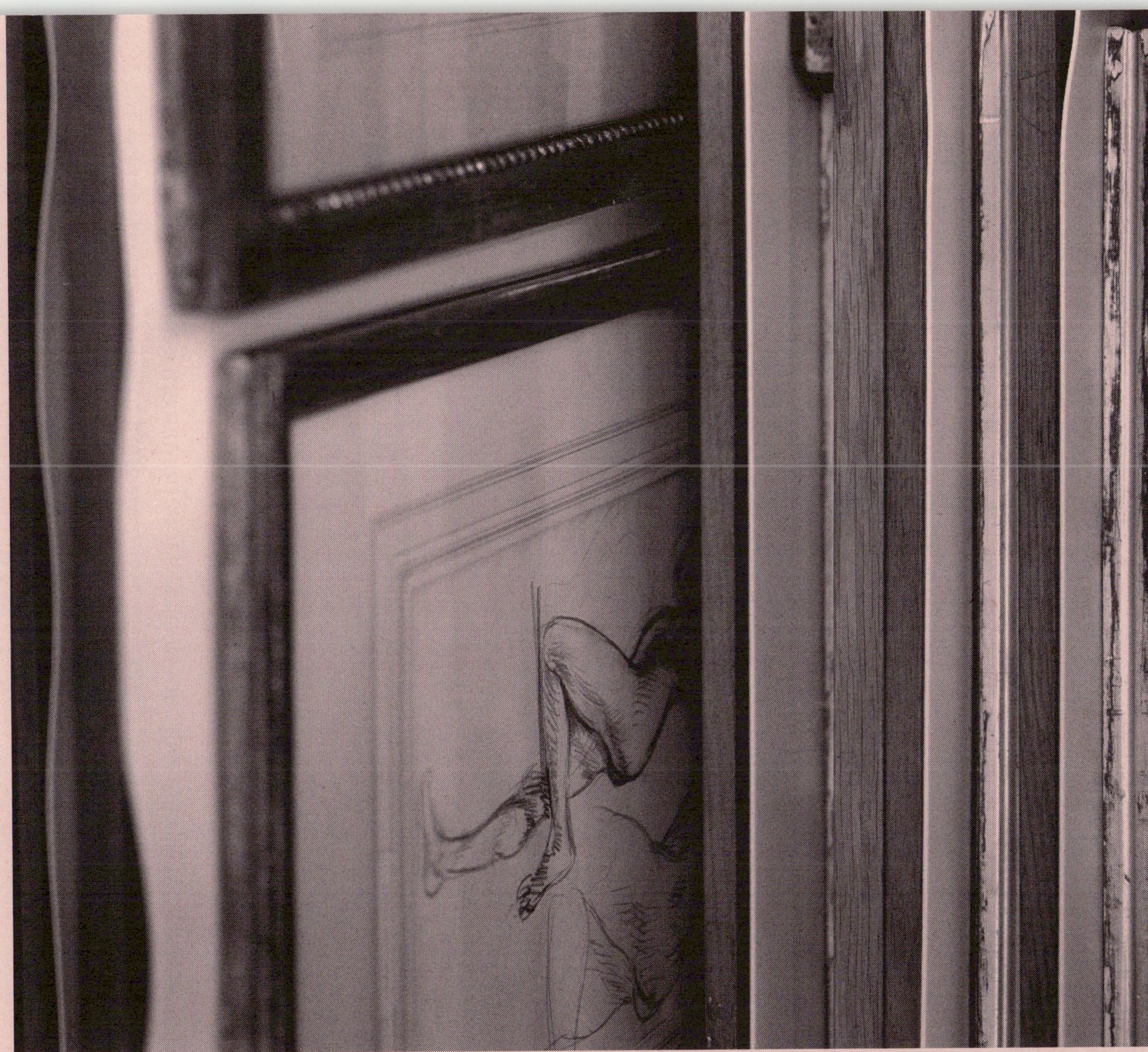

Louise Lawler, *Cabinet 2, Shelf 14*, 1997/1999

object became a dialectic in which neither pole can remain frozen in static opposition to its counterpart. The notions of fetishism and reification or "thingification" in Marxism attest to this. Historical materialism attempted—at times in crude and deterministic ways, to be sure—to think being as being in motion, in history, as never self-identical.

For Adorno, dialectics becomes properly materialist when the primacy of the object is established against idealist subject-centrism. While siding with the thingness of the object as that which remains an obstacle to complete human appropriation, Adorno also uses the term *Dinghaftigkeit* to critique the reification of human relations.[41] "The primacy of the object notwithstanding, the thingness of the world is also illusory. It tempts the subjects to ascribe to the things themselves the social conditions of their production. This is elaborated in Marx's chapter on the fetish."[42] Georg Lukács took Marx's notion of commodity fetishism (which will feature centrally in the first chapter of this book) as the basis for his theory of reification, or *Verdinglichung*—literally "thingification."[43] Aimé Césaire used the French cognate *chosification* to denote the objectification of colonized and racialized subjects—of which slavery, or the complete commodification of the human, is the most extreme manifestation.[44] More recently, Fred Moten pointedly noted that "the history of blackness is testament to the fact that objects can and do resist."[45] The objecthood of the enslaved Black sub-subject seemed to relegate it to a "dark," "benighted" past, yet Achille Mbembe suggests that it may in fact be a figure of the future:

> The Afrofuturist movement declares that humanism is now an obsolete category. Its exponents suggest that if we want to adequately describe the contemporary condition, we will have to refer to all the *objects/humans* and *humans/objects* of which the Black Man has been the prototype or the foreshadowing since the dawn of the modern era.[46]

The concept of reification has been suspected of evincing a crypto-idealist disparagement of the thinglike, but the thingness that is problematized is the specific thingness of the commodity fetish. What is crucial for Adorno is to combine "tenacious opposition against that which exists: against its thingness," with a staunch rejection of attempts to identify thingness as evil.[47] "In thingness there is an intermingling of both the object's unidentical side and the subjection of people under the prevailing forms of production—their own functional relations, which are obscure to them."[48] As fetish, the commodity appears endowed with autonomous life, as a kind of quasi-subject. The commodity is the modern object par excellence precisely because, as a product of alienated labor, it is then "subjectivized" by reified perception. In general, the problem of the object—including the artwork as object that is subject to positive art-historical knowledge—is precisely that it is too subjectified, too well integrated into a system of objects, while human relations, in turn, are objectified.

In his *Aesthetic Theory*, Adorno analyzes the modern artwork as an orchestrated dissonance of unresolvable antagonisms: content and form, mimesis and construction, subject and object—not, in other words, as idealist reconciliation. In one of many dialectical twists and turns, Adorno notes that it is the objective constitution of modern art that forces it to go through subjective mediation, even in the form of collective practices; thus the subjective part of the artwork is "a piece of objectivity."[49] This is not the place for an extensive reading or critique of Adorno's aesthetics, but one of its valid lessons is that concepts like "object" and "subject" need to be approached not as static entities forming rigid binaries, but as dynamic, operational abstractions that develop historically and get concretized analytically. The subject/object dichotomy, then, should be seen not as an error or illusion, but as an operative dialectic that is "a real reflection of the world of capital."[50]

Expanded Art History as Historical Formalism

Ultimately, the fight against "correlationism" is a fight against the aesthetic mode. Even when the aesthetic engages with the abstract, becoming a negative theology of the insensate, it always needs moments of concretion, of incarnation. This is precisely what puts it at odds with some of the object-oriented speculative realists. It is no wonder that a trendy proselytizer of object-oriented speculation such as Suhail Malik tries to "rescue" art from the aesthetic: since "contemporary art as the aesthetic experience of sense and value-making, as the co-constitution of the art object and subject, assumes correlationism and reproduces it," art must become post-contemporary by becoming post-aesthetic.[51] Even as it provides insecure (male) art students and aspirational edgelords with cool-sounding keywords, such para-theoretical freeport discourse robs contemporary subjects of tools for cognitive mapping, for navigating the networked real abstractions and their overdetermined articulations, for coming to terms with the disjunctions between distributed hyperobjects and their local effects, with the objectification of the human and the subjectification of the planet.[52]

With *Forms of Abstraction*, I want to stay with the trouble, to tarry with the aesthetic and with art as a mode of aesthetic practice that is always imperfect and compromised but has specific qualities and implications precisely for the ways it navigates degrees and mixtures of abstraction and concretions. I conceive of these two volumes as a form of expanded art history, or—to use a Clausewitzian formula—as a continuation of art history by other means: the means of critical aesthetic theory. In what amounts to a sketch for a historical formalism, I will analyze the *preformation* of subjects and objects, of things and persons, of artistic and social forms, of projects and networks, by what Sohn-Rethel (echoing Marx) has termed the real abstraction of the value-form. However, I will supplement this with an analysis of other real abstractions; in particular, those of the law and of technoscience.[53] The capitalist value-form molds the world and does so in conjunction with the formal schemata of the law and technoscience.

While I argue that certain dominant schemata continue to structure subjects and objects, relations and collaborations, I certainly do not mean this as a totalizing indictment. To analyze is not to affirm. I look for cracks and contradictions, for critical assemblages and immanent alternatives (however tentative and compromised), for different relations and forms of life in a collapsing economic, political, and cultural world order.

The structure of this volume consists of six chapters in three pairs. The first pair amounts to an introductory section on the artwork as mysterious fetish object that allows for a theorization of regimes of (re)production and objecthood more generally. The central section, comprising chapters three and four, homes in on the value-form as real abstraction that informs the artwork, and on two other strands of real abstraction next to the economic one: juridical and technoscientific. The last two chapters take this as the basis for an analysis of art practices that intervene in the nuclear regime as global hyperobject, and of the world as a global laboratory in which no form of life remains unaltered. The focus is on artworks that concretize the transformation of matter and of life by interlocking forms of real abstraction.

Personafications shifts the direction of the inquiry and starts from the human subject's formalization in "ordered ranks of personhood." While the factories in Bangladesh or China continue to produce the physical goods, their symbolic and cultural value and thus—significantly—their price are determined by the vanguardists of immaterial labor: by post-Fordist auto-productivists whose *autos* is less self-determination than self-control. In an over-designed world, the ultimate in design may not be the design of objects but the *self-design* of the neoliberal, entrepreneurial subject—a subject that is as thoroughly shot through by the forms of economic, technoscientific, and juridical abstraction as the latest iPhone. The two, after all, are bound together in a cyborg assemblage.

The planet has been covered in a communications web that amounts to a dismal version of the planetary *noosphere* posited by Pierre Teilhard de Chardin, later taken up by Marshall McLuhan as the basis of his global village in the 1960s, and once more reexcavated during the heady days of 1990s net utopianism: "A globe, clothing itself with a brain."[54] By now, the global hive mind often seems to be dangerously psychotic and delusional. Meanwhile, owing to the energy that went into the production of this noosphere, the biosphere of an anthropocenic and "subjectified" Earth acts up in unprecedented, unpredictable ways. Subject to a surfeit of design, the planet becomes a quasi-subject that cannot be locked away in any freeport. In this situation, *Objections* asks to what extent we can still speak of objects that function as critical obstacles and obstructions today, and whether artworks can be productive stumbling blocks that halt or redirect the flows of data, opinion, and spin that constitute the global psychotic subject.

NOTES

1 Paul Chan, “Odysseus as Artist,” *Los Angeles Review of Books*, December 21, 2017, https://lareviewofbooks.org/article/odysseus-as-artist/.

2 See Sven Lütticken, “A Heteronomous Hobby: Report from the Netherlands,” *e-flux journal*, no. 22 (January 2011), http://www.e-flux.com/journal/view/205.

3 Theodor W. Adorno, *Aesthetic Theory*, trans. Robert Hullot-Kentor (London: Bloomsbury, 2013), 192. Foucault traced the rise of the form/content dichotomy back to his “classical epistème” of the seventeenth and eighteenth centuries, while acknowledging that it only became consolidated in the nineteenth century. Michel Foucault, *The Order of Things: An Archaeology of the Human Sciences* (1966) (New York: Routledge, 2002), 88.

4 Yve-Alain Bois, “Whose Formalism?,” *Art Bulletin* 78, no. 1 (March 1996): 11.

5 Paul Chan, “Our Data, Our Selves,” *Los Angeles Review of Books*, September 19, 2019, https://lareviewofbooks.org/article/our-data-our-selves/.

6 Yve-Alain Bois, “Formalism and Structuralism,” in *Art since 1900: Modernism, Antimodernism, Postmodernism*, ed. Hal Foster, Rosalind E. Krauss, Yve-Alain Bois, and Benjamin H. D. Buchloh (London: Thames & Hudson, 2004), 32–39.

7 Caroline Levine, *Forms: Whole, Rhythm, Hierarchy, Network* (Princeton, NJ: Princeton University Press, 2015), 14, 17. For a critique of Levine’s cursory identification of Marxism with a fetishization of deep structure over sensible forms as mere epiphenomena, see Carolyn Lesjak, “A Democracy of Forms: Levine, Latour and the New Formalism,” *Historical Materialism*, https://www.historicalmaterialism.org/book-review/democracy-forms-levine-latour-and-new-formalism.

8 Tom Holert, *Knowledge Beside Itself: Contemporary Art’s Epistemic Politics* (Berlin: Sternberg Press, 2020), 95.

9 For the notion of the pseudo-concrete, see Karel Kosík, *Die Dialektik*

des Konkreten: Eine Studie zur Problematik des Menschen und der Welt (Frankfurt am Main: Suhrkamp, 1967).

10 Karl Marx, "The Value-Form," appendix to the first German edition of *Capital*, vol. 1 (1867), trans. Mike Roth and Wal Suchting, https://www.marxists.org/archive/marx/works/1867-c1/appendix.htm. This appendix also contained the first version of Marx's account of commodity fetishism, which was later integrated into the main text, along with the theory of the value-form.

11 Karl Marx, *Capital: A Critique of Political Economy*, vol. 1, trans. Ben Fowkes (London: Penguin, 1976), 184.

12 For a different use of the term "historical formalism," see Heide de Mare, "Gedisciplineerd kijken: Van kunstgeschiedenis naar historisch formalisme," in *Kunstlicht* 20, nos. 3/4 (1999): 14–20. Through a discussion of developments in Dutch art history, De Mare proposes a renewal of art history through "historical formalism," or the combination of synchronic and diachronic methods. The latter do not include dialectical materialism, which was anathema in the highly depoliticized field of Dutch art history in the period in question.

13 W. J. T. Mitchell, *What Do Pictures Want? The Lives and Loves of Images* (Chicago: University of Chicago Press, 2005), 112.

14 Vilém Flusser, *The Shape of Things: A Philosophy of Design* (London: Reaktion Books, 1999), 58.

15 See Fred Moten, "Resistance of the Object: Aunt Hester's Scream," in *In the Break: The Aesthetics of the Black Radical Tradition* (Minneapolis: University of Minnesota Press, 2003), 1–24.

16 Slavs and Tatars, "Mo' Hamann Mo' Often," in *Bathhouse Quackeries* (Berlin: Motto, 2018), 13.

17 Bruno Latour, *Facing Gaia: Eight Lectures on the New Climate Regime*, trans. Catherine Porter (Cambridge: Polity, 2017), 17.

18 Latour, 18.

19 See Rosalind E. Krauss, *"A Voyage on the North Sea": Art in the Age of the Post-medium Condition* (London: Thames & Hudson, 1999).

20 Georg Simmel, "The Picture Frame: An Aesthetic Study" (1902), trans. Mark Ritter, *Theory, Culture & Society* 11 (1994): 11.

21 Simmel, 11.

22 Simmel, 14.

23 Clement Greenberg raised the specter of the artwork becoming an arbitrary object in "Modernist Painting" (1960), in *The Collected Essays and Criticism 4: Modernism with a Vengeance, 1957–1969*, ed. John O'Brian (Chicago: University of Chicago Press, 1993), 89.

24 Victor I. Stoichita, *The Self-Aware Image: An Insight into Early Modern Meta-painting*, trans. Anne-Marie Glasheen (Cambridge: Cambridge University Press, 1997).

25 Eugène Fromentin, *Les maîtres d'autrefois: Belgique-Hollande* (Paris: Plon, 1896), 225. All translations in this volume are mine unless otherwise noted.

26 "Buddha of the Bathroom" is the title of Louise Norton's essay in *Blind Man*, no. 2 (1917), which is dedicated entirely to the "Richard Mutt Case." In her autobiography, *I Shock Myself*, Beatrice Wood later recalled that at one point Duchamp and Stieglitz decided to rename *Fountain* the "Madonna of the Bathroom." Wood, *I Shock Myself* (Ojai, CA: Dillingham Press, 1985), 30.

27 Jan van Adrichem, "Willem de Rooij: The Bouquets (2002–2010)," in *Windflower: Perceptions of Nature* (Otterlo: Kröller-Müller Museum, 2011), 177–91. A related project is Kapwani Kiwanga's series "Flowers for Africa," where the artist has florists create bouquets based on those in photos relating to postwar decolonization in Africa, but in this case, the bouquets are left to wilt.

28 See *Deed: Certificates of Authenticity in Art*, ed. Susan Hapgood and Cornelia Laufin (Amsterdam: Roma Publications, 2011).

29 Melanie Gilligan and Marina Vishmidt, "Economic Subjectivities in Crisis," in *And Materials and Money and Crisis* (Cologne: Verlag der Buchhandlung Walther König, 2013), 98.

30 Latour, *Facing Gaia*, 93.

31 Alexander R. Galloway, "Theory Hot and Cold," October 28, 2018, http://cultureandcommunication.org/galloway/theory-hot-and-cold.

32 See Bruno Latour, *We Have Never Been Modern*, trans. Catherine Porter (Cambridge, MA: Harvard University Press, 1993).

33 Andreas Malm, *The Progress of This Storm: Nature and Society in a Warming World* (London: Verso, 2018), 89.

34 Joshua Clover, "The Rise and Fall of Biopolitics: A Response to Bruno Latour," *Critical Inquiry Blog*, March 29, 2020, https://critinq

.wordpress.com/2020/03/29/the-rise-and-fall-of-biopolitics-a-response-to-bruno-latour/.

35 See also Fredric Jameson, *Representing "Capital": A Reading of Volume One* (London: Verso, 2011), 30.

36 This term was coined by Quentin Meillassoux. See Graham Harman, *The Quadruple Object* (Winchester: Zero Books, 2011), 136–38.

37 For an excellent compendium of recent theoretical examinations of real abstraction, see *In the Mind but Not from There: Real Abstraction and Contemporary Art*, ed. Gean Moreno (London: Verso, 2019). I return to (various interlinked forms of) real abstraction in chapters three and four, which go into greater depth concerning Alfred Sohn-Rethel and contemporary theorists while also touching on slightly more heterodox sources that have informed my thinking on the matter—notably the artistic-theoretical work of Alexander Kluge and of Harun Farocki.

38 Harman, *The Quadruple Object*, 19.

39 Stefan Heidenreich, "Freeportism as Style and Ideology: Post-internet and Speculative Realism, Part II," *e-flux journal*, no. 73 (May 2016), https://www.e-flux.com/journal/73/60471/freeportism-as-style-and-ideology-post-internet-and-speculative-realism-part-ii/.

40 See Boris Groys, "Under the Gaze of Theory," *e-flux journal*, no. 35 (May 2012), https://www.e-flux.com/journal/35/68389/under-the-gaze-of-theory/.

41 Theodor W. Adorno, *Negative Dialektik* (1966; Frankfurt am Main: Suhrkamp, 1975), 192.

42 Adorno, 190. For English quotations from *Negative Dialektik*, I have adapted the relevant passages from E. B. Ashton's dismal translation, *Negative Dialectics* (London: Routledge & Kegan Paul, 1990).

43 Georg Lukács, *History and Class Consciousness: Studies in Marxist Dialectics* (1923), trans. Rodney Livingstone (Cambridge, MA: MIT Press, 1971). In his 1967 preface/self-criticism, Lukács argues that he had been wrong to equate alienation with "thingification"; the latter is unavoidable and does not *have* to be alienating (xxiv). Socialism would presumably create a different thingness from that of reified commodities.

44 See, for instance, Aimé Césaire, "Discours prononcé par Aimé

Césaire à Dakar le 6 avril 1966," *Gradhiva*, no. 10, 2009, https://journals.openedition.org/gradhiva/1604. In English translations of Césaire, "thingification" is used for *chosification*. On Césaire, Marx, and Lukács, see Nick Nesbitt, *Caribbean Critique: Antillean Critical Theory from Toussaint to Glissant* (Liverpool: Liverpool University Press, 2013), 309n1.

45 Moten, *In the Break*, 1.

46 Achille Mbembe, "Afrofuturism and the Becoming-Black of the World," in *Futurity Report*, ed. Eric C. H. de Bruyn and Sven Lütticken (Berlin: Sternberg Press, 2020), 206.

47 Adorno, *Negative Dialektik*, 190, 191.

48 Adorno, 192.

49 Adorno, *Aesthetic Theory*, 68–69.

50 Gilligan and Vishmidt, "Economic Subjectivities in Crisis," 98.

51 Suhail Malik, "Reason to Destroy Contemporary Art," *Spike Art Magazine*, no. 37 (Autumn 2013), https://www.spikeartmagazine.com/en/articles/reason-destroy-contemporary-art.

52 Timothy Morton's notion of the hyperobject is one of the more productive manifestations of object-oriented ontology; see chapter 5 in this volume.

53 See, in particular, chapters 3 and 4 in this volume.

54 Jennifer Cobb Kreisberg, "A Globe, Clothing Itself with a Brain," *Wired*, June 1, 1995, https://www.wired.com/1995/06/teilhard/.

Chapter 1

FETISHIZE THIS!

ARTIFACTS AND OTHER AGENTS AT THE EDGE OF ART

A project by the artist Gert Jan Kocken, *Judenporzellan*, focuses on a set of peculiar artifacts: porcelain monkeys that were supposedly imposed on the Enlightenment thinker Moses Mendelssohn, confronting him with the realm of the grossly sensuous. It was long believed that this eighteenth-century German Jewish author had been obliged to buy some twenty large porcelain monkeys because of a 1769 decree with which the Prussian king Frederick the Great forced "his" Jews to buy items from the Royal Porcelain Factory in exchange for certain "privileges." The story goes that Moses Mendelssohn had to buy the monkeys in order to get married; in 1862, the author Fanny Lewald, who knew Mendelssohn's granddaughter, wrote about encountering them at her friend's home.[1]

There are a number of problems with this narrative: the dates don't match, and in contrast to the Meissen Porcelain Manufactory, the Royal Porcelain Factory in Berlin does not appear to have produced such figures.[2] The story may be no more than a family legend. Owing to the Nazi reign and World War II, the figures have been lost, making it difficult to investigate them. Kocken has exhibited large-scale photos of two contested monkeys that may or may not have been Mendelssohn's, accompanied by documentation and posters of the photos that people can take home with them. Together,

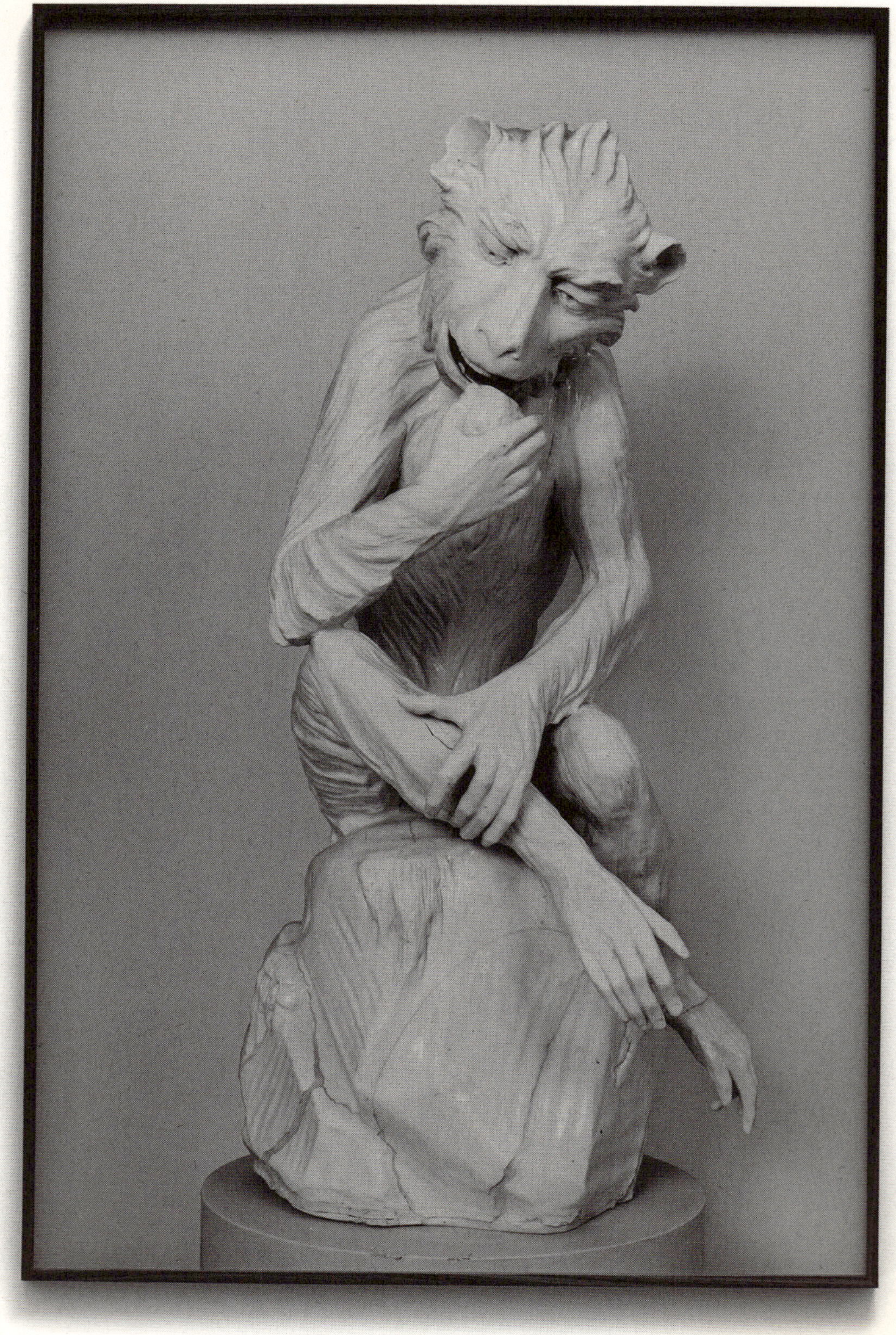

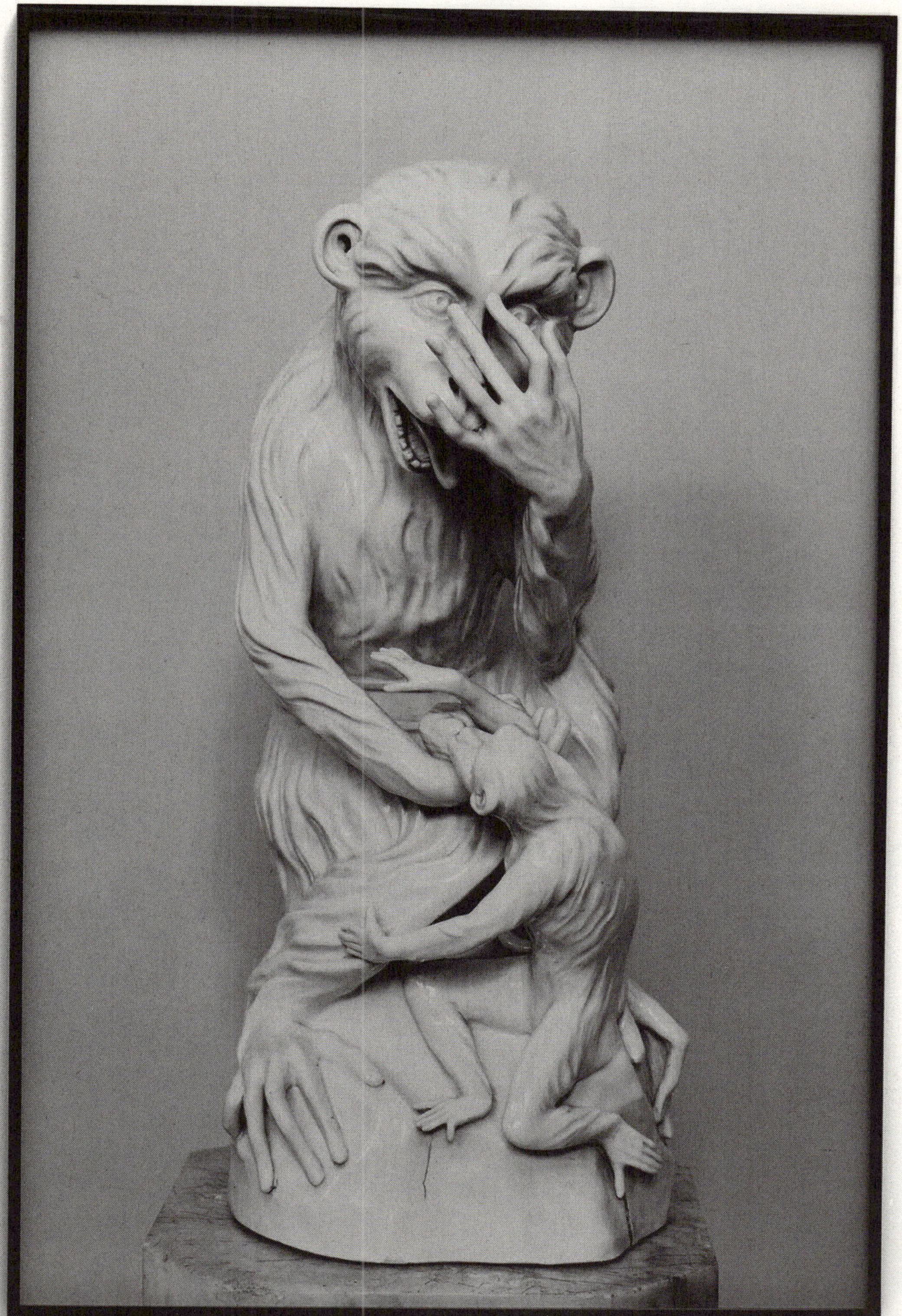

Gert Jan Kocken, *Judenporzellan*, 2009, details

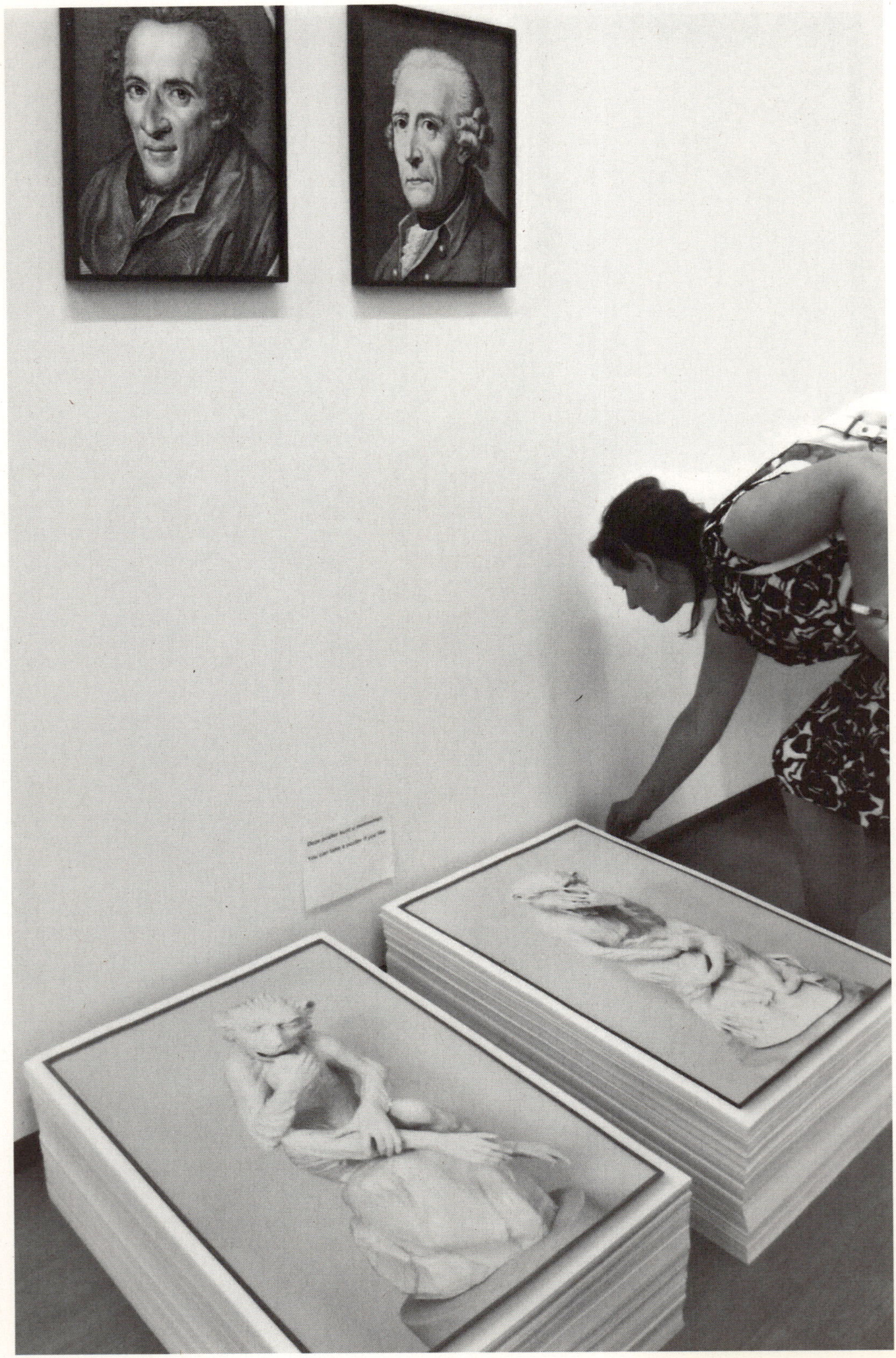

Gert Jan Kocken, *Judenporzellan*, 2009

these components invite a retelling, but also a reexamination of the "Mendelssohn monkey myth."

In her biography of the writer Rahel Varnhagen, written during the 1930s, Hannah Arendt notes that Mendelssohn's version of Enlightenment thinking made a strict separation between historical truth or facts on the one hand, and *Vernunftwahrheiten*, or truths of reason, on the other. History and society are not truly reasonable, as Mendelssohn may have experienced on a daily basis; hence, they lack legitimacy.[3] This is one specific articulation of the rift between reason and the world that necessitated the emergence of aesthetics as the field in which philosophy came to terms with the consequences of its own logocentric imperialism. Frederick the Great, the "philosopher king," found a way to make the aesthetic productive by making his Jewish subjects buy the products of his culture industry—porcelain manufacturing. The monkey myth may be so attractive and persistent because these cultural commodities are highly grotesque and because the monkey has always been a cipher of sensuousness unrestrained by reason and, as such, a mockery of the human subject. With the porcelain monkeys, the sensate and sensuous come home to haunt the Enlightenment as the *senseless.*

Fetishization

In the first volume of *Capital* (1867), Karl Marx theorized the commodity as a fetish. This was the term with which the Enlightenment categorized sub-aesthetic magical objects in "primitive" tribal societies in Africa. Theorists from Charles de Brosses to Hegel had used the term to denote the worship of seemingly "random" objects, often natural *objets trouvés,* in African cultures. In an 1842 article, Marx characterized fetishism in de Brosses's and Hegel's sense as "the religion of sensuous desire"—an earthbound religion before the abstractions of later belief systems.[4] That same year, Marx was planning a critical article on Christian art, which contained excerpts from books such as Carl Friedrich von Rumohr's *Italienische Forschungen* (Italian Studies, 1827–32), C. A. Böttiger's *Ideen zur Kunst-Mythologie* (Ideas on Art Mythology, 1826–36), Johann Jakob Grund's *Die Malerey der Griechen* (Painting of the Greeks, 1810), and de Brosses's classic 1760 treatise *Du culte des dieux fétiches* (On the Worship of Fetish Gods). The latter introduced the notion of fetishism as a distinct religious system preceding idolatry/polytheism and monotheism.[5]

The Portuguese term *feitiço* means "made by human hand." Referring to objects of witchcraft, it morphed into the pidgin term *fetisso* in the context of the colonial encounter with Africa in the late fifteenth century.[6] In this respect, fetish and artifact are virtually synonyms. Artifact, from the Italian *artefatto*, combines the Latin stem *arte* with *factum* for "made" or "produced": something "made with skill" by human ingenuity. In an etymological leap of faith, de Brosses linked the term *fétiche* to *chose fée* (fairy object, or magical object) to stress precisely that African fetishes were *chosen*, like readymades or objets trouvés, rather than *made*.[7] In a distorted manner, de Brosses's account may reflect the fact that many African religious practices revolved around magical, sacred substances that could be kept either in sculptures or in other objects, such as gourds.[8] There is thus always an element of cultural, semiotic labor—but not necessarily of object-making in a sculptural sense. The human mind may be a greater artificer than the human hand.

Marx also encountered the notion of fetishism elsewhere, notably in Hegel. For de Brosses and Hegel, fetishism denoted a state of religion and culture before the emergence of art in the true sense of the word. It was at a stage lower than idolatry, before humans formed matter, when they worshiped—according to de Brosses—random objects. For Hegel, consequently, fetishism had no place in the history of art;

at best, it belonged in the prehistory of religion.[9] However, the fetish's place outside the domain of "art proper" points precisely to an aesthetic problem that Hegelian idealism could address only indirectly: the problem of objects that appear to follow an obscure logic, that stand out from the natural world without reducing it to the status of passive receptacle for an ideal imprinted on it. If the artwork was for Hegel a *sinnliches Scheinen der Idee*, the fetish falls short of being the kind of spiritualized symbol that was the focus (indeed, the fetish) of idealist aesthetics.

Marx reformulated essential questions from idealist aesthetics—revolving around the relation between form and content and between concretion and abstraction—in social and economic terms. He appropriated the notion of fetishism to address an issue that is as aesthetic as it is political: while the value of commodities is determined by the labor invested in them, this labor does not "show up" in the object, whose value appears to be determined by its "social intercourse" with other commodities. It is an apparent autonomy of the value-form, of exchange-value, that produces the fetishistic effect. While the value of the religious fetish is supposedly intrinsic, the commodity's value is seemingly determined by the "social relations" entertained by different commodities; *in fact*, however, it is determined by the labor-time invested in their production.[10] This is the *Fetischcharakter der Ware*, or the fetishism of commodities.[11]

Lukács regarded Marx's commodity fetishism as an account of the "basic phenomenon of reification": human relations become *verdinglicht* as relations between artifacts.[12] On the other hand, the objects themselves arguably become subjectivized and animated in the process; the value-form comes to *inform* the commodity's *Naturalform*.[13] The uncanny and disturbing Mendelssohn apes hypostatize this subjectivation. While their history is murky and contradictory, the dominant narrative turns them into figures of fetishism. Having supposedly been imposed on the thinker as if by fate, these absolutist commodities become figures for the very state of fear and dependency that the feudal European societies of the eighteenth century projected on Africa. As Kafkaesque heirlooms, they appear to be stronger than their human owners. Kocken's remediation and recontextualization of these objects is also a redistribution of agency. As we are entering a post-democratic, neo-feudal state, we offset our inability to fundamentally challenge the system by keeping track of carbon footprints or slavery footprints—seeking to turn shiny commodities into problematic things whose social lives we can more fully engage with.

It is not usually acknowledged that the notion of fetishism also informs Marx's notion of *praxis*. In the "Theses on Feuerbach" (1845), Marx famously defined praxis as "human sensuous activity," and he came to think of his own work as a philosophy of praxis, and as philosophy-as-praxis. The phrasing clearly recalls his definition of fetishism three years prior, but with a crucial twist: desire becomes activity. Thus, we have two seemingly opposed strands emerging from his early readings on fetishism. On the one hand, there is the familiar trope of the commodity fetish, based on alienated wage labor that does not "show" in the commodity; hence its illusory autonomy as fetish, whereas its value is, in fact, determined by labor. On the other hand, praxis can be thought of as an "activated fetishism," or *fetishization* as activity rather than fetishism as a state. Such fetishization does not merely remain entangled in the world through desire, but seeks to actively transform it. This active fetishism goes against and beyond labor.[14] Wage labor is commodified and alienated praxis—just as commodity fetishism is a reification of praxis as *fetishization*, as activity.[15]

As Jean Baudrillard noted in 1972:

> [The term fetishism] has undergone a curious semantic distortion. Today it refers to a force, a supernatural property of the object and

> hence to a similar magical potential in the subject, through schemas of projection and capture, alienation and reappropriation. But originally it signified exactly the opposite: a *fabrication*, an artifact, a labour of appearances and signs.[16]

The real object of Baudrillard's critique is Marx and his notion of commodity fetishism. In contrast to what Baudrillard suggests, Marx and his followers always emphasized that the commodity fetish is, in fact, fabricated, the product of (hidden) labor, which has to be uncovered through analysis and action. Furthermore, as suggested in the above, Marx's notion of praxis can be interpreted in terms of active fetishization (as opposed to fetishism as state). To be sure, Baudrillard's own version of such fetishistic activity reflects the semiotic turn in the humanities and the rise of immaterial labor: he interprets *fainctise* as trickery, as the "cultural sign labor" that produces the fetish.[17] Here, labor is the work of signification. However, in the 1970s and after, Baudrillard would give ever more totalizing accounts of "the code," whose semiotic oppositions seemed to be programmed a priori, without any room for human agency. Baudrillard came to fetishize the fetishism of the code.[18]

Qua critique of Marx, Latour is Baudrillard's true heir. Latour argues that in modern thought—and this very much includes Marx and Marxism—the object is forever being interpreted as a fetish that is *both* too powerful *and* completely powerless, having an uncanny power over the subject even while being a hollow illusion. Modern theory has it both ways, to make sure that the critic is "always right": "When he or she debunks the claims of the fetishist by showing the work of his or her hands [...] or when he or she debunks the naïve belief in freedom by showing the weight of determination."[19] After all, the subject "is either so powerful that he or she can create everything out of his or her own labor [...] or nothing but a mere receptacle for the forces of determinations known by natural and social sciences." Meanwhile, the subject's other half, the object, "is either nothing but a screen on which to project human free will [...] or so powerful that it causally determines what humans think and do."[20]

Critiquing this "double operation of critique," Latour argues that "to believe that these terms describe anything at all about the real world amounts to taking an abstraction for a description."[21] The moderns end up with an account of reality that is a "portrait of humans parading against a background of things."[22] While Latour throws some of the fundamental operations of modern thought into sharp relief, Alexander Galloway has argued that his attack on critique amounts to a disabling double denial:

> Denying Kant he dismisses the kind of inquiry that would plumb the conditions of possibility for the present state of affairs, in the hopes of auto-position via better self-clarification; denying Marx he shuns the kind of inquiry that reveals the structure of antagonism generating these affairs, in the hopes of destroying them and generating a different configuration. In short, antagonism safely resides *inside* Latour's world, but his system omits antagonism *against* the world.[23]

Dismissing radical politics as being rooted in modern fallacies, Latour has often appeared as a defender of the neoliberal status quo—even as, in his recent work on the Anthropocene, he addresses its consequences with his usual conceptual tools.[24]

The critical oscillation attacked by Latour springs from the messy dialectic of objectivation and subjectivation; precisely, the more critical moderns *did* theorize impurity and hybridity, but with more eye for contradiction, conflict, and transformation than Latour. The issue is not one of the critic having it both ways, variously debunking the subject or the object. Rather, what is at stake here is the foundational instability that necessitates a perpetual problematization of objecthood and subjectivity, and of different forms and modalities of agency, as part of an ongoing critical praxis that cannot remove itself from the equation and put all antagonism at a remove. Take a particularly intriguing passage from the *Grundrisse*, in which Marx writes on the "production of consumption" (and here, as elsewhere, Marx's political economy takes up tropes and problems from aesthetic theory): "Production thus not only creates an object for the subject, but also a subject for the object. [...] It thus produces the object of consumption, the manner of consumption and the motive of consumption. Consumption likewise produces the producer's inclination by beckoning to him as an aim-determining need."[25] While Marx's vision of the overcoming of alienation and the achievement of the true human essence in the communist society of the future can obviously be criticized for its essentialist assumptions, his writings have the great value of analyzing object-subject relations in nineteenth-century capitalism as social relations that enact a highly unstable dialectic: a dialectic that cannot be wished away, and that any *praxis* is entangled in and needs to engage with in some manner.

Some of today's "speculative theorists" attack aesthetics as remaining within the framework of Kantian "correlationism." Armen Avanessian, for instance, critiques Kantian epistemology's "correlation between subject and object, of pure reason and intuition."[26] While the *Critique of Pure Reason* "limits the space of our experience to what can be thought, to the conditions of the possibility of our thinking," aesthetic experience has to step into the breach—without altering the fundamental parameters.[27] Avanessian argues that what is needed is not an aesthetics (which is apparently irredeemably Kantian) but a *poetics* that "refers to a making of something in which the boundary from non-being to being is crossed," and that this "poietic praxis transcends pure thinking and materializes whenever it makes its object, and be it a praxis of pure thinking."[28] However, Marx and many Marxists—among others—already considered praxis in such terms. Aesthetics was never limited to theorizing a certain kind of rarefied experience; it encompassed aesthetic practice as well as theory. It was *fetishization*: the making, unmaking, and remaking of things.

Du culte muséal des objets fétiches

In the early nineteenth century, Hegel noted that it had become impossible to kneel down and worship not only in front of sculptures of the Greek deities but also before images of God, Christ, or Mary.[29] Religious and philosophical thought had moved beyond human-made images of the absolute in anthropomorphic form; however, the "worship" of such images as works of art was a growing industry. The Romantic "cult of art" was setting artworks apart from other artifacts more drastically than before. This was both an enrichment and an impoverishment. The precondition for this Romantic cult was expropriation.

As Quatremère de Quincy discusses with some concern in 1796, owing to Napoleon's conquests and the emergence of the public art museum, works were being torn from their traditional networks of social relations and cultural habits at an unprecedented rate. Quatremère's intervention was aimed directly against the French state requisitioning artworks in occupied countries and transporting them to France, where the Louvre was to house masterpieces from the Ghent Altarpiece to the Laocoön.[30] Such a museum brought out certain qualities in its holdings while suppressing others. An abstraction machine, the museum extracts artifacts from their former social lives and creates new relations among them as artworks.[31]

Today's museums are being reconceptualized as old divisions—between, for instance, art and design or Western art and non-Western artifacts—are increasingly contested. Concurrently, there is a renewed theoretical interest in the agency of things and objects as agents or actants.[32] The time is ripe, then, for a reconsideration of the ways in which museified objects functioned, the kinds of lives they led, and the forms of secondary agency that were permitted or withheld from them by different museological conventions and protocols. Do certain arcane modern concepts and practices still hold a use-value in an age in which we can enter the Louvre not just in Paris but also in Abu Dhabi? We might say, with Brian Holmes, that the modern museological regime was based on "the notion that an object, by its distinction from all others, can serve as a mirror for an equally singular and independent subject."[33] The artwork was able to function as such a mirror precisely because it appeared to be uniquely endowed with a subjectivity of its own. It was a mesmerizing subject-object that was tantalizingly close to, yet ultimately distinct from, "primitive" magical fetishes and the fetishism of the commodity.

In historicizing art, Hegel was concerned with differentiating between various epochs in which art was able to achieve this sensuous manifestation of the ideal, to a greater or lesser extent. In the "symbolic" art of ancient Egypt, form remained mute and random, incapable of truly expressing its content. In classical Greece, form and content were in harmony, but this equilibrium was fragile and finally shattered when Christianity introduced a spiritualized conception of the world that could never be fully made sensate. While it was true that the abstract God of the Israelites incarnated in the material and visible form of Jesus Christ, the spiritual does not appear in Jesus the way it does in the Greek gods. The Greek gods were anthropomorphic *Erscheinungen* of the *Geist*. Here, art was indeed a *sinnliches Scheinen der Idee* at a moment when Spirit had not truly come to self-awareness in the form of the idea of subjective freedom.

This is the core of Christianity for Hegel: in contrast to the Greco-Roman gods as generic, idealized humans, the Christian God the Father incarnates as a particular and "accidental" mortal subject, the Son. It is the death and resurrection of the Son as the Holy Spirit that marks the dialectical overcoming of nature and the subjective transmogrification of the world.[34] The degree of subjective spiritualization that has been achieved with Christianity causes a crisis of form. Hegel argues that (religious) *love* may provide the only possible form for a subjective Christian art (here, one can think of medieval poetry and epics). What certainly does not work is trying to idealize the "accidental" body of Christ in a classical manner.

While Hegel appreciated the great art of the Renaissance, he argued that it was surplus to requirement from a strictly Christian point of view and that it heralded the autonomization of art. Having been formed by Prussian Protestantism, Hegel sometimes suggests that Catholic culture was not too dissimilar from the fetishism of African tribes that worshiped seemingly random objects.[35] He notes that "it is one thing for the mind to have before it a mere thing—such as the Host per se, a piece of stone or wood, or a wretched daub—but quite another thing for it to contemplate a painting, rich in thought and sentiment, or a beautiful work of sculpture, where soul holds converse with soul and Spirit with Spirit." He continues that, from the point of view of the Catholic Church, "the coarsest, ugliest, poorest representations serve their purpose just as well—or, in fact, better."[36] Better, that is, than a Raphael painting. "Thus Art in its very nature transcended the principle of the Church. Since the former is only a matter of sensuous representation, it is at first regarded as a harmless and indifferent matter. The Church, therefore, continued to follow it until the free Spirit from which art originated, advanced to thought and science; at that point, a separation ensued."[37]

Following Luther, the Catholic Church became truly obsolete, as it remained mired in superstitious attachment to form and matter ("Gebundensein an ein Sinnliches, an ein gemeines Ding").[38] While

Christianity is too spiritual to become fully sensate in art, Catholicism fetishized the base matter of the ingested host, which was supposedly the body of the Son. While the art of the Renaissance constituted a sensuous emancipation from Catholic fetishism, the Reformation allowed Spirit to realize as subjective freedom, untrammeled by external form. Together, the Reformation and the Renaissance ended Catholic fetishism. While they allowed the "autonomous" to soar, art itself was soon surpassed by philosophy and science. Hence, as Hegel famously put it in what has become known as his "end of art" thesis, "art, considered in its highest vocation, is and remains for us a thing of the past."[39]

By the early twentieth century, however, it was precisely the supposedly "disappearing" world of tribal culture that was supposed to reinvigorate and "spiritualize" modern art, and to reinfuse commodity fetishism with aboriginal magic. Artists, critics, dealers, and collectors revalued certain types of African objects (and later Oceanian and so on) as genuine works of art. This process spans from the early appropriation work by Cubists and Expressionists via Marius de Zayas's pioneering exhibition of "African Negro Art" at the Photo-Secession in New York in 1914 and Carl Einstein's 1915 book *Negerplastik* (Negro Sculpture) to the Surrealists' profound appreciation for ethnographica and the 1935 "African Negro Art" exhibition at the Museum of Modern Art (MoMA). The term "fetish" continued to be used, but the concept of "random objects worshiped by Africans" was now adapted and identified with specific types of objects—in particular, "nail fetishes" (wooden sculptures riddled with nails).[40]

This had an added attraction for the Dadaists and Surrealists since it suggested that what had been newly reconceptualized as African *art* could be used to challenge the conventions of Western academic art. Closely associated with Charles Ratton's Parisian gallery of African and tribal art and subscribing to the Communist Party's anti-imperialist stance, the Surrealists contributed to a

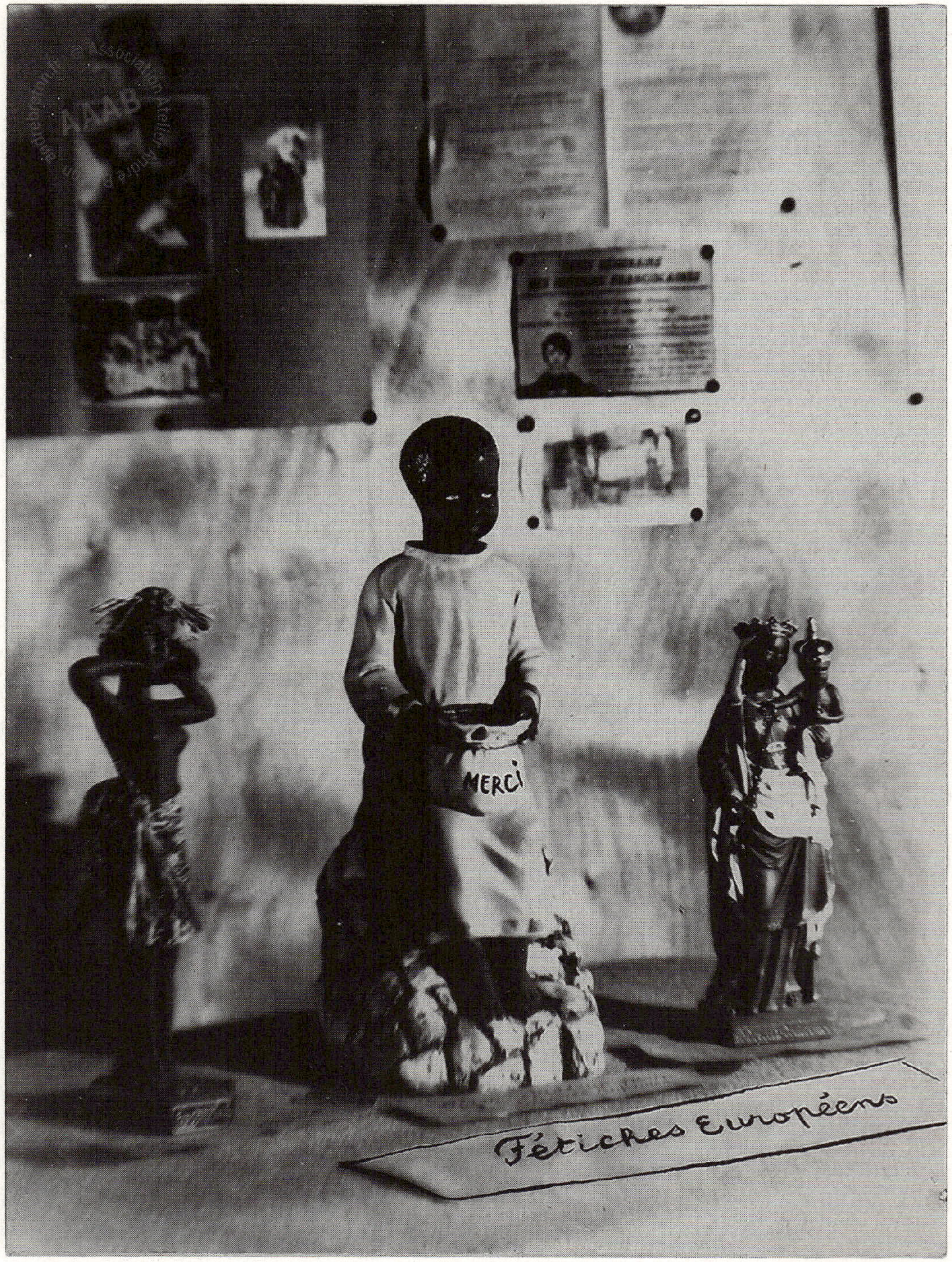

"European colonial fetishes" on display in the exhibition "La vérité sur les colonies," Paris, 1931

Comintern-backed anti-colonial exhibition by showing kitschy relics of colonial Catholicism as "European fetishes."[41] Such a case shows how immanent critiques by artists who were—as Europeans—ideologically and economically entangled in Western imperialism could grow into fundamental contestations.[42]

This is not to say that primitivist projections vanished overnight. After World War II, artists such as Barnett Newman continued the modernist tendency of privileging the "primitive fetish" as being more aesthetically productive than most Western art: "The artist today has more feeling and consequently more understanding for a Marquesas islands fetish than for the Greek figure."[43] Newman asserted a hierarchy between art and nonart within the realm of non-Western artifacts: the works of (male) Native American visual artists had to be separated from the craft of "women basket weavers," and it should be clear that "the God image, not pottery, was the first manual act."[44] This division should be seen in conjunction with the dividing line that Newman sought to draw between art and everyday (design) objects—the latter being bad objects, over-designed hosts devoid of transubstantiative power.

Newman was fiercely critical of Duchamp's work as well as the Bauhaus ideology that held sway at museums such as MoMA, which had organized the exhibitions "Useful Objects of American Design under $10" (1940) and "Good Design" (1951). Equating the readymade with the exhibition of design objects, Newman bemoaned the fact that "we now have museums that show screwdrivers and automobiles and paintings. […] I feel that it's time for the Museum of Modern Art, for instance, to put on an exhibition of machine guns."[45] For Newman, showcasing the work of "Bauhaus screwdriver designers" at MoMA was a category mistake—just as it was a category mistake to regard the products of (female) basket weavers as art.[46] It would be easy to pillory Newman for his unquestioned binaries and macho posturing;

what matters in the present context is that his writings give a good sense of the structural instability of the whole categorical apparatus of art and of objects suitable for "museification."

For Newman, the readymade, the Bauhaus screwdriver, and the handwoven basket negatively define the modernist artwork, which transcends those artifacts' mundaneness. The modern work of art is more akin to the "Marquesas islands fetish" in refusing use-value and asserting its sensuous plenitude. For Adorno, the artwork is a strange and somewhat dysfunctional—or excessively functional—commodity, precisely insofar as it still has traits of the religious fetish and thus goes beyond mere commodity fetishism.[47] This suggests, Stewart Martin stresses, that art is "a residual survival of magical fetishism within a modern culture of commodity fetishism," and that "the fetishism of art is distinct from the fetishism of magic as well as from the fetishism of commodities."[48] This is the point at which it would be productive to return to the root meaning of the term "fetish" as something that has been fabricated, and to counteract a certain "fetishization of the fetish" with a Marxian focus on *fetishization* as making, as practice.

Idealist aesthetics had promised reconciliation under the aegis of the subject, but the idealist compromise was always shaky—and much of modern art would be a kind of mutual haunting of object and subject, as in Duchamp's readymades and Surrealist objets trouvés. Furthermore, the privileging of a limited class of artworks that transcend the mundane objecthood of regular artifacts was challenged by such practices.[49] In Hegel's aesthetics, there was a chasm between the host or kitsch relics on the one hand, and a Raphael painting on the other. In the twentieth century, this distinction was *reincorporated into art itself* with Duchamp's readymades. The readymade is an industrial artifact chosen by the artist, who comes up with "a new thought for that object."[50] As John Roberts has argued, this also means that two forms of labor overlay one another—traditionally identified as "productive" labor and artistic labor.[51]

Duchamp's artistic work is indeed a semiotic operation. The commodity object becomes its own sign, and over time, its sign-value—to use a Baudrillardian term—vastly outperforms its original price. Via Jeff Koons and Damien Hirst, the readymade has become identified with the speculative bubbles of contemporary art, in which the artistic fetish is all but subsumed under the commodity fetish. In recent years, many of the most compelling artistic projects seek to transform the Duchampian artifact-turned-artwork back (or forward) into another kind of artifact.

Entrist Tactics and Exit Strategies

Arjun Appadurai has advocated a "methodological fetishism" that would consist in following "the things themselves, for their meanings are inscribed in their forms, their uses, their trajectories."[52] Here I will briefly discuss some trajectories that cross the line between contemporary art and nonart in one direction or another. Duchamp asked himself whether there could be *works* that would not be works *of art*.[53] In the case of museums, clearly many are not museums *of art*. During the last ten to twenty years, it has become common for artists to do projects in slightly dusty ethnographic, natural history, or community museums.

In the late 1960s, the artist Lothar Baumgarten started investigating display strategies in ethnographic museums—resulting, for instance, in a slide piece based on the Pitt Rivers Museum in Oxford (*Unsettled Objects*, 1968–69). These forays were not the result of invitations from the institutions.[54] In recent decades, however, it has become quite common for artists to receive invitations from curators of "nonart" museums, like Clémentine Deliss during her tenure at the

Weltkulturen Museum in Frankfurt am Main, or sometimes from third parties, such as freelance curators. Strategies, display and viewing habits, and conceptual frameworks from the sphere of contemporary art are then imported into the nonart museum. What is the purpose of such an exercise?

In a context where curators feel the need to address the colonial and imperialist nature of institutions, their collections, and their modes of ordering the world, the "task" of the artist is often implicitly, or explicitly, to provide a "fresh" and "critical" perspective, to rearrange the collection, to provide other ways of looking and structuring. It is no surprise that when the Royal Museum for Central Africa in Tervuren (outside Brussels) first started to seriously consider its role as a colonial relic, the exhibition project "ExitCongoMuseum" (2000) drafted contemporary artistic practices to provide critical perspectives.[55]

As abstraction machines, modern museums privilege scopic relations between individualized viewers and decontextualized objects. Around 1800, for instance, the rocks in the Teylers Museum in Haarlem—an Enlightenment institution—were put in display cases. Previously, the museum had privileged active handling and participation by the visitors, but now the relation with the items in the collection became primarily visual or scopic.[56] The modernist museum exacerbated this privileging of the visual, and Willem de Rooij's exhibition "Intolerance" (2010–11) at the Neue Nationalgalerie in Berlin intensified it to the point where it became self-reflexive. The installation combined Hawaiian feathered artifacts from the ethnological museum in Dahlem with the work of seventeenth-century Dutch "bird painter" Melchior d'Hondecoeter.[57] Both types of object were status symbols in their respective societies, and they were both implicated in early forms of global trade. D'Hondecoeter's paintings, for example, show exotic birds that had been imported to the Dutch Republic from other continents.

While such parallels did not make the montage of these two specific groups of objects less stark or striking, they were subjected to similar museological procedures. The code that De Rooij employed for this exhibition was that of the perfect white cube, of the museum as decontextualization tool or abstraction machine. Displayed without much additional information in well-lit cases set into the same wall on which d'Hondecoeter's paintings were hung, the Hawaiian artifacts were shown as objects that are as aesthetically rich and valid as the Dutch painter's work. This re-performing of modernist museological conventions creates an experience hovering between half-forgotten familiarity and irritating estrangement. However, it does not explain the actual processes of accumulation and deterritorialization related to the works.

By contrast, the exhibition "The Potosí Principle" (2010–11), curated by Alice Creischer, Max Jorge Hinderer Cruz, and Andreas Siekmann, was a sprawling assemblage of artifacts and artworks that primarily came from South America.[58] The core was constituted by Baroque paintings from Potosí, a silver mining town in Bolivia that was key to the Spanish colonial economy. The curators linked this site of "primitive accumulation" to its contemporary equivalents in Latin America, China, and the global art world.[59]

"The Potosí Principle" foregrounded the relation of the extraction of value from the soil and from people with the production of visual artifacts, such as the Baroque paintings that function both as propaganda and yet another form of accumulation. Hung on scaffolding and accompanied by a seemingly nonhierarchical mix of texts and diagrams, the paintings were fetishized not as masterpieces worthy of high-art status (they are usually seen as "derivative" colonial works) but as indices of larger political, economic, and cultural processes. "The Potosí Principle" used the art space as a site that can show, combine, and reflect on a wide variety of objects and images. This engagement with objects is as aesthetic as it is political—"aesthetic" not in the sense of an aestheticist fixation on a few choice qualities of a few choice artifacts, but in the more fundamental sense of a sounding out of the potential as well as limits of sensuous presence and visibility.

Is this still art as we thought we knew it, and is the context still that of an *art museum*? The Museum of American Art, a project by a Serbian artist who uses the name "Walter Benjamin" and other aliases, tries to undermine the art space from within. The original Berlin museum and its various "franchises" present reproductions and re-presentations of classic modern artworks and museum displays. If De Rooij is interested in the potential of the modern museum and gallery to abstract the works displayed in it, the Museum of American Art's meta-installations are presented within the narrative that the age of the modern museum and art is over. As "Walter Benjamin" puts it:

> Art museums didn't always exist—they are basically a recent invention, and it seems they have now exhausted their purpose, become obsolete, alongside the very notion of art. A few of them might be preserved and conserved as examples of what once was art and the art museum, thus closing the other end at some point. But most of the existing museums would have to transform into another kind of institution of memory. [...] Those places could use any kind of exhibits/artifacts: "original works of art," replicas, copies, facsimiles, documents, objects, moving images. Regardless of what their previous meanings were, the character of these artifacts would now be closer to the notion of "specimen" than to the notion of "work of art."[60]

The Museum of American Art appropriates or copies modern "masterpieces" and creates full-scale or reduced copies of classic modern museum spaces, from MoMA exhibitions to El Lissitzky's *Kabinett der Abstrakten* in Hannover and the US Pavilion at the 1962 Venice

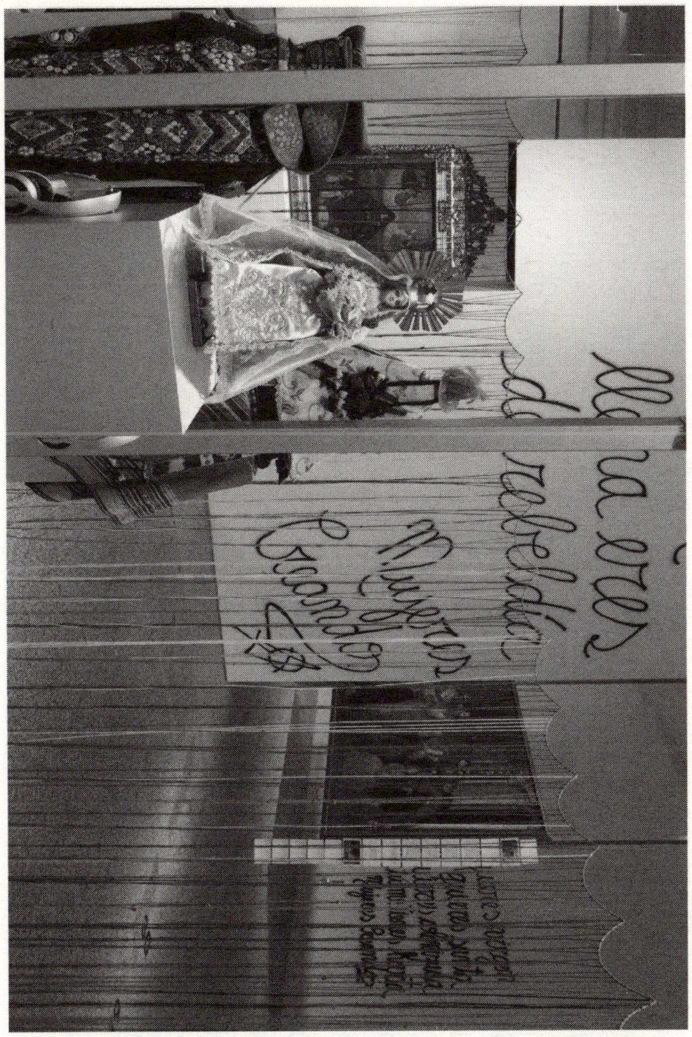

"The Potosí Principle," Museo Nacional Centro de Arte Reina Sofía, Madrid, 2010–11

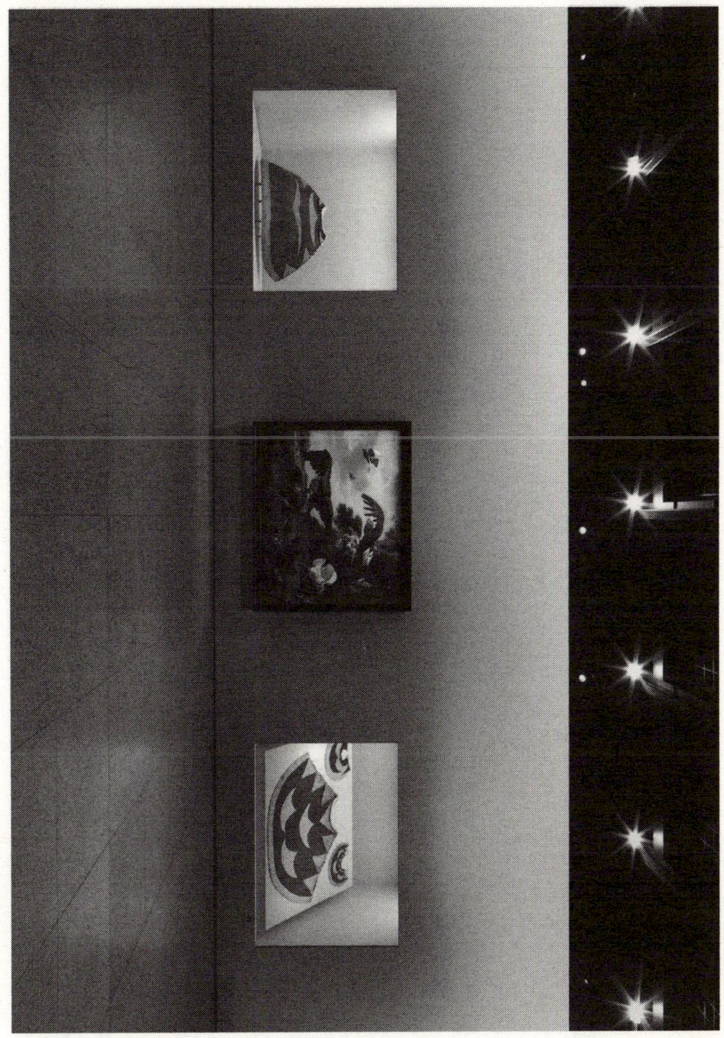

Willem de Rooij, "Intolerance," Neue Nationalgalerie, Berlin, 2010–11

Biennale. Going back further in history, the museum has also (re) presented depictions of the Belvedere gallery at the Vatican, where, during the Renaissance, popes began to display rediscovered antique statues such as the Laocoön and the Apollo Belvedere. "In today's terms, we would consider these statues to be the first readymades and, in fact, the first objects of art."[61] But if such artifacts were the first readymades, then what would contemporary artworks be for future post-art institutions? A kind of neo-ethnographica? Or, in fact, *liberated readymades* that are no longer all about the art/nonart distinction and auratization and hyper-reification, but about bringing out a wider set of qualities and conditions, as in "The Potosí Principle"?

At the Van Abbemuseum in Eindhoven, the Museum of American Art has exhibited installations dealing both with modernist museum displays and the Vatican's Belvedere gallery. "Walter Benjamin's" historical narrative seems to provide a script for the Van Abbemuseum, which has often given copies pride of place and is intent on using the museum for other purposes than aesthetic self-celebration. Rather than a space of calm and critical reflection, as in De Rooij's practice, the museum becomes an agent for action.

One example of this was Tania Bruguera's transformation of the Van Abbemuseum into the Museum of Arte Útil (2013–14), which documented an array of activist practices and attempted to reintegrate art into society as something other than an excessively expensive commodity fetish.[62] Bruguera's Museum of Arte Útil rhetorically transformed the institution by putting wooden partitions in front of its white walls, suggesting a future in which art has been turned into a useful tool, and the museum has indeed been transformed into "another kind of institution of memory." Within this architecture, Bruguera presented documentation of important aesthetico-political practices from the 1960s to the present.

However, the whole conceptual framework and visual manifestation of her "museum" represented an unfortunate relapse into crude binaries: decadent aestheticism versus useful art; contemplation versus action; white walls versus rough wooden fences; the urinal as useless readymade versus the urinal as usable urinal. In fact, Bruguera quite literally put the Duchampian urinal back in the bathroom, both at the Queens Museum and, some time after the "Arte Útil" exhibition, at the Van Abbemuseum. When the latter subsequently made its bathrooms gender neutral, the prominently installed urinal was deemed too confrontational and was removed.

Instead of reversing the readymade in this nondialectical manner, wouldn't the more productive approach be to potentialize it? This would mean to allow the artifact to engage with its contradictions and the different forms of labor and practice that are embedded within it. The Arte Útil project is marked by theoretical and practical impoverishment rather than by any transformative aesthetic or sociopolitical potential. Regardless, Bruguera's insistence on more traffic between the context of art and other social frameworks and fields is to the point. The museum becomes a node in an indexical network that no longer revolves exclusively, or even primarily, around the preservation and presentation of an exclusive group of rare and precious objects.

Post-readymades and Neo-readymades

The Duchampian readymade redefined the artwork by engaging with preexisting commodity fetishes instead of making new works, and this has led to a higher degree of fetishism in some of its offspring, such as commodity art à la Koons. However, precisely by problematizing the nature of artistic creation in relation to industrial or manual labor, it also initiated a shift from the *artwork* as object to *art work*—art as work involving the production, reproduction, maintenance, and circulation

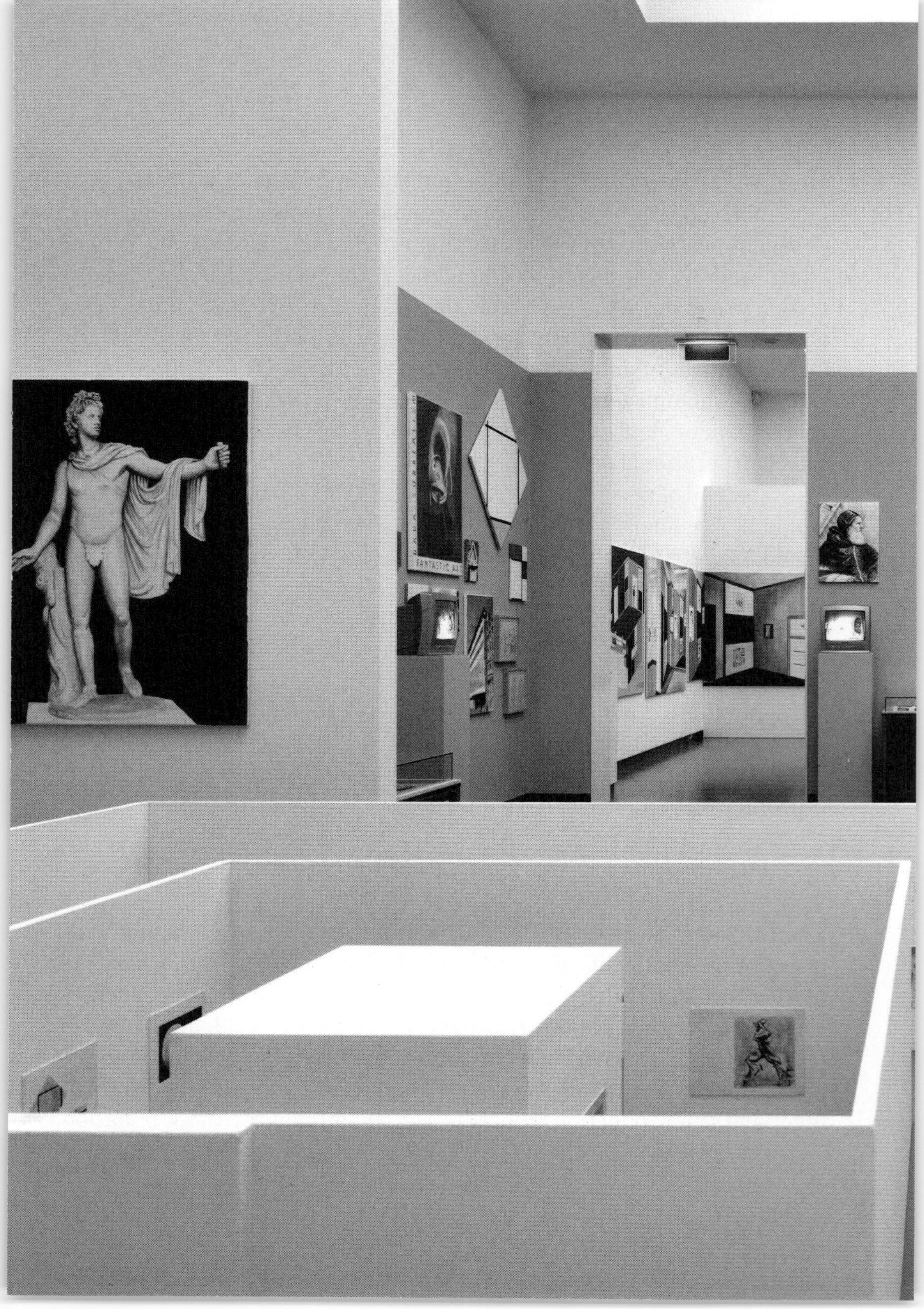

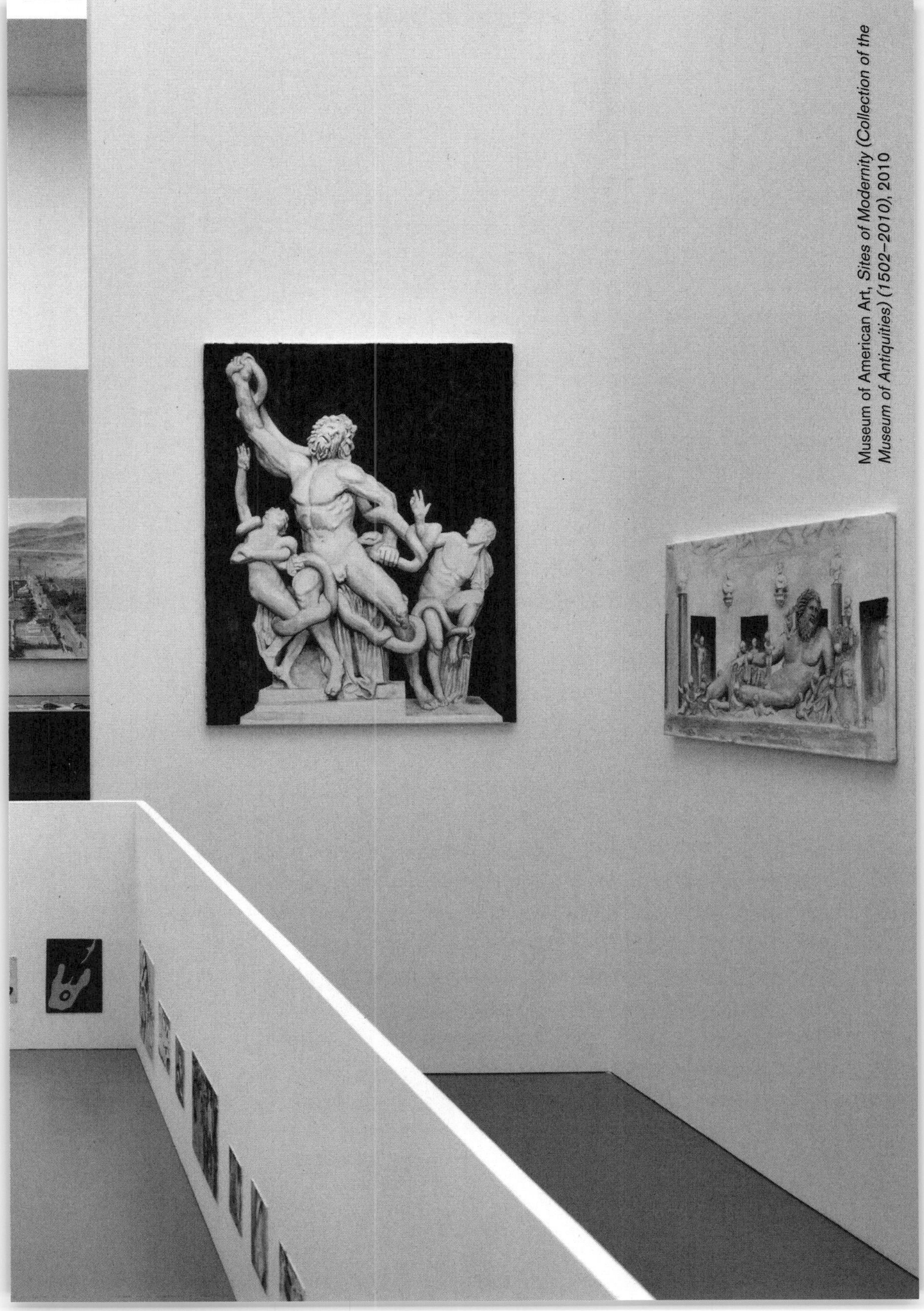

Museum of American Art, *Sites of Modernity (Collection of the Museum of Antiquities) (1502–2010)*, 2010

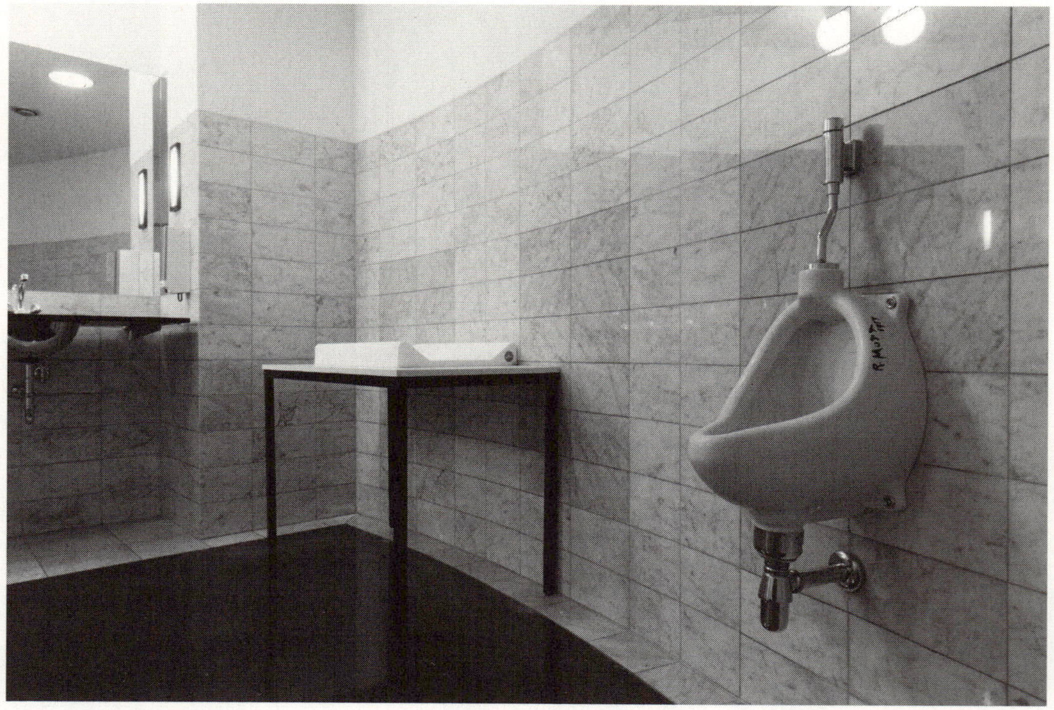

Tania Bruguera, *Arte Útil*, 2009/2016

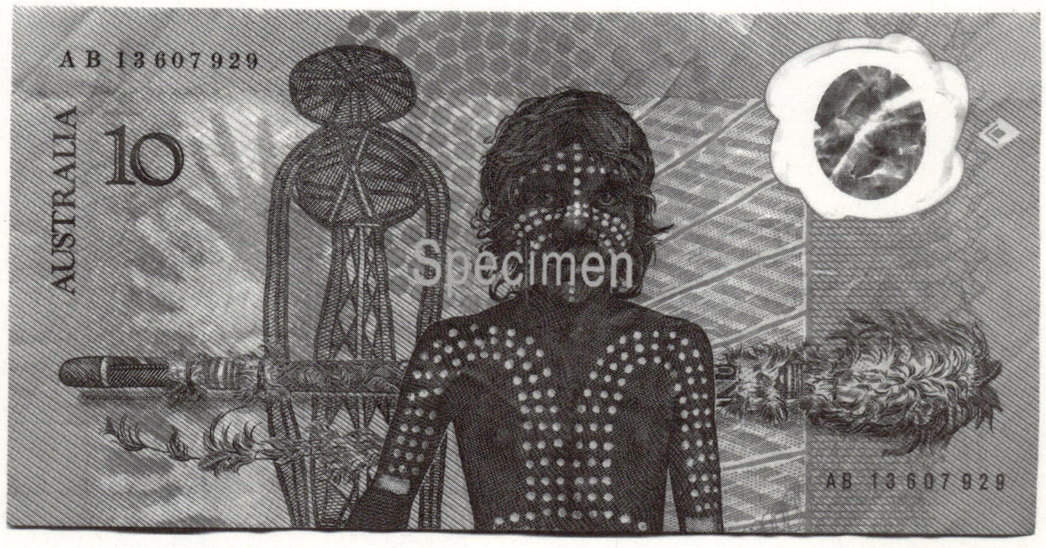

Agency, *Thing 001390 (Ten Dollar Bank Note)*, 2016

of a wide variety of fetishes. Who is more Duchampian: Koons, with his perfect stainless-steel bunnies, or Barbara Bloom, who, on the cover of the 1986 catalogue for "Damaged Goods" (the exhibition that helped launch Koons's career) showed a cleaning woman in a car salesroom, thus foregrounding the feminine maintenance work that goes into keeping fetish objects *shiny*?[63]

In his anthropological theory of art, Alfred Gell notes that artifacts are indexes in the Peircean sense: "Artefacts have the capacity to index their 'origins' in an act of *manufacture*."[64] Precisely insofar as they are *feitiços*, made by human hand, artworks and other artifacts "motivate abductions" about their meaning and function—about actual past meanings and functions and possible present and future meanings and functions.[65] The index is the social sign par excellence.[66] It cannot be relegated to a world of "pure" semiosis.[67] Insofar as they index their origins, artifacts or fetishes are also *temporal and historical signs.*

Ethnography and anthropology have often viewed other cultures and their artifacts as ahistorical, trapped in a perpetual present, but this is an ideologically motivated failure to engage with *other* histories. For Marx, the commodity fetish is a *broken index* insofar as it fails to reveal the real reasons for its "behavior" on the market. Many forms of critical aesthetic practice try to counteract this form of fetishism through active fetishization. "The Potosí Principle," for instance, treats artifacts as indexes that don't just point toward repressed origins but are also open to being re-performed, accruing new layers of labor and meaning—fetishes with a future.

A practice that embodies this open-ended re-performance is that of Agency, a Brussels-based platform for examining the modern regime of intellectual property, formed by Kobe Matthys in 1992. Agency collects "things" that have been subject to copyright litigation, and "calls [these] *things* forth from its list via varying assemblies inside exhibitions, performances, publications, etc."[68] These things are not necessarily single, physical objects—they range from computer-generated bingo cards and genetically engineered bacteria to cases pertaining to folklore, tradition, and tribal culture.[69]

For instance, *Thing 001635 (Australian Coat of Arms)* "concerns the conflict between indigenous elders and the Commonwealth about the use of totems in the Australian Coat of Arms." This case was discussed in Bétonsalon in Paris with a number of "concerned guests," including anthropologists. A related case, *Thing 001390 (Ten Dollar Bank Note)*, revolves around legal action by the sculptor Terry Yumbulul against the Reserve Bank of Australia and the Aboriginal Artists Agency Limited for violating his copyright. The agency had sold one of his ceremonial morning-star poles to the Australian Museum in Sydney and sublicensed the copyright to the bank to use the image on a ten-dollar note that commemorated the first European settlement in Australia.[70]

While Agency participates in exhibitions, its displays are only one aspect of the *assemblies* that it convenes around these "things." The assemblies bring together a disparate array of objects and subjects (or things and people). Usually, a "specimen" of one or more "things" is exhibited as part of the assembly, and there is a gathering during which experts and concerned parties debate the ins and outs of a particular case. Agency's artifacts and their uses, which have triggered legal actions, eventually generate Agency's assemblies, in which lawyers, artists, theorists, and other concerned parties discuss the thing in question—or become part of it.

The Heideggerian-Latourian meaning of "thing" as something that is a "matter of concern" is, of course, part of Agency's theoretical framework.[71] While such things have surprising agency, it is a secondary agency, dependent on human action and interpretation. In Agency's assemblies, the things trigger responses and become coproducers of discourse by eliciting statements from a variety of participants (via the invitations sent out by Matthys). Agency is not interested in incorporating these things into art as readymades. The point is not to "turn them into artworks," nor to reverse the procedure and "put the urinal back in the bathroom," but to examine semiotic artifacts through re-performing them and to problematize semiotic labor while engaging in it. In Agency's practice, it is a small step from a totem pole to a copyrighted algorithm or genetically engineered organism.

Marx's "dead labor" stored in machines and equipment seems uncannily alive. New products are now often an inextricable tangle of old and new patents and trademarks that enforce each other—knowledge extracted from traditional cultures and state-of-the-art laboratories (some privately funded, some state-funded), computing power and marketing strategies, and invisible sweatshops and automated high-tech plants. Nothing "purely analog" remains in a post-digital culture where the distinction between online and offline has become extremely fuzzy. As the theorist Florian Cramer has argued, the post-digital artifact is indexical to the core: "The 'maker movement'—as manifested in fab labs, but also at zine fairs—represents a shift from the symbolic, as the preferred semiotic mode of digital systems (and of which the login is the perfect example), toward the indexical: from code to traces, and from text to context."[72]

Whether they use digital technology or not, many contemporary practices conceive of the fetish as a thing that is subject to continuous remaking or re-performance. While this "circulationist" logic has deep roots in the analog culture industry, its logic was exacerbated and liberated by digitization. In the process, the artwork has been reconceptualized as *art work* that engages with the indexical trajectories of fetishes and the conflicts embedded in them—tracing, showing, and discussing them in art spaces. Methodological fetishism engages with such post-digital trajectories, including the geographical and cultural distances traversed by digital fetishes.

Sometimes the operations and transformations that are involved raise more questions than they care to answer. A case in point is Renzo Martens's Institute for Human Activities (IHA), which is trying to turn a palm-oil plantation in the Democratic Republic of Congo (DRC) into an art center using the rhetoric and logic of gentrification as well as the creative industries and Richard Florida's "creative class." To fund this development, Martens presents sculptures made by former plantation workers in Western gallery and museum shows—not the original clay sculptures, but 3-D prints in chocolate. These cacao neo-fetishes are combined with sparse, suggestive, and mystifying information about the entire "chain" of the production process, particularly the situation at the IHA's site in the DRC. In 2020, Martens released the film *White Cube*, chronicling his work with the IHA and the creation of a "white cube" gallery on the plantation site—still implementing Florida's script.

In an earlier film, *Episode III: Enjoy Poverty* (2008), Martens played himself as a neocolonial figure with a messiah complex who tries to get Africans to profit from their own poverty by taking their own pictures and selling them to Western agencies and media. In the film, we watch the predictable failure of this scheme. Now we are invited to believe that IHA is qualitatively different; that it is a serious attempt to effect change. Martens, however, still uses tired strategies of overidentification that run counter to this, such as accepting chocolate by Barry Callebaut (a company that isn't known for its ethics) and including large wall texts that read "Made possible by Barry Callebaut"—asking us to accept this as cheeky critique that obviates further criticisms. And while Martens rightly stresses that the art world and its role in gentrified Western metropolises depend on the disavowal of its connections to sites of colonial and neocolonial extraction and accumulation—the disavowal of the export of violence from the centers to the margins—how can a "good" form of gentrification be brought about?

Gentrification is not a cure for underdevelopment; it's a machine for the reproduction of inequality and displacement through wealth redistribution and the production of new class distinctions.[73] Even if Martens were to succeed in bringing gentrification to this site in the DRC, it changes nothing about the mechanism. If he really were successful, the site would become as unaffordable for artists and intellectuals, or workers, as Manhattan or much of London. But gentrification is not even given a proper chance (shades of *Enjoy Poverty*). Rather than collaborating with existing art initiatives, Martens decided to create his own and to designate former plantation workers as his living readymades. Using their sculptures, he produces chocolate techno-fetishes that garner high visibility for himself and the IHA, even though they barely sell, thus failing to generate funding for the art center at the plantation.

Some of Martens's designated artists produce striking pieces. Thomas Leba's work, in particular, stands out when exhibited—but it stands out in a context devised by Martens as an artist operating with a degree of symbolic capital and discursive presence that is unobtainable to his neo-plantation workers. In contrast to the Showroom and the Otolith Collective's collaboration with the Chimurenga group from Cape Town, or the activities of the Arts Collaboratory network, this is no meeting of equals.[74] The sculptors have no control over the means of production and the appearance of the final pieces. With these techno-fetishes, Martens seems to indulge in the contemporary take on the fetish while ultimately reverting to a much more conventional and conservative fetishism. Sculptures are extracted from the DRC, but now via digitization. In the process, they are modulated and re-performed, but primarily by a Dutch artist in the context of his own project.

Group Affinity[75]

When Martens had an IHA show at KW Institute for Contemporary Art in Berlin in 2015, he created a showroom of sculptures and a generic office space, which supposedly functioned "as a contact point and an open platform, which creates a market for the exhibited works, generates visibility and credibility, raises funds, convinces volunteers, and assembles knowledge—all in the interest of the plantation's long-term gentrification."[76] But this was clearly an instrumentalist "open platform" attempting to generate visibility for artistic commodity fetishes that generate income. It put a discursive and collaborative spin on a showroom—labeling it a "showroom" is another instance of Martens flaunting his critical self-awareness, as though this would preempt any critique of the stratagems in question. The contrast with the discursive space created by Chimurenga at the Showroom in London, on the invitation of the Otolith Collective, is again instructive. In "The Chimurenga Library," the group, which edits a "pan-African gazette," was able to articulate and problematize its own practice, including discussing the creative industries and gentrification.[77]

In some of its more relevant incarnations, the contemporary exhibition is no longer a display of (supposedly precious) artifacts. One German curator has put it in drastic terms: "These days, the only valid exhibitions are workshops or seminars or self-constituting reading groups."[78] In an age when everything appears to be subject to curation, museums and related institutions are no longer primarily in the business of collecting and curating artifacts. Following artifacts' indexical traces into a contested past and divergent futures, such institutions collect and curate social relations. These social relations obviously include artifacts as well as the humans that made them or whose ancestors made them, or whose ancestors stole or bought them, or those who have some other interest in the matter. Institutions that house the spoils of colonial plunder, such as the British Museum in London, have to engage with the living cultures that once produced their possessions.[79]

In other cases, the index in question is not a *work* but a *worker*, not a thing but a person. Following the appropriated "ethnographic" objects, migrants from all over the world come to metropolitan centers in the West to find legal or illegal employment—often as cleaners, domestic workers, or builders. In a first step, the *artwork* as fetish object (*faictise*) was redefined by focusing on the *art work* (the actual *faire*, the labor) that produced the object in the first place, and that keeps re-performing and circulating it. Now, the focus shifts from the work to the worker—and not just the "art worker" in a narrow sense, nor even people who are legally allowed to work.

Displaced surplus populations come to the West; such migrants and refugees—objectified by the legal and security apparatus, and given a residency permit or citizenship or relegated to the shadow economy—become living indexes. The same can be said of the descendants of slaves or colonized people whose families have been in the West for generations. Strictly speaking, we are *all* indexes of our own (pre) history, but this condition stands out more when the distance between point of departure and current position (in historical, cultural-geographic, or economic terms) is greater, and when the migration was undertaken under duress or constraints.

Kader Attia has created numerous works with sundry relics of the colonial era: an installation of shelves with nineteenth-century magazine front pages of the colonial Other as well as more recent "war on terror" images in the same vein, or a display of twentieth-century Algerian Berber jewelry that includes French coins in an apparent attempt by the colonized to appropriate the colonial power's *mana*. The video diptych *The Body's Legacies, Part 1: The Objects* and *The Body's Legacies, Part 2: The Postcolonial Body* (both 2018) is particularly compelling in this context. Attia is an artist whose work is grounded in procedures of collage, assemblage, and montage, and these videos present sequences of speakers who complement and, at times, contradict and critique each other.[80]

The Body's Legacies, Part 1: The Objects deals with the forced colonial-era displacement of people as well as of objects, the objectification of people, and the projection of human traits onto objects: at one point, a French collector of ethnographica accidentally refers to "ces gens" (those people) instead of "ces objets." The film contains stories about the meaning and social function that various "fetishes" had and have for the communities from which they were stolen, even while some speakers stress that the appropriated objects now have different and multiple meanings and that there is no way back. The Austrian ethnologist Gerhard Kubik blithely tells of his complicity in theft: while working in southeastern Angola in 1965, it came to his attention that a traditional healer had been arrested by the Portuguese authorities for *feiticeiria*, or witchcraft, and that his objects had been confiscated. Kubik then made a deal with the authorities: the man would be released, and his possessions ("very beautiful carvings") would be sent to a museum so that he would no longer be in a position to use them.

Discussing the French president's seeming commitment to restituting artworks to Africa, one of the speakers in *The Objects* wonders if this is also sending a subliminal message to ethno-nationalists and fascists: if the objects return, should African immigrants likewise go back to "where they belong"? In *The Body's Legacies, Part 2: The Postcolonial Body,* a collection of French artists and intellectuals of mostly African descent uses the case of Théo Luhaka, a young man brutalized by the French police, to examine what it means to be a person of color in France today, with a body both invisible and all too visible. In the film, Olivier Marboeuf characterizes this as "the body that has survived"—it somehow refused to be erased and is present as a zombie of colonialism. Marboeuf and other postcolonial subjects in the video speak as more than talking heads: their bodies, postures, and gestures index their histories in a variety of ways. They speak the language of the colonizer, but their *parole* is a very particular use of the *langue française*, infusing it with unrepresented experiences.

Attia shot some of the footage in La Colonie, in Paris—the decolonial space for lectures, debates, and cultural events he founded. When opening the 2018 "White West" symposium at La Colonie on the resurgence of fascism—during which extracts from *The Body's Legacies* were screened—Attia quoted from social media messages by a certain Mathieu Wagener, who extolled the right-wing Identitarian movement and disputed Attia's right as someone who is not "truly French," who belongs to the *cafards* from the Maghreb, to voice any kind of critique. The intellectuals and activists in the film recall their immigrant parents' desires to assimilate and "be invisible," with the second generation no longer playing the role of the "good immigrant" by speaking up. Contra Wagener, this is precisely what makes these vocal descendants of immigrants "truly French." Meanwhile, the postcolonial human body still indexes its difference, its unwanted presence.

Recent years have seen a proliferation of coalitions and projects in art with "illegal" as well as "legal" immigrants and refugees, acknowledging that art-world denizens, such as artists and curators, are frequently dependent on their labor (as domestic workers and nannies). From Bruguera's long-term Immigrant Movement International project in New York to the work of Dutch artists and intellectuals with cleaners, domestic workers, and the "rejected" asylum seekers of the We Are Here group, activist assemblages and assemblies proliferate. It can be a serious challenge to forge a "group subject" when its participants are so diverse. It hardly needs saying that an undocumented migrant who does not know where they will spend the night is in a dramatically different position from a curator or unpaid intern. The 2020 COVID-19 crisis exacerbated these problems, with the juridically, economically, and socially precarious often running out of options when it came to shelter and food. That La Colonie did not survive the lockdown (it was no longer able to make the rent) has a certain "canary in the coal mine" quality to it.

The point is not to minimize such crucial differences, which can be the difference between life and death, but to assert that we are all denizens of the global Potosí. The extreme subjectivation of cultural and intellectual workers is as problematic as the objectification of "disposable" immigrants, of whom there is always fresh supply. (But is the same not true of artists, curators, and critics?) There is a pressing need to assert the agency of human cooperation and the reality of the human subject as a living fetish who, in being or risking becoming human surplus, is both less and much more than a worker.

If Marx's account of commodity fetishism condenses two illusions—that of the *sensuousness of commodities* and that of the *autonomy of the value-form*—from living labor, and if Adorno's aesthetic theory privileges the first illusion and deploys it against the second, art after Duchamp sees a Baudrillardian triumph of the fetishism of the code.[81] The *labor of signification* does not seem to matter anymore in this realm of coded immanence, in which signifiers get shuffled around endlessly. As should be evident from the above, I certainly *do* accord agency to human praxis—which is always a hybrid practice, a cyborg practice, involving technology and "dead labor." However, in terms of economic value, the rise of sign-value in the age of branding does indeed appear to give a new autonomy to economic value.

Marx attempted to dispel the illusion of commodity fetishism by proving that the commodity's value is rooted in human labor. Whether such an operation is still possible under conditions of post-Fordism will be a question occupying us in the coming chapters. As consumers and users, we add value to brands in ways that seem

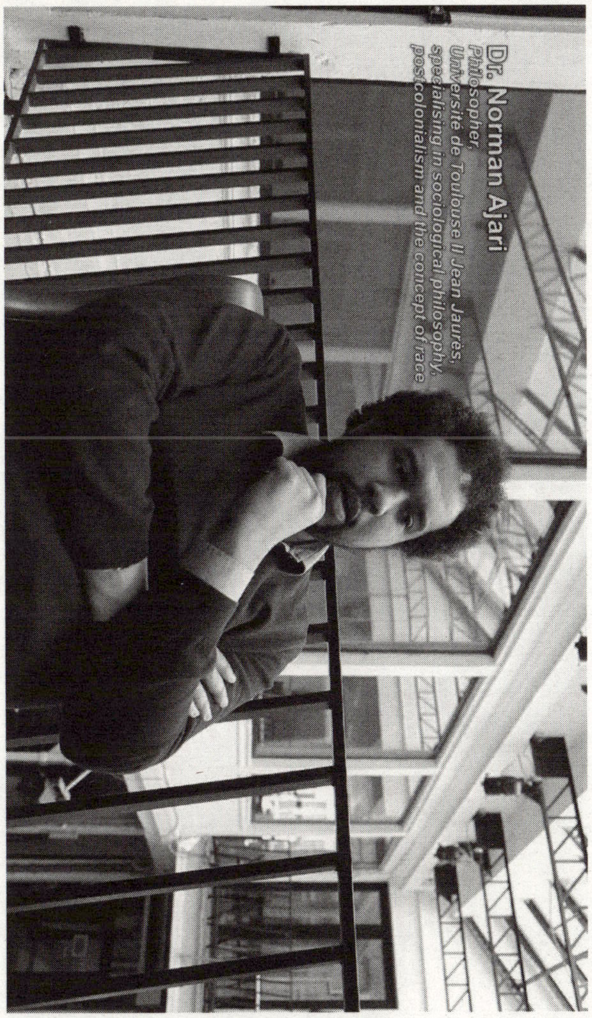

Still from Kader Attia, *The Body's Legacies, Part 2: The Postcolonial Body*, 2018

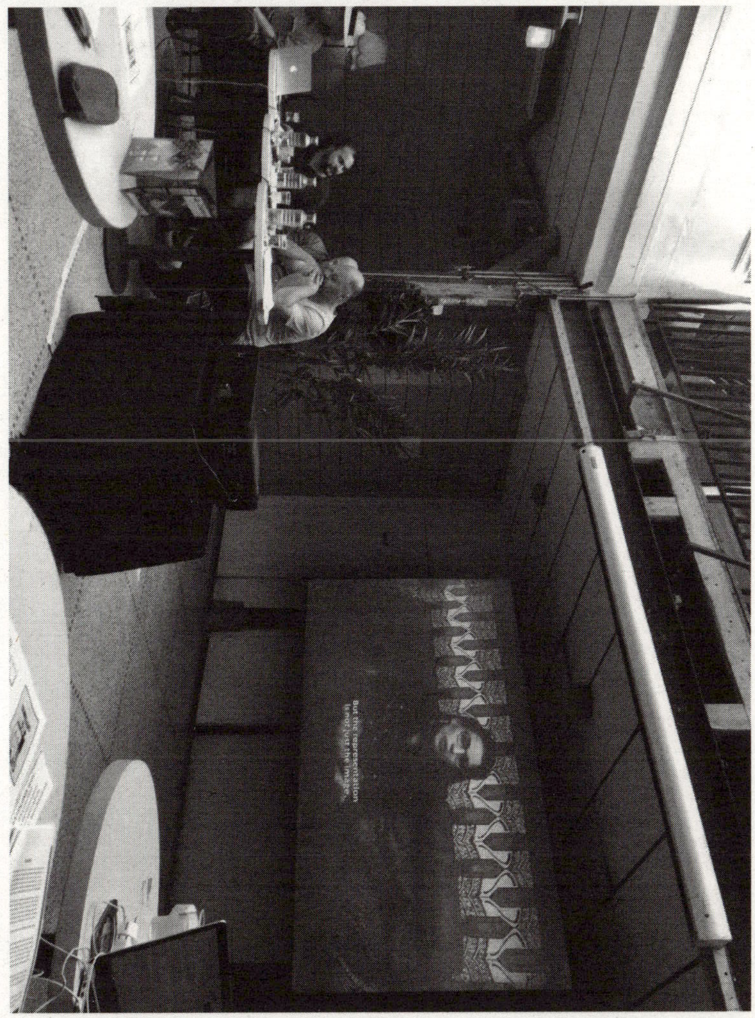

Kader Attia screening an extract from *The Body's Legacies, Part 2: The Postcolonial Body* (2018), at the symposium "The White West," La Colonie, Paris, May 2018

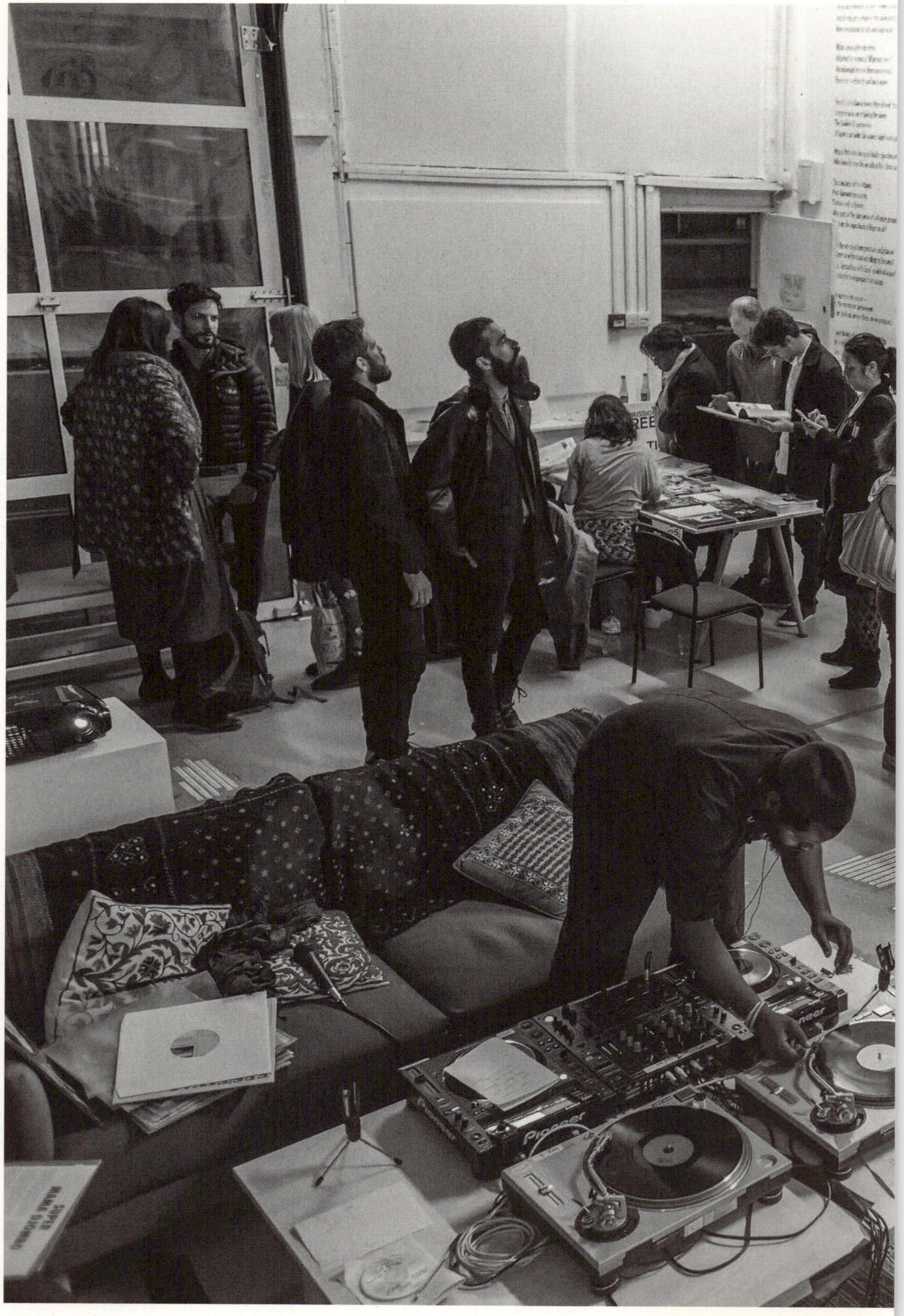

"The Chimurenga Library," The Showroom, London, 2015

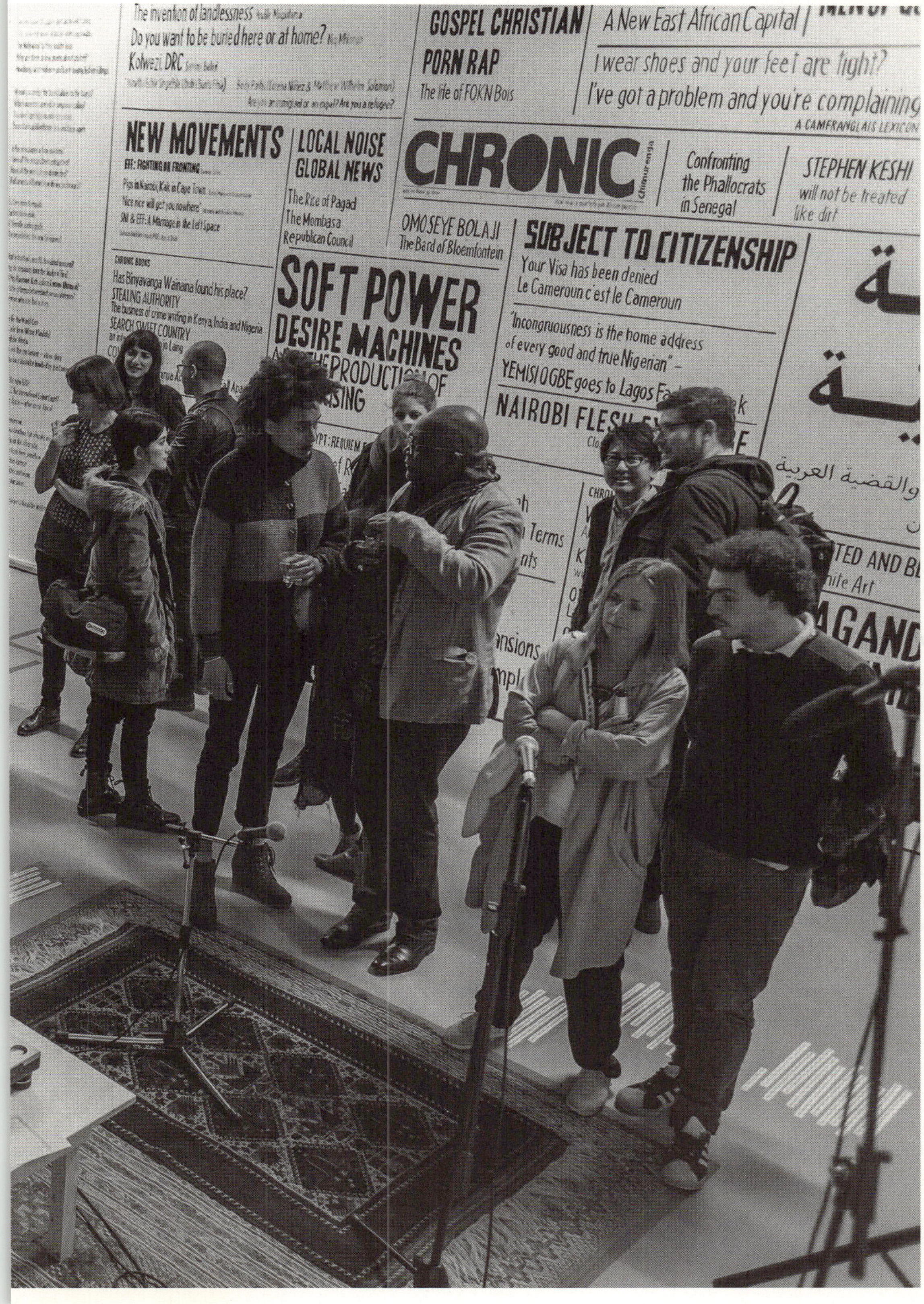
The invention of landlessness
Do you want to be buried here or at home?
Kolwezi, DRC
GOSPEL CHRISTIAN
PORN RAP
The life of FOKN Bois
A New East African Capital
I wear shoes and your feet are tight?
I've got a problem and you're complaining
A CAMFRANGLAIS LEXICON
NEW MOVEMENTS
LOCAL NOISE
GLOBAL NEWS
The Rise of Pagad
The Mombasa Republican Council
CHRONIC
Confronting the Phallocrats in Senegal
STEPHEN KESHI
will not be treated like dirt
OMOSEYE BOLAJI
The Bard of Bloemfontein
SUBJECT TO CITIZENSHIP
Your Visa has been denied
Le Cameroun c'est le Cameroun
SOFT POWER
DESIRE MACHINES
Has Binyavanga Wainaina found his place?
STEALING AUTHORITY
The business of crime writing in Kenya, India and Nigeria
"Incongruousness is the home address of every good and true Nigerian" –
NAIROBI FLESH

barely quantifiable. Our practices of fetishization may make a cultural and social difference, but what is its precise economic value? Some accounts see the source of value in *form* itself—form imprinted on fungible materials, branding brute matter.

NOTES

1 A quote from Fanny Lewald's *Meine Lebensgeschichte* (1862) opens the sourcebook compiled by Gert Jan Kocken to accompany *Judenporzellan* in exhibitions, for instance, at Stedelijk Museum Bureau Amsterdam in 2009.

2 See Patrick Föhl, "Die Porzellanaffen des Moses Mendelssohn: Nachprüfung einer Legende," in *"Ein Traum, was Sonst?" Preußische Tugenden* (Göttingen: Wallstein, 2002), 59–67, which is included in the sourcebook that accompanies Kocken's photographs.

3 Hannah Arendt, *Rahel Varnhagen: Lebensgeschichte einer deutschen Jüdin aus der Romantik* (Munich: Piper, 2010), 25–26, 42–43. Written in 1933 but only published in 1959, Arendt's book is marked throughout by her firsthand experience of the more recent history of the German Jews—to the point where this later history appears as inexorable fate, and all historical steps toward Jewish emancipation in Germany appear futile from the beginning.

4 William Pietz, "Fetishism and Materialism," in *Fetishism as Cultural Discourse*, ed. Emily Apter and William Pietz (Ithaca, NY: Cornell University Press, 1993), 133–34.

5 Margaret A. Rose, *Marx's Lost Aesthetic: Karl Marx and the Visual Arts* (Cambridge: Cambridge University Press, 1984), 62.

6 On the history of these terms, see William Pietz, "The Problem of the Fetish II: The Origin of the Fetish," *RES: Anthropology and Aesthetics*, no. 13 (Spring 1987): 23–45. More recently, see also Rosalind C. Morris and Daniel H. Leonard, *The Returns of Fetishism: Charles de Brosses and the Afterlives of an Idea* (Chicago: University of Chicago Press, 2017), especially Leonard's introduction (1–39), for an incisive characterization of de Brosses's overall project.

7 Charles de Brosses, *Du culte des dieux fétiches, ou parallèle de l'ancienne religion de l'Egypte avec la religion actuelle de Nigritie* (1760; Paris: Fayard, 1988), 15.

8 See, for instance, Karl-Heinz Kohl, *Die Macht der Dinge: Geschichten und Theorie sakraler Objekte* (Munich: C.H. Beck, 2003), 191–94.

9 See G. W. F. Hegel, *Vorlesungen über die Philosophie der Geschichte*

(Frankfurt am Main: Suhrkamp, 1986), 284–85; and Hegel, *Vorlesungen über die Philosophie der Religion I* (Frankfurt am Main: Suhrkamp, 1986), 282–84, 295.

10 See, of course, the famous section on the fetishism of commodities in chap. 1, sec. 4 of Karl Marx, *Capital: A Critique of Political Economy*, vol. 1, trans. Ben Fowkes (London: Penguin, 1976), 163–77. In the first German edition of 1867, a shorter version of Marx's comments on commodity fetishism was to be found in the appendix on the value-form.

11 Rosalind C. Morris makes much of the fact that the original German version of the heading "The Fetishism of Commodities" reads "Der Fetischkarakter der Ware" and asserts that "Marx rarely used the term 'fetishism' (*Fetischismus*), except in explicit reference to religion." Morris, "After de Brosses: Fetishism, Translation, Comparativism, Critique," in *The Returns of Fetishism*, 188. The point is precisely that Marx's notion of the commodity fetish is a polemical appropriation of the concept of the religious fetish, and where there is a fetish, there is fetishism (at least since de Brosses). Hence, Marx states: "Dies nenne ich den Fetischismus, der den Arbeitsprodukten anklebt, sobald sie als Waren produziert werden, und der daher von der Warenproduktion unzertrennlich ist." Karl Marx, *Das Kapital*, in *Marx-Engels-Werke*, Bd. 23 (Berlin: Dietz, 1962), 86–87. In the original 1867 German version, Marx uses the term *Fetischismus* repeatedly.

12 Georg Lukács, *History and Class Consciousness: Studies in Marxist Dialectics* (1923), trans. Rodney Livingstone (Cambridge, MA: MIT Press, 1971), 86.

13 This would be the "animist" reading of commodity fetishism; see *Animism (Volume I)*, ed. Anselm Franke (Berlin: Sternberg Press, 2010), 35, 46–47.

14 The "Theses on Feuerbach" may be "early Marx," but Herbert Marcuse rightly insisted that early Marx's insights "find their place, structurally, *after Capital*, not merely because they convey the image of socialist man, but also because they presuppose Marx' full analysis of capitalist society." Marcuse, "Cultural Revolution" (ca. 1970), in *Towards a Critical Theory of Society*, vol. 2 of *Collected Papers, ed.* Douglas Kellner (London: Routledge, 2001), 129.

15 On praxis and labor, see also Josefine Wikström, "Practice Comes before Labour: An Attempt to Read Performance through Marx's Notion of Practice," *Performance Research: A Journal of the Performing Arts* 17, no. 6 (2012), http://doi.org/10.1080/13528165.2013.775753.

16 Jean Baudrillard, *For a Critique of the Political Economy of the Sign* (1972), trans. Charles Levin (St. Louis, MO: Telos Press, 1981), 91.

17 Baudrillard, 91. The term *fainctise* in Baudrillard's original French is rendered by Levin as "faking."

18 The decisive work is Baudrillard's *Symbolic Exchange and Death* (1976), which established a rigid opposition between precapitalist "symbolic exchange" and the equivalence of signs in the age of simulation.

19 Bruno Latour, "Why Has Critique Run Out of Steam? From Matters of Fact to Matters of Concern," *Critical Inquiry* 30 (Winter 2004): 240 (fig. 4).

20 Latour, 241 (fig. 5).

21 Bruno Latour, *Facing Gaia: Eight Lectures on the New Climatic Regime*, trans. Catherine Porter (Cambridge: Polity, 2017), 58.

22 Latour, 58.

23 Alexander R. Galloway, "Theory Hot and Cold," October 28, 2018, http://cultureandcommunication. org/galloway/theory-hot-and-cold.

24 Bruno Latour, *We Have Never Been Modern*, trans. Catherine Porter (Cambridge, MA: Harvard University Press, 1993), 40, 44.

25 Karl Marx, *Grundrisse: Foundations for the Critique of Political Economy (Rough Draft)*, trans. Martin Nicolaus (London: Penguin, 1993), 92.

26 Armen Avanessian, "The Speculative End of the Aesthetic Regime," *Texte zur Kunst*, no. 93 (March 2014): 56.

27 Avanessian, 56.

28 Avanessian, 56–58.

29 G. W. F. Hegel, *Vorlesungen über die Ästhetik I* (Frankfurt am Main: Suhrkamp, 1986), 142.

30 Antoine Quatremère de Quincy, *Lettres à Miranda sur le déplacement des monuments de l'art de l'Italie* (1796; Paris: Macula, 1989). Quatremère's analysis could, of course, be extended with even

more justification to the violent appropriation of artifacts from regions occupied by the European colonial powers—which accompanied the violence directly inflicted on these regions' inhabitants.

31 I used the term *abstraheringsmachine* in relation to an article by Wouter Davidts on the Centre Pompidou and Tate Modern; see Sven Lütticken, "Total participatie," *De Witte Raaf*, no. 101 (January–February 2003), 1.

32 Bruno Latour uses "actant" as a more "neutral" alternative for the irredeemably human-sounding "agent" or "actor."

33 Brian Holmes, "Artistic Autonomy and the Communication Society," *Third Text* 18, no. 6 (2004): 548.

34 In the preceding, I synthesize passages from Hegel's *Philosophie der Geschichte*, esp. 305, 387, 391–93.

35 See the similarities between Hegel's discussion of the Catholic cult in the passage below and his account of African fetishism in *Philosophie der Religion*, 295. Ethnologist Karl-Heinz Kohl argues that what Europeans interpreted as fetishism was, in fact, not dissimilar from the Catholic cult of relics in *Die Macht der Dinge*, 15–98. Kohl also emphasizes the long process of hybridization, during which African cultures appropriated elements from the colonizers' Catholic religion.

36 Hegel, *Philosophie der Geschichte*, 488–89; translation adapted from *Lectures on the Philosophy of History*, trans. John Sibree (London: G. Bell & Sons, 1914), 426.

37 Hegel, 489 (adapted from Sibree's translation, 426–27).

38 Hegel, 493.

39 Hegel, *Vorlesungen über die Ästhetik I*, 25. The different versions of Hegel's "end of art" narrative (and his account of history in general) in his various lecture series are not always fully consistent with each other, but here I do not focus on the discrepancies.

40 Kohl argues that these nail fetishes are the product of the encounter between African tribal cultures and the Catholicism of the European colonizers. Kohl, *Die Macht der Dinge*, 19–20, 194.

41 The Surrealist installation of "fétiches européens" was part of "La vérité sur les colonies," the 1931 Communist International–organized exhibition in Paris to counter the "Colonial Exposition."

42 This is where I part ways with Ariella Aïsha Azoulay, who in *Potential History: Unlearning Imperialism* (London: Verso, 2019) never concedes that those operating immanently on the margins of colonial capitalism can make a meaningful difference. Her treatment of Carl Einstein is telling (92–93). Since Einstein's singular practice did *not* effect a clean break with European culture, his differences do not make a difference in Azoulay's book.

43 Barnett Newman, "The New Sense of Fate" (1948), in *Selected Writings and Interviews*, ed. John P. O'Neill (Berkeley: University of California Press, 1992), 165.

44 Newman, "The Ideographic Picture" (1947) and "The First Man Was an Artist" (1947), in *Selected Writings and Interviews*, 108 and 159.

45 Newman, "The Plasmic Image" (1945), in *Selected Writings and Interviews*, 245.

46 Newman, "Open Letter to William A. M. Burden, President of the Museum of Modern Art" (1953), in *Selected Writings and Interviews*, 39.

47 See Theodor W. Adorno, *Ästhetische Theorie* (Frankfurt am Main: Suhrkamp, 1970), 338.

48 Stewart Martin, "The Absolute Artwork Meets the Absolute Commodity," *Radical Philosophy*, no. 146 (November/December 2007): 22.

49 See Susan Vogel's pivotal exhibition catalogue *Art/Artifact: African Art in Anthropology Collections* (New York: Center for African Art, 1988).

50 "The Richard Mutt Case," *Blind Man*, no. 2 (May 1917): n.p.

51 John Roberts, *The Intangibilities of Form: Skill and Deskilling in Art after the Readymade* (London: Verso, 2007), 21–43.

52 Arjun Appadurai, "Introduction: Commodities and the Politics of Value," in *The Social Life of Things: Commodities in Cultural Perspective*, ed. Arjun Appadurai (Cambridge: Cambridge University Press, 1986), 5.

53 Marcel Duchamp, "À l'infinitif / 'Boîte blanche,'" in *Duchamp du signe*, ed. Michel Sanouillet and Elmer Peterson (Paris: Flammarion, 1994), 105.

54 On Baumgarten and ethnography, specifically his 2011 exhibition at Museum Folkwang, see Benjamin Meyer-Krahmer, "Who's Present in Presentation? On Lothar Baumgarten's *Evening of Time – Señores*

Naturales. Yanomami," in *Timing: On the Temporal Dimension of Exhibiting*, ed. Beatrice von Bismarck et al. (Berlin: Sternberg Press, 2014), 258–80.

55 The overall curatorial concept of "ExitCongoMuseum: A Century of Art with/without Papers" was by Boris Wastiau, who invited the artist Toma Muteba Luntumbue to curate the contemporary art section, in which he also participated. Among the other participants were Meschac Gaba, David Hammons, and Luc Tuymans.

56 Julia Noordegraaf, *Strategies of Display: Museum Presentation in Nineteenth- and Twentieth-Century Visual Culture* (Rotterdam: Museum Boijmans Van Beuningen, 2012), 9. On the Teylers Museum, see Mark Dion, "Füllung des Naturhistorischen Museums," *Texte zur Kunst*, no. 20 (November 1995): 75–86.

57 "Intolerance" was accompanied by a boxed three-part catalogue, with a volume dedicated to, respectively, Melchior d'Hondecoeter, Hawaiian featherwork, and De Rooij and his exhibition.

58 "The Potosí Principle: How Can We Sing the Song of the Lord in an Alien Land?" was shown at Museo Nacional Centro de Arte Reina Sofía in Madrid, Haus der Kulturen der Welt in Berlin, and the Museo Nacional de Arte and Museo Nacional de Etnografía y Folklore in La Paz.

59 See various essays in *The Potosí Principle: How Can We Sing the Song of the Lord in an Alien Land?*, ed. Alice Creischer, Max Jorge Hinderer, and Andreas Siekmann (Cologne: Verlag der Buchhandlung Walther König, 2010).

60 "Walter Benjamin," "The Way beyond 'Art'" (2010), in *Recent Writings* (Vancouver: New Documents, 2013), 67–68. This text was originally published in the first issue of *The Copyist*, a publication accompanying the Van Abbemuseum's project "Play Van Abbe" (2009–11).

61 "Walter Benjamin," "The Unmaking of Art" (2011), in *Recent Writings*, 132. See also Steven ten Thije, "The Joys of Meta: On the Museum of American Art," *Afterall*, no. 37 (Autumn/Winter 2014), http://www.afterall.org/journal/issue.37/the-joy-of-meta_on-the-museum-of-american-art.

62 The Museum of Arte Útil was on view at the Van Abbemuseum, Eindhoven, from December 2013 to March 2014. See https://vanabbemuseum.nl/en/programme/programme/museum-of-arte-util/.

63 See Sven Lütticken, “Shine and Schein,” *e-flux journal*, no. 61 (January 2015), http://www.e-flux.com/journal/shine-and-schein/.

64 Alfred Gell, *Art and Agency: An Anthropological Theory* (Oxford: Oxford University Press, 1998), 23. Indexicality is, of course, not an exclusive property of artifacts; they can be indexical, symbolic, and iconic.

65 Gell, 28.

66 Referencing the title of Eliseo Verón’s study *La semiosis social* (1993), So-Hyun Ahn calls the form of semiosis proper to the index “social semiosis.” Ahn, “Le sens de l’espace muséal: Analyse sémiotique des éléments muséographiques” (PhD diss., Jean Moulin University Lyon 3, 2010), 81. After Rosalind Krauss’s classic two-part “Notes on the Index,” in *The Originality of the Avant-Garde, and Other Modernist Myths* (Cambridge, MA: MIT Press, 1986), 196–219, the most ambitious recent attempt to accord the category of the index a central role for cultural analysis is Diedrich Diederichsen, *Körpertreffer: Zur Ästhetik der nachpopulären Künste* (Berlin: Suhrkamp, 2017).

67 Unlike the autonomous semiotic system posited by Baudrillard in his desire to define fetishism in systemic terms, as the fetishism of the code, forgetting his own remarks about the “made” quality of the *feitiço*.

68 “Agency,” Les Laboratoires d’Aubervilliers, http://www.leslaboratoires.org/en/artiste/agency/assemblee-les-laboratoires-d-aubervilliers.

69 In the case of *Thing 000773 (Pseudomonas)*, the patented organism has a strong link with traditional knowledge—its detoxifying properties had been used in India for centuries. See chapter 6 in this volume.

70 While the artist consented to the museum sale, he contested the use of his sculpture on the banknote, which was highly controversial in his community. During the court case, “Roy Marika, the senior male member of the Rirratjingu clan […] understood that Mr Yumbulul had the right to make the Morning Star Pole for ceremonial purposes and also for sale to places such as museums in order to educate people. […] Mr Marika said that the subject of mass reproduction of paintings and important objects is very sensitive because it takes the ability and right to produce and supervise the production of these objects out of the hands of the Aboriginal people” (quoted from Agency’s file on *Thing 001390*). However, the judge ruled that

because Yumbulul had signed an agreement with the agency that provided for this kind of transaction, he could not claim to have been misled, and his case was dismissed.

71 See, for instance, *Making Things Public: Atmospheres of Democracy*, ed. Bruno Latour and Peter Weibel (London: MIT Press, 2005).

72 Florian Cramer, "What Is Post-digital?," *APRJA* 3, no. 1 (2014), http://www.aprja.net/?p=1318.

73 See Stefano Harney and Tonika Sealy, "Creative Industries as Underdevelopment," *Chimurenga Chronic*, March 2015, 48.

74 These projects acknowledge that the participants are not economic, social, and political equals; thus, democratic and egalitarian forms of collaboration become all the more important.

75 "Group Affinity" was the title of a summer school and subsequent exhibition co-organized by Casco and Kunstverein Munich in 2011.

76 Taken from the exhibition's press release, http://www.kw-berlin.de/media/files/00_renzo-martens_press-kit_en.pdf (link discontinued).

77 See "The Chimurenga Library," October–November 2015, http://www.theshowroom.org/exhibitions/the-chimurenga-library; the *Chimurenga Chronic* was available at the exhibition.

78 "Man kann eigentlich nur noch Ausstellungen machen, die Workshops sind oder Seminare oder selbstermächtigende Bildungsgruppen." Tim Caspar Boehme, "Gekommen, um im Betonberg zu bleiben," *die tageszeitung*, September 15, 2012, http://www.taz.de/1/archiv/digitaz/artikel/?ressort=ku&dig=2012/09/15/a0054.

79 On the British Museum and Australian Aboriginal culture, see Paul Daley, "Preservation or Plunder? The Battle over the British Museum's Indigenous Australian Show," *Guardian*, April 9, 2015, http://www.theguardian.com/artanddesign/2015/apr/09/indigenous-australians-enduring-civilisation-british-museum-repatriation.

80 Attia's 2020 video installation *The Object's Interlacing* can be seen as further development of *The Body's Legacies, Part 1: The Objects*, continuing the artist's dialogic inquiry into the histories of plundered and displaced objects as well as the changing cultures and societies that have some kind of stake in them.

81 On the two illusions contained in Marx's analysis of commodity fetishism, see Martin, "The Absolute Artwork," 22–23.

Chapter 2

GHOSTS OF THINGS, OR

THE UNIVERSAL MUSEUM OF PLASTER CASTS

If the fetish indexes its origins, the commodity fetish is indeed a broken index. The commodity's value appears to be determined by its "social intercourse" with other commodities; it is not evident to the "fetishist" that the commodity's value is, in fact, the result of the amount of socially necessary labor that went into its production. In contrast to the symbol or the icon, according to Charles Sanders Peirce, the index signifies through physical contiguity. A footprint indexes that somebody has been there; a wind vane indexes the wind. As Diedrich Diederichsen has put it, the index shouts from reality but does not say much at first.[1] It only starts to signify through interpretation. But what if the index is not even recognized, if its shout goes unheard? The commodity's value appears not to be *faictise*, that is, not made by human hand. Marx's project—that of the labor theory of value—is to restore the indexical link. However, this does not amount to some kind of fetishization of the handmade. As opposed to Ruskin or Morris, Marx had little time for medievalizing nostalgia.

Marx's exchange-value is quantity to use-value's quality; it is abstraction to use-value's concretion.[2] As "concrete useful labour,"[3] work creates use-values. However, when we are dealing with abstract labor in the form of labor-power sold by the worker to the capitalist, this produces exchange-value. On the one hand, we have work that creates use-value, as a necessary condition for the subsistence and reproduction of humankind, independent of the socially produced division of labor. On the other hand, there is "abstract labor" or human labor-power in general, which is subject to the division of labor and made measurable and compatible as a commodity in its own right.

Workers sell their labor-power, their generalized and abstract labor, for a certain amount of money. Any "functioning" commodity must have a use-value, or possibly several different use-values to different people; otherwise, it would be a failed commodity, never to find a buyer. Therefore, "use-value" need not refer only to objects that have a clear "practical" function—such as coats, cars, or cornflakes. In fact, Marx states categorically, "Nothing can be a value without being an object of utility. If the thing is useless, so is the labour contained in it; the labour does not count as labour, and therefore creates no value."[4]

Marx does not attempt to restore the indexical link in the sense of showcasing individual craft in the object, as Arts and Crafts and related movements that were critical of industrial alienation sought to do. The labor on which Marx focuses is quantifiable, socially necessary abstract labor. In the process, the fetish moves from the realm of the singular (this rock, that tree, that sculpture) to the multiple, quantifiable, and replicable (raw linen or linen coats; raw iron and wrought iron or cast-iron objects). Marx often draws his examples from key industrial sectors and technologies, such as the textile industry, with its programmable Jacquard looms, and the iron industry. He also took notes on cast iron, without ever expounding on it in print.[5] In the nineteenth century, cast iron replaced a number of traditional materials and was used on a large scale in architecture (including cotton mills), and on a smaller scale for household objects.

Western thinking about objecthood and design has been shaped by ancient philosophy, in particular, Aristotle's hylomorphism. In his *Metaphysics*, Aristotle intervened in the antique debate over substance and accidents by distinguishing between *hyle* (matter) and *morphe* (form), with the latter being the prime mover, the soul that shaped the body provided by raw matter. Nineteenth-century cast iron was an *operational hylomorphism*, providing a relatively effortless transition from design to mold to the mass materialization of the form. The indexical procedure of casting was perfect for generating any number of forms in any number of styles. Among the definitive artifacts of the era are catalogues of casts. Major ironworks like W. Macfarlane & Co. Ltd. had sumptuous showrooms that were Benjaminian *Traumhäuser*—phantasmagoric condensations of the world of the arcades. Macfarlane and Coalbrookdale also published extravagant illustrated catalogues. As Paul Dobraszczyk has argued, the technical possibility of providing customers with virtually identical copies of designed objects and the economico-juridical need for copyright protection of one's design conspired to make such catalogues desirable and even necessary.[6]

In the nineteenth century, Augustus Pugin condemned cast-iron ornaments (based on Greek or Gothic forms derived from other materials) as a "sham," "showy," and "meretricious," while Ruskin lambasted the material as "Operative Deceit."[7] Such ethico-aesthetic criticism of capitalist commodities is linked to the rise of the notion of "truth to materials," which found its first great exponent in Gottfried Semper.[8] Ultimately, this doctrine would triumph in modernism, and help to end the reign of historicist cast-iron objects, ornaments, and architecture. It is telling that many modernists preferred wrought iron over cast iron. Modern plastics, however, have led to a resurgence of casting in manufacturing—the vast majority of everyday plastic objects are made with molds. Hence it should come as no surprise that the second half of the twentieth century saw a resurgence of Aristotelian hylomorphism in theories of design and technology such as Vilém Flusser's, which effectively collapsed the value-form with the visible, plastic form.

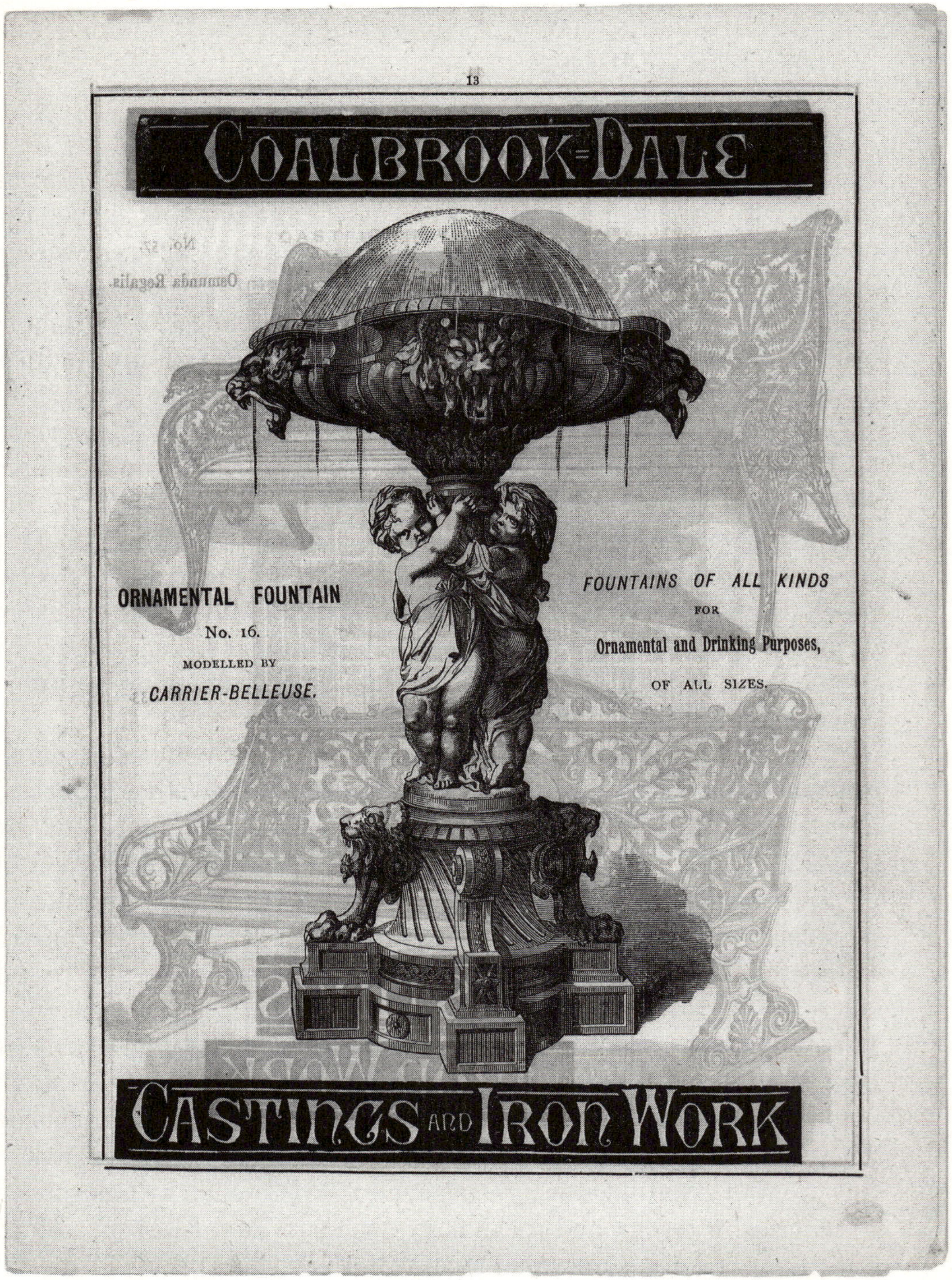

Page from the *Coalbrookdale Illustrated Spring Catalogue* (1888)

For Flusser, design is the imprinting of matter (*hyle*) with a form (*morphe*), and the value of a ballpoint pen derives from this form.[9] By contrast, in his philosophy of technical objects, Gilbert Simondon stressed that form does not somehow magically incarnate in matter, it is rather the result of complex processes of individuation—even in the case of something as seemingly simple as molding clay into bricks. We are always dealing with *prepared matter* and with already *materialized forms* (such as a mold), mediated by a third factor that classic hylomorphism leaves out: human social labor. For Simondon, this Aristotelian blind spot suggests that the hyle/morphe distinction reflects the one between the craftsperson/slave on the one hand, and the free person/designer on the other.[10] Simondon's point here recalls Marx's observation in *Capital* that while Aristotle made some headway with the analysis of value, he fell short of understanding the basis of value in "equal human labour." Marx continues:

> Greek society was founded on the labour of slaves, hence had as its natural basis the inequality of men and their labour-powers. The secret of the expression of value, namely the equality and equivalence of all kinds of labour because and insofar as they are human labour in general, could not be deciphered until the concept of human equality has already acquired the permanence of a fixed popular opinion.[11]

From nineteenth-century cast iron to twentieth-century plastics, then, casting was an essential method. In both cases, *production* is essentially mechanical *reproduction*: the difference is that cast-iron objects sometimes also mimicked historical examples, while plastic objects tend to reproduce an "up-to-date" prototype. Mass production *is* reproduction; catalogues illustrating the products add another layer of reproduction. Modern art, of course, being predicated on handcrafted, unique fetish objects, long struggled with the rise of mechanical (re)production. Given the role of indexical casting in industrial capitalism, it is not surprising that some artists should have engaged with the plaster cast as the quintessential artistic—but still suspect, precisely for its mechanical nature—form of casting.

That Old Thing, Mechanical Reproduction

Throughout Europe, one can see the scattered remains of what once was a prominent type of cultural institution: the collection of plaster casts from ancient (especially Greek and Roman) sculptures. In the nineteenth century, the golden age of cast collections, they played two essential functions. On the one hand, in the context of museums, they could give the "general public" an overview of the history of sculpture that no collection of originals could offer. On the other hand, in the context of art academies, they provided students with materials to copy and, ultimately, emulate. These two overlapping functions both came under pressure in the decades around 1900. Once omnipresent, plaster casts were relegated to the status of an embarrassment by modernism—something utterly old-fashioned, inartistic, and alien to living art.

After spending most of the twentieth century in the wilderness, with more and more cast collections suffering from neglect or active destruction up to the 1960s and 1970s, the plaster cast seems to be subject to a certain revaluation. A number of collections have been restored or reconstructed and newly installed—Munich being prominent among these. Does this mean that the plaster cast has now been normalized, that it has become a well-behaved footnote of cultural history? I would argue that its historical status remains contradictory and, therefore, interesting.

As a method of mechanical reproduction that has been practiced since time immemorial, casting—whether in plaster or another material—

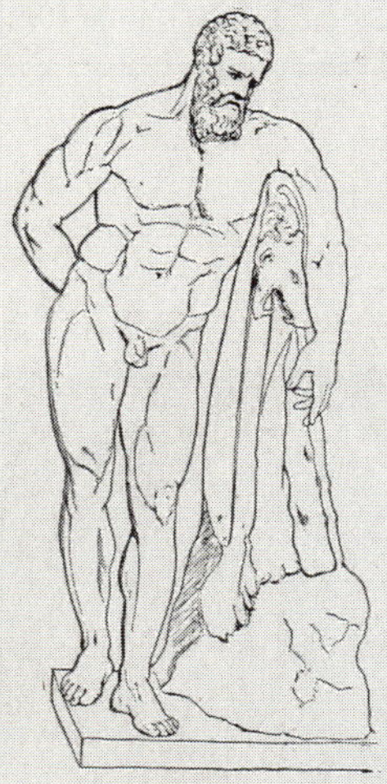
754

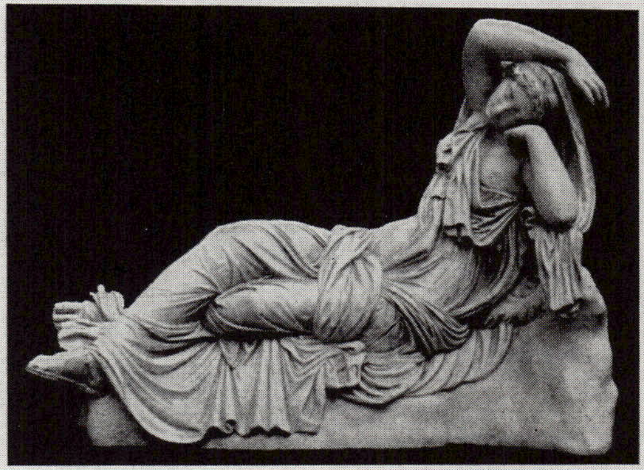
755

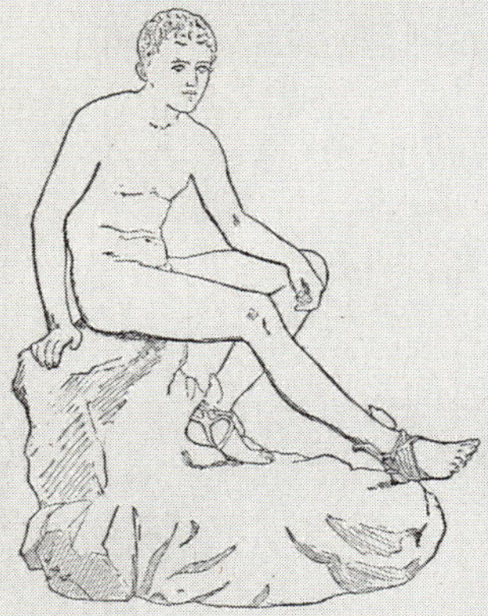
758

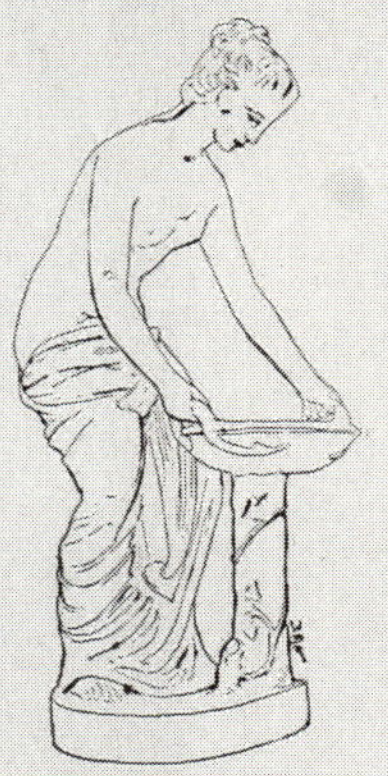
759, 759 A

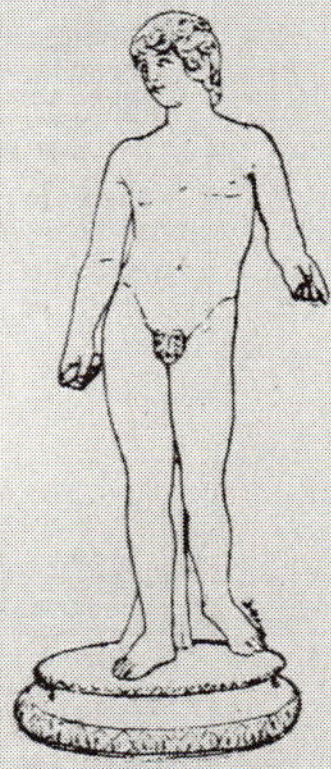
760

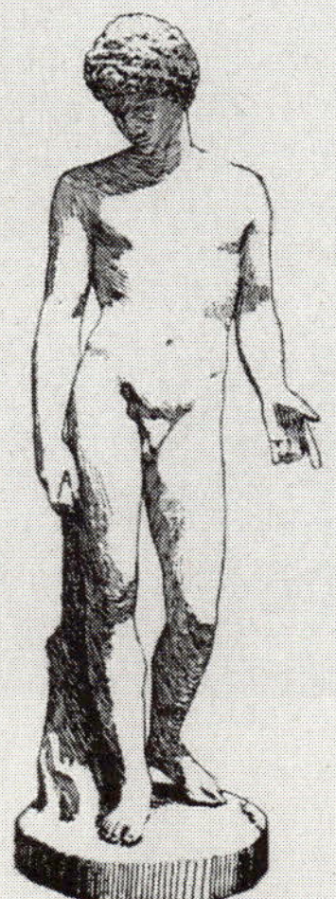
761

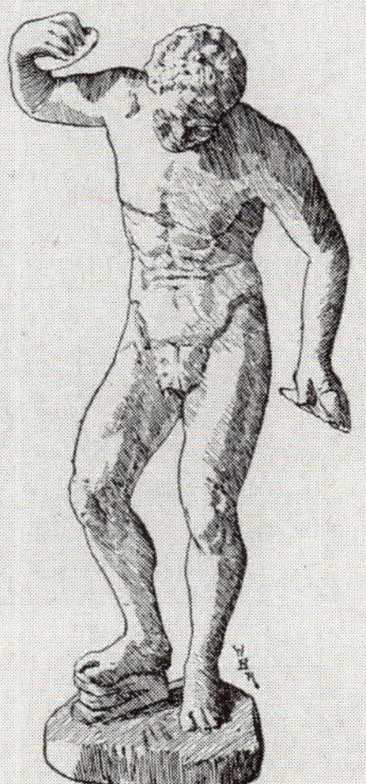
762, 763

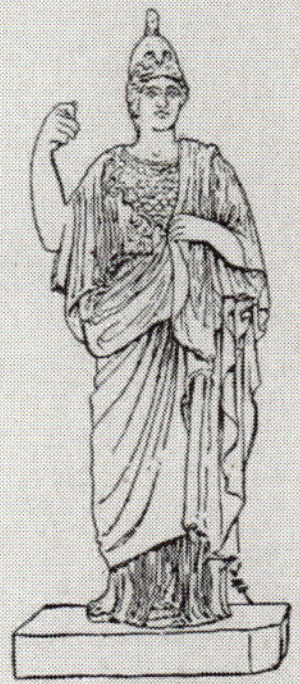
783

Page from P. P. Caproni and Brother, *Catalogue of Plaster Cast Reproductions from Antique, Medieval and Modern Sculpture* (1901)

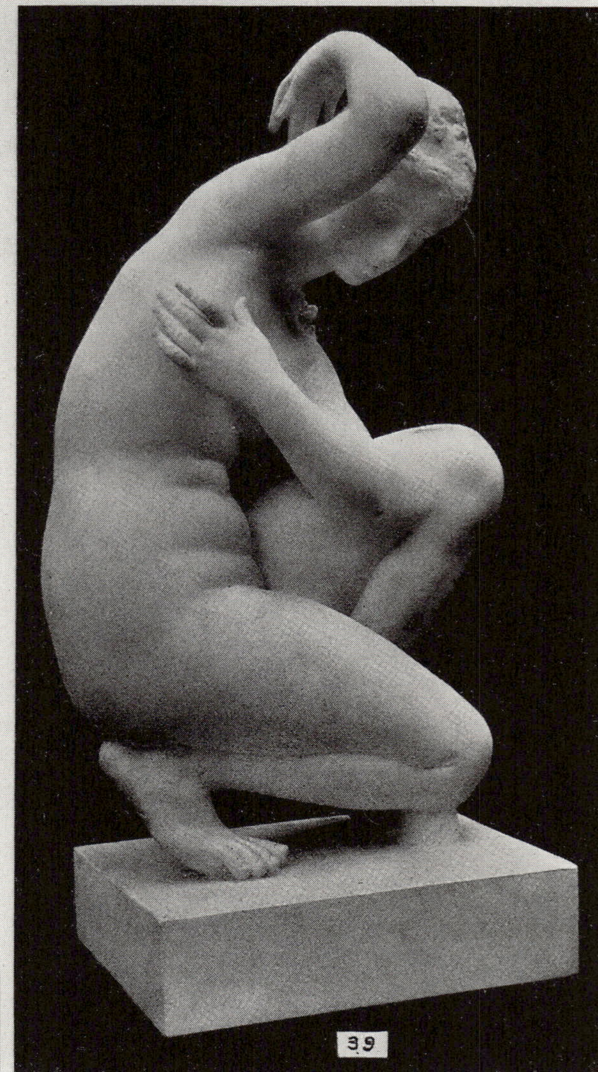
39

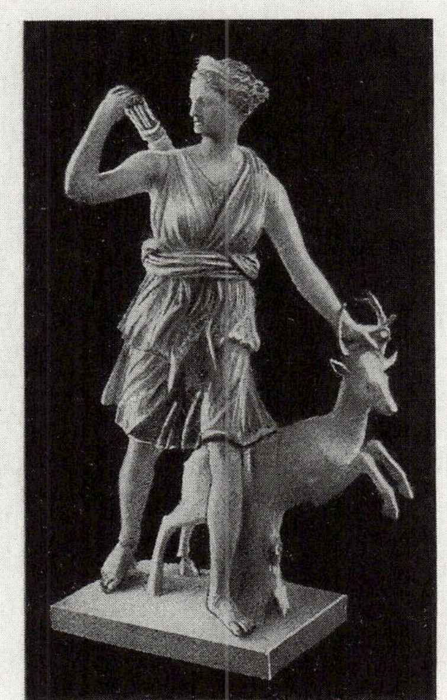

44

No. 39 Venus Crouching ....2 ft. 7 in. $25.00
(Original in Louvre, Paris.)

Diana of Versailles. This figure is also known as the Goddess of the Chase. The date of discovery is unknown. The original is in the Louvre, Paris.

No. 44	Diana of Versailles....................................	7 ft.	$100.00
No. 44A	" "	4 "	40.00
No. 44B	" "	3 "	20.00

Page from P. P. Caproni and Brother, *Catalogue of Plaster Cast Reproductions from Antique, Medieval and Modern Sculpture* (1901)

can be termed both archaic and prophetic. Perhaps the fervor with which plaster casts and cast collections were attacked as anachronisms in the twentieth century was a symptom of uneasiness concerning the growth of mechanical reproduction in the modern era. Perhaps the *Unheimlichkeit* of cast collections was due as much to their futurist as to their old-fashioned traits.[12]

As Georges Didi-Huberman has emphasized, the casting of bodies or body parts was used by Renaissance sculptors such as Donatello, but it was frowned upon by humanist art theorists such as Vasari.[13] As casting was a mechanical procedure, it frustrated art's attempt to become accepted as one of the liberal arts—something with which sculpture, as a more physical art than painting, had greater difficulty anyway.[14] Renaissance art theory placed a high value on imitation; artists were to copy works by their great predecessors, but this was not a mechanical process. Imitation should not be slavish, and it had to lead to compositions that modify the examples that have been used. Though this was, to a significant degree, a manual affair, the hand was guided by the mind, by a lofty conception, and this was a fundamental difference with (apparently) merely mechanical practices such as casting.

Even so, Renaissance art was unthinkable without various forms of (semi)mechanical reproduction, including woodcuts and engravings and casts of revered antique statues. A culture developed in which the Apollo Belvedere, the Laocoön, and the other revered masterpieces of ancient art from the Vatican's Belvedere Courtyard (and from the Capitoline Hill) were sought after to make molds and casts. Around 1540, Primaticcio, court painter of François I, was in Rome making plaster molds from the most famous antique sculptures, which were sent to France. In France, bronze casts for Fontainebleau were then made from these molds. Bronze casts were, of course, more difficult and expensive to make than plaster ones, so the slightly less wealthy opted for plaster casts, but even this was rare in the sixteenth century.

But casts after antique statues not only provided impressive decorations for the abodes of the rich and powerful, they were also important teaching aids. Sculptors could learn much from studying casts as "stand-ins" for the originals. When Louis XIV set up the French Academy in Rome in 1666, one of its prime tasks was to make various sorts of copies to be sent back to Paris: marble copies made by young, aspiring artists as well as casts.[15] Since the transportation of brittle casts was a dangerous, expensive enterprise, from the late eighteenth century, an increasing amount of casts were produced in northern Europe (where the buyers were) from molds that had traveled across the Alps.[16]

By this time, the white surfaces of plaster casts had come to be appreciated as much as the more irregular marble surfaces of the originals, *and sometimes more so.* Previously, plaster casts were considered to be inferior by far to bronze casts, but Johann Joachim Winckelmann sang the praises of white as the color that reflects the most rays and is perceived and therefore adds beauty to an already beautiful body. These are the humble beginnings of aesthetic hierarchies that would eventually become the dogma of "scientific racism," enshrining whiteness alongside facial features among the characteristics that demonstrates the superiority of the "White Man" and legitimized colonialism.[17] Greek sculptures and their Roman copies, originally painted, had been whitewashed over time. In the classicist imaginary, a sculpture such as the Apollo Belvedere constituted an aesthetic ideal precisely because it represented a noble "Greek profile" in white marble—and as such, it could be visually juxtaposed to "negro" and simian heads, as in a notorious nineteenth-century illustration.[18]

Nothing was whiter than a new plaster cast. Fresh white plaster seems to transubstantiate flesh and turn it into the idea of flesh.[19] Plaster casts thus allowed Neoclassicist artists and art lovers to study a purified kind of sculpture, almost dematerialized yet three-dimensional, which could also be studied from all angles and even turned around. Winckelmann and Goethe got their first substantial taste of antique sculpture at the Skulpturenhalle in Mannheim in their native Germany. In his autobiography *Dichtung und Wahrheit*, Goethe fondly reminisced how, as a young man, he first entered this cast collection with its "forest of statues" that could be lit in various ways and turned on their pedestals—great advantages over the originals. Here, he finally saw the Laocoön group about which he'd read so much—in Leipzig, he had only seen a cast of Laocoön himself, not the entire group.[20] When Goethe went to Italy, he made sure to visit the Farsetti collection of plaster casts in Venice in 1786, making the acquaintance of some works that had not been present in the Mannheim collection.[21] When in Rome, he visited a caster's workshop, where he saw "together what is dispersed throughout Rome, which is immensely useful for comparisons."[22]

Cast collections allowed Goethe and others to see and compare dispersed works. As André Malraux noted, cast collections are, in this respect, comparable to the "imaginary museum" constituted by photography in the nineteenth and twentieth centuries. Both go beyond copying existing museums and, in fact, form an "imaginary museum" of reproductions:

> Museums of casts and copies too bring together dispersed works: they chose more freely than other museums […]. They have more force than an album [of photographs], but not the virus which dissolves everything in favor of style. This stems from reduction in size and, often, from the absence of volume, and always from the proximity and succession of plates, makes a style come alive similar to a sped-up film that makes a plant come alive.[23]

In *Le musée imaginaire*—which was translated into English rather freely as *The Museum without Walls*—Malraux argues that the "real" museum was increasingly supplanted by the imaginary museum of photography. However, the physical art museum itself came *after* the imaginary museum of plaster casts, and my own work as well as that of Claudia Bahmer and Walter Grasskamp has sought to reinstate this historical background to Malraux's work.[24] For a while, the art museum—as the modern institution whose characteristics were defined between the 1790s and the 1930s—coexisted with this plaster cast museum. When a museum was opened in the Louvre in the wake of the French Revolution, there were two collections of plaster casts, both having been supplied by the French Academy in Rome: the royal collection and the one owned by the Académie Royale de Peinture et de Sculpture.[25]

However, Napoleon's conquests went hand in hand with the requisition of works of art from occupied countries, which were deported to the Louvre. The famous antique sculptures from the Belvedere arrived in Paris in a festive procession in July 1798. In the Louvre museum, which was called the Musée Napoléon from 1803 on, the cast collection lost its necessity: the plasters were supplanted by their originals. At least in the case of the Tiber and Nile statues from the Vatican, the originals were in fact exhibited in the very places where the copies had been installed from 1692 to 1793.[26] The imaginary museum of plaster casts was made real, as the real works of art became stand-ins for their own reproductions. When the original works of art had to be returned in 1815, the creation of a museum of plaster casts became, once again, a priority.[27] Throughout the nineteenth century, the Louvre housed several museums of casts with varying contents.

From the sixteenth to the early nineteenth century, there was a small canon of "antique masterpieces"—those from the Belvedere being most canonical of all. However, in the decades around 1800, the idea slowly sank in that most of the revered statues—such as the Apollo Belvedere—were not originals by Greek artists but Roman copies. With the arrival of the Parthenon marbles in London and other discoveries, the status of sculptures from the Belvedere receded, and earlier, authentic Greek works became more focal. But while extending backward in time, the imaginary museum also moved forward into the Middle Ages and the Renaissance. By the last decades of the nineteenth century, museums such as the Musée de Sculpture Comparée in the Trocadéro, the Victoria and Albert Museum in London, and the Rijksmuseum in Amsterdam were actively engaged in these fields, which seemed more relevant to contemporary culture after the demise of Neoclassicism. Frequently, such casts would also be tinted in a naturalistic fashion.

Naturalism was, of course, also de rigueur for the casting of live models. While it had long been a suspicion hanging over the heads of sculptures that their more naturalistic works were (based on) casts, rather than on a truly creative synthesis, castings from life (or from death) provided study material for artists and art students. By the end of the nineteenth century, the Gipsformerei in Berlin, for one, was actively implicated in the fabrication and dissemination of ethnographic casts made from colonial subjects, who often had little agency in the matter. One 1906 letter shows a Prussian anthropologist fretting over the correct coloration of a cast of a South African "Bushman": replication of the actual skin color of the man would not give a realistic impression, as he would normally be covered in dirt, and the cast should reflect this. This colonial casting of those deemed to represent a lower, near-simian rung on the evolutionary ladder is the obverse of classicism and its cult of idealized white bodies, as embodied by the Apollo Belvedere and its many casts: the dark side of the aesthetic ideal.[28]

Two Imprints

Like art history, anthropology used photographs for its classificatory and anthropometric aims. Across disciplines, the rise of the imaginary museum of photography was unstoppable. As a method of mechanical reproduction, the cast does, in fact, share certain characteristics with photography. Both the cast and the photograph are imprints. The cast is the positive print of the negative mold, just as the analog photo print is a positive of a negative that is a photochemical imprint made by briefly opening the aperture. In Peirce's categorization of signs as icon, index, or symbol, it is the indexicality of both cast and photo that stands out. An index is a sign that has some causal connection with the object to which it points—a footprint "points to" the foot that made it by imprinting itself on the sand, and a weather vane points out the direction of the wind.[29]

Icons are signs that physically resemble what they stand for. This is not necessarily the case for indices, as the weather vane does not resemble the wind. Casts and photographic imprints form a special subset: their very indexicality makes them appear as "natural images," as perfect likenesses, or *vera icones.* The reference to the Christian notion of the "vera icon" is not a frivolous aside, for the legend of the "Veronica" image is a proto-photographic myth. In fact, the Shroud of Turin, which has supposedly been in direct contact with the body of Christ, only really became a religious and cultural icon once a photographic negative had been made in 1898. It was only in the negative that the image of the body became really apparent.[30] One could, therefore, say with Didi-Huberman that, in the case of both photo and cast, "the element of *contact* remains a guarantee of uniqueness, authenticity and power—and therefore of aura."[31] Mechanical reproduction, then, does not forcibly destroy aura, as Benjamin claimed—and Malraux's *musée imaginaire* was, to a large extent, a critical response to Benjamin.

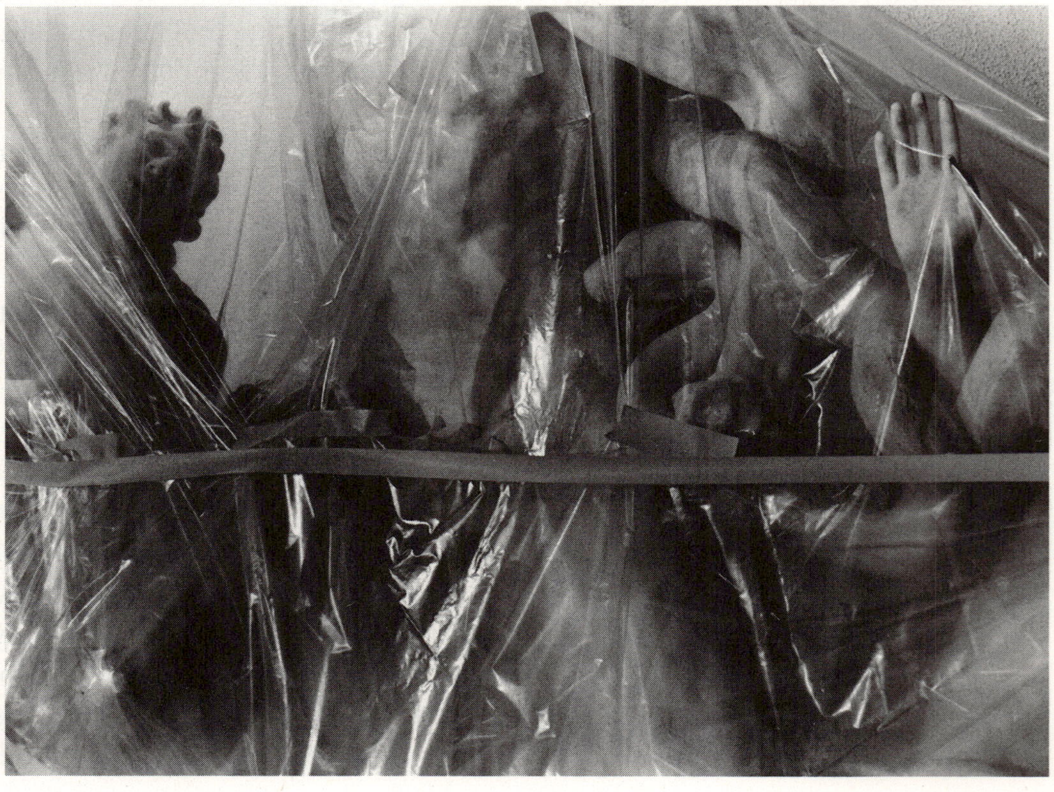

Louise Lawler, *Storage*, 1984

Douglas Crimp's 1993 book *On the Museum's Ruins* contains a series of photographs by Louise Lawler of casts after antique sculptures such as the Munich Glyptothek's Barberini Faun (ca. 220 BC) and Fallen Warrior (ca. 490–480 BC; from the eastern pediment of the Aegina temple). Removed from the Metropolitan Museum of Art in 1938, Lawler documented them as stored and (partly) restored relics at the Queens Museum.[32] On the one hand, these casts are the embarrassing relics of a patriarchal and imperialist culture that has modernized its appearances, but they also anticipate the use of photomechanical reproduction by artists such as Robert Rauschenberg and Andy Warhol, or Lawler herself—a development that Crimp, referencing Benjamin as well as Malraux, sees as throwing the modern museum as a storehouse of "originals" into a fundamental crisis. As with Benjamin's prediction about the destruction of aura, this has hardly been borne out by the course of events. However, the rise of photographic reproduction *did* contribute to the decline of the plaster cast. Why, then, did the photograph succeed where the cast failed?

Photography constituted a much more perfect musée imaginare than cast collections had because it was far freer in selecting, enlarging, and combining images, and, in fact, in *turning objects into images*: "These miniatures, these frescos, these stained-glass windows, these tapestries, these Scythian plaques, these details, these drawings, these Greek vases, even the sculptures, have become plates. What have they lost? Their object-quality. What have they gained? The greatest stylistic significance they can attain."[33] In the photographic musée imaginaire, works were often cropped, reduced to fragments that call attention to style. Because works of different sizes and materials were all reduced to the same size and to two-dimensionality, this emphasis on style was even more pronounced. Whereas the cast collection remained doggedly faithful to the objects' sizes, even as it replaced precious materials with that simulacrum of materiality that is plaster, photography enjoyed greater autonomy vis-à-vis the object and dematerialized it while still transmitting an unbelievable wealth of detail.

Photography became a crucial tool for the developing discipline of art history. Exhibitions such as the 1877 Dresden retrospective of Hans Holbein combined originals with photographs of Holbein paintings that were absent.[34] In 1875 (the fifth centennial of Michelangelo's birth), an exhibition was organized in the Accademia in Florence in which the *David* was the only authentic piece—other sculptures were present as plaster casts, arranged around the central figure of the *David*, while drawings and frescos were presented as photographs. The whole ensemble amounted to an imaginary museum combining an ancient technique of reproduction (casting) with a modern one (photography), and one original work. In the wake of the exhibition, a Michelangelo museum following the same principle opened in 1882.[35]

More fundamentally, as Francis Haskell has stressed, the possibility to compare works through photographs triggered a desire to compare the originals and, thus, for the genre of the old-master exhibition. As far as museums' permanent collections were concerned, these were supposed to consist of originals. In discussions about the Rijksmuseum and its plaster cast collection in the late 1910s, what stands out is how marginalized cast collections have become in the age of the *authentic object*.[36] These "ghosts of things," as the art historian Willem Vogelsang called them, were uncanny presences in the museum of originals.[37] Many agreed that, in theory, they could be teaching aids for art historians, just as they had been for art schools and craft schools, but in practice, there were great obstacles. Since they should not be combined with the originals, they required separate museums, and precisely because museums were now seen as repositories of authentic masterpieces, such cast collections, in fact, became "ghosts of museums," spectral doubles of the real thing.

Photography never really seemed a threat to the authentic object because it so patently dematerialized it, even as it reproduced it down to its minute details and blemishes. And crucially, photography could reproduce *painting*: a medium that became more and more dominant as classicist aesthetics waned, and one that Hegel considered to be that of Christian art par excellence, being more spiritual and subjective than sculpture. For an idealist such as Hegel, the whole classicist enterprise ultimately rested on a fallacy: it was impossible to return to or revive classical Greek sculpture, as that stage in the development of Spirit was irretrievably lost.[38] With its idealized human bodies in stone or bronze, classical Greek art represented the pinnacle of art, a happy medium between spirit and matter, subject and object. Christian art, on the other hand, was subjective and soulful. Painting was the perfect medium for modern subjectivism, and antique sculpture looked cold and objective by comparison.[39]

While Hegel noted that the greatest Christian art presented a subjective or spiritualized view of God's creation, recent art had tended to disintegrate into two opposed tendencies: either extreme, solipsistic subjectivism or minute attention to external details.[40] The public announcement of the invention of photography took place eight years after Hegel's death, but his analysis of the logic of "modern" art resonates with the new medium. Its seemingly slavish faithfulness was its boon and its bane; for many artists and critics, a photochemical imprint could never be art, as it failed to idealize or subjectify reality. However, photographers soon sought to demonstrate that they could use the medium to poetic effect. Photographic imprints on paper or celluloid differ from the three-dimensional imprints of casts. While a photograph can give a complete view of a painting or print as well as show a detail or an installation view with several works, it obviously cannot pretend to reproduce a sculpture in three dimensions. Instead, it shows it at a specific time and place, in a certain light, from a point of view that emphasizes particular characteristics.

This meant that photographs could show sculptures in their context, thus fortifying their aura. It also meant that photographers could use sculptures in compositions that underlined their own creative role. Edward Steichen's renditions of works by Rodin are perhaps the most famous examples. For Steichen and the other "pictorialist" photographers associated with the review *Camera Work*, the aim was to show that photography was as rich as painting and could cover both sides of the coin: poetic suggestion of a higher reality as well as objective rendering of physical reality. Like many others in the decades before him, Rodin exhibited plasters at the Salon in Paris and other exhibitions and turned his studio into a plaster cast museum. For all his aesthetic innovations, Rodin's plaster-centric production process was profoundly indebted to the Neoclassical sculpture of ca. 1800.

Antonio Canova, who, as a young apprentice, had first encountered the masterpieces of antique sculpture in the cast collection of the Palazzo Farsetti in Venice, was foremost among them. Canova perfected a process beginning with small *bozzetti* in clay and culminating in a full-scale plaster cast from a clay model. These plaster casts could then be displayed in his studio or elsewhere until a buyer was found, who would finance the execution of the piece in marble. The "original plaster" would thus serve as both an enticement for the customer to buy a certain piece and the model for the final piece.[41] For the creation of the marble, the plaster would be covered in "points," where thin nails were inserted in crucial spots. Subsequently, a pointing machine (consisting of a wooden framework with adjustable arms ending in metal needles) was used to register the coordinates and then to transfer the points (the coordinates) to the marble block.[42] Thus, a mechanical reproduction (a plaster cast of a clay model, the "original plaster") was used to create a reproduction in marble—

in a process that was manual, but with some mechanical and industrial elements. This semi-industrial practice was justified by the Neoclassicist aesthetic, which placed the highest value on the artist's lofty conception, and less on his personal touch, which threatened to make a piece too individual and personal. As Romanticism and its modernist legacy triumphed, Canova's way of working was increasingly regarded as inartistic.

Though Rodin's artistic practice was in part shaped by a mechanical reproduction process, he was at pains to keep things fluid. He often made different plasters or worked on them by dipping the pieces—if they were heads or small figures—into liquid plaster, thus creating an irregular new surface (on which he could do further work).[43] For the reproductions of these plasters in other materials, and in spite of the mystique surrounding his unique touch, Rodin relied on specialized founders (for bronzes) and on studio assistants under his surveillance (for marbles). One of the foundries was the Maison Barbedienne, which operated as Collas and Barbedienne from 1838 until 1850, after which Ferdinand Barbedienne and his successors continued without Antoine Collas. They specialized in the "reduction" of famous sculptures, producing (bronze) casts in miniature. To achieve faithful models that could then be molded and cast, they used a kind of pantograph apparatus devised by Collas—a refinement of the pointing machine used by Canova and others before, now allowing for changes in scale (reductions and enlargements). When others produced knock-offs of their reproductions (by remolding their casts), Barbedienne sued for copyright infringement. However, the judges considered the products to be mere mechanical reproductions, not worthy of protection.[44] Nonetheless casts of "public domain" works such as the Laocoön or the Apollo Belvedere (with which an 1845 Collas and Barbedienne catalogue opens) were clearly a different category from the *oeuvres contemporaines* by Bosio and Rude listed later.[45] The works of those recognized artists were protected by copyright, and neither Barbedienne nor others could simply churn out copies; contracts were developed that specified the rights of the artist and his "publisher." As the hold of classicism waned, the importance of modern sculpture soon outstripped that of ancient art.[46]

Judith Ickowicz, who discusses this case, stresses that French intellectual property law has always insisted that only true artworks that show the imprint (*l'empreinte*) of their creator's personality can be protected.[47] The language is, of course, highly suggestive: the work needs to index the creator's personality, and in visual art, this has traditionally manifested itself via the hand, via the artist's unique touch. Rodin always took care to ensure that his works showed ample evidence of his personal touch, even when they were cast or "imprinted" using the same methods as classicist sculptures with their smooth surfaces.

Under Barbedienne's successor Gustave Le Blanc, Rodin signed a contract with the firm that gave them the exclusive rights to some of the artist's most famous pieces—including *The Kiss* (1882). Rodin sent Barbedienne concerned letters about rumors that others were counterfeiting the works in question.[48] The artist's closest collaborator concerning the reduction (and the enlargement) of his pieces, however, was sculptor Henri Lebossé, who used a version of the Collas apparatus.[49] In his atmospheric photo print *Rodin—The Thinker* (1902), which is, in fact, a composite of several exposures, Steichen showed Rodin in front of his white marble Victor Hugo bust and opposite his large bronze piece *The Thinker* (1880/1902)—a work in whose production Lebossé was closely involved.[50] The sculptures seem like visions, transfigured matter, willed into form by the artist-thinker, sprung from his mind. Classicism may have been a thing of the past, but its idealization of the sculpture as all but immaterial vision reached an apex in Steichen's staging of Rodin.

On the occasion of the 1981–82 exhibition "Rodin Rediscovered" at the National Gallery of Art in Washington, DC, which examined Rodin's working process and Lebossé's role, Rosalind Krauss noted: "Rodin's relation to the casting of his sculpture could only be called remote. Much of it was done in foundries to which Rodin never went while the production was in progress; he never worked on or retouched the waxes from which the final bronzes were cast, never supervised or regulated either the finishing or the patination, and in the end never checked the pieces before they were crated to be shipped to the client or dealer who had bought them."[51] Krauss's real targets in the piece were modernist conceptions of originality and authenticity. Acknowledging that "Rodin strikes one as the very last artist to introduce to the subject, so popular was he during his lifetime, so celebrated, and so quickly induced to participate in the transformation of his own work into kitsch," Krauss insisted that Rodin's "position deep in the ethos of mechanical reproduction" was one in which "the concept of the 'authentic bronze cast'" made little sense to him.[52] This made him the perfect vehicle for a critical rethinking of modernist dogma.

Krauss's intervention reflected her engagement with the more overt use of mass (re)production in art since the 1960s. In Martha Buskirk's terminology, the work of art's realization became *contingent* when Minimalist artists adopted forms of quasi-industrial production processes by farming out the construction of their work to workshops, and Pop and Conceptual artists embraced screen printing, photography, and written instructions.[53]

On the one hand, this seemed to spell the end of modernist notions of originality and authenticity. Some of the appropriation art discussed by Krauss in her text, such as Sherrie Levine's "rephotography" of modernist photographs, was a critical deconstruction of the notion that there is a direct indexical link between an authorial genius and an authenticated work bearing his or her imprint. On the other hand,

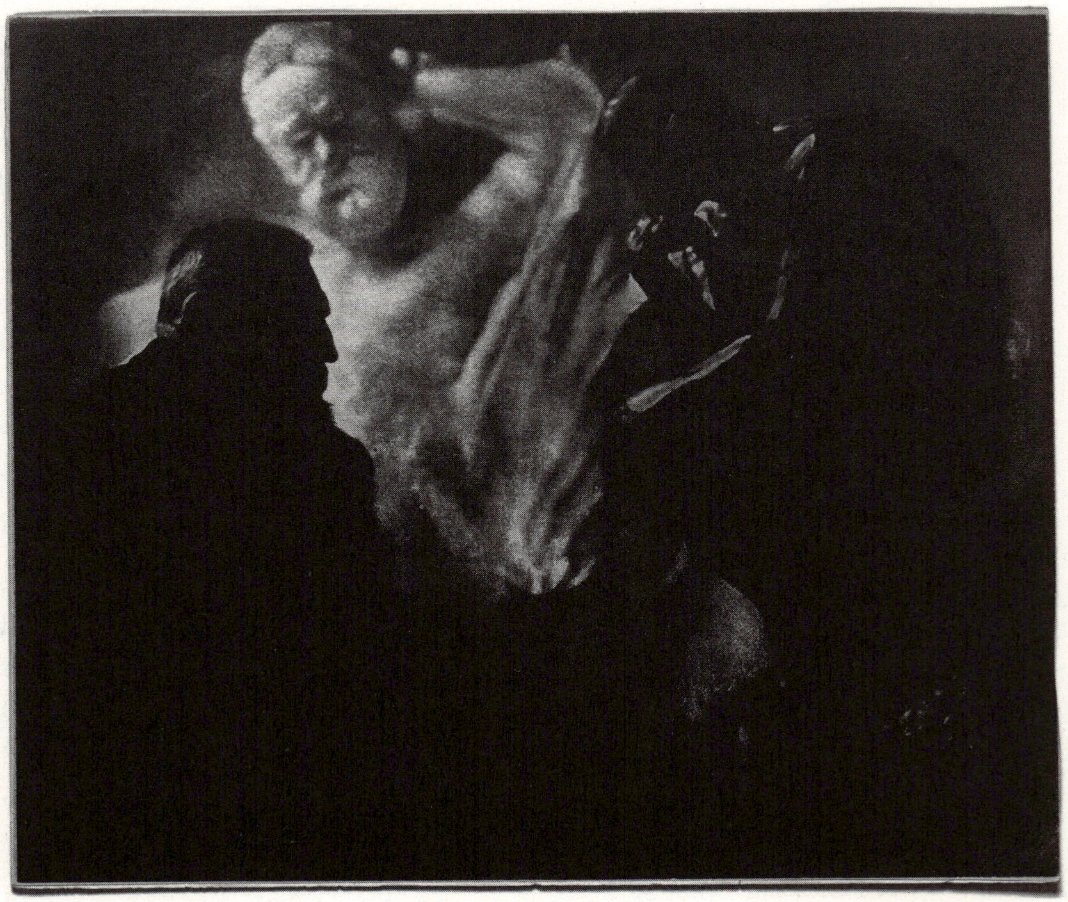

Edward J. Steichen, *Rodin—The Thinker*, 1902

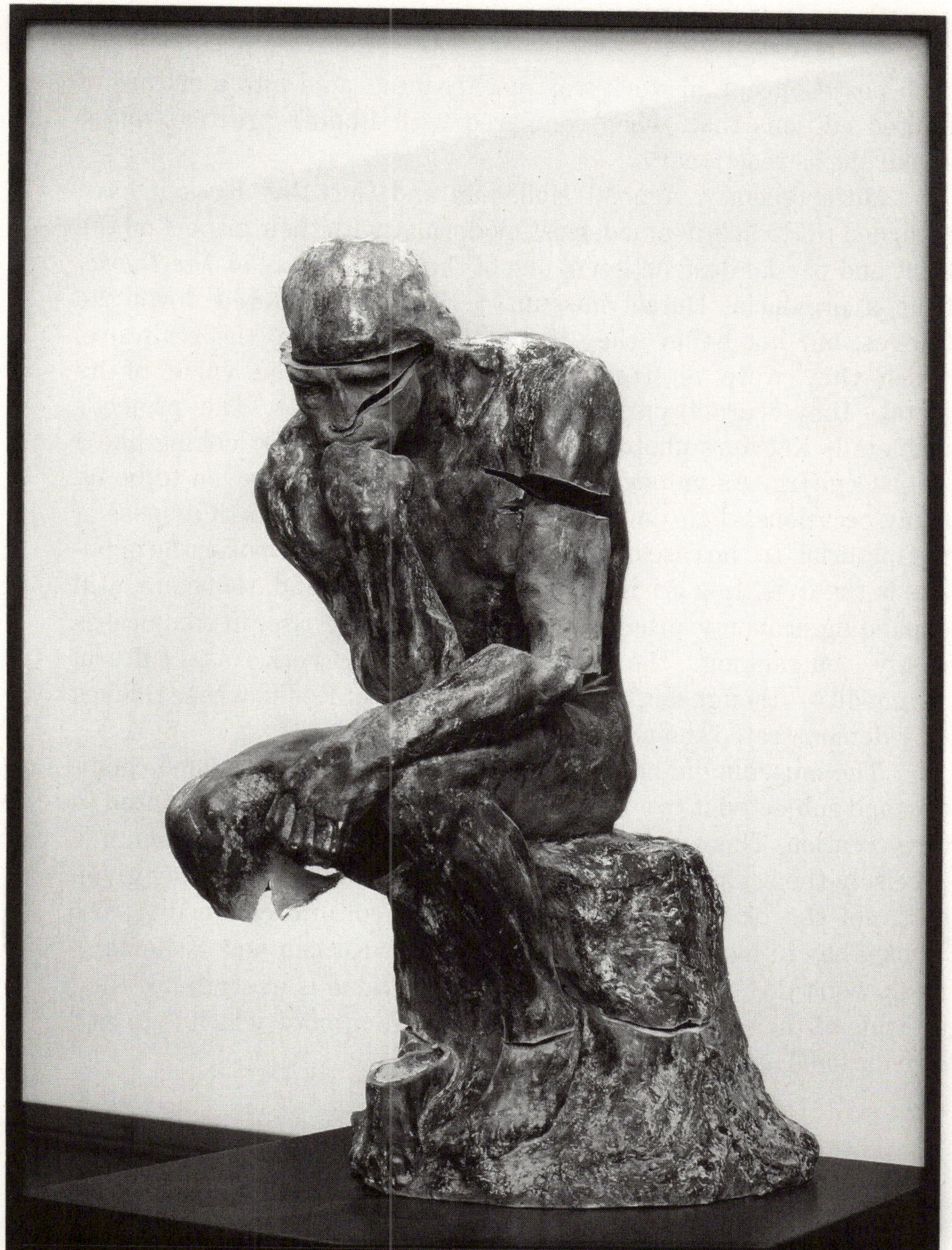

Arnoud Holleman and Gert Jan Kocken, *Broken Thinker*, 2016

such post-Conceptual work was quickly integrated into a culture of limited editions that, when compared with Rodin's practice, might strike one as reactionary.

More recently, Arnoud Holleman and Gert Jan Kocken have returned to Rodin's nonmodernist modernity with their project on the theft and partial destruction of one of the bronze casts of *The Thinker* from a provincial Dutch museum.[54] The police tracked down the thieves, but not before they had started cutting up the sculpture, which they were interested in exclusively for the value of its metal—they were bronze thieves, not art thieves. The project's emblem is Kocken's photograph of the retrieved work looking like a Cubist cyborg. As vulnerable as plaster casts have proven to be on many occasions, their downfall was often the sheer worthlessness of the material. In the case of a bronze cast such as *The Thinker*, the opposite is the case. In a crisis-ridden but globalizing and, therefore, still expanding economy, prices for metals are on the rise, in some cases vastly outranking the price of the artwork as cultural commodity—though not, of course, in the case of Rodin, whose thieves only demonstrated their own ignorance.

The museum did not want to keep the work in its ruined condition and subjected it to a restoration process that almost amounted to a re-creation. This suggests that what is valuable to the museum is precisely the sculpture-as-icon—not the historical "life" of any given cast, not the *biography of the object*. As a cultural commodity, *The Thinker* has to look exactly like *The Thinker*. Kocken and Holleman's freak won't do.[55] In semio-capitalism, sign-value is everything—and the side of the sign that triumphs is Peirce's *symbol*, which is to say, conventional and codified meaning.

Limited Editions and Viewing Copies

Aby Warburg once called Flemish tapestries—early reproductive media that disseminated compositions throughout Europe—“automobile Bilderfahrzeuge” (automobile visual vehicles).[56] Later media have proven to be rather more powerful “visual vehicles,” capable of being produced on a Fordist assembly line. But rather than have the work travel to the viewer—an increasing tendency throughout the nineteenth and twentieth centuries—in the case of video or film pieces in contemporary art, the viewer has to travel to the work installed in a gallery or museum. Artists and dealers had been struggling for decades to get the principle of the limited edition (common enough in prints and sculptures) accepted in the case of film and video art, but their success remained restricted while it was still a matter of selling film reels or video cassettes. Buyers proved reluctant to buy these items at “art prices.” It was only with “the advent of high-quality, low-cost video projection and its tremendous institutional endorsement from the early 1990s onward” that things changed.[57]

This economy of the rarefied object leads to a proliferation of viewing copies as a means of granting access to work beyond the “official” limited editions and outside of the exhibition context. In a way, “viewing copies” do not really exist—their spectral status is owed to the art world’s economy of artificial scarcity and the severe limitations it imposes on the movement of images. While many in the art world cling on to their archive of DVDs, the hard-copy viewing copy is already obsolete, already a dead medium, having been replaced by password-protected online “viewing links.” Whether as physical artifact or as link, the viewing copy is the obverse of the limited edition: as a copy given or loaned to “art-world professionals” for documentation or research purposes, it can never be shown in public. It expands the reach of the work of art, but confidentially and in semi-secrecy. It is precisely this eccentric status of the viewing copy within the economy of art—which itself has an equally exceptional status within contemporary capitalism—that makes it an exemplary object, a *theoretical object*, par excellence.

In "The Work of Art in the Age of Mechanical Reproduction," Walter Benjamin makes a remark that effectively undermines his suggestion that the new media of photography and (especially) film will necessarily diminish the "cult value" and aura of artistic works. After all, as Benjamin admits, Hollywood's star system creates a new, artificial aura by carefully constructing the big stars' "personalities," leading to a "cult of the movie star."[58] Essential for this cult was limiting the stars' availability—the studios knew that too much exposure posed the danger of profanation.

Like certain cult images that are only removed from their shrine during important festivities, the great stars were shown to the public only under carefully controlled conditions. One did not see Greta Garbo in an endless stream of B pictures, only in a few choice productions. Such films were first shown in the most prestigious of "first-run" theaters, then gradually trickled down to other cinemas. Whereas Hollywood created scarcity and aura within a medium of mass reproduction, largely through crafting the star's persona and maintaining their distance from the audience, the art world has developed a different way of imparting aura to film and video. The dialectic of de- and re-auratization is more complex than Benjamin allowed for—Malraux's use of photography in his imaginary museum was already a case in point.

Many artists proffer a seemingly legitimate reason for being anxious about the circulation of their work: it is meant to be seen under very specific conditions in a gallery space. While this desire for "proper" installation complies with the art world's mystificatory economy of exclusivity, which still uses as its ultimate model the unique cult image in its sacred precinct, it is, of course, understandable that artists would want their work to be seen under the right conditions. However, it is a mistake to think that these must be the only conditions under which a work can ever be seen. In an age in which everyone is used to seeing moving images in degraded forms online, viewers have a great capacity for "correcting" these conditions in their minds, for imagining the "proper" presentation. Seeing shaky illegal copy of the latest blockbuster on a laptop does not really damage the film; if anything, knowing that it must be so much better when seen under optimal conditions can only increase its aura.

Films and videos are special kinds of artifacts, of objects. In modern philosophy, the object was that which resisted—but ultimately yielded to—the subject's active, transformative power; or, in a positive register, it was the result of the subject's active fetishism, its sensuous praxis. Movement, temporality, was on the side of the subject. With modern moving images, the dialectic is more iterative, as films and videos—once produced—need to be performed and re-performed in order to be seen. A film reel, video cassette, DVD, or .MOV file is fairly useless unless activated. Writing about digital technology, Hans Dieter Huber and Boris Groys have emphasized that code is nothing unless it is actualized or embodied—performed in some manner: "Unlike traditional image media such as paintings or drawings," Huber argues, "digital works exist in two completely different forms—the state of notation and the state of performance."[59]

Groys makes similar claims, but both authors' conceptions are overly binary; in their theories, the digital file that is being performed seems to come out of nowhere. In such a theory, the focus is on consumption as an act of performance, but the production of the file remains opaque; the file comes to take on divine qualities, becoming pure transcendence. Seeking to create a more encompassing and dialectical model, Boris Čućković Berger has differentiated between the source, the executant, and the production process. "In computer-related discourse, the term 'source' usually refers to the software's source code, a textual listing of commands."[60] However, in Čućković Berger's model, it refers to "production categories established and employed in the making of the object," while the "executant" is "a conventionalized mode of executing or performing the source."[61] As for "contemporary examples of the source-executant relation," one could think of "a digitally printed image as the executant of the computer file (its source), a digital scan as the executant of an old photograph (its source), a web page as an executant of all the digital images, texts, animations and sounds that function as its source material."[62] Interested in open-source production, Čućković Berger draws attention to modes of production in which (technological or cultural) source codes are not protected by copyright. For instance, the animated film *Elephants Dream*, which was made using open-source 3-D models and textures.

As objects become informational, they become more contingent upon performance—under specific economic and juridical working conditions. The source-executant-production model can be used to show parallels as well as contradictions between the digital production mode and contemporary art. It is true that "art keeps a track of copies, while popular culture does not."[63] Popular culture favors unlimited editions, but both art and mass culture fight piracy—illegal copies. Like the culture industry, art seeks to limit and regulate the performance of sources, the production of executant. In art, *certificates* authenticate specific versions.[64] Superflex polemically applied the open-source software idea to a relief by Sol LeWitt in their 2010 *Free Sol LeWitt* project, for which they installed a workshop producing copies of the piece in the Van Abbemuseum, Eindhoven. The piece, of course, contributes to the aura and brand of Superflex as collective author; their practice navigates the contradictions of contemporary cultural capitalism from the inside.

Post-internet Plaster

In 2012, the Kunstverein München hosted the exhibition "The Imaginary Museum," combining plaster casts from the Munich Abgusssammlung—which used to be housed in the spaces now occupied by the Kunstverein—with works by contemporary artists. One project, represented through a number of related digital prints and a video, was Sean Snyder's *Index* (2008–9), which staged a complex dialectic of de- and rematerialization. For *Index*, Snyder digitized his entire archive, in the process doing away with material media such as tapes, films, photo prints, and even CDs and DVDs. The ultimate goal was the creation of an indexed online version of all of his work. While the work was not realized as originally envisaged, he has developed an idiosyncratic open-source method that involves a variety of websites with names such as mnemosynedrone.io and braunschweigterrier.info.[65]

The operation also generated new black-and-white images in several categories. One type of *Index*-related digital print depicts various material media, such as film reels and DVDs, now obsolete. Another consists of digital prints of Snyder's analog photographs—resurrected, as it were, after their autos-da-fé. A third category shows corrupted image files, more noise than signal. Finally, there are works such as *CCD Digital Image Sensor (5 Layers)*, a separate piece that came out of the work on *Index*, and which was shown in Munich. These large black-and-white prints show the five layers of a digital sensor that translates light into data: images of granularity, seemingly formless patterns of pure information, material indices of the destruction of old physical media, and analog formats.

Digitization is a further mobilization, a further deterritorialization of images. Louise Lawler's photo *Hand on Her Back* (1997/1998), taken at an art academy, shows a cast of a Crouching Venus on a wheeled cart, making it mobile for study from all angles. The title picks up on

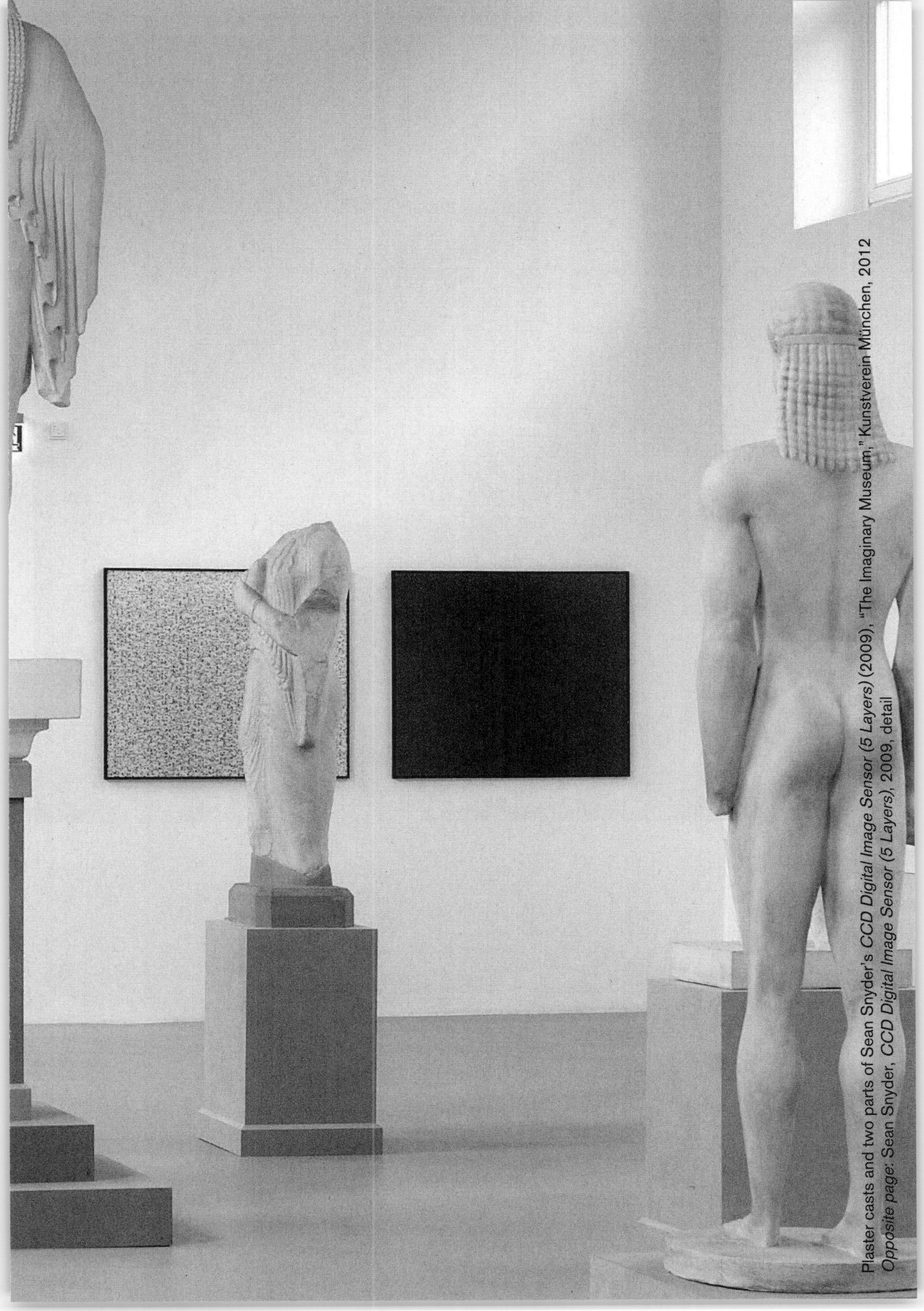

Plaster casts and two parts of Sean Snyder's *CCD Digital Image Sensor (5 Layers)* (2009), "The Imaginary Museum," Kunstverein München, 2012
Opposite page: Sean Snyder, *CCD Digital Image Sensor (5 Layers)*, 2009, detail

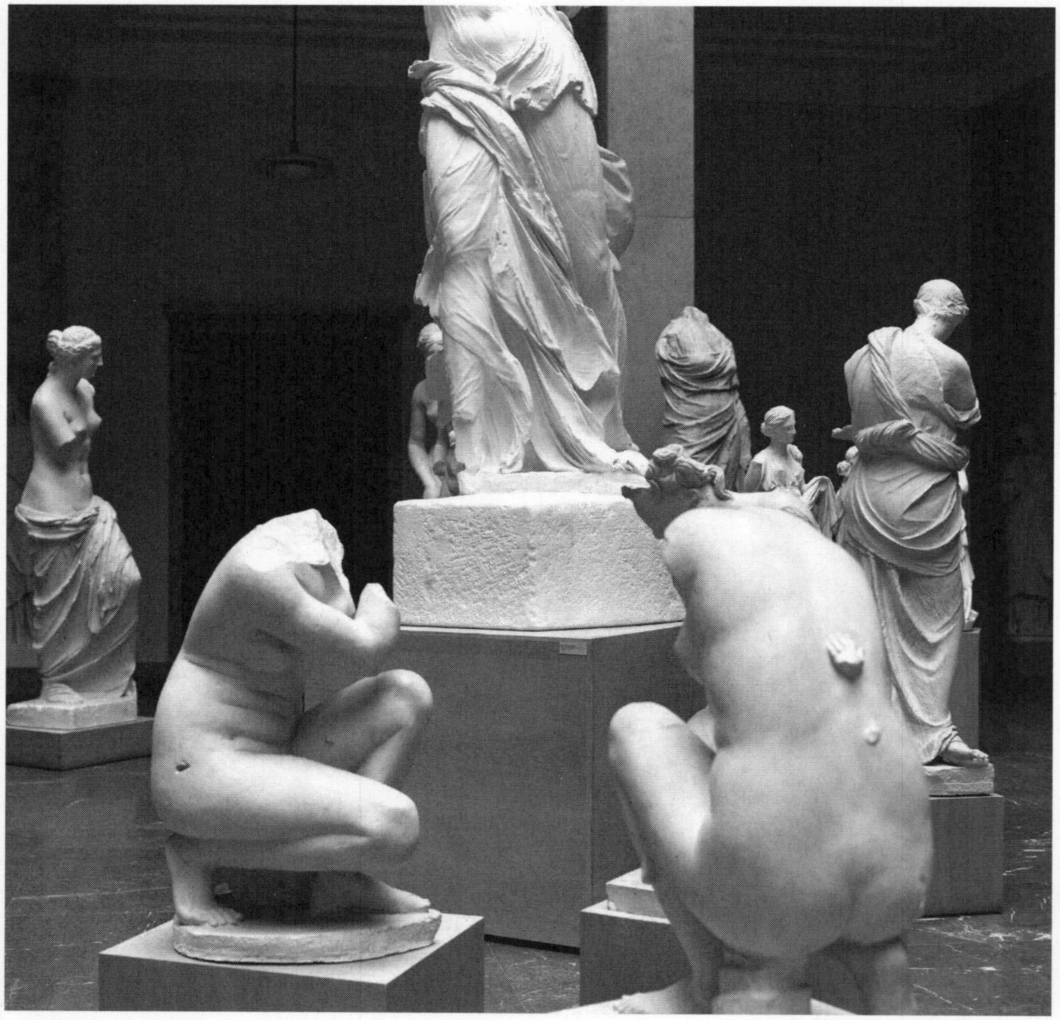

Louise Lawler, *She Wasn't Always a Statue (A)*, 1996/1997

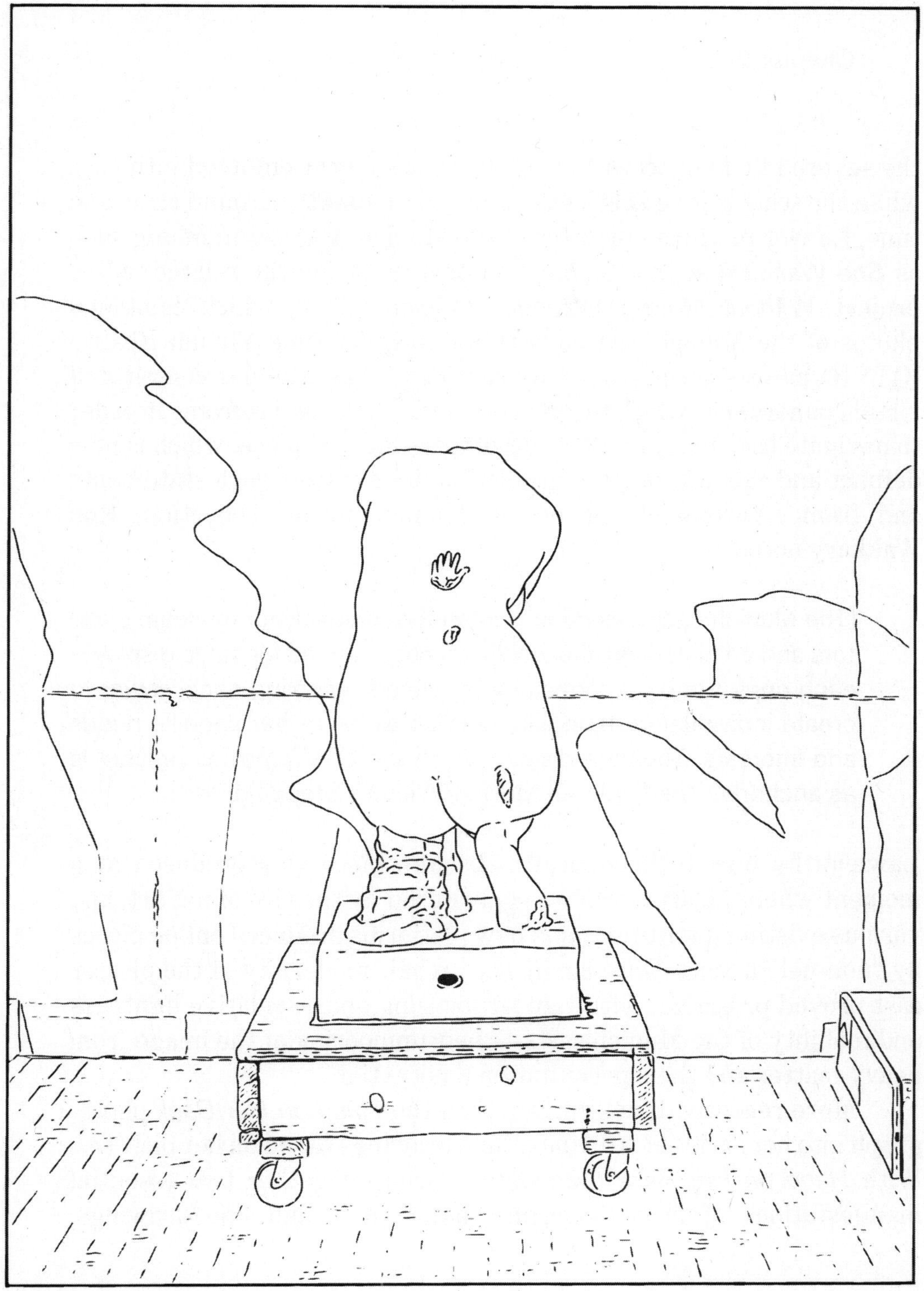

Louise Lawler, *Hand on Her Back (traced)*, 1997/1998/2013

the severed little hand on Venus's back to suggest enforced intimacy, while the wheels give this Venus a certain mobility. Around the same time, Lawler produced pictures of the Munich Abgusssammlung such as *She Wasn't Always a Statue (A)* (1996/1997) and the related online project *Without Moving/Without Stopping* (1998), which combined photos of the Munich cast collection into QuickTime Virtual Reality (QTVR) movies accompanied by captions. These movies constituted virtual panoramas, which the viewer had to frame and reframe in order to navigate the space. In a text accompanying this piece, which is now defunct and can now only be gleaned indirectly from such statements and from Lawler's photos of the Munich plaster collection, Ron Wakkary noted:

> [The Munich cast collection is intended] primarily for museum curators and art historians, the works are not arranged for static display—each copy sits on a pedestal with wheels, enabling each viewer to create individual groupings according to his or her specific needs and interests. Thus the display which the QTVR movies present is as anchorless as "Without Moving/Without Stopping."[66]

Lawler's by now technologically obsolete piece was produced at a moment when the art world was galvanized by the rise of net art, and various existing institutions and new platforms produced online pieces by "non-net" artists. Once again, the archaic modernity of the plaster cast proved prescient, with Lawler focusing on the relative lightness and mobility of the Munich casts—their unmooring of the image from heavy matter and their permutational potential.

More recently, Lawler integrated the *Hand on Her Back* photograph into her series of "tracings," line drawings based on her pictures. With *Hand on Her Back (traced)*, she brings together two essential manifestations of Neoclassicism: plaster casts and line drawings, which both appear to purify matter and reduce form to its essence. With their "dematerializing" aesthetic, Neoclassicists could be seen as unwitting prophets of today's semiotic capitalism. While Snyder's *Index* can be read as a grotesque realization of the neo-idealist ideology of dematerialization through digital technology, any digital remediation of analog media is also always a reformatting (and, as shown by the obsolescence of QTVR, subsequent digital reformatting is frequently necessary). When Snyder rematerializes his digital photographs of destroyed physical media, or shows his digital videos on bulky old-school monitors, or exhibits black-and-white printouts of digitized artworks from the Rijksmuseum website, it is clear that he is not interested in linear narratives about leaving matter behind in favor of some digital Platonism.[67] Rather, he is profoundly invested in examining the formats, standards and protocols that structure digital as well as analog cultural artifacts, and the ISO standards that in turn regulate them—from aspect ratios to blockchain and distributed ledger technologies.

As an artist informed by the Conceptual practices of the 1960s and 1970s, Snyder uses blockchain as a contemporary version of the artist's certificate or the artist's contract. One case involved the transfer of a screenshot depicting a horizontal iTunes bar listing John Cage's "silent" composition *4′33″* (1952) as being for sale for €0.99. Snyder actually bought the digital file from iTunes, or more precisely, he licensed the file. If ownership has long been fundamental to the modern juridical regime, it is increasingly being replaced by a variety of license and lease contracts. Snyder made audio and video pieces using the file, and the screenshot became a framed and editioned photograph; an "artist's proof" of this piece was sold to the author of this book for €485.33, which is the production costs plus €0.99. The artist called this operation *Non-alchemical Transaction* (2017), logged it in the blockchain and called it an experiment in the "zero-method

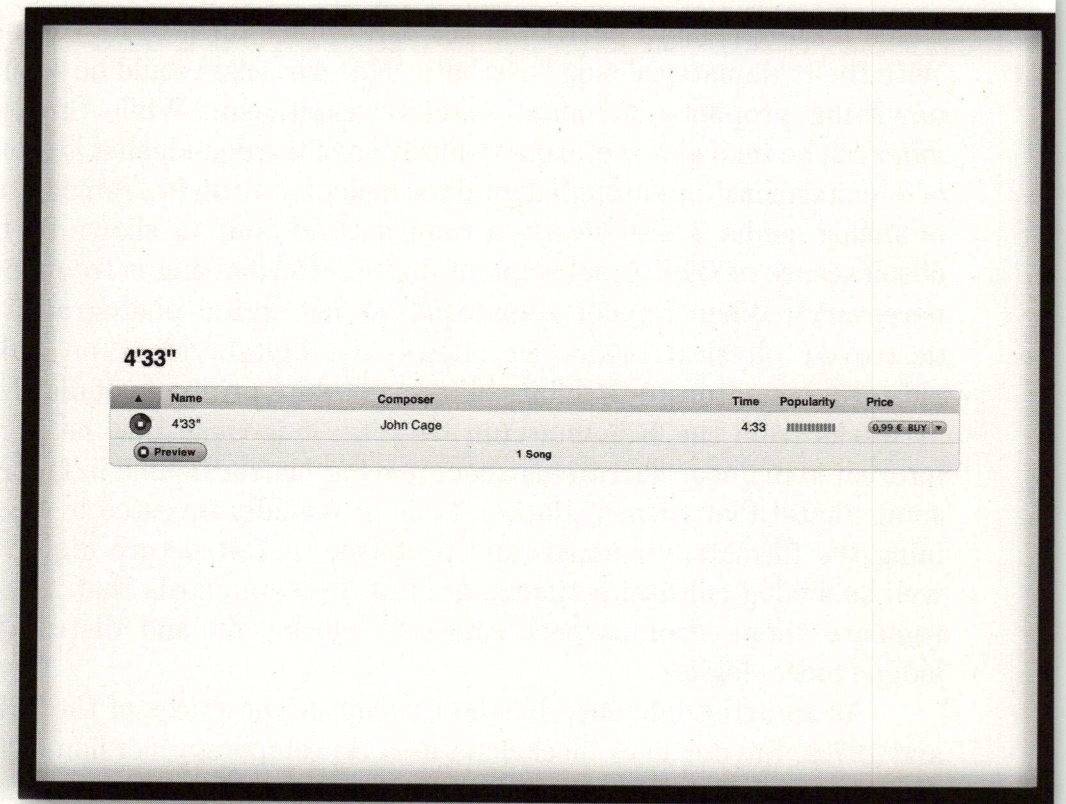

Sean Snyder, *0.99€*, 2015

of value exchange." A document provided by Snyder notes that the "fee for transferring 0,99€ via Western Union (transfer minimum 1€) amounts to 5€," and that a "re-mastered copy of the data purchased from Apple can be downloaded at http://mnemosyndrone.info for free."[68]

While blockchain platforms such as Codex "[open] the door for digital art as an investment through the introduction of digital scarcity," Snyder uses the technology to demystify the "alchemic transmutation" of transactions on the art market—while still keeping track of copies.[69] By contrast, Oliver Laric created a website in which 3-D scans of sculptures from a public collection in Lincoln, in the United Kingdom, can be downloaded and used for digital renderings or physical 3-D prints by anyone, as open-source code with a potentially infinite number of executants. Three-dimensional scanning is the new casting; some of the scanned objects were plaster, bronze, or resin casts to begin with. A significant number among them are Neoclassical sculptures by John Gibson and others. Laric has exhibited in cast collections and is profoundly invested in the examination of copies and versions, and in the connections between traditional plaster casting and 3-D printing. His interests also extend to the nineteenth-century inventor François Willème, whose "photosculpture" method tried to apply a Collas-like procedure to making 3-D portrait sculptures based on photos from multiple angles, functioning as a predecessor of today's techniques.[70]

Laric embraces kitsch, both with his own multicolored 3-D prints and in the form of other people's uses of the Lincoln scans, which he assiduously documents on the site and showcases during talks: a garden ornament, a magazine cover or ad, a background image in a Eurovision Song Contest performance, or an appearance in a Netflix series on the Roman Empire. With its quasi-Neoclassical black-and-white aesthetic, the website is a space of potentiality that is both actualized and brutally betrayed by the tatty executions that Laric appears to love (in contrast to Lawler, who usually leaves the uses of her tracings implicit).[71] In a freeware version that perhaps complements rather than challenges the proliferation of proprietary products, his project has the virtue of presenting almost a cartoon of a certain ideology of scannability and malleability: the birth of digital printing from the spirit of plaster.

We live inside a giant imaginary museum of plaster casts. In a kind of capitalist Platonism, the value of many contemporary commodities has come to be dependent on design and branding; commodities have become "culturalized." This is the neopolitical idealism of hyper-capitalism: with a strong brand such as Apple, with its iconic logo, the price consumers pay is determined only marginally by the salaries of Foxconn's slave-employees, or even by the value of increasingly contested materials such as coltan. It should come as no surprise that artists of the 1960s and 1970s rediscovered the plaster cast, from Giulio Paolini's use of antique sculptures in reflexive installations to Walter De Maria's casts of geometric forms arranged in patterns.[72] Art's "conceptual turn" in the period in which these artists participated is part and parcel of post-Fordism and the "semiotic turn" of capitalism. Like Apple, Conceptual art generates surplus-value through branding, through design.

None other than Jeff Koons encapsulated this in dialectical images when he used plaster casts from his "Gazing Ball" series for Louis Vuitton shop windows in 2017. The "Gazing Ball" works are shiny, white plaster casts based on classical sculptures, each incongruously outfitted with a reflective blue sphere, which traps beholder and sculpture in a bubble of warped surface and topological self-absorption. In a Christmastime window display, *Gazing Ball (Ariadne)* was also accessorized with Koons-designed Louis Vuitton bags sporting motifs from Manet's *Le déjeuner sur l'herbe* (1863). The classical cast becomes décor for a brand accessory. Our imaginary museum of plaster casts doubles as pricey gift shop.

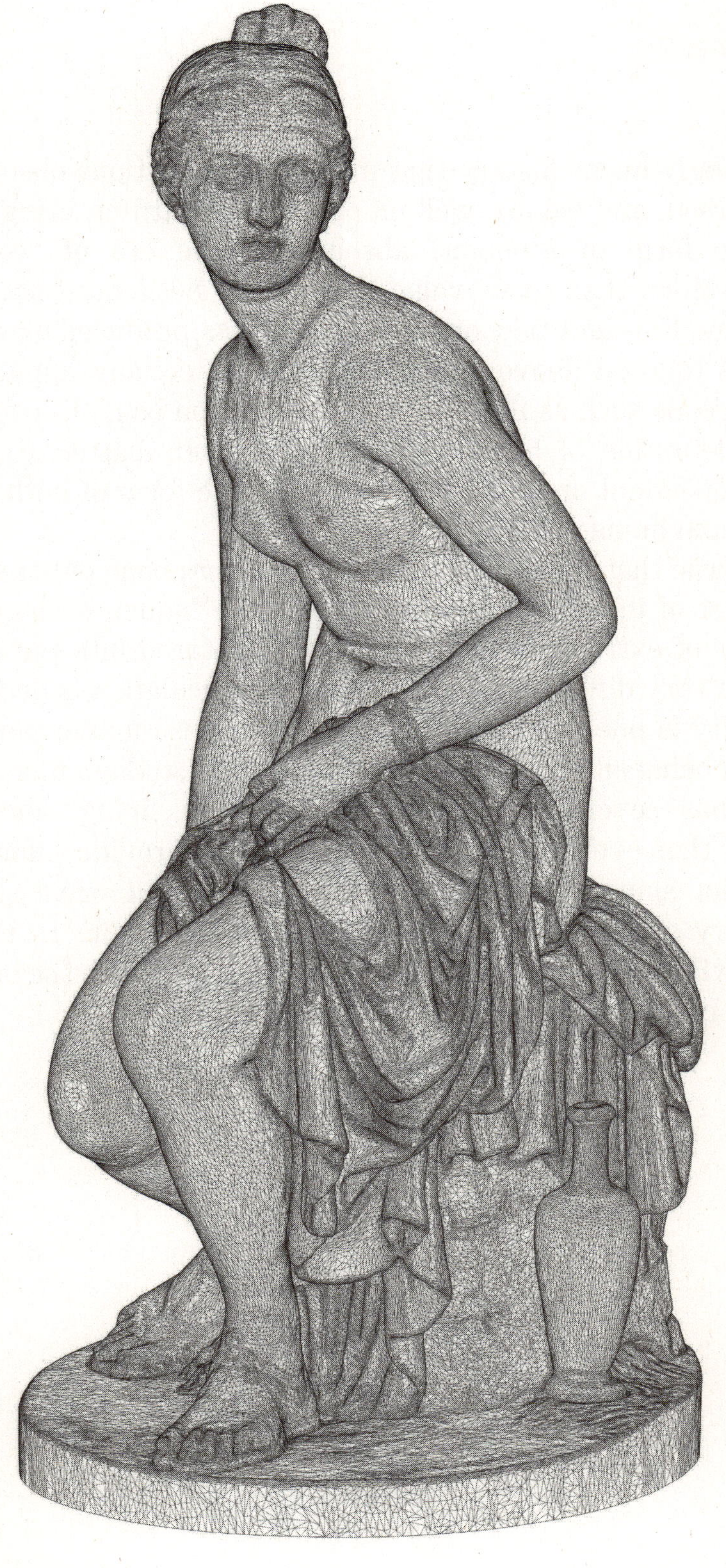

"Nymph Preparing for the Bath," threedscans.com

The seemingly linear history that made cast collections obsolete has been reversed, and we are well on our way toward entering a post-democratic form of economic absolutism—the era of "corporate rococo."[73] More than ever, value appears to be a mystery. In the branded age, Flusser's take on the value of mass-produced plastic ballpoint pens (quoted above) would seem to be equally applicable to premium goods such as iPhones or Louis Vuitton bags. But for all its idealist celebration of form or information over matter, capitalism remains dependent on a material basis—in the form of both natural resources and human labor.

It is true that the material value of a smartphone only makes up a small part of its price—but what about the hidden ecological and social costs of extractivism? If these were factored into the price, it would be a very different picture; that such calculation is de facto an impossibility is one aspect of the crisis of value. Furthermore, with production being either automated or outsourced, today's financialized economy has severed the indexical link with living labor more completely than ever. We may perform codes and provide value for the social media companies whose services we use, but what good is a labor theory of value if wage labor is on the way out? In the next chapter, I will analyze the crisis of the value-form through the informed things and conceptual objects of contemporary art.

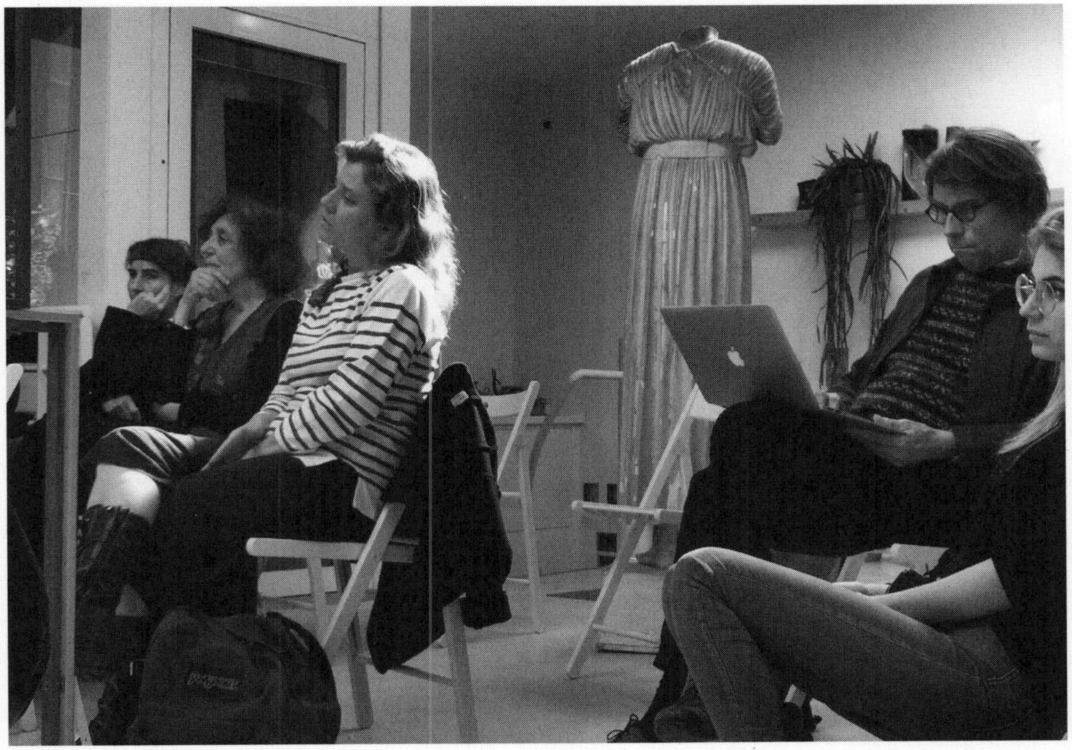

Plaster cast at Villa Vassilieff, Paris, 2016

NOTES

1 Diedrich Diederichsen, *Körpertreffer: Zur Ästhetik der nachpopulären Künste* (Berlin: Suhrkamp, 2017), 19.

2 The following paragraphs are based on the second chapter of Sven Lütticken, *Art and Autonomy: A Critical Reader* (London: Afterall, forthcoming), on which John Byrne did substantial work.

3 Karl Marx, *Capital: A Critique of Political Economy*, vol. 1, trans. Ben Fowkes (London: Penguin, 1976), 137.

4 Marx, 131.

5 See, in particular, Karl Marx, "Manuskripte zum zweiten Buch des 'Kapitals' 1868 bis 1881," in *Marx-Engels-Gesamtausgabe II*, Bd. 11 (Berlin: Akademie Verlag, 2008), 192–93.

6 Paul Dobraszczyk, *Iron, Ornament and Architecture in Victorian Britain: Myth and Modernity, Excess and Enchantment* (Farnham: Ashgate, 2014), 32–42.

7 Dobraszczyk, 11.

8 Gottfried Semper, *Style in the Technical and Tectonic Arts; or, Practical Aesthetics* (1860–63), trans. Harry Francis Mallgrave and Michael Robinson (Los Angeles: Getty Publications, 2004).

9 Vilém Flusser, "About the Word Design," in *The Shape of Things: A Philosophy of Design* (London: Reaktion Books, 1999), 20.

10 Gilbert Simondon, *L'individuation à la lumière des notions de forme et d'information* (1958; Grenoble: Jêrome Millon, 2013), 39–45, 51.

11 Marx, *Capital*, vol. 1, 151–52.

12 On casts as anachronisms, see Georges Didi-Huberman, *La ressemblance par contact: Archéologie, anachronisme et modernité de l'émpreinte* (Paris: Éditions de Minuit, 2008).

13 Didi-Huberman, 92–110.

14 See James Hall, *The World as Sculpture: The Changing Status of Sculpture from the Renaissance to the Present Day* (London: Chatto & Windus, 1999), 1–103.

15 Francis Haskell and Nicholas Penny, *Taste and the Antique: The Lure of Classical Sculpture 1500–1900* (New Haven, CT: Yale University Press, 1981), 37; and Geneviève Bresc-Bautier, "Copier

l'antique à la cour de Louis XIV," in *D'après l'antique*, ed. Jean-Pierre Cuzin et al. (Paris: Réunion des musées nationaux, 2000), 60–68.

16 See Charlotte Schreiter, "Moulded on the Best Originals of Rome: Eighteenth-Century Production of Plaster Casts of Antique Sculpture and Their Trade in Germany," in *Plaster Casts: Making, Collecting, and Displaying from Classical Antiquity to the Present*, ed. Rune Frederiksen and Eckart Marchand (Berlin: De Gruyter, 2010), 121–42.

17 Hall, *The World as Sculpture*, 74. The quotation is from the "Von dem Wesentlichen der Kunst" section of chap. 4 in *Geschichte der Kunst des Altertums*. More than Winckelmann, a key precursor or progenitor of scientific racism in the eighteenth century was Johann Friedrich Blumenbach, discussed in David Bindmann, *Ape to Apollo: Aesthetics and the Idea of Race in the 18th Century* (London: Reaktion Books, 2002), 190–201.

18 The 1801 illustration from an opus by J. J. Virey, and its later variants, are discussed and illustrated in Éric Michaud, *Les invasions barbares: Une généologie de l'histoire de l'art* (Paris: Gallimard, 2015), 82–86.

19 See also Alex Potts, *Flesh and the Ideal: Winckelmann and the Origins of Art History* (New Haven, CT: Yale University Press, 1994), i.a.,155–64.

20 Johann Wolfgang Goethe, *Aus meinem Leben: Dichtung und Wahrheit*, in *Gedenkausgabe der Werke, Briefe und Gespräche*, ed. Ernst Beutler, Bd. 10 (Stuttgart: Artemis Verlag, 1962), 548–49.

21 Johann Wolfgang Goethe, *Italienische Reise*, in *Gedenkausgabe*, Bd. 11, 94–96.

22 Goethe, 16.

23 André Malraux, *Les voix du silence* (Paris: Gallimard, 1951), 44. *Le musée imaginaire* was first published in book form in 1947, as the first volume of Malraux's *Psychologie de l'art*; the second version became part of *Les voix du silence* in 1951.

24 My research on cast collections and photography, on which this chapter is largely based, goes back to 2003 and an invitation by artist Krijn de Koning to write a text for the book accompanying his exhibition at the Musée des Moulages in Lyon. The book, however,

never went beyond mock-ups by the artist. A shortened version was published as Sven Lütticken, "Two Imaginary Museums: Plaster Casts and Photography," *Kunstlicht* 25, nos. 1/2 (2004): 4–9. A reworked, longer version was the catalogue essay for the exhibition "The Imaginary Museum" at Kunstverein München in 2012 (4–21). In the meantime, Claudia Bahner published some related reflections as "Fotos für alle: André Malraux (1901–1976)," in *Ideengeschichte der Bildwissenschaft: Siebzehn Porträts*, ed. Jörg Probst and Jost Philipp Klenner (n.p.: Suhrkamp, 2009), 179–91. I found out about Bahner's article belatedly through Walter Grasskamp's book *André Malraux und das imaginäre Museum: Die Weltkunst im Salon* (Munich: C.H. Beck, 2014), which references both Bahner and me.

25 The latter collection was quickly closed to the public and eventually moved. Predictably, the royal collection contained the small group of statues that had enjoyed the most prestige since the Renaissance: the Apollo Belvedere, the Laocoön, the Hercules Farnese, and the like. In this respect, it resembled other such imaginary museums—or the others resembled this one. Jean-Luc Martinez, "Les moulages en plâtre d'àprès l'antique du musée du Louvre: Une utopie du XIXe siècle," in Cuzin et al., *D'après l'antique*, 78–79.

26 Martinez, 79.

27 Martinez, 79.

28 Felix von Luschan to Anton von Dessauer, November 23, 1906, in *Near Life: The Gipsformerei—200 Years of Casting Plaster*, ed. Veronika Tocha et al. (Munich: Prestel, 2019), 89; see also 86–87 for evidence of successful resistance to Luschan's casting practices.

29 A classic text on indexicality in modern art is, of course, Rosalind E. Krauss, "Notes on the Index: Part 1" (1976), in *The Originality of the Avant-Garde, and Other Modernist Myths* (Cambridge, MA: MIT Press, 1986), 196–209.

30 See Hans Belting, *Das echte Bild: Bildfragen als Glaubensfragen* (Munich: C.H. Beck, 2005), 63–67.

31 Didi-Huberman, *La ressemblance par contact*, 49; see also 52–59.

32 See the sequence by Louise Lawler, in Douglas Crimp, *On the Museum's Ruins* (Cambridge, MA: MIT Press, 1993), 188–97;

and Douglas Crimp, "War Is Terror," in *Louise Lawler: Receptions*, ed. Roxanna Marcoci (New York: Museum of Modern Art, 2017), 52–44.

33 Malraux, *Les voix du silence*, 43–44.

34 Francis Haskell, *The Ephemeral Museum: Old Master Paintings and the Rise of the Art Exhibition* (New Haven, CT: Yale University Press, 2000), 92.

35 Marcella Anglani, "The Michelangelo Museum and the Evolution of the Galleria dell'Accademia from the Nineteenth to the Twentieth Century," in *The Accademia, Michelangelo, the Nineteenth Century (The Place for David 1)*, ed. Franca Falletti (Livorno: Sillabe, 1997), 37–53.

36 May Meurs, "De gipscollectie van het Rijksmuseum II: Opkomst en verval van een hulpmiddel voor het Nederlandse kunstonderwijs," *Bulletin van het Rijksmuseum* 50, no. 2 (2002): 272–76.

37 Meurs, 277.

38 See Johan Hartle, "Rightist Hobbies and the End of Art," *Open*, no. 23 (2012): 27–29.

39 G. W. F. Hegel, *Vorlesungen über die Ästhetik III* (Frankfurt am Main: Suhrkamp, 1970), 11–67.

40 G. W. F. Hegel, Vorlesungen über die Ästhetik II. Werke 14 (Frankfurt am Main: Suhrkamp, 1970), 239–40.

41 Fred Licht, *Canova* (New York: Abbeville Press, 1983), 224–27.

42 See Simona Rinaldi, "Canova and the French Practice of Using Pointing Machines," in *Amore e psiche a Milano* (Soveria Mannelli: Rubbettino, 2012), 120–27.

43 Albert E. Elsen, "When the Sculptures Were White: Rodin's Work in Plaster," in *Rodin Rediscovered* (Washington, DC: National Gallery of Art, 1981), 127–50.

44 Judith Ickowicz, *Le droit après la dématerialisation de l'oeuvre d'art* (Dijon: Les presses du réel, 2013), 129–31.

45 Société A. Collas & Barbedienne sales catalogue (Paris, 1845), https://gallica.bnf.fr/ark:/12148/bpt6k310003z.

46 Florence Rionet, "Introduction," in *La Maison Barbedienne: Correspondances d'artistes* (Paris: CTHS, 2008), 12–13, 23–16.

47 Ickowicz, *Le droit après la dématerialisation*, i.a., 136.

48 See letters (n.d., before 1899; and April 29, 1911) in Rionet, *La Maison Barbedienne*, 292–95.

49 Elsen, "Rodin's 'Perfect Collaborator,' Henri Lebossé," in *Rodin Rediscovered*, 249–59.

50 Executed by Steichen as a gum bichromate print, *Rodin—The Thinker* was published twice by *Camera Work*: as a half-tone reproduction in 1905, and as a photogravure in a special 1906 Steichen portfolio.

51 Rosalind E. Krauss, "The Originality of the Avant-Garde," in *Originality of the Avant-Garde*, 153. The show that sparked Krauss's comments was "Rodin Rediscovered."

52 Krauss, 157, 153.

53 Martha Buskirk, *The Contingent Object of Contemporary Art* (Cambridge, MA: MIT Press, 2003).

54 See http://www.brokenthinker.nl/.

55 The photograph was, however, exhibited at Singer Laren, in the Netherlands, in the 2011 exhibition "Rodin: De Denker denkt weer," which included the "restored" bronze cast as well as a number of Rodin's original plasters.

56 Aby Warburg, "Mnemosyne: Einleitung" (1929), in *Der Bilderatlas Mnemosyne*, ed. Martin Warnke and Claudia Brin (Berlin: Akademie Verlag, 2000), 5.

57 Erika Balsom, *After Uniqueness: A History of Film and Video Art in Circulation* (New York: Columbia University Press, 2017), 151. See also Balsom more generally on the rise of (limited) editions in film and video art.

58 Walter Benjamin, "The Work of Art in the Age of Mechanical Reproduction" (1936), in *Illuminations: Essays and Reflections*, ed. Hannah Arendt, trans. Harry Zohn (New York: Schocken Books, 1969), 231.

59 Hans Dieter Huber, "The Embodiment of Code" (2005), www.hgb-leipzig.de/artnine/huber/writings/embodiment.pdf; and Boris Groys, "Religion in the Age of Digital Reproduction," *e-flux journal*, no. 4 (March 2009), http://www.e-flux.com/journal/view/49.

60 Boris Čučković Berger, "The Open Source Cultural Object," *Leonardo Electronic Almanac* 20, no. 1 (January 2014): 29–30.

61 Čučković Berger, 29–30.

62 Čučković Berger, 29–30.

63 Ana Peraica, "Chauvinist and Elitist Obstacles around YouTube and Porntube: A Case Study of Home-Made Porn Defended as 'Video Art,'" in *Video Vortex Reader: Responses to YouTube*, ed. Geert Lovink and Sabine Niederer (Amsterdam: Institute of Network Cultures, 2008), 192.

64 On certificates, see Buskirk, *The Contingent Object of Contemporary Art*, 21–56; and *In Deed: Certificates of Authenticity in Art*, ed. Susan Hapgood and Cornelia Lauf (Amsterdam: Roma Publications, 2011).

65 "It is true that *Index* was also supposed to include a website. The whole idea was to give back the information. The material for the website was finished, but never uploaded. I am still considering it but also looking for the possibilities to finish the project." Sean Snyder, email to the author, July 1, 2013.

66 Ron Wakkary, text from the defunct net art piece *Without Moving / Without Stopping* (1998), archived at https://web.archive.org/web/19991011114005/http://stadiumweb.com:80/without_moving/without_stopping/information/wmws_info.html.

67 The monitors were used in "No Apocalypse, Not Now," Kölnischer Kunstverein, 2013; and the Rijksstudio printouts in "The Rembrandt and Ravachol Appreciation Society," at Rongwrong, Amsterdam, 2020.

68 Sean Snyder, *Non-alchemical Transaction (Artist's Proof)* (2017), author's personal archive.

69 Katya Michaels, "Crypto Art for the Crypto Wealthy: Engaging New Generation of Art Patrons," *U.Today*, August 17, 2018, https://u.today/crypto-art-for-the-crypto-wealthy-engaging-new-generation-of-art-patrons.

70 Laric had an exhibition called "Photoplastik" at Secession, Vienna, in 2016.

71 On some framed prints of Lawler's tracings, a few small fields have been colored in.

72 Paolini used plaster casts of antique statues, made to look as spotless and even as possible, in a large number of works throughout the decades; De Maria's major plaster piece is *The 2000 Sculpture* (1992).

73 The term is from contemporary plaster caster Stephan Dillemuth. See Werner von Delmont, *Corporate Rokoko und das Ende des bürgerlichen Projektes* (n.p.: Permanent Press, 2035 [*sic*]).

Chapter 3

Zachary Formwalt's film *An Unknown Quantity* (2015) is set in the former grain exchange of the 1903 Amsterdam exchange building, designed by Hendrik Berlage. Formwalt scanned the empty hall with a GigaPan camera, generating a hyperreal panning and zooming movement through frozen space.[1] In 1978, the grain exchange hall became the options exchange, five years after the founding of the pioneering Chicago Board Options Exchange. With neoliberal "deregulation" and accelerating digitization, derivatives such as options and futures (the first entailing the *right* and the second the *obligation* to sell an asset at a future date) became sought-after financial products.

Grain trading was a field in which futures contracts were established early on. As the voice-over in Formwalt's film puts it:

> For centuries, grain merchants had made these kinds of arrangements in order to protect themselves from bad harvests. If there was a shortage of grain, holding a contract with a price that had been agreed to, was of great value. [...] But these kinds of contracts were drawn up between two people and were not seen in themselves as tradable objects.[2]

This is exactly what happens when the options and futures on stocks came to be traded, and when tools such as the Black–Scholes model—developed in Chicago during the 1970s—make risk calculable and manageable.[3]

Part of Formwalt's voice-over concerns the development of the stock index. Such an index is a representation of movement: the movement of prices on the market. However, its indexicality is a mediated one; it is an abstraction based on cumulative results. First, the old stock ticker was digitized, and in the early 1980s, the stock index itself was turned into a financial product and traded on the options market.[4] But a stock index can be more than a speculative device in the financial sense. As is evident from Formwalt's work, it can be turned into a vehicle for theoretical speculation.

In 2011, Andrea Fraser published a graph titled *Index*, which shows a correlation between the rise in the Mei Moses All Art Index and rises in US income inequality and the S&P 500 Total Return Index during the same decades—financial indexicality times two. Correlation may not be causation, but it is clear that "deregulation" boosted the 1%—or the 0.1%—and the art market. In other words, "what has been good for art has been disastrous for the rest of the world."[5] In the wake of Donald Trump's election victory, Richard Prince disowned his $36,000 portrait of (and commission by) Ivanka Trump, but this incident highlights the role of "blue-chip" art as storage for surplus capital.[6] The autonomy of art has been realized perversely as that of a financialized product seemingly immune from crisis.

However, as Eric de Bruyn notes concerning Formwalt's work: as much as financial (media) technology may attempt to suppress noise, the "radical contingency of an uncertain future" will end up reasserting itself over algorithmic risk management.[7] The name Trump can stand for such contingency. Right up to the election, "liberal" denizens of the New York art world could not imagine anything but a Hillary Clinton victory. Neofascism in the United States, as elsewhere, is a symptom of the breakdown in the reproduction of the labor-capital relation, as surplus populations enter into a toxic relation with the populist representatives of surplus wealth.

For all the blindness of some of its protagonists, at its best, contemporary art *indexes* a crisis of value—not through direct physical or photochemical imprints, but by registering its shocks in problematic, sensate forms that allow us to discuss the transformations of the *value-form* itself. I will discuss contemporary visual art as a form of aesthetic practice that is speculative in more ways than one, constituting a series of speculative proposals as well as being a speculative investment.[8] The works and projects thus produced are exemplary objects—*choses de pensée*, thought-things.[9] Financialized art's seeming autonomy from crisis is, in fact, dependent on a careful concealment of the heteronomous factors that enable it, and from this acknowledgment starts much of the best aesthetic practice in and against the current regime.[10]

Value-Form and Symbolic Form

Marx's theory of value is as much a *formal theory* as a *labor theory of value.* As noted in the introduction, Marx distinguishes the commodity's natural form, which is "the form of the commodity's *body* itself, iron, linen, etc., its tangible, sensible form of existence" from its value-form, which is its "social form."[11] In Fredric Jameson's words, for Marx, exchange-value is "precisely mental if not spiritual: that is to say, pure form rather than content," in contrast to the qualitative and sensuous nature of use-value.[12] In a kind of adapted Aristotelianism, Marx notes that use-value is *substance*, whereas exchange-value is *form.*[13] It is the value-form—the commodity-form—that generates the fetishistic occlusion of value's basis in labor, leading to a false sense of autonomy of

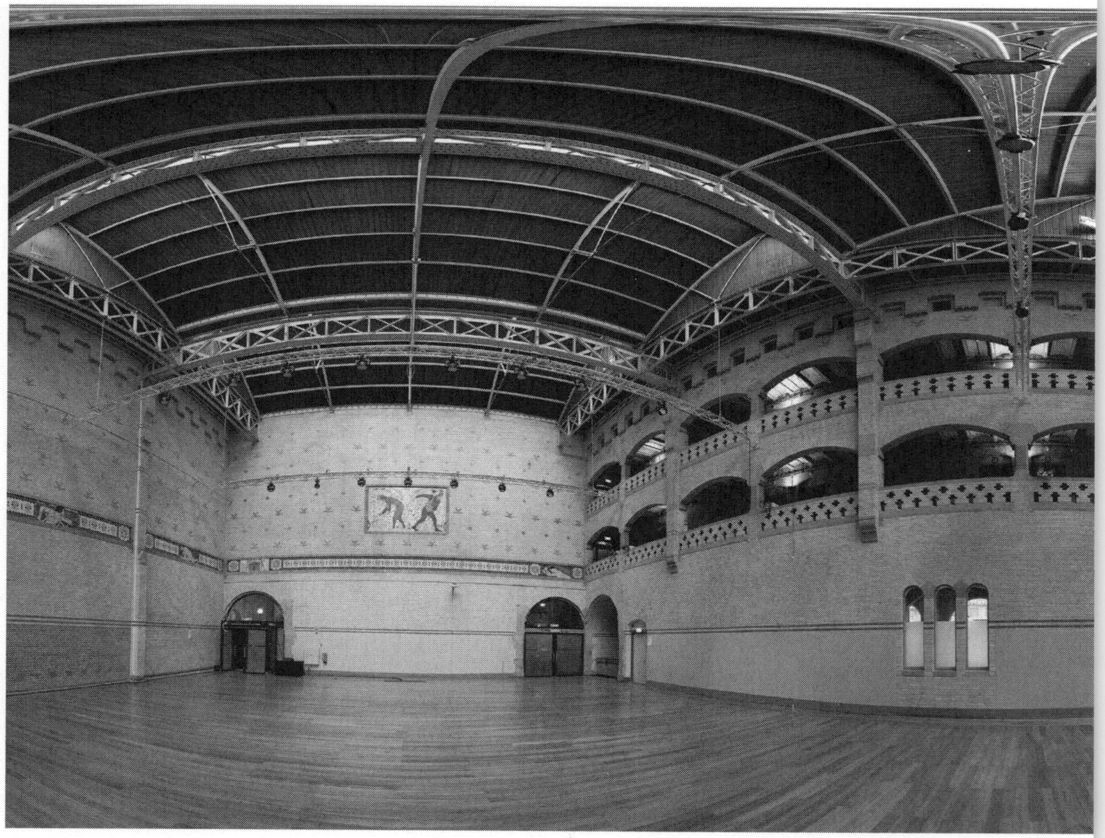

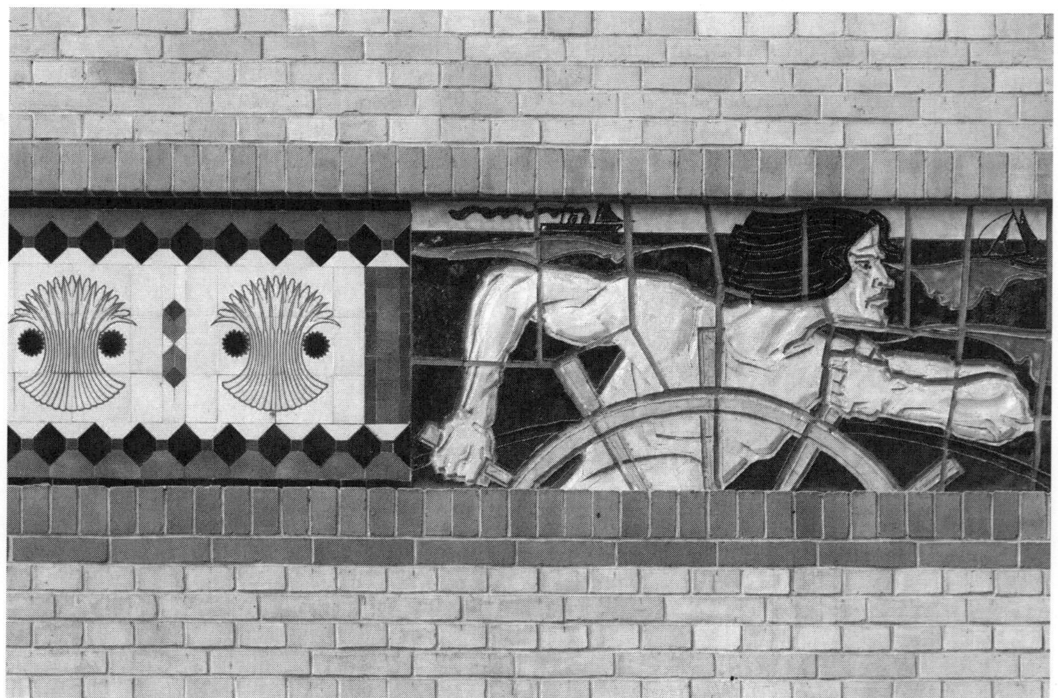

Stills from Zachary Formwalt, *An Unknown Quantity*, 2015

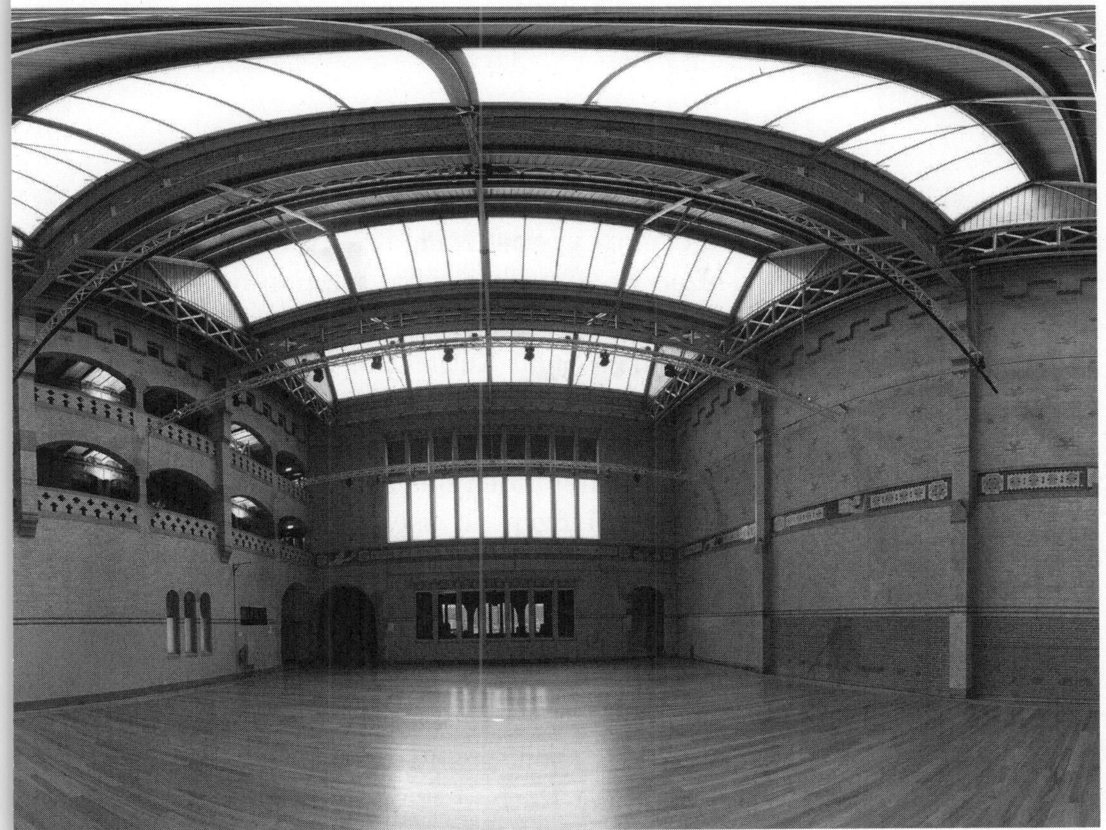

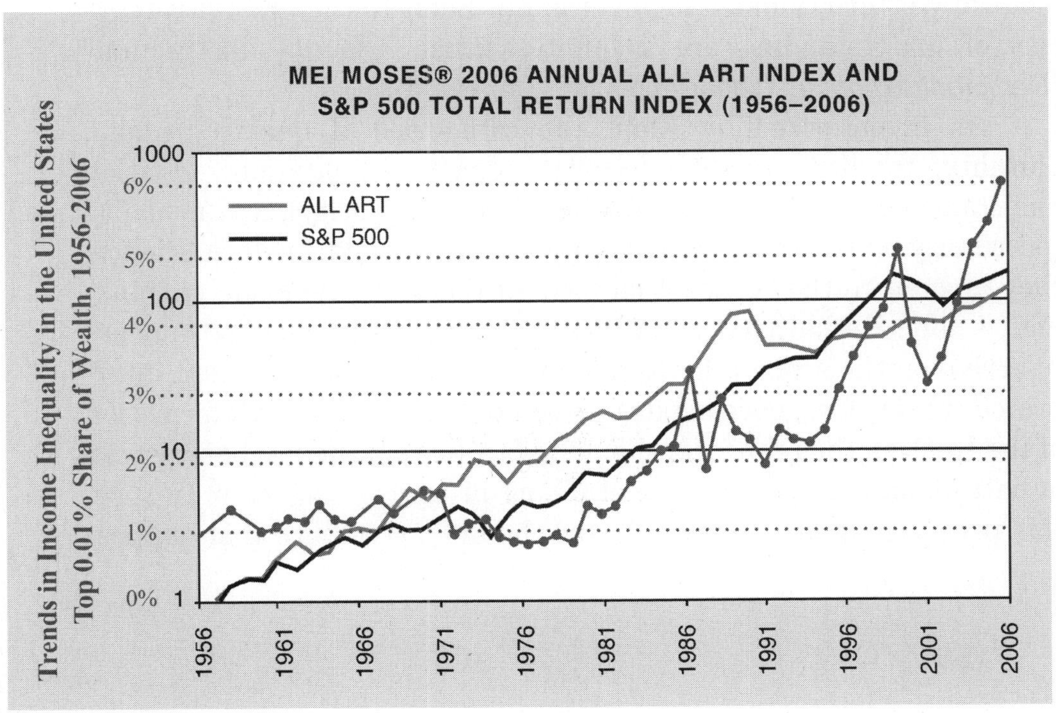

Andrea Fraser, *Index*, 2011

exchange-value.[14] The commodity fetish derives its appearance of autonomous life from exchange; money is not reified as a thing (copper coins, bank notes) but fetishized as a purely formal relation between things, as difference on the basis of equivalence.

As the German Marxist Alfred Sohn-Rethel put it: "The value-form denies and veils the quantitative relation of value to labour through the 'reified appearance [*gegenständlichen Schein*]' of commodity value."[15] Ultimately, money functions as the medium for "these formal properties abstracted from all use-value," for "pure formal abstractions."[16] Sohn-Rethel is perhaps the thinker who has made the most sustained study and use of Marx's concept of the value-form. This lifelong project, beginning in the interwar period, culminated in his 1970 opus *Intellectual and Manual Labour*, which he later revised a number of times, and in which he desublimates philosophical "thought abstractions" by linking them generically to the "real abstractions" of exchange and money.[17] Sohn-Rethel attempts to reveal the historically specific economic underpinnings of Kantianism and of modern Western thinking in general. For Sohn-Rethel, Kant's categories of understanding are a quintessential "thought abstraction" (*Denkabstraktion*) or "thought-form" (*Denkform*).

As inventorized by Kant, the categories of quantity (unity, plurality, totality), quality (reality, negation, limitation), relation (substance and accident, cause and effect, reciprocity), and modality (possibility, existence, necessity) lie at the basis of modern science; they amount to the "conceptual form of the scientific mode of thinking."[18] Sohn-Rethel argues that this preforming Kantian mind appears to arrive on the scene fully formed; it is *itself* preformed. Kant interpreted this preformation in purely mental terms, but this preformation of the Kantian thought-form should in fact be regarded as being *social* in nature, and as the outcome of a long historical process.[19] In turn, this pregiven apparatus constitutes the deep structure that supposedly preforms all of our perception and cognition. For Sohn-Rethel, by contrast, this preformation of the Kantian thought-form is *social* in nature. The Kantian thought-form is shaped by the value-form; the thought abstraction shaped by real abstraction. Because of the division between manual and intellectual labor, Sohn-Rethel argues, the intrinsic relationship between the two remains unnoticed.

Even while reading Marx and forging ties with Benjamin and Adorno, during the 1920s, Sohn-Rethel studied with the neo-Kantian philosopher Ernst Cassirer and witnessed the famous *Zauberberg*-style debate between Cassirer and Heidegger in Davos in 1929. Cassirer *pluralized* and *culturalized* Kant's framework of mental categories and transcendental schematism—the apparatus that structures our reality and occludes the *Ding an sich* as so much epistemological waste. Kant had given an idealist twist to old, Aristotelian debates about substance and attributes. Cassirer noted that Kant's thinking "keeps circling around the dualism of matter and form set forth in its beginnings, and [...] gradually changes and deepens the meaning of this opposition."[20] One could indeed discern a displacement of hylomorphism in Kantian a priori categories and transcendental schemata: the categories of understanding, on which Sohn-Rethel tended to focus, and the procedural rules or schemata that allow the subject to "apply" these to sense data, to inform data with them.[21] Cassirer, however, posited not a single schematism of the mind but rather a plurality of symbolic forms that each have their own innate logic, that structure the world in different ways: myth, for instance, or language, or science, or art. Late in his life, in a 1942 Yale lecture, he acknowledged Saussure's semiology as a kindred and compatible project, but Saussure's privileged sign system—natural language—was only one particular symbolic form for Cassirer.[22]

In the 1920s, the circle around Aby Warburg availed itself of Cassirer's notion for the purposes of art history and theory. In his famous essay "Perspective as Symbolic Form" (1924–25, published in 1927), Erwin Panofsky analyzed Renaissance perspective as a symbolic form that functioned as an "objectification of the subjective," but also the reverse.[23] Linear perspective first creates a distance between people and things, but it then "abolishes this distance by […] drawing this world of things, an autonomous world confronting the individual, into the eye."[24] The *obiectum* is appropriated by the subject. Long before Bruno Latour, Panofsky thus engaged with the Western tableau as a crucial device for producing a modern regime of subject-object relations. Whereas Latour interprets the painting as a window opening onto an object behind it, Panofsky focuses on the painting's surface—specifically, the perspectival grid. In the process, he dematerializes the artworks by abstracting perspective grids from the physical paintings; his diagrams seek to reveal the deep structure that relates objects to subject.

If *art as such* is a symbolic form, according to Cassirer, it seems rather curious that Panofsky would analyze a specific device within a particular type of art—Renaissance linear perspective—as a symbolic form. This could be seen as symptomatic lack of rigor, but also as a further specification, as a step in the labor of concretization. In fact, Cassirer's own listing of "myth and art, language and science" as the four fundamental symbolic forms is also curiously like a Borgesian encyclopedia, as the terms clearly overlap and are not comparable in every respect. The interrelations between the "linguistic sign" and the "mythical or artistic 'image,'" which can be articulated in linguistic signs, remain undialectical and approximate.[25]

In contrast to Cassirer's pluralization and culturalization of Kant's categorical apparatus, Sohn-Rethel sought to deconstruct its formalist universalism as an unacknowledged reflection of exchange. Dispensing with the natural form and noting that not an atom of matter has entered into the commodity qua value-form, he sought to demonstrate that the exchange process is marked by an abstraction from all material and sensuous qualities that prefigures and informs the operations of the Kantian mind. Much of this remains sketchy and speculative, though the second part of his book goes into further historical detail: while the Greeks and Romans had money and exchange, and thus produced a certain body of philosophical-scientific knowledge to mirror this real abstraction, it was only in the Renaissance that a truly capitalist economy based on the production of surplus-value emerged. It is this that put modern science on a trajectory that went far beyond the ancient world. However, as his critics have noted, Sohn-Rethel's account of real abstraction is exchange-centric; production hardly features.[26] Thus, much of what he says does indeed appear to be equally applicable to ancient Greece, medieval feudalism, or industrial capitalism. Indeed, the value-form itself is not distinctly capitalist; insofar as exchange-value is the form of value, it is transhistorical, and long predates capitalism. What is specific for capitalism is the role of abstract human labor as the determinant of value, and the dialectical relations that this establishes between value, exchange-value, and use-value. Marx himself noted that Aristotle, who analyzed the exchange between different commodities, lacked a proper concept of value because he lived in a slave society that had no notion of labor as consisting of equal, equivalent units.[27] The specifically *capitalist* value-form is the autonomized expression of labor-time. Commodity fetishism is a type of formalism: it occludes the role of labor to suggest that value is actually determined by being realized on the market.

In relation to *art*, Sohn-Rethel's exchange-centeredness makes a certain degree of theoretical sense. After all, is art not still fundamentally what it always was—"that old thing, art," having never been fully "modernized" and industrialized, and never been really and fully subsumed under capitalist production methods? However, as we have seen in the last chapter, archaic methods of reproduction (casting) can

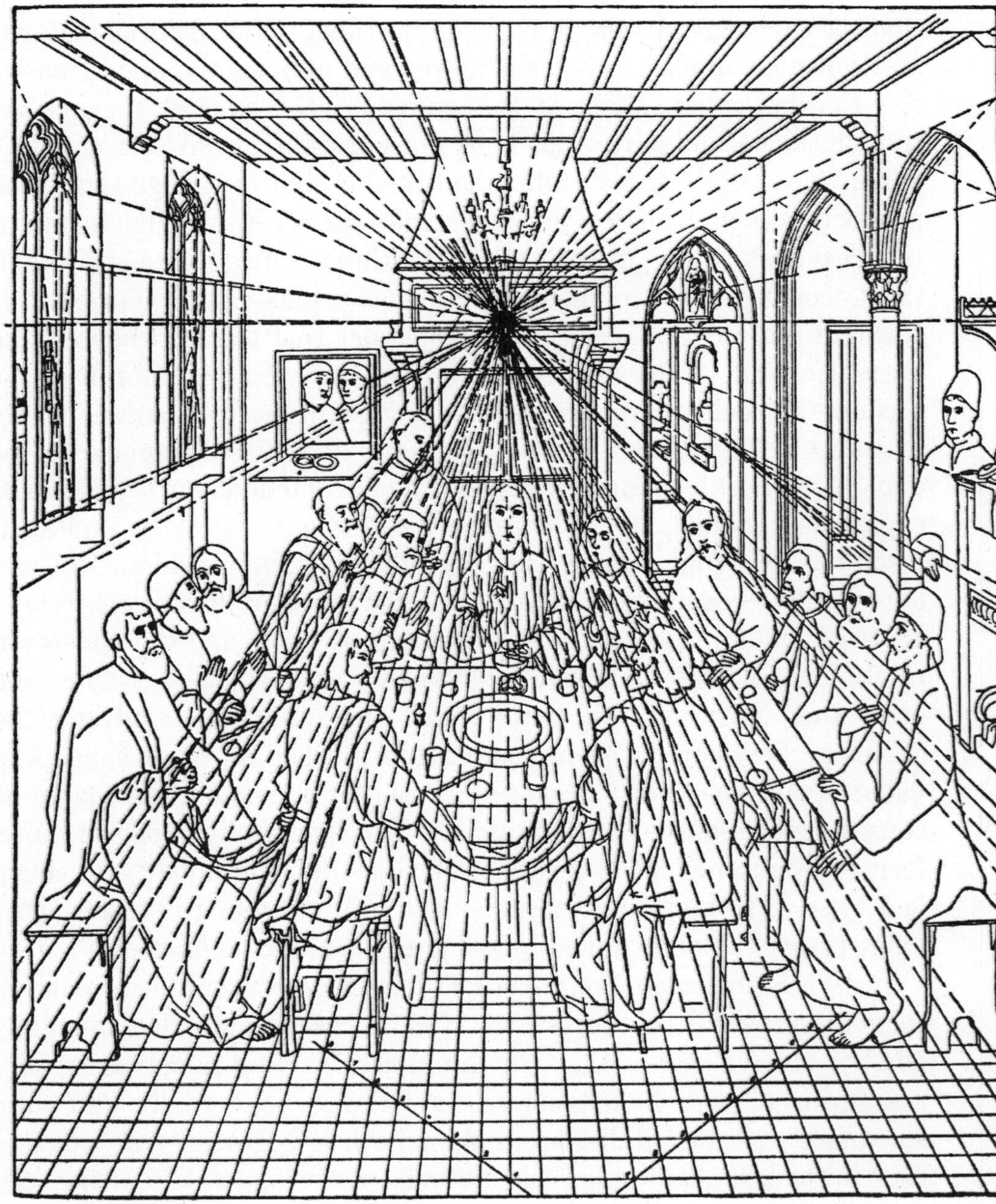

Erwin Panofsky's perspectival schema of the *Last Supper* of Dirk Bouts (Louvain, St. Peter, 1464–67)

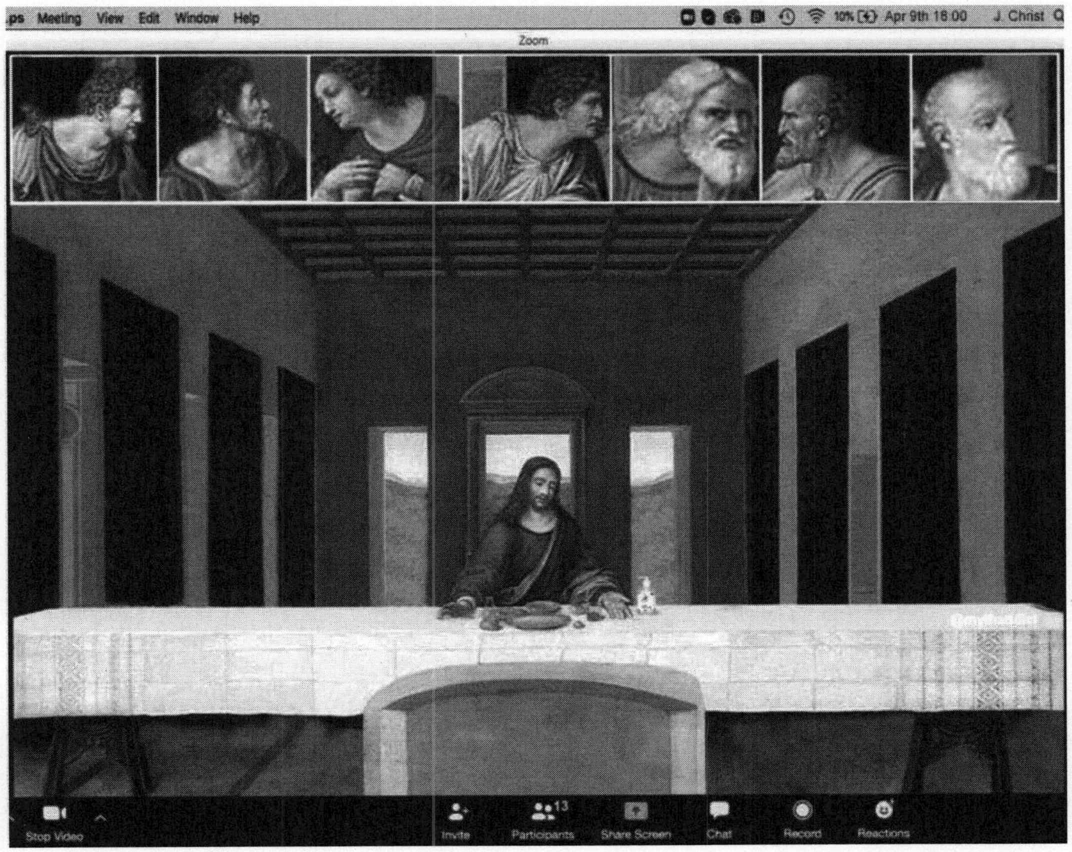

"The Last Zoom," COVID-19 lockdown meme, 2020

reveal themselves as incubators of mass production. Now that mass production is increasingly automated *and* moved offshore, the labor theory of value meets its limits in more than just art. In a culturalized economy, branded goods appear to make the fetishistic illusion of the autonomous value-form an operational reality. This, however, arguably spells trouble for a seemingly triumphant capitalism.

Sohn-Rethel raises the important question of the relation between Kantian "preformations" of the mind and the exchange form as "preforming" social structures. Both preformations—the real abstraction of economic exchange and the abstraction of thought—extirpate all sensuous concretion.[28] The disenfranchisement of qualitative sensory experience through quantitative abstraction thus plays a significant role in Sohn-Rethel's work, but his analysis also seems to exacerbate this tendency. He tends to equate sensate experience with irredeemably private sensations, and in this way, he is perhaps more indebted to classical bourgeois philosophy than he would care to admit:

> The commodity is not, like its use-value, the exclusive private datum of a solipsistic self, but belongs to a common world which is common to all the private selves. Although the perception is as multiple as the people perceiving it, its existence is one. If the existence of one object were divisible the object could indeed be owned simultaneously by separate owners. Each owner could not only experience the world as his "private datum" but own it as his exclusive property.[29]

Today, those "private data" are themselves socialized through commodification: we produce value for Facebook by sharing what used to be private. How do the real abstractions of exchange "preform" our embodied and social perception of the world? What can we really say we own anymore, and what happens (economically and socially) when we no longer sell our labor-power but spend our time freely? Are we productive workers? How is value generated when it is no longer clear what work is, and how much labor-time went into a commodity, and when brands create artificial scarcity by producing "limited editions"? In the "proper" commodity, according to Marx, value is determined by the socially necessary amount of labor needed for the production, though the value-form as pure equivalence masks this. Now exchange swallows up production. Are we dealing with an *operational commodity fetishism* in which value is generated in ways that cannot be tied back to labor-power and labor-time?

Art: An Exceptional Ism?

Marx's mature critique of political economy remained informed by Romanticism and, hence, by the aesthetic—for instance, in the discussion of use-value, which stands for the realm of the qualitative as opposed to quantifiable exchange-value. The defense of the qualitative and of non-equivalence was a crucial aspect of the modern aesthetic project, which generated two distinct forms of aestheticism. The first is the more familiar phenomenon of *l'art pour l'art* from Gautier and Whistler to Huysmans, Wilde, and beyond; the second, which could be termed "utilitarian aestheticism," was embodied in Ruskin's or Morris's attempts to reintegrate art into daily life and the realm of "useful" labor and artifacts. Both strands were attempts to soften the blows of industrial capitalism and counter the relentless triumph of abstract labor and exchange-value. Ruskin's invectives against Whistler's "paint-flinging" amounted to internecine squabbling. The moment in 1874 when a young Oscar Wilde pushed wheelbarrows full of paving stones as part of Ruskin's project to have his students pave a road in Hinksey, near Oxford, in celebration of healthy and unalienated manual labor, shows how closely these genealogies are intertwined.[30]

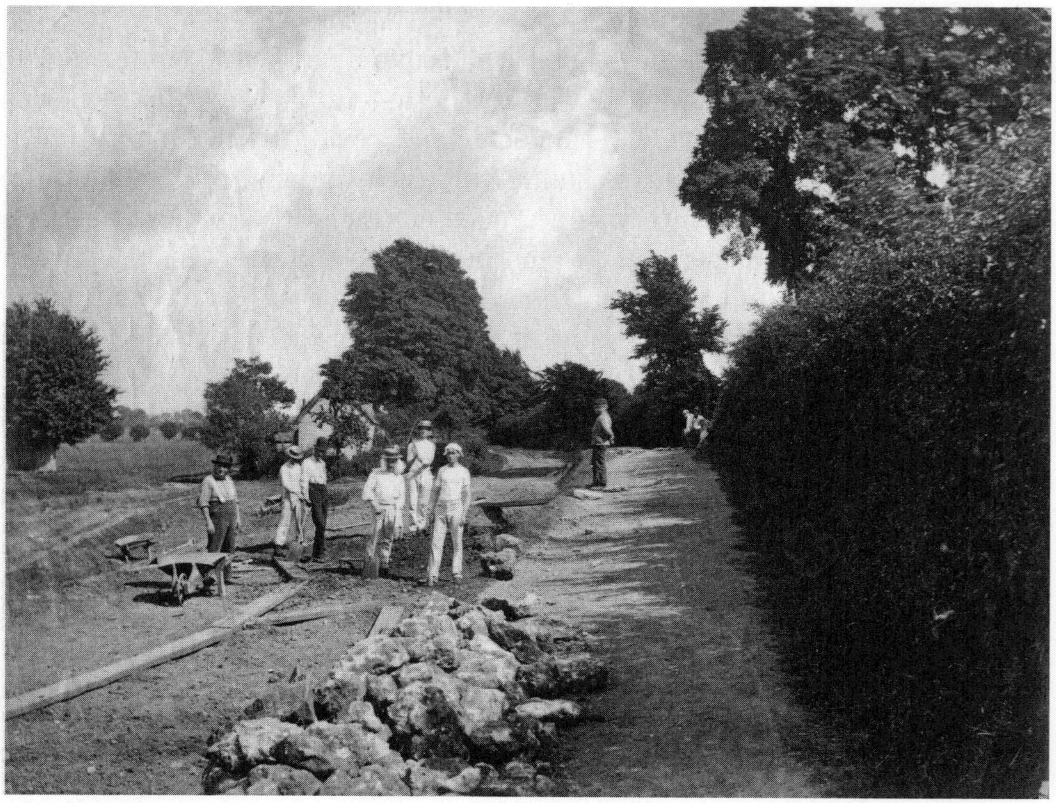

John Ruskin's gang of road builders in North Hinksey, June 1874

Marxist and non-Marxist theorists alike have long acknowledged that the artwork seems to behave differently from "normal" capitalist commodities. Clinging on to precapitalist modes of production, art is often deemed incompatible with the Marxian labor theory of value, according to which the real value of a commodity is determined by the "socially necessary labor-time" it represents.[31] Here, Marx uses "value" without any qualifier. This is the third term in a dialectical constellation alongside use-value and exchange-value, though it frequently gets lumped together with the latter. The components of the triad use-value/exchange-value/value relate to each other as substance/form/magnitude of value. Representing the spheres of private consumption, market exchange, and production, these concepts are each others' codependent dialectical counterparts.[32] The magnitude of value is measured in the "socially average" amount of units of labor-power needed for producing a type of commodity. [33] In order for a commodity to have value, it must also have a use-value, however rarefied it may be; and exchange-value is not autonomous, as the illusion of commodity fetishism would suggest, but is in fact based on the value of socially necessary labor-time. However, value not only presupposes use-value as its *conditio sine qua non*, but also needs exchange-value as its "mode of expression" or "form of appearance."[34] This is capitalist value formalism.

Crucially, Marx adapted Ricardo's labor theory of value by insisting that value is determined not by any specific skills or qualities of workmanship, but by abstract, homogenous units of labor-power:

> The total labour-power of society, which is manifested in the values of the world of commodities, counts here as one homogeneous mass of human labour-power, although composed of innumerable individual units of labour-power. Each of these units is the same as any other, to the extent that it has the character of a socially average

> unit of labour-power and acts as such; i.e. only needs, in order to produce a commodity, the labour-time which is necessary on an average, or in other words is socially necessary. Socially necessary labour-time is the labour-time required to produce any use-value under the conditions of production normal for a given society and with the average degree of skill an intensity of labour prevalent in that society.[35]

Profit, of course, springs from what is added to socially necessary labor-time: surplus labor performed by the worker. Clearly, it was difficult for Marx to integrate art into this theory of value. Most artists did not sell their labor-power to a capitalist who could pocket the surplus-value, but rather worked in an artisanal manner, selling their works directly. While any work may be productive of use-values, only labor that generates surplus-value for capital is "productive" in Marx's technical sense—which is to say, productive of *value* for capital:

> Milton, who wrote *Paradise Lost*, was an unproductive worker. On the other hand, a writer who turns out work for his publisher in factory style is a productive worker. Milton produced *Paradise Lost* as a silkworm produces silk, as the activity of his own nature. He later sold his product for £5 and thus became a merchant. But the literary proletarian of Leipzig who produces books, such as compendia on political economy, at the behest of his publisher is pretty nearly a productive worker since his production is taken over by capital and only occurs in order to increase it. A singer who sings like a bird is an unproductive worker. If she sells her song for money, she is to that extent a wage labourer or merchant. But if the same singer is engaged by an entrepreneur who makes her sing to make money, then she becomes a productive worker, since she produces capital directly. A schoolmaster who instructs others is not a productive

> worker. But a schoolmaster who works for wages in an institution along with others, using his own labour to increase the money of the entrepreneur who owns the knowledge-mongering institution, is a productive worker. But for the most part, work of this sort has scarcely reached the stage of being subsumed even formally under capital, and belongs essentially to a transitional stage.[36]

In this respect, as Dave Beech has noted in his study *Art and Value*, modern art presents the paradoxical spectacle of commodification without true commodities. That is to say, works of art are *simple commodities* to which commodification remains external and a posteriori; their production process is not truly capitalist.[37] Art may have been subsumed formally, but not in its productive logic. *Art and Value* is an extended critique of Western Marxism's absent economy of art: "Western Marxism has always used every device it can find to associate art with capitalism without having to conduct the economic analysis that could establish such associations as [either] substantial or superficial."[38]

Beech attempts a "shift from a theory of art's exceptionalism based on choices and consumer behaviour to one based on artistic production and art's relation to capital," criticizing his predecessors for failing to address the fundamental logic of commodification.[39] However, Beech has a rather rigid conception of what constitutes "properly" capitalist production while refusing to acknowledge that capitalism itself appears increasingly "exceptional" from the perspective of the labor theory of value. It is precisely this constellation that makes art a potentially privileged field of inquiry, even as much of it sinks into collector-pleasing irrelevance. Beech argues that, on the level of production, visual art has mostly remained a matter of artisanal production of simple commodities, and that even when artists involve assistants in the making of the work, this work "is not commodity production according to the labour theory of value."[40] This is because the work is insufficiently standardized, and these art factories "do not require economizing measures, and they do not determine the prices of artworks."[41] These prices are rather determined by critics, curators, other artists, and even collectors.[42] Beech notes that the value added to the artwork by such actors remains "external to the commodity," but does it?[43] And at what point does the economic exception become the norm? Has that old thing, art, now become the covert model of today's branded goods and curated experiences?

Arguing that it is "strange within the labour theory of value to think that an act of consumption added value to a product," Beech maintains that "no value is added at all, even though the prices of artworks appreciate. The difference in price is not extracted from labor but, as Marx puts it when talking about trade as a zero sum game, is 'coaxed' out of the pockets of another capitalist."[44] While it is indeed important to acknowledge the particularities of the art market, with its gatekeepers and its "value-adding" experts, are we not living through an economic moment in which such work is becoming ever more fundamental to the economy at large? If the kind of work performed by experts in art spells trouble for the labor theory of value, then what of fashion bloggers, YouTube and Instagram influencers, Facebook users, and all sorts of online likers and linkers? The "prosumer" of communicative capitalism has thrown processes of art-world valorization into a bit of a tailspin. In the age of websites that function as "algorithmic moodboards"—from MutualArt and Artfacts to *DIS Magazine*—the conventional chain of artist-critic-curator-dealer-collector is in tatters.[45] If anything, an algorithm-collector complex seems to be emerging. Here, as elsewhere, Beech comes across as curiously classicist in failing to address such developments.

In marked contrast to Beech, Diedrich Diederichsen has launched a spirited attempt to save the labor theory of value for the analysis of art.[46] Diederichsen effectively tries to normalize art by creating a more encompassing labor theory of value, arguing that the value of an artwork is created not simply by the artist, but also, in part, by other parties that invest their time—critics, collectors, all kinds of viewers. Taking up his work on the indexical basis of postwar cultural production, Diederichsen also argues that the question with art is how much of the time that has been "stored" in the work "can then be 'read out' in a narrowly technical as well as an aesthetic sense?"[47] Diederichsen does not really explain how the time "stored" in the artwork can be read or retrieved. In addition to indexical audio or video recordings, he argues that time can also be stored in other ways, for instance by being encased in an object, such as a painting or in a score, or in the embodied memory or performers.[48]

Surely, here we are here dealing with "stored time" that cannot ever be quantified. Even if we were to know that a painting took twenty-seven hours to paint, its style might suggest far greater haste, or a vast expanse of glacial time, or a montage of different temporalities and durations. And how are the time and value added by critics and collectors to be "read" from the work? Tautologically, via the price it fetches at auction? And is the time enclosed in a score the four minutes and thirty-three seconds that it takes to be performed, or the lifetime of aesthetic decisions leading up to that work, or indeed the cumulative investment of everyone who has ever heard (of) the piece? This all amounts to an infinitely elastic *durée*, or an ineffable intensity—not Marx's "socially necessary labor-time."

In 1971, Antonio Negri already noted a "disconnection between work and labor value/exchange value" in the postwar welfare state, and technological, economic, and social developments since then have only exacerbated this crisis of value.[49] In subsequent decades, Negri and other thinkers associated with (post-)Operaism and autonomism were among the most attentive theorists of this disconnection. For Autonomia, "the worker is always powerful."[50] As Negri puts it in a recent article: "Without the worker's activity, there is no production of value. Capitalism does not exist without workers' productive power. [...] To affirm the *class as a subject*, to build it in a process of subjectivation, is the first and most important of Marx's contributions, to anyone becoming aware of exploitation and who is willing to fight it."[51] For Operaismo and Autonomia, the task is always to recast the crisis of value and of capitalism in terms of agency and class composition: if capitalism reduces workers to unskilled labor ("the mass worker"), or to precarity or surplus status, or releases them from wage labor into the individualized realm of "immaterial labor," these are so many signs of capitalism having painted itself into a corner. In responding to workers' autonomy by ramping up automation and outsourcing production, capitalism comes to depend more than ever on intellectual and technical workers that can become (part of) a new revolutionary subject. If the project of revolutionary working-class struggle became problematic in the wake of the West's deindustrialization, post-Operaist autonomism triumphed theoretically/rhetorically precisely because it sketched an alternative multitudinous subject as replacement for the old working class, and decreed the necessity and inevitability of proletarian or precarian struggle—of emancipatory human praxis.[52]

For the *Wertkritik* (value critique) developed by the German Krisis group, Operaist/autonomist accounts of the crisis of labor and value remain both too anecdotal and too voluntarist, failing to address the fundamental logic and systemic crisis of capitalism.[53] There was a "double Marx," as Robert Kurz liked to say, and for all their digging in the *Grundrisse*, the Italians ultimately sided with the exoteric one of *The Communist Manifesto* and of workers' emancipation. In contrast with the Operaist-autonomist lineage and its focus on activism and transformation, the value critics opted for "Marx no. 2," the theorist of the value-form and of abstract labor.[54] Engaging with capitalism's intrinsic logic they approach value itself as an "automatic subject" that is pitted against that of the working class and its struggle against the reduction of human activity to alienating abstract labor.[55]

Wertkritik is marked by the pessimism of the intellect, post-Operaism by the voluntarism of the imagination. Both strands of theory articulate the crisis of value, looking toward the abolition of labor-time as its measure, and toward the end of labor itself.[56] *Wertkritiker* such as Kurz have noted a breakdown in value production owing to the increasingly technological nature and socialization of labor. In line with Kurz, Anselm Jappe has argued that the calculation of the labor invested in a single commodity becomes a de facto impossibility.[57] Even if one were to try to identify all constituent factors, the question would be what to include and what not. Is a fashionista "liking" posts by Louis Vuitton working or not? Or both, or neither? One much-remarked characteristic of post-Fordism is that the distinction between labor and leisure has eroded in many sectors. "The measurability of labor presupposes that the individual subject is always either working or not working. It is impossible to measure labor-time that is mixed with other activities," as Jappe puts it.[58] Trying to reestablish the labor theory of value by widening the net—by including what was previously thought of as nonlabor—is not necessarily going to result in convincing calculations.

Other products are, of course, available. If the labor theory of value is untenable, then what about neoclassical economics and marginal utility theory? I will return to this in the next volume; for now, I want to stay with the labor theory of value to argue that its crisis is indexical—that it is directly linked to the crisis of the economic system itself. Arguing that the socialization and technologization of production "simply" means that the calculation of the labor invested in a single commodity gets more complex fails to do justice to the cumulative effects of the scattering and diffusion of labor, which undermine such distinctions between productive and reproductive or unproductive *in practice*.

If the labor theory of value meets its limits in art, as Beech argues, then why stop there? If the theory falters on the "micro level" of art as a specific type of commodity, we need to acknowledge that art now has a status fundamentally different than in 1890, 1920, or 1950. On the one hand, certain artists and artworks realize baffling prices—and garner a lot of media attention in the process—while, on the other hand, precarious and badly remunerated "creative" work proliferates. These are both symptoms of a crisis of labor and a crisis of value that seems to fall outside of Beech's self-defined purview. My point in critiquing Beech's "classicism" is not, as Marina Vishmidt has suggested, that I wish to "settle" for an "equally well-worn" account of the real subsumption of art under capital.[59] That would indeed be banal. Rather than diagnosing art's complete subsumption, I'm interested in how both contemporary art's financialized status and alternative or critical artistic practices articulate a crisis of labor and value. The point is not some totalizing gesture, but rather an analysis of the contradictions, tensions, and breakdowns that capitalism's intrinsic logic—or immanent drive—generates.

From Whistler to Morris, from Jorn to Beuys, art has been conceived (in different and frequently incompatible ways) in terms of *practice against labor*. In the modern division of labor, the artist's job was to perform qualitative acts as a stand-in for liberated human activity, for true praxis, under capitalist conditions. The artist was a specialist of the qualitative in the realm of quantity—as another modern specialism, but one that took the form of an exception. Needless to say, conservative ideologies of the aesthetic exploited the tentative nature of the aesthetic promise, its relegation to the status of a harmless daydream. Still, as can be seen from Marx's gloss on Milton, artistic "work against labor" always contained within it a potential for politicization. Standing for the aesthetic promise of unalienated work, Milton-the-silkworm remains an indictment of the present, both archaic and a figure of the future.

Productive and Reproductive Labor; Incorporation and Exclusion

At this point I should acknowledge that there is some debate concerning the question whether Marx's theory of value actually *is* the labor theory of value that is usually ascribed to him: a "strong" labor theory that supposes we could somehow calculate the labor-time in any commodity, and hence "directly" establish its price. This is what many socialist schemes tried to do: do away with exchange-value, and calculate price in labor-time rather than in money. Diane Elson has argued that this is a misreading of Marx, who was skeptical of such schemes.[60] Socially necessary labor-time—and what is "necessary" is defined by Marx as that which allows people and organizations to survive under historically specific economic conditions—is an abstraction, an average, that cannot be established by tallying up working hours in a factory. Such socially necessary labor-time is "not a ready-made prerequisite but an emerging result" in the process of exchange, according to Marx.[61] "Social labour-time exists in these commodities in a latent state, so to speak, and becomes evident only in the course of their exchange."[62]

While *value* as defined by Marx could be seen as materialist demystification of exchange-value (through the famous descent into the hidden abode of production), this value needs to be *realized through* exchange. Even in those cases where it appears to be possible to calculate the amount of labor that has gone into the making of a commodity (x workers have worked on it for x amount of time), this is a false concretion. Value is the *socially necessary* amount of labor-time, meaning that an inefficient factory produces goods that cost more than what they are worth. However, the socially necessary amount is an average that only manifests itself *through exchange*. This is exchange understood in a post-fetishistic sense: not as autonomous from labor, but as its mediated manifestation. As Elson puts it, "Values cannot be calculated or observed independently of prices."[63] So much for the great "socialist calculation debate." Insofar as labor is at the heart of Marx's account of value it remains a labor theory, it is an *indirect labor theory of value* that offers no shortcuts for complex processes of transformation and realization. The dialectic of substance, form, and measure cannot be abrogated.

In this sense, Wertkritik may depend on too orthodox a notion of the "labor theory of value" in order to demonstrate its breakdown in the present. If direct calculation of value through labor-time was never an option, what has changed? One difference lies precisely in the operationalization of the value-form. The appearance of autonomous prices creates its own reality when commodities become incommensurable. With cultural commodities from iPhones to Gerhard Richter paintings, fetishism is operational—a form of fetishization that creates new economic and social realities.[64] Designed and branded products show the value-form informing and remaking the material world, the *Naturalform*. The value-form becomes an operational morphe. In semiocapitalism, labor-power as composed of homogeneous units is a *necessary condition* for value, just as use-value is, but it no longer fully informs it. Labor-power may be "encrypted in the commodity," but the codebook has been lost.[65]

Updating the labor theory of value for products such as Apple laptops, tablets, or phones, Wu Ming have argued that such commodities' hidden costs need to be taken into account—for instance, the dirty and unhealthy disposal of junked devices in Africa: "Being these rapidly obsolescent commodities, and particularly, commodities whose obsolescence is *planned*, this work is *already embodied in them* since the beginning of the cycle."[66] I will leave to one side the question of whether this can salvage the "direct" labor theory of value, and whether it has any consequences for Marx's "indirect" theory. What is crucial about Wu Ming's example is surely that such forms of labor—and even more so the ecological costs that accrue—are not actually factored into the equation of any company. They are "outsourced" to society—in ways that show the persistence of colonial inequality and the unequal distribution of what Rob Nixon calls "slow violence." Here we should heed David Harvey's insistence that Marx's term "socially necessary labour-time" puts *society* on the agenda. Instead of positing an autonomous play of "market forces," or even an automatic subject of value, we would do well to remember that what is socially necessary is socially determined—and thus also open to contestation.[67]

It has long been an autonomist contention that to demand that "hidden" labor be factored into production costs and the value of commodities would strike at the root of capitalism. The autonomist-feminist Wages for Housework campaign (1972–77) revolved around such a demand.[68] As noted by Kerstin Stakemeier, Wages for Housework transposed "a struggle for autonomy *into* a social realm deemed heteronomous."[69] In recent years, this campaign has been invoked by Laurel Ptak's website Wages for Facebook, which contains a scrolling text with a manifesto-like demand to quantify and remunerate the value produced by each Facebook user.[70] If the value of Facebook is indeed "proportional to the square of the number of its users," as Metcalfe's law has it, this means that the value of an individual user's quasi labor can and will fluctuate greatly.[71] Demanding wages for Facebook users is a threat to the business model as much as demands for factoring in ecological costs would be. Both are unrealistic at present—however, even as governments and their corporate backers resist the incorporation of certain costs, capitalism's exclusions come back to haunt it in the form of restless surplus populations.

Capitalism thrives on a dialectic of incorporation and exclusion. The frequently violent process of incorporation was characterized by Marx as *original* or *primitive* accumulation, associated with

> those moments when great masses of men are suddenly and forcibly torn from their means of subsistence, and hurled as free and

> "unattached" proletarians on the labour-market. The expropriation of the agricultural producer, of the peasant, from the soil, is the basis of the whole process. The history of this expropriation, in different countries, assumes different aspects, and runs through its various phases in different orders of succession, and at different periods. In England alone, which we take as our example, has it the classic form.[72]

Marx here refers to land enclosure; land that was previously in common use was used to graze sheep for wool production, thus separating people from the land:

> The great feudal lords, in their defiant opposition to the king and Parliament, created an incomparably larger proletariat by forcibly driving the peasantry from the land, to which the latter had the same feudal title as the lords themselves, and by usurpation of the common lands. The rapid expansion of wool manufacture in Flanders and the corresponding rise in the price of wool in England provided the direct impulse for these evictions. The old nobility had been devoured by the great feudal wars. The new nobility was the child of its time, for which money was the power of all powers. Transformation of arable land into sheep-walks was therefore its slogan. [...] A comparison between the writings of Chancellor Fortescue and Thomas More reveals the gulf between the fifteenth and the sixteenth centuries. As Thornton rightly says, the English working class was precipitated without any transitional stages from its golden age to its iron age.[73]

For Marx, primitive accumulation was a "historical process of divorcing the producer from the means of production"; this also meant divorcing that producer from incorporating into capitalism.[74] The shepherd has no option but to sell his labor, and sheep themselves have been incorporated in capitalist production. This traumatic, catastrophic development is referenced in Thomas More's *Utopia* (1517), where an evocation of the topsy-turvy world of early sixteenth-century England, in which placid sheep have become devouring monsters, provides a contrast for the more rational (at times, frighteningly so) social organization in Utopia.[75]

The island of Utopia was, of course, situated by More in the New World; thus, one scene of primitive accumulation is linked to another. Indeed, Massimo De Angelis argues that Marx's "discussion of primitive accumulation in England" must necessarily lead to an analysis of "distant lands, to the extent these areas are linked and subordinated to the process of accumulation in England," for instance, through the slave trade and its impact on British ports.[76] Marx had certainly not been blind to the colonial dimension of primitive accumulation. He stressed that the "discovery of gold and silver in America, the extirpation, enslavement and entombment in mines of the indigenous population, the beginnings of the conquest and plunder of India, and the conversion of Africa into a preserve for the commercial hunting of blackskins" are "the chief moments of primitive accumulation."[77] These moments "can be assigned in particular to Spain, Portugal, Holland, France and England, in more or less chronological order."[78] Already in Marx, then, there is the sense that primitive accumulation cannot be limited to any single, "classic" moment, but is, in fact, an ongoing process as long as there are "outsides" to capitalism.

However, De Angelis notes:

> [Slavery] did not entail a classic-Marxist model of transition applied to Africa from feudalism to capitalism. This model, that was common Marxist orthodoxy until not long ago, by emphasizing the role played by land enclosures in the "transition" from feudal to a capitalist mode of production in England, has contributed to turn the concept of primitive accumulation into a corner-stone of a monumental building generally referred to as "stage theory." Instead, the example of the

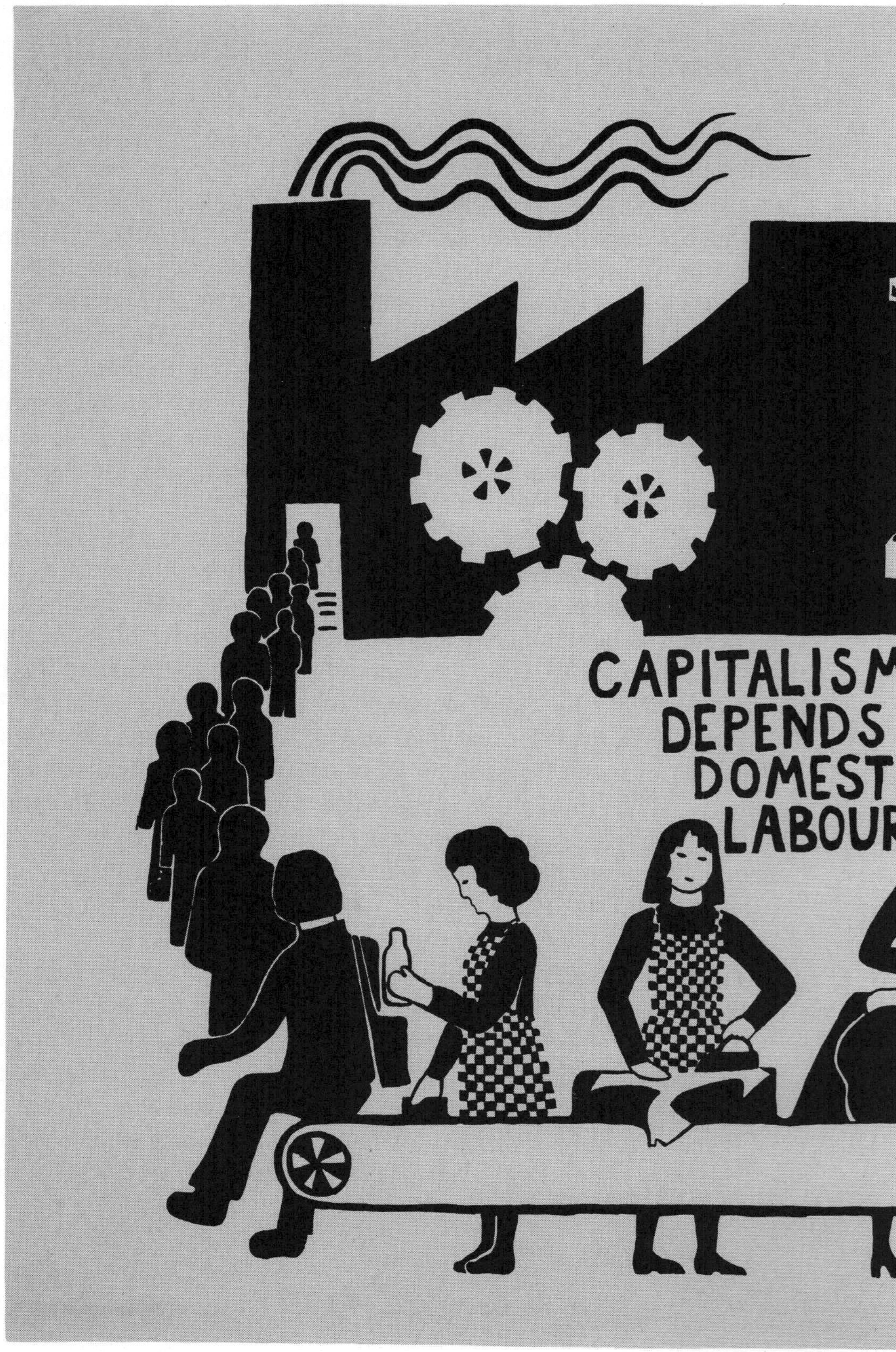

See Red Women's Workshop, *Capitalism Also Depends on Domestic Labour*, 1975

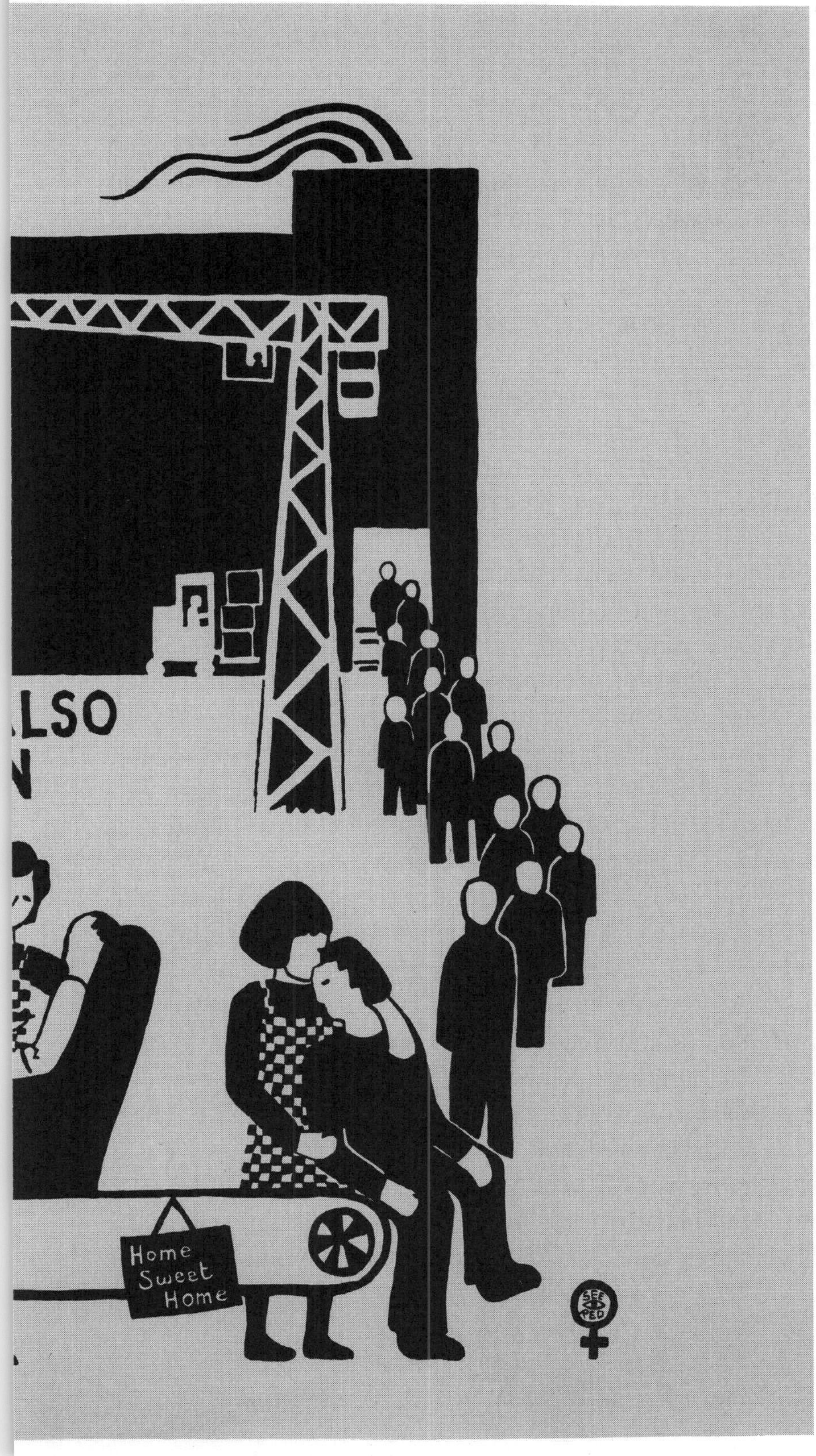
Home
Sweet
Home

> slave trade shows that primitive accumulation may occur through the interaction between North and South, an international division of labour, the destruction of African communities, and enslavement.[79]

Silvia Federici has likewise deployed the concept of primitive accumulation to unseat Marxist orthodoxies, using it to analyze the historical exclusion of women from the emerging capitalist economy. This genealogical project, which she has developed since the second half of the 1970s, provides the historical background for the Wages for Housework campaign—in which Federici was centrally involved.[80] In *Caliban and the Witch*, Federici argues that primitive accumulation and the enclosure of the commons in the early sixteenth century went hand in hand with a new sexual division of labor, with women being relegated to a "private" sphere of reproductive work and excluded from wage labor.[81]

In arguing that the value of commodities—including labor-power itself—is determined by the amount of labor socially necessary to produce them, Marx acknowledged the time necessary for maintaining and reproducing the labor-power of the workforce.[82] Overall, however, Marxism failed to do justice to the sphere of reproduction as integral to the production process in general, thus becoming complicit in women's relegation to the domestic sphere as a supposedly extra-economic supplement. In the 1940s, the American feminist Mary Inman launched a fierce debate in the US Communist Party by insisting that "under capitalism, housewives' work, in a majority of cases, is necessary to the process of producing and distributing commodities," and is thus productive labor.[83] In founding documents of the Wages for Housework campaign, such as Mariarosa Dalla Costa and Selma James's *The Power of Women and the Subversion of the Community* (1972), we likewise see an insistence that housework is productive.[84]

In the sense that housework is necessary for capitalist society to function, this is of course true. A 1975 poster by the London-based See

Red Women's Workshop makes this basic point in visual terms: women support and "mend" the men and send them back to the devouring mechanism of the factory.[85] However, when Federici later synthesized 1970s feminist and Marxist debates and took them as a point of departure for historical research into primitive accumulation, she argued that reproductive work under capitalism is useful and valuable precisely *insofar as it is treated as an immanent exception.*[86] It is productive in the broad social sense insofar as it is not regarded as "productive labor" in the direct economic sense. In Jason Moore's terminology, we might distinguish between *exploitation* through wage labor and the direct, unwaged *appropriation* of labor and energy.[87] The former is as crucial as the latter.

In parallel with the feminist autonomism that emerged in the early 1970s, Mierle Laderman Ukeles's 1969 *Manifesto for Maintenance Art* and related pieces, such as her 1973 cleaning of the Wadsworth Atheneum Museum of Art in Hartford, Connecticut, aligned art practice as "unproductive" work with "reproductive," feminized housework.[88] In a different aesthetic register and production mode, Jean-Luc Godard and Anne-Marie Miéville's television series *Six fois deux* (1976) constituted a critique of the division between productive and reproductive labor as well as the division of labor in general, and the separation between labor and leisure. Part 3A reflects on photography: professional photographers get paid, as do photo models, but not people in the Third World whose misery is equally photogenic: "Magazines from all over the world made a fortune from Vietnam." Part 3B is dedicated to Marcel, a watchmaker and amateur 8 mm filmmaker who insists that his hobby is pure relaxation and very different from work, yet the footage of him tinkering with film shows hand gestures that are strikingly similar to those of his job.

Programmatically, in part 1A Godard has a job interview with a cleaner—a woman who has long worked at the local Gaumont cinema in the kind of role that Ukeles took on. Progressively turning the job interview into a questioning of the division of labor, Godard insistently suggests that there may be no need for her job to be limited to cleaning: Why could she not take a more active role in the operations of Sonimage and, for instance, take a film to screen it in China? Both Ukeles and Godard/Miéville engage with forms of salaried reproductive labor—cleaning staff.

Wages for Housework centered on unwaged work; the activists thought of their program as a kind of impossible demand that capitalists would be unwilling and unable to implement, and which would, thus, stand to "explode the system" under the pressure of the oppositional alliances that such demands could bring together. For Federici, hidden unremunerated labor has revolutionary potential, as is evident from her quote from John McMurtry's *The Cancer State of Capitalism*: "The emerging liberative agent in the Third World is the unwaged force of women who are not yet disconnected from the life economy by their work. They serve life not commodity production. They are the hidden underpinning of the world economy and the wage equivalent of their life-serving work is estimated at $16 trillion."[89] Clearly, then, this project also has a (de)colonial dimension, and anti-colonial struggle had indeed been an impetus for the international Wages for Housework campaign, as it suggested that the Marxian analysis of labor needed to be expanded beyond the traditional focus on waged labor in factories and include unwaged forms of labor both in the Global South and at home, in the home.[90]

The attack on capitalism's incorporated exclusions also takes the form of an insistence on the debt amassed by (former) colonial powers. If the nations and corporations had *paid* for what they robbed, things would have been very different. Here, again, we see the dialectic of incorporation and exclusion: primitive accumulation functions by insisting that what it appropriates is nature, reduced to so much raw material.

The enslaved body—the objectified and racialized subject—has been one such material. Denise Ferreira da Silva insists that colonial debt is unpayable because of the fact that we are dealing (in her terminology) not with an *exploitative* appropriation of partial value created through wage labor, but with an *expropriative* appropriation of total value created through slave labor.[91] Capitalism can only thrive as long as permanent primitive accumulation is ongoing, as long as there is an immanent outside that can be incorporated materially without having to factor as economic *cost*. Exploitation needs appropriation as its supplement.

Extending reflections by C. L. R. James, Sylvia Wynter has differentiated between three value producers: the slave, whom she identifies with "circulation for accumulation"; the worker, or "production for accumulation"; and the consumer, or "consumption for accumulation."[92] Marx himself was well aware that while slavery has ancient roots, in early modernity the plantation system was integrated into capitalist production: "The method of production which [the slave-owning capitalist introduces] has not arisen out of slavery but is grafted on to it. In this case the same person is capitalist and landowner."[93] One could argue, however, that Marx ultimately continued to privilege wage labor, and did not pay sufficient attention to such immanent exceptions. It is of course a key criticism of feminists like Federici that Marxism's focus on "productive labor" has been complicit with capitalism's exclusionary definition of what counts as "properly economic." Capitalism has always depended on realms that are cast in the role of the extra-economic—of "cheap nature," which Moore defines as the "releasing [of] new sources of free or low-cost human or extra-human natures for capital" through "the interlocking agencies of capital, science, and empire."[94]

If reproductive labor and slave labor are the constitutive exclusions of capitalism, Achille Mbembe has argued that a condition previously limited to enslaved Africans is in the process of being universalized:

> We now observe a trend towards the universalization of the condition once reserved for Blacks, but as part of a process of *inversion*. This condition used to entail reducing the person to a thing, an object, a piece of merchandise that could be sold, bought or owned. The production of "subjects of race" certainly continues, but the modalities have changed. Today's Negro is no longer only a person from Africa, characterized by his sun-burnished color ("the surface Negro"). Today's "underlying negro" (in lowercase) is a subaltern category of humanity, a subaltern *kind of humanity*, the superfluous and almost surplus component that capital hardly needs, and which seems doomed to zoning and expulsion [...]. The "underlying negro" is this software-driven humanity's Other, a new figure of the species that is so typical of the new age of capitalism, where self-reification is the best chance we have to achieve self-capitalization.[95]

While it would be absurd and obscene to suggest some kind of equivalence between such radically different forms of "unproductive labor" as housework, slave labor, and artistic work, Mbembe's notion of the "underlying negro" points toward the emergence of new surplus populations that no longer fit any traditional category. They are a blurry exception, a sprawl of lives that may generate value for the masters of the world without *producing* value that will show up in the GDP. Such production can, for instance, take the form of debt—indebtedness is big business. As with Dirk Scheringa's DSB Bank and its subprime loans, the profits can then be invested in art. Within the condition indicated by Mbembe, then, there is no *identity* or *equivalence* of various exceptions and exclusions, but rather *complicitness*.

At the same time as formerly productive workers become surplus, there is a transformation of what was deemed unproductive work into profitable activity. Like the unpaid labor of housewives, the paid work of cleaners and other maintenance staff is unproductive in orthodox Marxist terms; it does not directly contribute to the production of surplus-value. In recent decades, private and public sectors alike have increasingly outsourced cleaning to specialized companies. In such cases, as Jappe argues, formerly unproductive labor *does* become productive—but only on the micro level of the companies in question, *not* on the macro level of the entire economy. The rise of the "service industries" or "tertiarization" has certainly resulted in profits for these companies in particular, but not at a systemic level.[96] Thus, privatization and outsourcing reveal themselves not as part of capitalism's dynamism, but as contributing to a movement toward stasis. The same can be said of networked forms of "self-reification" on social media that generate what Shoshana Zuboff calls "behavioural surplus"—a surplus based on aggregated data trails left by users.[97]

In their *Anatomy of an AI System*, Kate Crawford and Vladan Joler have analyzed the Amazon Echo as "an anatomical map of human labor, data and planetary resources."[98] The Echo not only results from cheap labor and cheap nature but also produces them; it is at the forefront of a new wave of extractivism that quantifies the world in the form of datasets. Analyzing the interdependence of different factors in systemic terms, Crawford and Joler do not themselves attempt to quantify them, rather noting that the entire edifice is built on the obfuscation of the actual environmental and social costs. Furthermore, in their text and in the diagram (the actual map), they register not only invisible labor but also *free labor* by users. Work proliferates, but the work in question is not necessarily waged or paid labor.

Today we are witnessing much anguish over the rise of automation and the looming obsolescence of many types of jobs. To some extent, this is a repeat of debates during the postwar era. In 1964, in the Operaist journal *Quaderni Rossi*, Raniero Panzieri revisited Marx's account of the realization of surplus-value in relation to technology and capitalist planning. Technology—such as computers that can vastly outperform human workers—increases productivity. As the output of each worker's labor grows and the relative surplus-value rises, this is offset by the smaller number of people needed.[99] Leaving aside the intricacies of Marx's contentious theorem of "the tendency of the profit rate to fall" and its various Operaist and *wertkritische* interpretations, an economy with large surplus (unemployed) populations clearly poses problems.

While a debt-based economy may gloss over this for some time (until the next subprime crash), the profit rate will indeed drop when a large section of the population has no income or spending money. In response to the actual decline in profit rates during the 1970s, neoliberal politics since Reagan and Thatcher has involved wealth redistribution through "deregulation" and speculation. Here differentiation between micro and macro levels is indeed crucial: while value may be produced in "unproductive" sectors such as art, this amounts to redistribution on the macro level of the global economy as a whole. And just how unbalanced can society become in economic terms before something has to give—before matters of value and socially necessary labor are (perhaps violently) renegotiated? Surplus populations face off against a capitalist system thriving on value that has become autonomous from labor; it is this rift that constitutes the crisis of value and labor alike. The intriguingly coiffed symptoms of this crisis have dominated the news cycle for some time.

Art between Service and Asset

With a growing tertiary sector promising to make unproductive labor profitable, some artists adopted a service- rather than production-based model of art. The notion of "art as service" came to the fore in the nascent Reagan era, as art became commodified and financialized to an unprecedented degree. When artists Christopher D'Arcangelo and Peter Nadin did construction jobs in the late 1970s, plastering apartments and suchlike, they sent invitations to view the results of their work in the style of an art-world opening (a masculine counterpart of Ukeles's maintenance art), always listing the amount of labor-time: "The product of four days work may be seen on June 16th, 1978, between 12 noon and 5 PM. At 99 Prince St. N.Y.C., 5th floor, West."[100] This activity culminated in the opening of a project space at 84 West Broadway, on November 9, 1978, with the initial presentation being their "30 Days Work"—the labor-time invested in the refurbishment by D'Arcangelo and Nadin, together with Nick Lawson.

In 1983, a few years after D'Arcangelo's death, Nadin cofounded the Offices of Fend, Fitzgibbon, Holzer, Nadin, Prince & Winters, which advertised "practical esthetic services adaptable to client situation." The nature of these services remained somewhat sketchy, though some prefigure Peter Fend's later Ocean Earth Construction and Development Corporation.[101] A much more fully elaborated model of "artistic services" was developed by Andrea Fraser in the early 1990s, when she published a number of prospectuses outlining her services for individuals as well as not-for-profit and for-profit institutions, and coorganized a symposium and documentary exhibition titled "Services" with Helmut Draxler.[102]

If one takes the stance of value criticism—whose theoretical elaborations come at the cost of an almost Adornian aloofness—such service-based art practices can appear as instances of the same capitalist logic as the object-based art they oppose. However, "service art" may be of interest precisely because it is at the forefront of commodification, exacerbates its contradictions, and seeks to create space for critical practice by doing so. In his work *Some Cleaning* (2013), the dancer and choreographer Adam Linder sits in an art space, talking to the gallerists and visitors, and occasionally jumping up to perform movements akin to window-cleaning or dusting. Referencing Ukeles,

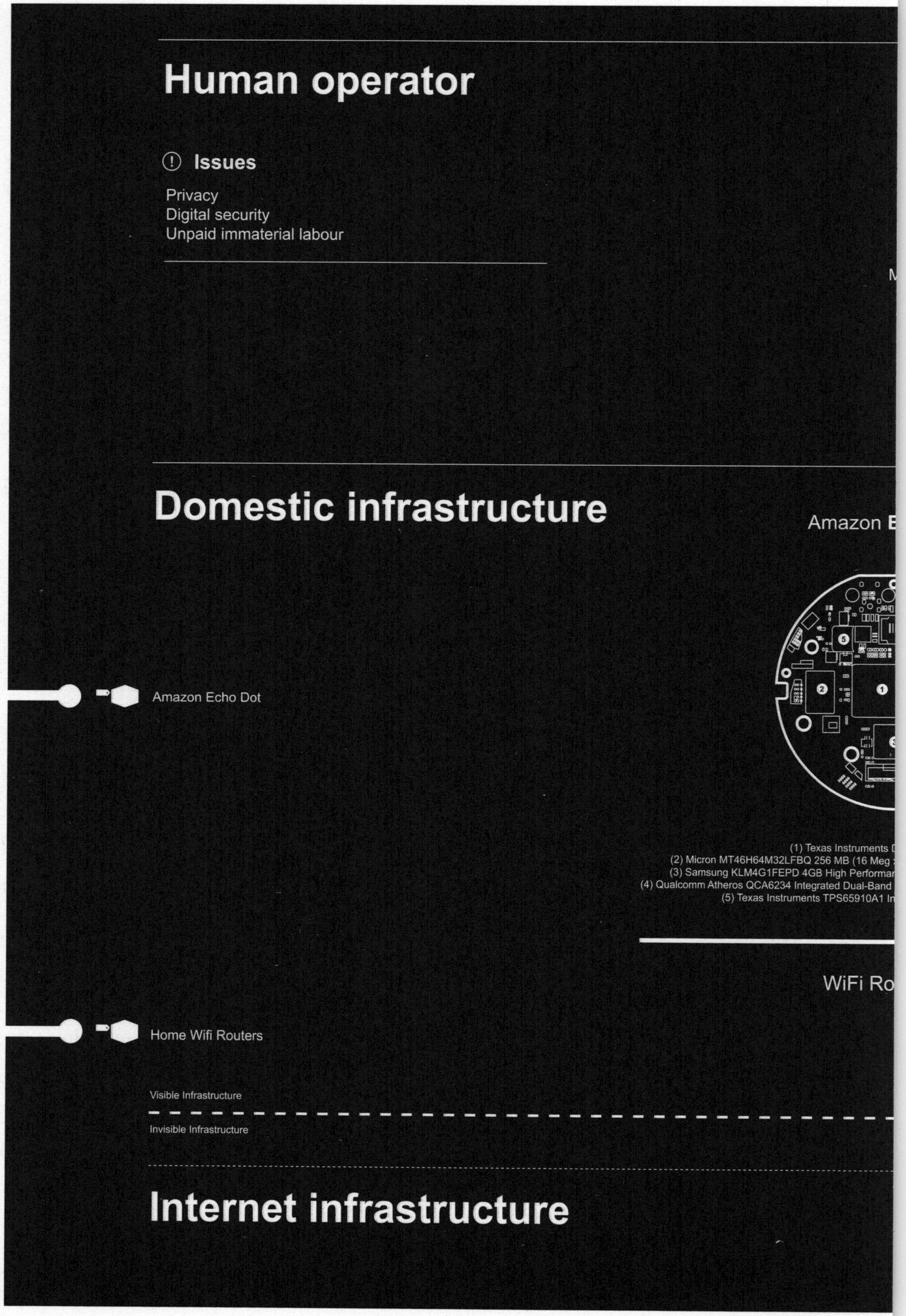

Kate Crawford and Vladan Joler, *Anatomy of an AI System*, 2018, detail

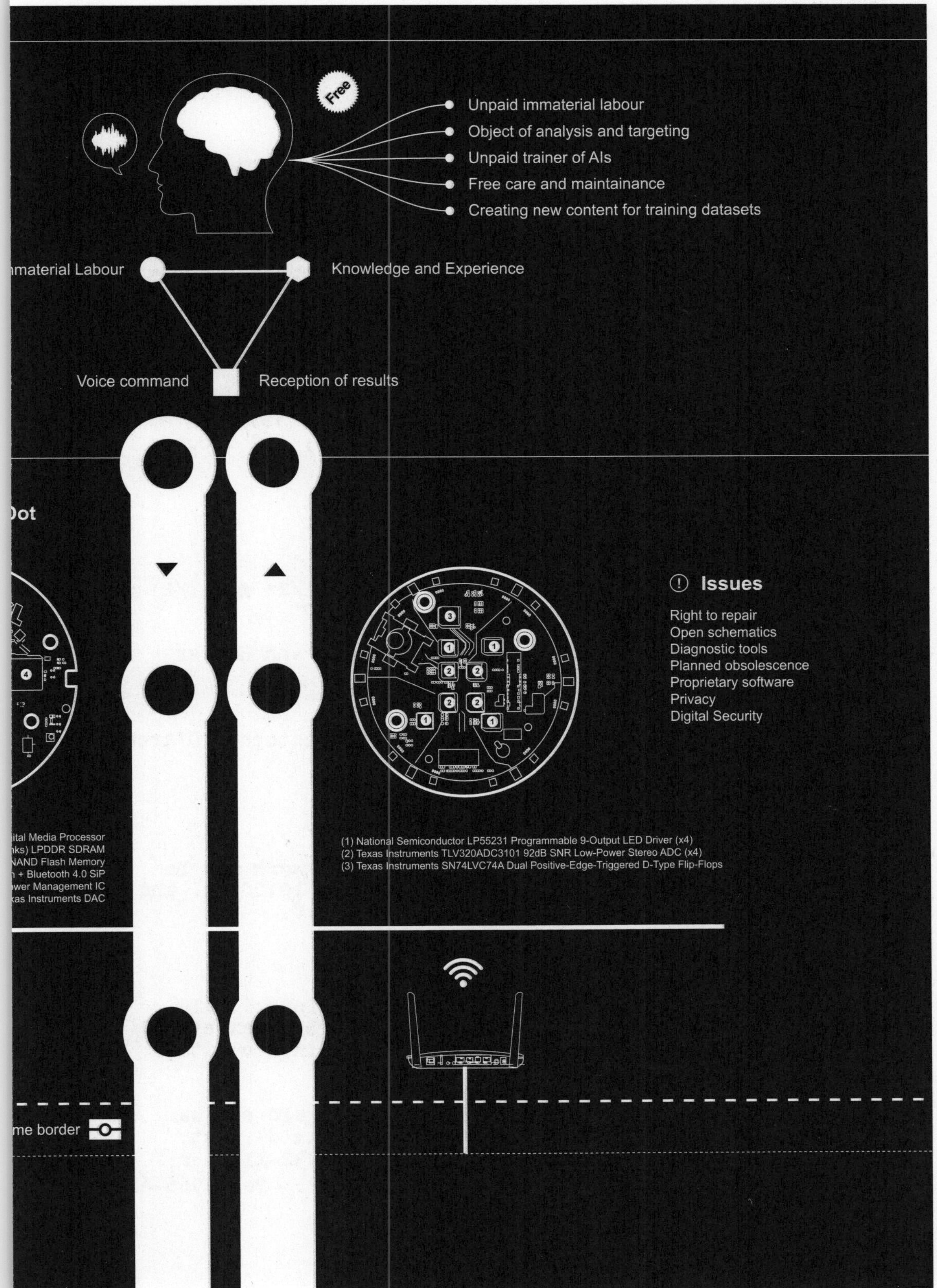
Free
Unpaid immaterial labour
Object of analysis and targeting
Unpaid trainer of AIs
Free care and maintainance
Creating new content for training datasets
nmaterial Labour
Knowledge and Experience
Voice command
Reception of results
Dot
Issues
Right to repair
Open schematics
Diagnostic tools
Planned obsolescence
Proprietary software
Privacy
Digital Security
ital Media Processor
nks) LPDDR SDRAM
NAND Flash Memory
n + Bluetooth 4.0 SiP
ower Management IC
xas Instruments DAC
(1) National Semiconductor LP55231 Programmable 9-Output LED Driver (x4)
(2) Texas Instruments TLV320ADC3101 92dB SNR Low-Power Stereo ADC (x4)
(3) Texas Instruments SN74LVC74A Dual Positive-Edge-Triggered D-Type Flip-Flops
me border

Nine days work:

9I2 sq. ft. 38' X 24'

Function by Louise Lawler

Design by function

Execution by Peter Nadin and Christopher D'Arcangeloº

Materials: Celatex, Drywall, Lath, and Nails

Purchased by Louise Lawler

The product of nine days work may be seen on January 23rd and 30th, I978, between 3:00 and 6:00pm. at 407 Greenwich St. N.Y.C., 3rd floor, front.

Five and a half days work:

2,548 sq. ft., 22' x 11' x 10', 12 1/2' x 6 1/2' x 10', 12 1/2' x 6 1/2' x 10'

Function by Jeane, Philip, Mia, and Ann Harper

Design by function

Execution by Robert Janiger and Christopher D'Arcangeloº

Materials: Plaster and Latex paint

Purchased by Jeane and Philip Harper

The product of five and a half days work may be seen on January 17th, 1978, between 10:00 am. and 5 pm., at 166 1/2 East 81st St. N.Y.C.

ºWe have joined together to execute functional constructions and to alter or refurbish existing structures as a means of surviving in a capitalist economy.

Peter Nadin and Christopher D'Arcangelo can be contacted to execute future works at: 84 West Broadway N.Y.C., N.Y. 10007. Tel. 732-1153 or 260 Elizabeth St. N.Y.C., N.Y. 10012. Tel. 966-6139

Peter Nadin and Christopher D'Arcangelo, announcement of refurbishments, 1978

D'Arcangelo, Nadin, and Fraser, art historian Sabeth Buchmann notes that Linder and the gallery have drawn up a contract for selling the piece that is "reminiscent of classical conventions of conceptualism as well as of institutional critique associated with what's called 'service art.'"[103] This contract stipulates that the hourly rate is that of cleaners rather than of performers.

While some artists live in project-based precariousness, others produce exclusive commodities for the storage and speculative multiplication of wealth. Some who have participated in the creation of the project-driven art economy have also contributed to its transformation into a speculative asset; these are by no means completely distinct genealogies. In 1996, looking back at the Art Workers' Coalition (AWC) hearings of the late 1960s and at the Projansky/Siegelaub contract for art sales, which gave the artist a stake in future resales, Fraser noted: "What was radical about the AWC's proposed protections was the duplicitous condition of art's value that they uncovered: they implied a radical splitting of artwork into tangible and intangible value. And this in turn implied a redefinition of artwork from a commercial product or good to a service product—in this case, intellectual property."[104] Fraser's terminology here may be somewhat imprecise, but it is true that the conceptual becoming-contingent of the artwork's material realization and the politicized focus on the artist's continuing stake in the work as their intellectual property could be seen as being fully part of art's transformation into a speculative asset; it's just that the artist, too, should be a shareholder.

An awareness of this implication can be seen in certain works by Hans Haacke. While the well-known *Manet-Projekt '74* (1974) caused a scandal because its panels detailed the provenance of a Manet still life, a related work by Haacke is, in some respects, more revealing. *Manet-Projekt '74* revealed the public secret that the chairman of the Wallraf-Richartz-Museum, who had recently purchased the painting, had a shady past as a banker in the Third Reich. This foregrounded the failed denazification of West Germany; in many cases, the old elite was the new elite. Haacke's *Seurat's "Les Poseuses" (Small Version), 1888–1975* (1975) is more future-oriented. The form of the piece is the same: a reproduction of the painting and text panels detailing its history. In this case, this history results in the work's acquisition by Artemis S.A., a Luxembourg-based art investment company, who then sold it on to the dealer Heinz Berggruen—who would himself soon become a board member of Artemis. A painting that is unique and indivisible in material terms nonetheless becomes an asset that investors can own shares in. The value-form emancipates itself from the natural form, even while the latter remains important as a physical guarantee. The era of freeport art announces itself.

It is in mimicry of art investment companies that the art project Real Flow—devised by a group that includes Suhail Malik and Christopher Kulendran Thomas—purports to "[pave] the way to art's sublime future by offering tailor-made financial solutions." Specifically, they note that "art's potential is stifled by its entrenchment in a terrestrial, illiquid commodity form" and is "weighed down by the gravity of obsolete historical identifications."[105] Using Romantic-idealist verbiage, they claim that financialization offers the prospect of a purified, rarefied, truly sublime art beyond distinct form or embodiment, an art of financial air. In order to achieve this, Real Flow offers "instruments" that allow for a decoupling of the artwork from its physical incarnation. Different permutations of the art as object/property and as financial asset are possible—so that, for instance, a collector uninterested in "the burden of handling or possessing an artwork" can deal with it as a virtual asset.[106]

Is art, then, an asset class? Beech is critical of accounts of visual art's transformation into an asset. While noting that "artworks which are less like conventional art commodities (paintings, sculptures, prints) take on forms that belong to assets (documents, contracts, certificates)," he maintains that even while art "has developed since the 1980s as an asset class, included in investment portfolios," it remains exceptional and anomalous on this level, too.[107] However, if artworks are not stocks or options or futures, this is precisely why they can function as a distinct kind of asset—one with deliciously little regulatory oversight. At Deloitte's ninth annual Art & Finance Conference at the Van Gogh Museum (!) in Amsterdam, one panel was dedicated to the subject of "Monetising—Why and how to turn your fine art collection into a working asset." Here issues of "art-secured lending" were discussed by speakers, including the president and CEO (ex-Bloomberg) of Athena Art Finance, a "specialty lender for the art market providing non-recourse financing against art as collateral." Another speaker was the CEO (ex-KPMG) of a group that "invests in rare art pieces for investment purposes and currently advises some of the largest art funds in the world."[108]

In its focus on financial liquefaction, Real Flow seems to transmutate the Adornian "mimesis of the hardened and alienated" into a captive mimicry vis-à-vis the automatic subject of finance capital.[109] The toxicity of its overidentification stratagems notwithstanding, Real Flow does introduce a factor that Beech consistently minimizes: historical change. Real Flow acknowledges both that art has become an asset of sorts and that it is an impure one; this is what it seeks to remedy, in however illusory a manner. The project pushes the transformation of artworks into "documents, contracts, certificates" to a grotesquely logical conclusion—though by now, the booming market for digital artworks in the form of non-fungible tokens (NFTs) logged in the blockchain makes Real Flow seem almost quaint.

Beech's insistence that "the appreciation of artworks as assets, whether paltry or spectacular, appears to be independent of the production of new value" is valuable, but one could extend it to other

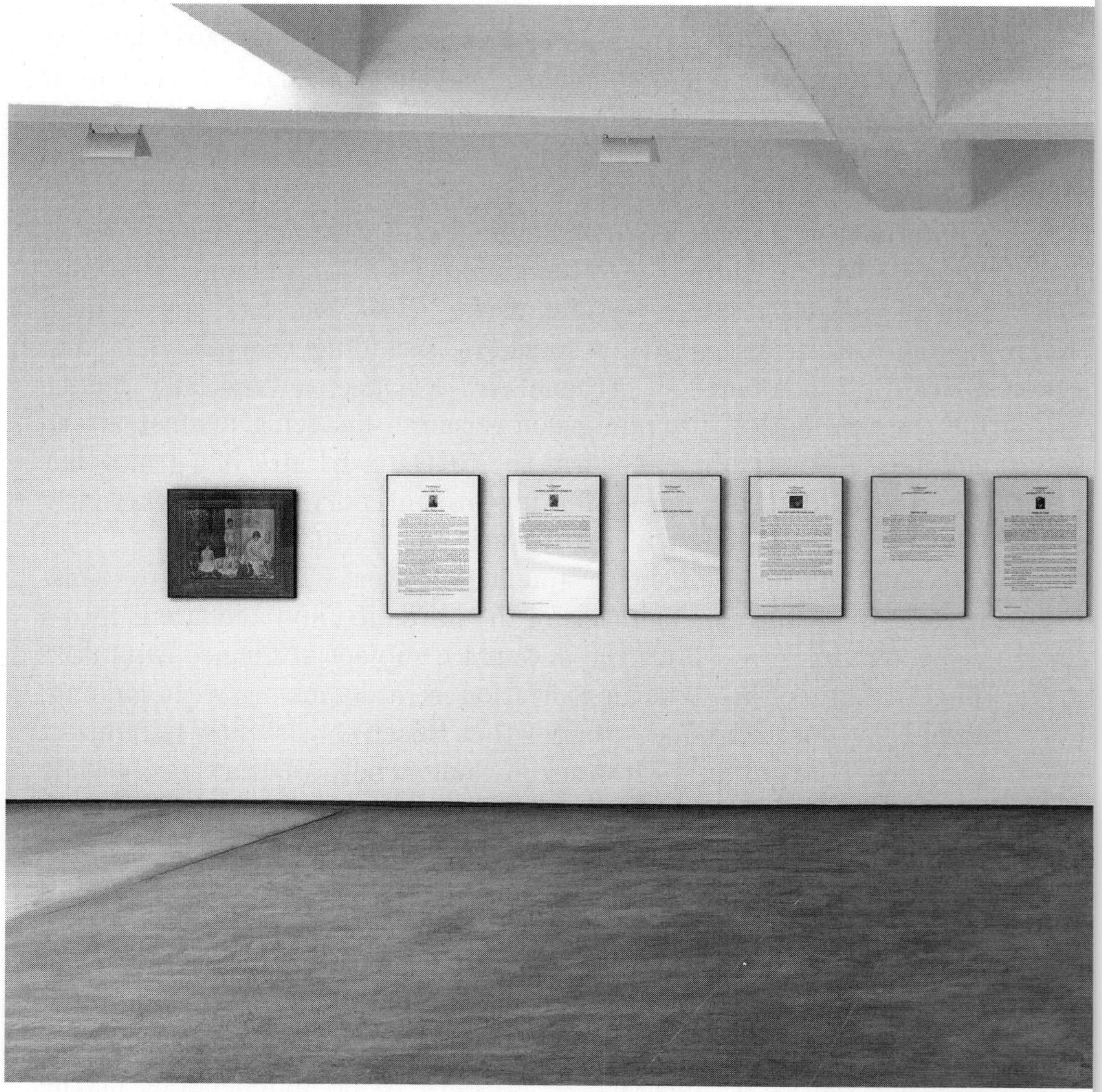

Hans Haacke, *Seurat's "Les Poseuses" (Small Version), 1888–1975*, 1975, installation view

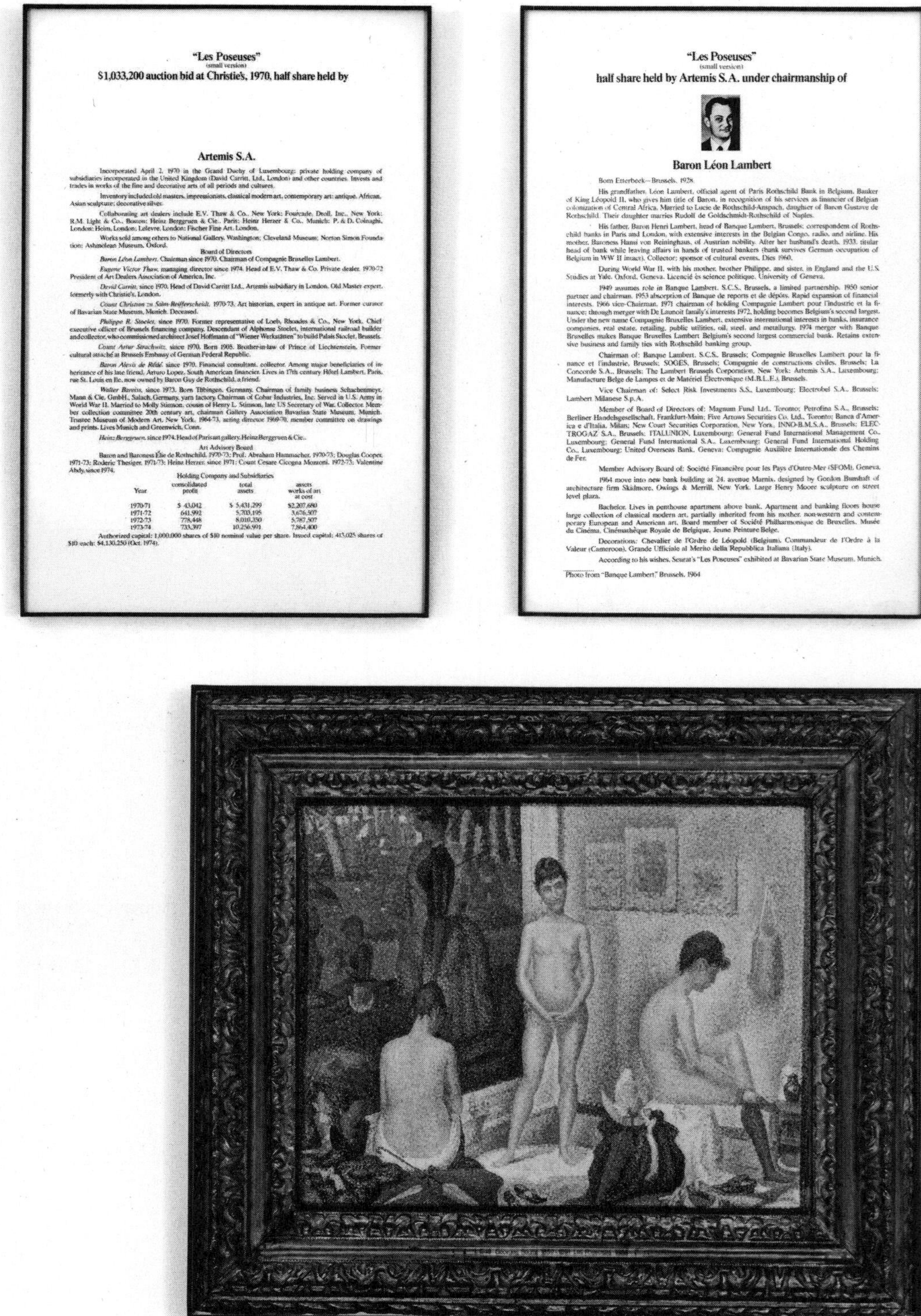

Hans Haacke, *Seurat's "Les Poseuses" (Small Version), 1888–1975*, 1975, details

"Les Poseuses"

(small version)

purchased 1971 for unknown amount (part in art works) by

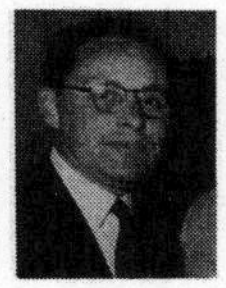

Heinz Berggruen

Born 1914 in Berlin, Germany.

Studies art history in Berlin and Toulouse, France, graduating there with equivalent of Master of Fine Art degree. In late 1930's moves to California. Postgraduate studies in art history at Berkeley. Assistant Curator of San Francisco Museum of Art. Writes art criticism for *San Francisco Chronicle.* Works at 1939 World Exposition on Treasure Island, San Francisco.

Marries Lilian Zellerbach of prominent San Francisco paper manufacturing family. Birth of son John Berggruen 1943 (now art dealer in San Francisco). Birth of daughter Helen, 1945.

After World War II, service in US Army. Stationed in England and Germany. Works for German language US Army publication in Munich.

Around 1947 move to Paris via Zurich. Employed by cultural division of UNESCO. In late 1940's, starts dealing in art books and prints. Becomes art dealer. Berggruen & Cie, now at 70, rue de l'Université, develops into one of major Parisian art dealers in modern art, particularly Ecole de Paris.

Lives Ile St. Louis, Paris, and on château near Pontoise. Owns large collection.

1974 elected member of the Board of Directors of Artemis S.A., a Luxembourg-based art investment holding company. Chevalier of Legion of Honor.

His purchase of Seurat's *Les Poseuses* at "impressive profit" to Artemis S.A. (annual report). Painting now on anonymous loan in Bavarian State Museum, Munich.

Photo from "Art in America," 1963

sectors of the "creative" economy.[110] Value production increasingly makes way for value extraction and redistribution—and financialized art plays its part in this redistribution process. Welcome to the Van Gogh Museum, dear investors. The question is not so much whether this or that iteration of the labor theory of value falters vis-à-vis art or today's "creative economy," but whether value creation in this economy is in crisis. When the idea of universal basic income is embraced not just by the likes of Negri but also by Silicon Valley entrepreneurs eager to make up for the loss of jobs wrought by their technological breakthroughs, it is hard to avoid the conclusion that the crisis is deep and accelerating.[111]

Exchange-value can be said to attain a certain autonomy and inform the creation of value, on a micro scale and to the detriment of other economic sectors or regions. However, Marxological debates about the labor-time invested in this smartphone or that artwork are ultimately less relevant than the crisis of the labor/value complex on the macro level. As less living labor is needed and more precarians slide into surplus-labor status, what is "socially necessary" is contested between the complicit opposites of free-market ideologues and neo-fascist protectionists. The fight against immigrants and other scapegoats intensifies, and the value of work and of life is up in the air.

Practice Makes Imperfect

Many practices today are marked either by enthusiastic participation or by some form of supposedly tactical overidentification. From Real Flow to artist Jonas Lund's algorithm that produces a curatorial ranking, these acts of mimicry result in a dismal form of capitalist realism. However, it is important to look beyond this. If there is one fundamental problem with many economic and sociological accounts of art, it is that they treat art as a mute object of study. Art is rarely accepted as a form of praxis that might itself have discursive insights to add—sometimes precisely by problematizing all-too-perfect models.

In certain cases, this takes the form of projects that, in the tattered relation between labor and value, side with labor. This is the case, for instance, in the aforementioned collaborations with "reproductive" domestic workers, or in Gulf Labor's engagement with the "productive" male construction workers building institutions such as the (now postponed or canceled) Guggenheim Abu Dhabi under conditions of de facto slavery—marked by a general lack of rights, passport confiscation, and debt from "recruitment fees."[112]

Without attempting to arrive at the "true" value of the Abu Dhabi Guggenheim as an architectural icon and franchise of a global institutional brand, several posters and other pieces made by artists in the context of Gulf Labor attempt to quantify various factors, and emphasize jarring pay gaps. A newspaper ad by Andrea Fraser for week forty-five of the "52 Weeks of Gulf Labor" campaign, lists the budget as "potentially unlimited"; the total construction budget of the Saadiyat Island museum complex (20,000,000,000€); former Guggenheim director Thomas Krens's severance bonus (1,500,000€); current director Richard Armstrong's salary (560,000€); the Abu Dhabi GDP per capita (77,000€); and the monthly wage of Guggenheim Abu Dhabi construction workers (132€). In "creative," "cultural," "semiotic," or "communicative" capitalism, physical labor is made as invisible and disposable as possible, whether in iPhone factories or at building sites. The question in Fraser's ad—"Who's building the Guggenheim Abu Dhabi?"—emphasizes the literal construction of the institution over other kinds of labor involved, such as that of architects, artists, or managers.[113]

Antje Ehmann and Harun Farocki took a more generalist and somewhat scattershot approach with their project "Labour in a Single Shot," originally taking place during 2011–14 in the form of a series of workshops in fifteen major cities on different continents, during which

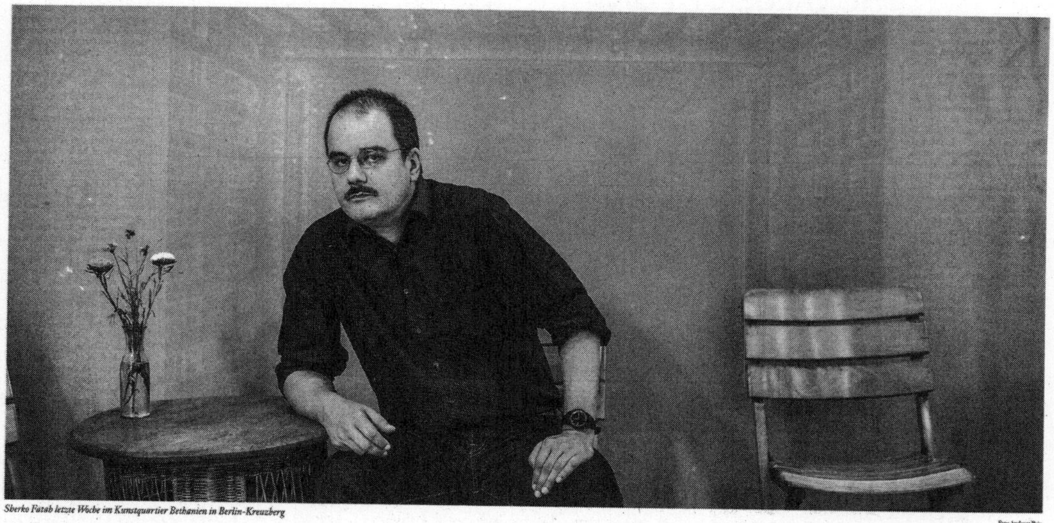

Sherko Fatah letzte Woche im Kunstquartier Bethanien in Berlin-Kreuzberg

Der Westen ist weich, der Osten fast ohne Hoffnung

Über den großen deutschen Erzähler Sherko Fatah. Und über den Crash der Kulturen: in seinem Kopf, seinem Roman. Und im Nordirak

Was ist in uns, wenn nichts mehr um uns ist? Was ist der Kern von uns, der Kern der Geschichten, die wir gehört haben ein Leben lang? Die Geschichten der Eltern, die Geschichten des Landes, in dem wir aufgewachsen sind? Was bleibt am Ende, in der Einsamkeit, in der Leere, wenn wir abgemagert sind, bis aufs Skelett der tiefsten, der intensivsten Erfahrungen unseres Lebens? Was sind wir?

Sherko Fatah, 50, ist ein Abmagerungskünstler der Geschichte. Er führt seine Figuren ans Ende ihrer Welt, an den Gegenpol ihrer bisherigen Erfahrungen und sieht zu, was ihnen geschieht. Er ist ein realitätsbegeisterter Phantast, ein Weltbeschreiber an Orten der Leere. Fast alle seine Bücher spielen im Nordirak, im Grenzgebiet zu Syrien und der Türkei, wo täglich neue Grenzen entstehen, wo die verschiedensten Völker und Religionen mal miteinander leben, mal gegeneinander, sich ermorden, hassen oder ignorieren. Die Protagonisten seiner Romane sind gefallene Gotteskrieger, Glücksucher, Stürzende, die von einem Pol der Welt zum anderen geraten, vom Westen in den Anti-Westen oder umgekehrt, und die in jener anderen Welt alles in Frage stellen, was zuvor die Grundlage aller ihrer Überzeugungen war. Systemkarambolage im Kopf. Explosion. Auslöschung.

Sherko Fatah erzählt die spannendsten und spannungsreichsten Geschichten in der deutschen Literatur der Gegenwart. Er stammt, wie viele der besten unserer Autoren im Jetzt, aus vielen Herkunftswelten. 1964 kam er in Ost-Berlin zur Welt, seine Mutter stammt aus Masuren, sein Vater aus dem Norden des Iraks. Mit einem Stipendium war der als Student in die DDR gekommen und geblieben. Er war nicht Teil der Nomenklatura, hatte aber, mit irakischem Pass, das unschätzbare Privileg, zu reisen, wohin er wollte. 1975 siedelte die Familie zunächst nach Wien und dann nach West-Berlin über. Oft lebte die Familie aber monatelang auch im Irak. Von Welt zu Welt, von System zu System zu wechseln, gehört für Sherko Fatah also zum Leben dazu. Aber ursprünglich lernte er die Welt und was man von ihr wissen muss in den Geschichten kennen, die er von seinem Vater hörte, wenn der von einer seiner Reisen zurückgekehrt war. Die Welt als Erzählung.

So ist er selbst zum Erzähler geworden. In dessen Geschichten sich abstrakte Politik in Erzählung verwandelt, Anschauung, Abenteuer, Lebendigkeit. „Für mich war es schon immer so", hat Fatah vor einiger Zeit in der F.A.Z. geschrieben: „Alle paar Jahre wieder fand ich Geschichten, ausführlich erzählt oder auch nur beiläufig fallengelassen von Verwandten, die in der Krisenregion Irak leben, in den brandaktuellen Meldungen zur Weltpolitik wieder." Während der westliche Fernsehzuschauer so lange nichts von der Existenz einer Armee namens IS gehört hat, bis diese Truppen plötzlich ganze Landstriche und Städte besetzen und ein eigenes Kalifat errichten, sind die Vorläufer dieser Organisation längst schon Teil von Fatahs Romanwelt gewesen. So auch in seinem neuen Roman „Der letzte Ort", der in dieser Woche erscheint und in dem der Emir, also der Befehlshaber einer Vorgängerorganisation der IS, sein Land und dessen Feinde so erklärt: „‚Ich erzähle dir etwas über Eindringlinge', sagt Abdul. ‚Es geht längst nicht mehr nur um die Kreuzfahrer, die Amerikaner und Briten, die hier hereingeströmt sind. Die Eindringlinge in Mesopotamien sind schon viel länger da. Im Norden die verwestlichten Kurden, sie sind eine wahre Plage. Ebenso wie die Turkmenen. Dazu kommen die Ungläubigen, die es noch immer gibt in diesem Land, Christen. Die gefährlichste Gruppe aber, und zugleich die größte sind die Häretiker, die sich selbst Schiiten nennen. Jene, bei denen ihr vorher wart und von denen wir euch übernommen haben, weil sie einfach zu dumm waren, etwas mit euch anzufangen.'"

Die, denen jener Abdul die Feinde seines Landes so geduldig erklärt, sind Albert und Osama, zwei junge Männer, die im Irak entführt worden sind, die von einem verlassenen Ort zum nächsten transportiert, von Terrorgruppe zu Terrorgruppe weitergereicht wurden, um schließlich hier, beim letzten Emir, am fernsten Ort der Welt anzukommen. Und etwas über Feindschaften zu hören. Den wahren Glauben und die falsche Welt. Albert ist Deutscher, ein wankelmütiges Wilhelm-Meisterchen, einer, der in den Irak geflohen ist, ein typischer Westler, der sich selber sucht oder sich loswerden will. Der nicht als Krieger kommt, nein, der helfen will, das kulturelle Erbe des Iraks zu retten, zu bewahren. Ein Vorhaben, das im Land selbst auf Unverständnis stößt: „Ein Mann aus dem Westen kommt hierher, es herrscht Krieg, er fährt durch die Gegend und kümmert sich um alte Steine. Was soll das?"

Der sich das fragt, ist Osama, Alberts Übersetzer. Er stammt aus einer liberalen irakischen Familie, fühlt sich von jeher zur westlichen Welt hingezogen und gilt im eigenen Land als absoluter Verräter, Kollaborateur mit den Besatzern. Fremdling im eigenen Land. Fatahs Roman ist über weite Strecken beinahe ein Kammerspiel. Gespräch zwischen zwei Entführten, Albert und Osama, Männer aus unterschiedlichen Welten, die von der Welt des anderen magisch angezogen wurden und die nun im existentiellen Gespräch über ihre Wurzeln, ihre Erinnerungen, ihre Wünsche an die Grenzen des Verständnisses gelangen. Sie wollen sich nah sein, und je mehr sie reden, je bedrohlicher die Welt um sie herum wird, desto fremder werden sie einander.

Bis zur Verzweiflung versucht Osama, den weichen Westling zu verstehen. Warum ist er wirklich hierher gekommen? Irgendwann will er es gar nicht mehr aus eigenem Interesse wissen, es geht vielmehr ums Überleben. Die Entführer glauben die lächerliche Steinbewahrer-Geschichte nicht und halten Albert für einen Agenten und mit ihm auch Osama. So dringt der Übersetzer immer tiefer in die Herkunftsgeschichte Alberts ein, um seine Reise zu verstehen und sie somit auch den Entführern verständlich zu machen. Es fällt ihm schwer. Alberts Geschichte geht zurück in die DDR, zu seinem Vater, der Profiteur des Systems, gläubiger Sozialist gewesen ist, der Auslandsreisen machte, der Familie davon erzählte und der den Fall der Mauer als Sturz ins Leere erlebte. Der überzeugt ist, dass den Menschen heute der Widerstand fehlt, die Reibung, die Abgrenzung, die Mauer, die die eine Welt von der anderen trennt. Er sieht in der Ge-

ANDREA FRASER

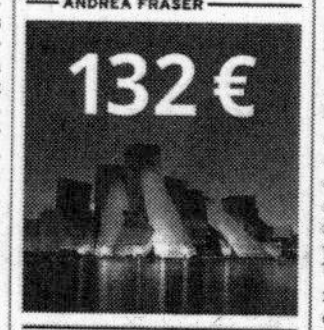

genwart nur Beliebigkeit und Leere. Gegen diesen Vater hatte nicht Albert gekämpft, sondern zunächst seine geliebte Schwester Mila. Die aus Protest zu hungern begann, die anarchistische Widerstandsposen pflegte, den Vater in den Wahnsinn trieb. Und die Albert irgendwann einmal einen toten Skorpion hinter Glas schenkte. Gefrorene Wüste, totes Abenteuer, Gefahr in Plexiglas gesichert. Irgendwann war der Skorpion verschwunden. Und Alberts ewiger Wunsch, die Wüste zu sehen, musste Wirklichkeit werden.

Osama findet in diesen Geschichten nichts, was sich gegenüber den Entführern für Albert verwenden ließe. Er, der eigentlich voller Sympathie für den weichen Westler war, verliert beinahe den Glauben: „Das nennt ihr Freiheit. Jeder macht den Unsinn, der ihm gerade einfällt, und so werdet ihr alt. Und damit es hier genau so wird, schickt ihr eure Panzer her."

Einmal, durch einen plötzlichen Glücksfall, gelingt es Albert insgeheim, eine E-Mail an seine Schwester Mila zu schreiben. Er schreibt ihr, unter Todesgefahr, den Anfang des Romans „Kidnapped" von Robert Louis Stevenson, um sie auf seine Situation aufmerksam zu machen. Osama, begeistert von Alberts Mut, fragt ihn, was er geschrieben habe. Albert zitiert aus dem Kopf: „I will begin the story of my adventures with a certain morning . . ." Das ist der Moment, in dem Osama am Verstand dieses westlichen Würstchens zweifelt. Was hat er gemacht? Einen Roman zitiert? Ist er verrückt? Wir brauchen Hilfe! Hubschrauber! Rettung! Jetzt! „Er verstand sie nicht, diese idealistischen, gut ausgebildeten, mutigen, wohlgenährten Kinder. Wie stolz musste dieser Deutsche auf die Exklusivität seiner Nachricht sein, noch dazu, da er sie an eine ferne Schwester schicken konnte, die so etwas war wie seine verbotene Geliebte. Das sind fliegende Menschen, dachte Osama. Sie sind wahrhaftig frei, so frei, dass sie sich verirren."

Fatahs Inszenierung dieses Kammerspiels ist genial. Die Gespräche, die Annäherungen, die Sympathien, die Grenzen der Verständigung, die immer wieder zu Tage tretende Fremdheit, die größer zu werden scheint, je näher man sich kommt, das ist phänomenal erzählt.

„Zu Hause war es mir näher, als es mir hier je sein könnte", denkt Albert so für sich. „Dort war das Fremde Abwechslung, Ausweis von Modernität." Es ist die große Stärke Fatahs, diese deutsche Fremdheitssehnsucht nicht als Kriegs- und Abenteuerkitsch zu entlarven, sondern als aus guten Gründen entstehende, tiefe Wünsche ernst zu nehmen. Sie zerschellen dann eben nur an der politischen, wirklich fremden Realität vor Ort.

Wenn man mit Sherko Fatah über die politische Gegenwart spricht, weiß er so wenige Lösungen wie wir. Er weiß nicht, ob man früh in Syrien hätte militärisch eingreifen müssen, statt nur die Chemiewaffen zu zerstören. Er weiß nicht, ob die Offensive der IS jetzt in letzter Konsequenz vor allem zur Gründung des neuen Kurdenstaates führen wird, weiß nicht, wie die Grenzen bald verlaufen werden. Sein Vater und viele Verwandte leben noch im Nordirak in Sulaimania, einer großen Stadt im Nordosten, die nicht direkt von den aktuellen Kämpfen betroffen ist. Wenn er mit seiner Familie vor Ort telefoniert, wissen die auch nicht mehr, als das, was sie im Fernsehen sehen. Da sind 50 Kilometer Entfernung so viel wie 5000.

Sherko Fatah weiß nicht, wie eine Lösung aussehen könnte. Er glaubt an Europa. Er glaubt, dass die europäische Idee neu erzählt werden muss. Wie jede politische Idee, damit sie Kraft gewinnt, so viel Kraft, dass sie am Ende siegt.

VOLKER WEIDERMANN

Sherko Fatah: „Der letzte Ort". Luchterhand, 280 Seiten, 19,99 Euro

ANDREA FRASER

Wer baut das Guggenheim Abu Dhabi?

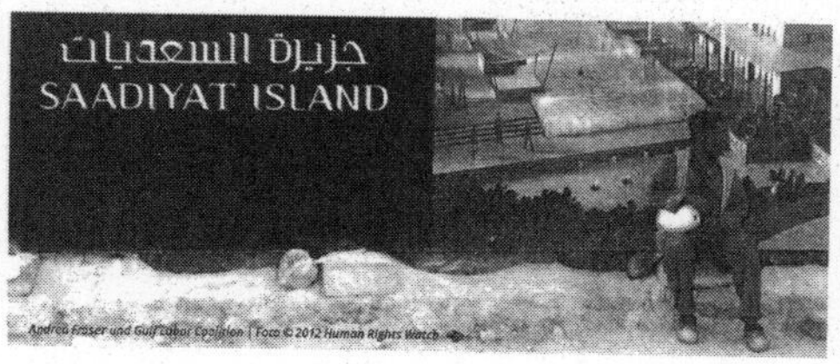

Ankaufsbudget des Guggenheim Abu Dhabi	"potentiell unbeschränkt"
Geschätzte Baukosten für den Saadiyat Island Museumskomplex	€ 20.000.000.000
Abfindungsbonus des ehemaligen Direktors Thomas Krens	€ 1.500.000
Jahresgehalt des derzeitigen Guggenheim Direktors Richard Armstrong	€ 560.000
Bruttoinlandsprodukt Abu Dhabis pro Einwohner (Schätzung S&P, 2014)	€ 77.000
Monatliches Gehalt eines Bauarbeiters des Guggenheim Abu Dhabi	€ 132

Lesen Sie die Berichte & unterzeichnen Sie die Petition: gulflabor.org

Andrea Fraser, *132 €*, 2014

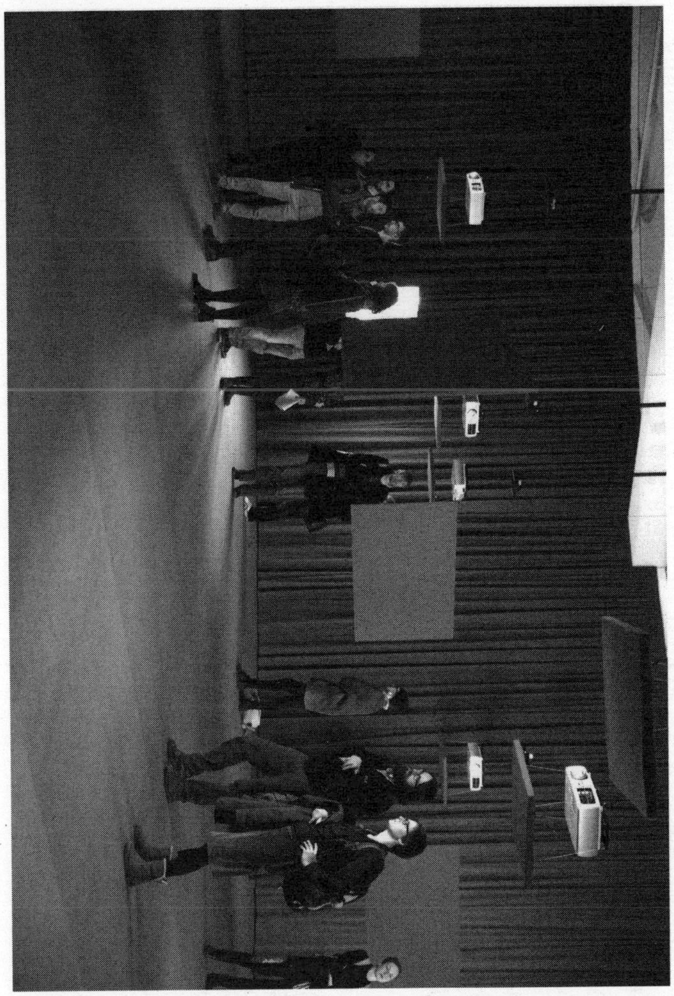

Harun Farocki and Antje Ehmann, “Labour in a Single Shot,” Haus der Kulturen der Welt, Berlin, 2015

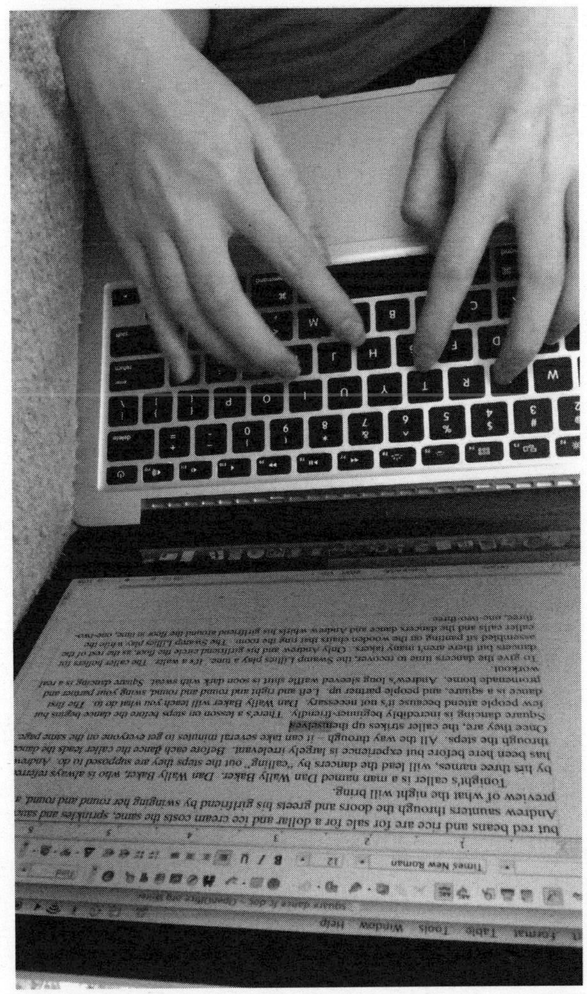

Still from Nicole Teeny, *The Writer*, Boston, 2013

the participants were asked to represent a type of work in a single continuous take of one to two minutes. In early 2015, after Farocki's death the previous year, the project was exhibited at the Haus der Kulturen der Welt (HKW) in Berlin.[114] The main exhibition space contained a screen for each of the fifteen cities, showing a selection of single-shot films, and also, behind a curtain, a thematic selection on sixteen monitors. Here the focus was on the motif of "workers leaving the factory," the subject of the first film by the Lumière brothers in 1895, which Farocki had previously explored in a 1995 video essay, and in the 2006 installation *Workers Leaving the Factory in Eleven Decades*.

At HKW, *Workers Leaving the Factory in Eleven Decades* was mirrored by a new installation in which the Lumière film was shown alongside "remakes" made by workshop participants in the project's fifteen cities. This geographic displacement of cinema's "primal scene" evokes what was an important inspiration for Farocki: the long single take of workers leaving an Egyptian factory in Straub-Huillet's *Too Early/Too Late* (1981).[115] However, in the "fifteen cities" installation, not all the sites were actual factories: they included shopping malls and construction sites. Many of the other films show street performers and other "picturesque" occupations. Industrial labor is scarce on the ground; there are a few interesting instances of domestic labor, though, curiously, it does not feature as a category on the project's website. The search function for the film archive on the project's website—which keeps evolving, as new workshops started being organized from 2017 on—has no "finance" category, though there is one for "monitor work."[116]

In Nicole Teeny's *The Writer* (Boston, 2013), the camera pans across a messy apartment floor to show a young woman lying on a bed with her MacBook, diligently typing on the tilted laptop, working in a place associated with escape from work—with a voice-over letting us hear the unfolding text. Meanwhile, *Data Center* by Markus Bauer, Susanne Dzeik, and Rene Paulokat (Berlin, 2012) shows a maintenance worker doing his rounds inside one of the centers hosting servers that keep the cloud afloat.[117] However, less "advanced" forms of work can hardly be said to be any less contemporary; they function as part of the same global economy with all its inequities. It is contemporaneity itself that is asynchronous and fractured. One film that manages to condense this into a single shot is Cristián Silva-Avária's *The City, the Runners and the Fisherman* (Rio de Janeiro, 2012), which shows a solitary fisherman on a small boat casting his net in the background, slowly drifting in the bay, while glimpses of mobile urban professionals race by on colorful bikes in the foreground. Here, a form of montage has been incorporated into the single shot itself, and the result is, at the very least, compellingly suggestive.

On the whole, "Labour in a Single Shot" convincingly represents the impurity of the global economy, in which ancient professions coexist with laptop labor, but it hardly functions as a cognitive map of contemporary capitalism and its vectorial, violently transformative powers.[118] Furthermore, while some of the workshop participants have strong practices in their own right, their work is largely subsumed under Ehmann and Farocki's double curatorship-as-authorship—and within the latter, Farocki is usually foregrounded. While the result was more than the sum of its parts, the legal status of the individual films and the remuneration of their makers remained unaddressed and opaque. With its networked approach, the project was hyper-contemporary in a way that Ehmann and Farocki never fully acknowledged: here artistic labor became a scattered and aggregate condition that reflected, without fully reflecting *on*, the ways in which networked capitalism transforms human labor and the creation of value, subsuming unpaid or badly remunerated work under the aura of brand names.

As labor and value spiral into an ever-deeper crisis, practices of *commoning* come to embody the aesthetic as well as political promise of immanent exceptions. Is it any wonder that art, seeing its exceptionalism eroding, latches on to commonist theory and practice? In 2013, the Utrecht-based art space Casco organized a "Conversation Market" in the shopping mall Hoog Catharijne, with artist Aimée Zito Lema providing newly built versions of De Stijl designer Gerrit Rietveld's crate furniture as the setting—a project titled, after Rietveld, "Sitting Is a Verb." Casco's practice has been informed by feminists such as Federici, and in this case, particularly by the duo J. K. Gibson-Graham's notion of community economies, taking as its motto their slogan: "The economy is something we do, not just something that does things to us." Gibson-Graham insist that the capitalist part of the economy is just the tip of an iceberg. Above the water level stand "wage labor, market exchange of commodities, and capitalist enterprise." Below, we find a much messier informal economy—a mix of "not for market" and "not monetized" activity, including gifts and volunteer work, barter, noncapitalist cooperatives, self-employment, and child labor.[119] Here, one may also think of Nancy Fraser's insistence that capitalism has always been more than "an economy" in a narrow sense, and that it is "necessary to talk about the 'non-economic' background conditions that enabled such an 'economic system' to exist."[120]

Artistic appropriations of notions of the commons and of community economics can, of course, be criticized as naïve. We might wonder if something such as the Casco "Conversation Market" does not relapse into a precritical understanding of the extra-economic zone of social activity as being truly outside capitalism—rather than as an immanent exception, as the zone of appropriation that helps constitute and maintain it, and that has increasingly been reincorporated into the economic part of society. In fact, Casco's "Conversation Market" was an intervention by invitation—part of the shopping mall's rebranding of itself through art.[121] And is the supposed size of the "hidden," informal part of Gibson-Graham's iceberg metaphor fooling us about the pervasiveness of capitalism in society as a whole? As Jappe notes, a collapse of capitalism would have much more drastic consequences for the majority of the population now than it would have had around 1900.[122]

Nonetheless, in however scoutlike a manner, these practices (or proposals for practices) attack the crisis of value and the concomitant crisis of labor head-on. While Casco's "Conversation Market" was essentially a barely structured exchange of half-formed thoughts between whomever showed up, such projects ultimately do contribute to opening up a conversation on value—the value we place on monetary and financial value itself.

In the context of the Institute of Network Cultures' MoneyLab project, some of the more technologically minded actors in this field have attempted "the radical reinvention of money itself," on the basis of a critical engagement with cryptocurrencies, and the blockchain technology behind them. They have attempted to counter the frequently right-wing technolibertarian discourse associated with these technologies by sketching the outlines of a much more fundamentally alternative form of money. In Bitcoin, as a MoneyLab contributor argues, the asset function of money trumps the exchange function, meaning that it essentially becomes a derivative—an option or futures contract.[123] By contrast, Tiziana Terranova and others have proposed a "commoncoin" that would lose value over time to counter this speculative aspect. While this proposal is neither the first nor the last word on the matter, it at least opens up the conversation beyond the "there are alternatives" baseline of contemporary ideology. Terranova and Andrea Fumagalli insist that the crisis of value and of capitalism should not lead to primitivism:

> The notion of a bad, fake financialization opposed to the real economy is contested both by activist anthropologists of the financial world, but also by post-workerist Marxists who, as we have seen, consider financialization as the answer of capital to the crisis of measure—

> that is the inability to measure productivity on the basis of the labor theory of value. Financialization has a potential: it reveals how money can function as an intervention and that it can also account for different ways of organizing the production and distribution of wealth, which is alternative to both socialism (state) and market (capital).[124]

In contrast to the merely theoretical radicalism of the value critics, Commoncoin is an attempt to devise a postcapitalist tactic that will help to accelerate the crisis even while reshaping social and economic structures in ways that go beyond a simple "taking over."

If Commoncoin would have devaluation built into its DNA, then what about art? Given art's capture as exceptional asset, writer Andrea Phillips has argued for its "devaluation" as a political process through which "we dispossess ourselves of value as an economic and aspirational asset class."[125] She advocates a transformation of art education to this end, and suggests that there may be uses of artistic skills that allow artists to make a living in ways "that do not necessitate individualized value as a form of capital expansion."[126] Such proposals can easily be brushed aside as half-baked speculations far removed from practical steps, but making sense of the crisis of value and revalorizing value may itself be a crucial form of praxis.

In it growing dysfunction, spluttering financialized global capitalism contains the seeds of a postcapitalist future that could either be dominated by catastrophic collapse—economic, but also ecological and social collapse—or by a consciously shaped alternative. The window for intervention is closing, as ecological and social violence intensifies. The real challenge is only beginning to be understood: to transvaluate value and rethink and reimagine what counts as socially necessary, and socially desirable.

NOTES

1 See Joshua Simon, "In Face of Capital," in *Zachary Formwalt: Three Exchanges* (Amsterdam: Roma Publications, 2015), 155–64.

2 Voice-over, in Zachary Formwalt, *An Unknown Quantity* (2015), in *Three Exchanges*, 168.

3 In Brian Holmes's words, the Black–Scholes model "lent rigor to option pricing, so it looked more like science and less like gambling. On the other [hand], it showed a path toward the automated calculation of dynamic hedges for complex derivative contracts." Holmes, "Information's Metropolis: Chicago and the New Nature of Global Finance," in *Volatile Smile*, ed. Beate Geissler and Oliver Sann (Nürnberg: Verlag für moderne Kunst, 2014), 35.

4 Paraphrased from the voice-over in Formwalt's *An Unknown Quantity*.

5 Andrea Fraser, "L'1%, C'est Moi," *Texte zur Kunst*, no. 83 (September 2011): 122.

6 Benjamin Sutton, "Richard Prince Disowns His Ivanka Trump Portrait, Possibly Increasing Its Value," *Hyperallergic*, January 13, 2017, https://hyperallergic.com/351403/richard-prince-disowns-his-ivanka-trump-portrait-possibly-increasing-its-value/.

7 Eric C. H. de Bruyn, "Three Exchanges," in *Three Exchanges*, 73.

8 See also Marina Vishmidt, *Speculation as a Mode of Production: Forms of Value Subjectivity in Art and Capital* (Leiden: Brill, 2018).

9 Jacques Rancière, *L'inconscient esthétique* (Paris: Galilée, 2001), 12.

10 For an analysis of a number of such practices, see Max Haiven, *Art after Money, Money after Art* (London: Pluto Press, 2018).

11 Karl Marx, "The Value-Form," appendix to the first German edition of *Capital*, vol. 1 (1867), trans. Mike Roth and Wal Suchting, https://www.marxists.org/archive/marx/works/1867-c1/appendix.htm. Similar formulations are in *Capital: A Critique of Political Economy*, vol. 1, trans. Ben Fowkes (London: Penguin, 1976), 138–44.

12 Fredric Jameson, *Representing "Capital": A Reading of Volume One* (London: Verso, 2011), 35.

13 Marx, *Capital*, vol. 1, 126–31.

14 Marx, *Capital*, vol. 1, 163–77.

15 "Die Wertform verleugnet und verschleiert den Grössenbezug des Werts zur Arbeit durch den 'gegenständlichen Schein' des Warenwerts." Alfred Sohn-Rethel, *Geistige und körperliche Arbeit: Zur Theorie der gesellschaftlichen Synthesis*, rev. ed. (Frankfurt am Main: Suhrkamp, 1972), 77. Unless otherwise noted, all quotations of Sohn-Rethel are my translations of the 1972 German edition, which was revised and expanded in response to the book's critical reception. The English version of Sohn-Rethel's book, *Intellectual and Manual Labour*, is an anglicized reworking rather than a pure translation; it sometimes adds clarifications, but in many ways, it is an inferior digest of the original. I refer to the English version only when it contains a particularly apt expression of one of Sohn-Rethel's crucial points.

The "versioning" didn't stop there: Sohn-Rethel published a third German edition in 1989, which is remarkable for an acknowledgment of Cassirer's work that is missing from previous editions.

16 "Diese vom Gebrauchswert abstrahierten Formeigenschaften"; "reine Formabstraktionen." Sohn-Rethel, 20–21.

17 Sohn-Rethel, 38–42.

18 Sohn-Rethel, 30–40; the term "Begriffsform der naturwissenschaftlichen Denkart" appears on 37.

19 Sohn-Rethel, 22.

20 Ernst Cassirer, *The Philosophy of Symbolic Forms*, vol. 3, *The Phenomenology of Knowledge*, trans. Ralph Manheim (New Haven, CT: Yale University Press, 1957), 7.

21 Yuk Hui, *On the Existence of Digital Objects* (Minneapolis: University of Minnesota Press, 2016), 6–8.

22 Steve G. Lofts, *Ernst Cassirer: A "Repetition" of Modernity* (Albany, NY: SUNY Press, 2000), 227n5.

23 Erwin Panofsky, *Perspective as Symbolic Form*, trans. Christopher S. Wood (New York: Zone Books, 1991), 66.

24 Panofsky, 67.

25 Ernst Cassirer, *The Philosophy of Symbolic Forms*, vol. 1, *Language*, trans. Ralph Manheim (New Haven, CT: Yale University Press, 1955), 106.

26 Anselm Jappe, "Sohn-Rethel and the Origin of 'Real Abstraction':

A Critique of Production or a Critique of Circulation?," *Historical Materialism* 21, no. 1 (2013): 3–14; see also the relevant part in Sohn-Rethel, *Geistige und körperliche Arbeit*, 123–73.

27 Marx, *Capital*, vol. 1, 151—152.

28 Sohn-Rethel, *Geistige und körperliche Arbeit*, i.a., 81, 88–89.

29 Alfred Sohn-Rethel, *Intellectual and Manual Labour: A Critique of Epistemology* (London: Macmillan, 1978), 43; and the (more or less) equivalent passage in *Geistige und körperliche Arbeit*, 70.

30 For a recent restatement of utilitarian aestheticism that takes cues from John Ruskin, see *What's the Use?: Constellations of Art, History, and Knowledge*, ed. Nick Aikens, Thomas Lange, Jorinde Seijdel, Steven ten Thije (Amsterdam: Valiz, 2016).

31 Marx, *Capital*, vol. 1, 129. In these short quotations, the British spelling of "labour" has been adjusted.

32 David Harvey, *A Companion to Marx's "Capital"* (London: Verso, 2010), 24.

33 Marx, *Capital*, vol. 1, 129.

34 Marx, 127.

35 Marx, 129.

36 Marx, 1044.

37 Dave Beech, *Art and Value: Art's Economic Exceptionalism in Classical, Neoclassical and Marxist Economics* (Leiden: Brill, 2015), 9–11. In emphasizing the economic exceptionalism of art, Beech builds on John Roberts, *The Intangibilities of Form: Skill and Deskilling in Art after the Readymade* (London: Verso, 2007).

38 Beech, 219.

39 Beech, 22.

40 Beech, 311.

41 Beech, 311.

42 Beech omits to mention the latter. Today, the act of being collected by a major art collector can itself add to a work's value.

43 Beech, 311, 312.

44 Beech, 311–12.

45 I take the phrase "algorithmic moodboard" from a work in progress by Melanie Gilligan and Marina Vishmidt.

46 Diedrich Diederichsen, *On (Surplus) Value in Art* (Rotterdam:

Witte de With Publishers, 2008). See Beech's response in *Art and Value*, 20–22.

47 Diedrich Diederichsen, *(Over)production and Value* (Berlin: Sternberg Press, 2017), 11. Diederichsen's move is reminiscent of Romano Alquati's early 1960s analysis of labor as information, which will be discussed in the next chapter.

48 Diederichsen, 14.

49 Antonio Negri, "Crisis of the Planner State: Communism and Revolutionary Organization" (1971), in *Books for Burning: Between Civil War and Democracy in 1970s Italy* (London: Verso, 2005), 24. See also Matteo Pasquinelli, "Capital Thinks Too: The Idea of the Common in the Age of Machine Intelligence," *Open!*, December 11, 2015, https://onlineopen.org/capital-thinks-too.

50 Antonio Negri, "Starting Again from Marx," *Radical Philosophy* 2, no. 3 (December 2018), https://www.radicalphilosophy.com/article/starting-again-from-marx.

51 Negri, "Starting Again from Marx."

52 See Steve Wright, *Storming Heaven: Class Composition and Struggle in Italian Autonomist Marxism*, 2nd ed. (London: Pluto Press, 2017), 149–62.

53 For an English-language anthology of Wertkritiker writings, see *Marxism and the Critique of Value*, ed. Neil Larsen, Mathias Nilges, Josh Robinson, and Nicholas Brown (Chicago: MCM Publishing, 2014). For a critique of Operaism, Negri, and Hardt from the perspective of Wertkritik, see Anselm Jappe, *Die Abenteuer der Ware: Für eine neue Wertkritik* (Münster: Unrast Verlag, 2005), 235–40.

54 Robert Kurz, "Der doppelte Marx," *Exit!*, https://www.exit-online.org/link.php?tabelle=autoren&posnr=50. See also Kurz, *Geld ohne Wert: Grundrisse zu einer Transformation der politischen Ökonomie* (Berlin: Horlemann, 2012), 11–45.

55 In *Capital*, vol. 1, Marx notes that "in the circulation M-C-M both the money and the commodity function only as different modes of existence of value itself," which "is constantly changing from one form into the other, without becoming lost in this movement; it thus becomes transformed into an automatic subject" (255). The notion has been taken up with considerable enthusiasm by Wertkritiker and

associated authors. See, for instance, *Das automatische Subjekt bei Marx*, ed. Hans-Georg Bensch and Frank Kuhne (Lüneburg: Klampen, 1998); and Jappe, *Die Abenteuer der Ware*, 80–88.

56 Jappe, *Die Abenteuer der Ware*, 104–5. See also Gruppe Krisis, "Manifest gegen die Arbeit," December 31, 1999, http://www.krisis.org/1999/manifest-gegen-die-arbeit/.

57 Jappe, 126.

58 Jappe, 105.

59 Vishmidt, *Speculation as a Mode of Production*, 132.

60 Diane Elson, "The Value Theory of Labour," in *Value: The Representation of Labour in Capitalism*, ed. Diane Elson (1979; London: Verso, 2015), 135–36.

61 Karl Marx, *A Contribution to the Critique of Political Economy* (1857), in *Marx and Engels Collected Works*, vol. 29 (New York: International Publishers, 1987), 286; quoted in Elson, 136.

62 Marx, 286; quoted in Elson, 136.

63 Elson, 136.

64 The next chapter will revolve around the becoming-operational of abstraction, which can be said to culminate in operational fetishism under networked and financialized capitalism.

65 Haiven, *Art after Money, Money after Art*, 37.

66 Wu Ming 1, "Fetishism of Digital Commodities and Hidden Exploitation: The Cases of Amazon and Apple," *libcom.org*, December 6, 2011, https://libcom.org/library/fetishism-digital-commodities-hidden-exploitation-cases-amazon-apple.

67 Harvey, *A Companion to Marx's "Capital,"* 20–21.

68 Wages for Housework can be regarded as a networked campaign waged by a few key players with local groups in various countries/cities. For the most complete historical account to date, see Louise Toupin, *Wages for Housework: A History of an International Feminist Movement, 1972–77* (Vancouver: UBC Press, 2018).

69 Kerstin Stakemeier, "(Not) More Autonomy," in *Art Production beyond the Art Market?*, ed. Karen van den Berg, et al. (Berlin: Sternberg Press, 2013), 22.

70 Laurel Ptak, Wages for Facebook project/campaign, http://wagesforfacebook.com.

71 Jodi Dean discusses Metcalfe's law in *The Communist Horizon* (London: Verso, 2012), 129.

72 Marx, *Capital*, vol. 1, 878–79. Marx's term is *ursprüngliche Akkumulation*, rendered in English (somewhat unfortunately) as primitive accumulation. To make matters more complicated, Marx's title refers to a *sogenannte usprüngliche Akkumulation*, or "so-called primitive accumulation." This has to do with Marx's debunking of dominant liberal myths concerning precapitalist accumulation, which posited the emergence of a divide between haves and have-nots owing to the latter's innate laziness. Against such mythmaking, Marx maintains that "in actual history, it is a notorious fact that conquest, enslavement, robbery, murder, in short, force, play the greatest part" (874), and he proceeds to analyze the process in detail.

73 Marx, 878–79.

74 Marx, 875.

75 The passage is part of the first chapter of Thomas More's *Utopia*, "Discourses of Raphael Hythloday, of the Best State of a Commonwealth."

76 Massimo De Angelis, "Marx's Theory of Primitive Accumulation: A Suggested Reinterpretation," UEL, Department of Economics, Working Paper, no. 21, May 2000, http://citeseerx.ist.psu.edu/viewdoc/download?doi=10.1.1.200.9435&rep=rep1&type=pdf.

77 Marx, *Capital*, vol. 1, 915.

78 Marx, 915.

79 De Angelis, "Marx's Theory of Primitive Accumulation."

80 The first result of this project, Federici and Leopoldina Fortunati's *Il grande Calibano*, was published in 1984 (Milan: Franco Angeli).

81 Silvia Federici, *Caliban and the Witch: Women, the Body and Primitive Accumulation* (Brooklyn, NY: Autonomedia, 2004).

82 See for instance Marx, *Capital*, vol. 1, 341. The notion of reproduction plays a complex role in Marx's work, referring to the cyclical processes through which society and the economy maintain themselves. In this respect, the later focus on "reproductive labor" by Marxist feminists is more limited.

83 Mary Inman, *In Women's Defense* (Los Angeles: Committee to Organize the Advancement of Women, 1940), 136.

84 Mariarosa Dalla Costa and Selma James, *The Power of Women and the Subversion of the Community* (Bristol: Falling Wall Press, 1972). See also Silvia Federici's 1975 essay "Wages against Housework," in *Revolution at Point Zero: Housework, Reproduction, and Feminist Struggle* (Oakland, CA: PM Press, 2012), 15–22.

85 *See Red Women's Workshop: Feminist Posters 1974–1990* (London: Four Corners Books, 2016), ix–xiii, 48–49.

86 Federici's exchange with German scholar Maria Mies should be noted here; Mies's 1986 *Patriarchy and Accumulation on a World Scale* is a counterpart to Federici's *Caliban and the Witch.*

87 Jason W. Moore, *Capitalism in the Web of Life: Ecology and the Accumulation of Capital* (London: Verso, 2015), 54.

88 On the Wadsworth piece and its various components, see the exhibition booklet http://www.thewadsworth.org/wp-content/uploads/2011/06/Matrix-137.pdf.

89 Federici, "The Reproduction of Labor Power in the Global Economy and the Unfinished Feminist Revolution" (2008), in *Revolution at Point Zero*, 92.

90 See also Federici, "Introduction," in *Revolution at Point Zero*, 6–7.

91 Denise Ferreira da Silva, "Unpayable Debt: Reading Scenes of Value against the Arrow of Time," in *The documenta 14 Reader*, ed. Quinn Latimer and Adam Szymczyk (Munich: Prestel, 2017), 106.

92 Sylvia Wynter, "Beyond the Categories of the Master Conception: The Counterdoctrine of Jamesian Poiesis," in *C. L. R. James's Caribbean*, ed. Paul Buhle and Paget Henry (Durham, NC: Duke University Press, 1992), 81–82.

93 Karl Marx, chap. 12 of "Theories of Surplus-Value" (1861–63), https://www.marxists.org/archive/marx/works/1863/theories-surplus-value/ch12.htm.

94 Moore, *Capitalism in the Web of Life*, 53.

95 Achille Mbembe, "Afrofuturism and the Becoming-Black of the World," in *Futurity Report*, ed. Eric C. H. de Bruyn and Sven Lütticken (Berlin: Sternberg Press, 2020), 209.

96 Jappe, Die Abenteuer der Ware, 130–31.

97 Shoshana Zuboff, *The Age of Surveillance Capitalism: The Fight for the Future at the New Frontier of Power* (London: Profile Books, 2019).

98 Kate Crawford and Vladan Joler, "Anatomy of an AI System: The Amazon Echo as an Anatomical Map of Human Labor, Data and Planetary Resources," *AI Now Institute and Share Lab*, September 7, 2018, https://anatomyof.ai/.

99 Raniero Panzieri, "Plusvalore e pianificazione," *Quaderni Rossi*, no. 4 (July 1964): 257–88. Published in English as "Surplus Value and Planning," trans. Julian Bees (1976), http://zerowork.org/Panzieri Planning.html.

100 The best documentation of these activities was published by artist Ben Kinmont as *Project Series: Christopher D'Arcangelo* (Paris: Antinomian Press, 2005), http://www.airdeparis.com/download /benkinmont/.

101 See Greg Allen, "The Offices of Fend, Fitzgibbon, Holzer, Nadin, Prince & Winters," April 16, 2013, https://greg.org/archive/2013 /04/16/the-offices-of-fend-fitzgibbon-holzer-nadin-prince-winters .html; and Leah Pires, "We All Know What the Problems Are, but Who Now Meets Them Directly? Aesthetic Services circa 1980," *Counter-Signals*, no. 3 (Fall 2018/Winter 2019): 210–29.

102 The original iteration was at the Kunstraum der Leuphana Universität Lüneburg, where the project and its implications were the subject of the 2014 conference "Art and Its Frames."

103 Sabeth Buchmann, "Art as (un-)Specific Work as (un-)Specific Labor" (lecture, "But Something's Missing: Marxist Art History between Possibility and Necessity" conference, mumok, Vienna, December 15, 2015), lecture manuscript.

104 Andrea Fraser, "What's Intangible, Transitory, Mediating, Participatory, and Rendered in the Public Sphere? Part II" (1996), in *Museum Highlights: The Writings of Andrea Fraser*, ed. Alexander Alberro (Cambridge, MA: MIT Press, 2007), 61.

105 Real Flow, *Art Is the Sublime Asset*, prospectus (March 1, 2015), 3, http://www.p-exclamation.com/wp-content/uploads/Real-Flow.pdf.

106 Real Flow, 8.

107 Beech, *Art and Value*, 303, 304, 306.

108 Deloitte's 9th Art & Finance Conference, Amsterdam, April 21, 2016, conference booklet, https://www2.deloitte.com/content /dam/Deloitte/lu/Documents/financial-services/artandfinance/lu

-en-artandfinancereport-booklet-21042016.pdf.

109 See also Kerstin Stakemeier, "Exchangeables: Aesthetics against Art," *Texte zur Kunst*, no. 98 (June 2015): 124–42.

110 Beech, *Art and Value*, 307.

111 Antonio Negri and Raúl Sánchez Cedillo, "The New Left in Europe Needs to Be Radical—and European," *Guardian*, February 27, 2015, https://www.theguardian.com/commentisfree/2015/feb/27/new-left-europe-greece-democratic-capitalism-nato; and Jathan Sadowski, "Why Silicon Valley Is Embracing Universal Basic Income," *Guardian*, June 22, 2016, https://www.theguardian.com/technology/2016/jun/22/silicon-valley-universal-basic-income-y-combinator.

112 See *The Gulf: High Culture / Hard Labor*, ed. Andrew Ross (New York: OR Books, 2015).

113 Andrea Fraser, *132 €*, week 45 of "52 Weeks of Gulf Labor," published as an advertisement in *Frankfurter Allgemeine Sonntagszeitung*, August 17, 2014.

114 "Labour in a Single Shot," Haus der Kulturen der Welt, Berlin, 2015, https://www.hkw.de/en/programm/projekte/2015/eine_einstellung_zur_arbeit/eine_einstellung_zur_arbeit_start.php.

115 Harun Farocki, "Wie soll man das nennen, was ich vermisse?," in *Suchbilder: Visuelle Kultur zwischen Algorithmen und Archiven*, ed. Wolfgang Ernst, Stefan Heidenreich and Ute Holl (Berlin: Kulturverlag Kadmos, 2003), 18–19.

116 See https://www.labour-in-a-single-shot.net/en/films/.

117 The film archive on the project website also contains another, less successful film on the same subject.

118 Fredric Jameson's concept of cognitive mapping has been revisited and expanded upon in Alberto Toscano and Jeff Kinkle, *Cartographies of the Absolute* (Winchester: Zero Books, 2015).

119 J. K. Gibson-Graham, *A Postcapitalist Politics* (Minneapolis: University of Minnesota Press, 2006), 69–70. The diagram was originally devised by Community Economies Collective in 2001 and drawn by Ken Byrne.

120 Nancy Fraser, "Behind Marx's Hidden Abode," in *New Left Review*, no. 86 (2014): 66.

121 “Call of the Mall,” Hoog Catharijne, Utrecht, June 20–September 22, 2013.

122 Jappe, *Die Abenteuer der Ware*, 138.

123 David Golumbia, “Bitcoin as Politics: Distributed Right-Wing Extremism,” in *MoneyLab Reader: An Intervention in Digital Economies*, ed. Geert Lovink, Nathaniel Tkacz, and Patricia de Vries (Amsterdam: Institute of Network Cultures, 2015), 118–31.

124 Tiziana Terranova and Andrea Fumagalli, “Financial Capital and the Money of the Common: The Case of Commoncoin,” in Lovink et al., *MoneyLab Reader*, 153.

125 Andrea Phillips, “Devaluation,” *Parse*, no. 2 (November 2015), https://parsejournal.com/article/devaluation/.

126 Phillips, “Devaluation.”

Chapter 4

The triumph of art as an increasingly normative exception undermines the (relative and ideologized) autonomy on which art's exceptional status and value were based. If more and more commodities now function in a manner that mirrors the artwork's monetary autonomization vis-à-vis labor-power and labor-time, this is largely through the added value of designed brand identities. The triumph of art propels the aestheticization of the world through design and branding—from Louis Vuitton to Apple, from starchitects to "influencers." It is through design that value remakes the sensible world; in Marx's terms, which I discussed in the introduction, the value-form reshapes the commodity's physical or natural form.

The sublation of art's autonomy through design was an intrinsic part of the modern aesthetic project. In *Design and Crime* (2002), Hal Foster traced the roots of today's "total design" to modern attempts to reconcile art and life via design in Art Nouveau and the Bauhaus: "So, yes, the world of total design is hardly new—imagined in Art Nouveau, it was retooled in the Bauhaus, and spread through institutional clones and commercial knock-offs ever since—but it only seems to be achieved in our own pan-capitalist present."[1] Total design includes exhibition design, graphic design, information design, bio-design, self-design: everything and the kitchen sink. If there is a problem with Foster's take on this, it is not that it is too totalizing but rather that it is insufficiently total. His analysis addresses design as commodity fetish but not as omnipresent process, as a productive operation that we all participate in willy-nilly—and that may, at times, be converted into critical aesthetic practice.

As the universal agent of what I will here analyze as *concrete abstraction*, and as the medium of its formal implementation, design is not so much an autonomous and specific discipline as a process of calibration and a constantly adapted set of protocols and procedures for applying abstraction. As a mid-nineteenth-century instruction book called *The Practical Draughtsman's Book of Industrial Design, and Machinist's and Engineer's Drawing Companion* put it:

> Industrial Design is destined to become a universal language; for in our material age of rapid transition from abstract, to applied, Science—in the midst of our extraordinary tendency towards the perfection of the means of conversion, or manufacturing production—it must soon pass current in every land. It is, indeed, the medium between Thought and Execution.[2]

From nineteenth-century industrial design to the total design-ification of the present, design is the medium through which the forms of economic, juridical, and technoscientific abstraction are progressively integrated in practice and transform the natural form of the world. It is in the mode of design that aesthetic practice, negating and sublating "autonomous art," has become operational and executable. However, if the project was art's sublation through design, what has actually occurred its realization as design. The self-overcoming of art turns into its self-actualization. In the resulting "creative economy," already discussed in the previous chapter, the crucial question is how to enact concrete abstraction against its protocol; how to perform its *preformations* otherwise.

The Birth of Design from the Spirit of Modern Art

In his work on aspect ratios and ISO standards, Sean Snyder investigates fundamental ways in which the world is shaped. The International Organization for Standardization regulates everything from the size of hotel key cards to the Internet of Things.[3] Such standards function as a kind of operational Kantian schematism. Different aspect ratios of screens—which, by now, have also been incorporated into the ISO framework—likewise shape our field of vision. In his 2016 exhibition "Aspect Ratio/Dispositif," the work *Aspect Ratio (Vanishing Point)* (2015–16) consisted of framed prints, one of which reproduced Malevich's *Black Square* (1915) in aspect ratio 16:9. Stretching the painting (the black square itself plus its white border), Snyder pressed Malevich's "zero of form" into a "landscape" format.

The show also included square stickers of a QR code, as well as a video projection *Mnemosynedrone (Metadata)* (2015–16), which shows QR codes in various states of being stretched horizontally to fit the screen. Snyder's QR codes may lead to his own websites or nowhere at all; one site begins with a simple animation of *Black Square*, then its negative in white, and then a QR code.[4] The QR code—a carefully regulated format that needs to be machine-legible—is staged by Snyder as the contemporary equivalent of the modernist *Black Square*: a machinic abstraction that not so much replaces mundane reality with a nonobjective vision as it "augments" reality in formatted and patented ways.

Recently, the *Black Square* has been reframed as a "racist joke" owing to the Tretyakov Gallery's assertion that an X-ray revealed that Malevich had once inscribed the painting with a joke based on Paul Bilhaud and Alphonse Allais's mock-abstract monochromes with titles referring to "negroes fighting in a cellar at night." Thus, the work is reclaimed for representation.[5] Irrespective of whether the erased

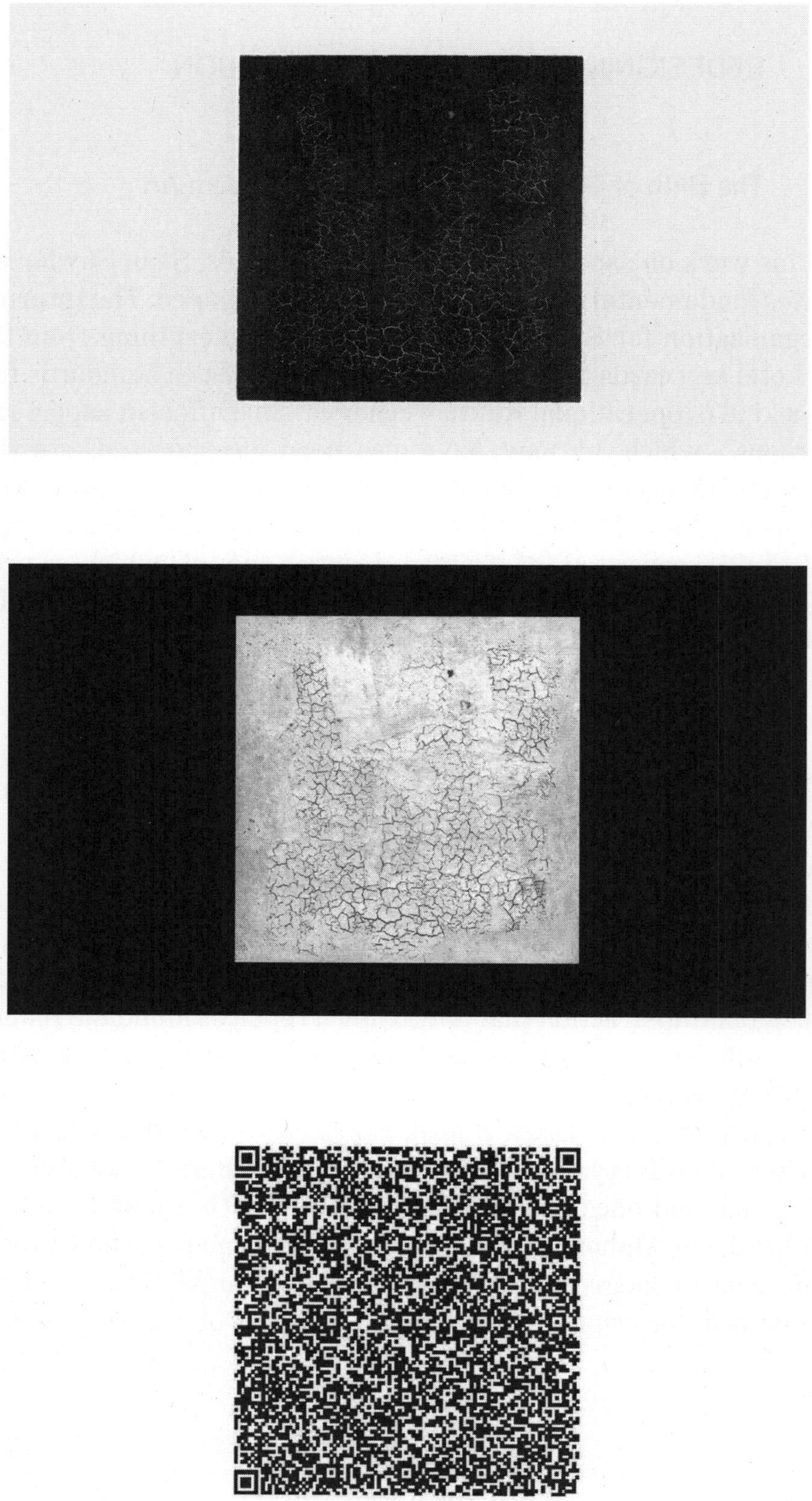

Stills from an MP4 movie on Sean Snyder's (now defunct) website, https://mnemosynedrone.io

inscription was by Malevich himself or by some anonymous vandal, the *Black Square* is shaped by this deletion, by the absence of reference. This exemplifies the second stage in a historical sequence analyzed by Fredric Jameson on the basis of Giovanni Arrighi's *The Long Twentieth Century* (1994): a triad of realism, modernism, and postmodernism that mirrors Marx's cycle of M-C-M.[6] The first phase is marked by trade and, aesthetically, by realism. To restate this in my own words: in the realm of realism, the value-form is grasped not as such but through commodities and acts of exchange, and the subjectivities thus formed. What is brought out is not the rule of equivalence but the manifold, specific *effects* of equivalence in a world intent on maintaining certain social hierarchies and conventions. Even so, in what one could term a modernist reading of Balzac, one critic has pointed out that a single page of Balzac's prose often contains up to twenty or thirty numbers, like mystical signs indicating that money as common denominator consumes all objects. The financial investors described by Balzac "do not partake in a company's actual substance," being "nihilists who have even turned their backs on nothingness."[7] Thus, he painstakingly details a world in which everything already melts into thin air.

Jameson insists that whereas with realist literature, exchange-value "provoked a new interest in the properties of objects," it is only with modernism that "the processes of the new industrial city, very much including the abstract flows of money, determine a whole new and more abstract way of thinking, radically different from the object world of the older merchant cities and countryside."[8] He continues:

> [Under modernism,] equivalence has as its result a withdrawal from older notions of stable substances and their unifying identifications. Thus, if all these objects have become equivalent as commodities,

> if money has leveled their intrinsic differences as individual things, one may now purchase as it were their various, henceforth semiautonomous, qualities or perceptual features; and both colour and shape free themselves from their former vehicles and come to live independent existences as fields of perception and as artistic raw materials.[9]

Elsewhere, Jameson has argued that "the abstractions of modern art can be said to have reflected the first-degree abstractions of the commodity form itself, as objects lost their intrinsic use-value and were replaced by a different kind of social currency: modernist spiritualisms vied with modernist materialisms to render the "theological mysteries" (Marx's term) of this new object world.[10] Such connections were not just made decades after the fact. In his unfinished 1930s book *Die Fabrikation der Fiktionen*, Carl Einstein compared the "archaic" use of metaphors in modern poetry—as well as philosophy—to the liquefaction of the material world by capitalist exchange:

> The metaphorical strings contain another archaism. The different conditions and things slip into one another and are evaluated evenly. One sign can replace the other randomly. And so the mana wanders serenely from humans into things, from animals into stones. A similar neutralization of concrete things or persona is administered by the capitalist. He defigures humans and objects by the means of abstract money, which is his mana. Poets and capitalists are dynamists and are seeking out a maximum of mobility.[11]

Quoting this passage, Kerstin Stakemeier notes that the metaphor-laden aesthetic mode comes to function as a "figure of capital" and "its boundless ability to homologize all things living and dead under the value of form."[12] Art's sensate forms can deny and occlude—and perhaps, at times, negate—their preformation by real abstraction, yet art can also foreground those very preformations and use them as aesthetic material.

With postmodernism as the cultural logic of finance capital, we reach a new level of abstraction. What is needed, Jameson avers, is "an account of abstraction in which the new deterritorialized postmodern contents are to an older modernist autonomization as global financial speculation is to an older kind of banking and credit."[13] This account is compelling but perhaps insufficiently attentive to the dialectic of abstraction and concretion in modernism. Do abstract paintings, while they free color and line, not end up as precious still-life objects in their own right? Abstract art is bewitchingly concrete. It oscillates between sign and mark, between articulation and evasion, between meaning and muteness. What is said, what is intimated, what is obscured and occluded in modernist abstraction?

For some years, the artist Riet Wijnen has been producing written "conversations" on abstraction that are composed of statements attributed to various historical figures (or to organizations such as the group Abstraction-Création), resulting in polyphonic dialogues. The ongoing series "Sixteen Conversations on Abstraction" provides data that is then "programmed" into a tablelike, horizontal sculpture titled *Sculpture Sixteen Conversations on Abstraction*. Here the characters from the conversations are encoded red, the locations yellow, the topics mint green, and key terms blue. The sculpture will keep changing as the number of conversations grows. A tabulating table, *Sculpture Sixteen Conversations on Abstraction* is like an analog computer for which only Wijnen seems to have the code. Looking at it involves attempts to decipher its structural logic and moments of giving up and siding with enjoyment, with *jouissance* over analysis.

In 2013, Wijnen published a booklet with sometimes contradictory "facts" on the life and work of the painter Marlow Moss—often considered a Mondrian epigone, and born Marjorie Jewel Moss.[14] Is it

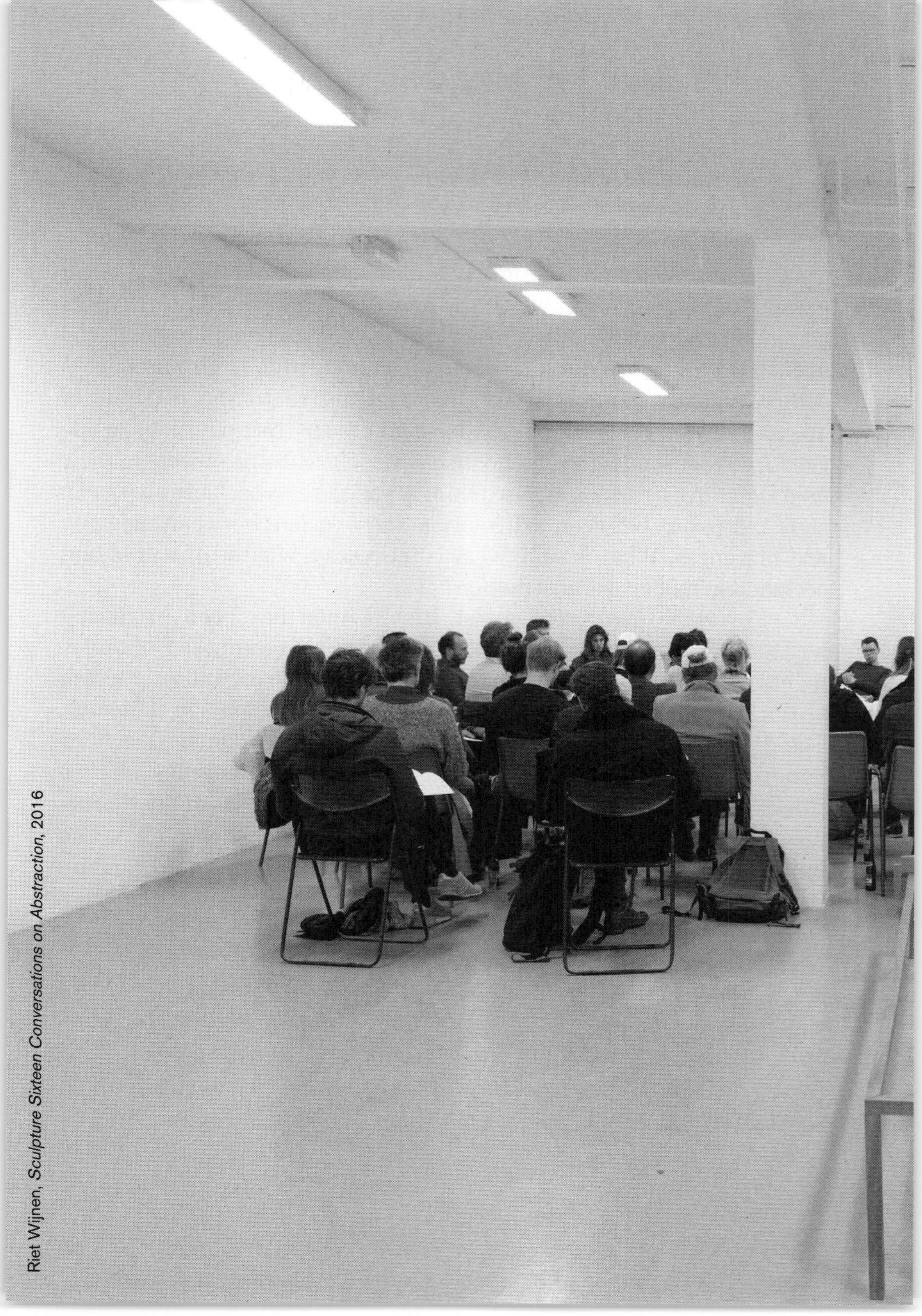

Riet Wijnen, *Sculpture Sixteen Conversations on Abstraction*, 2016

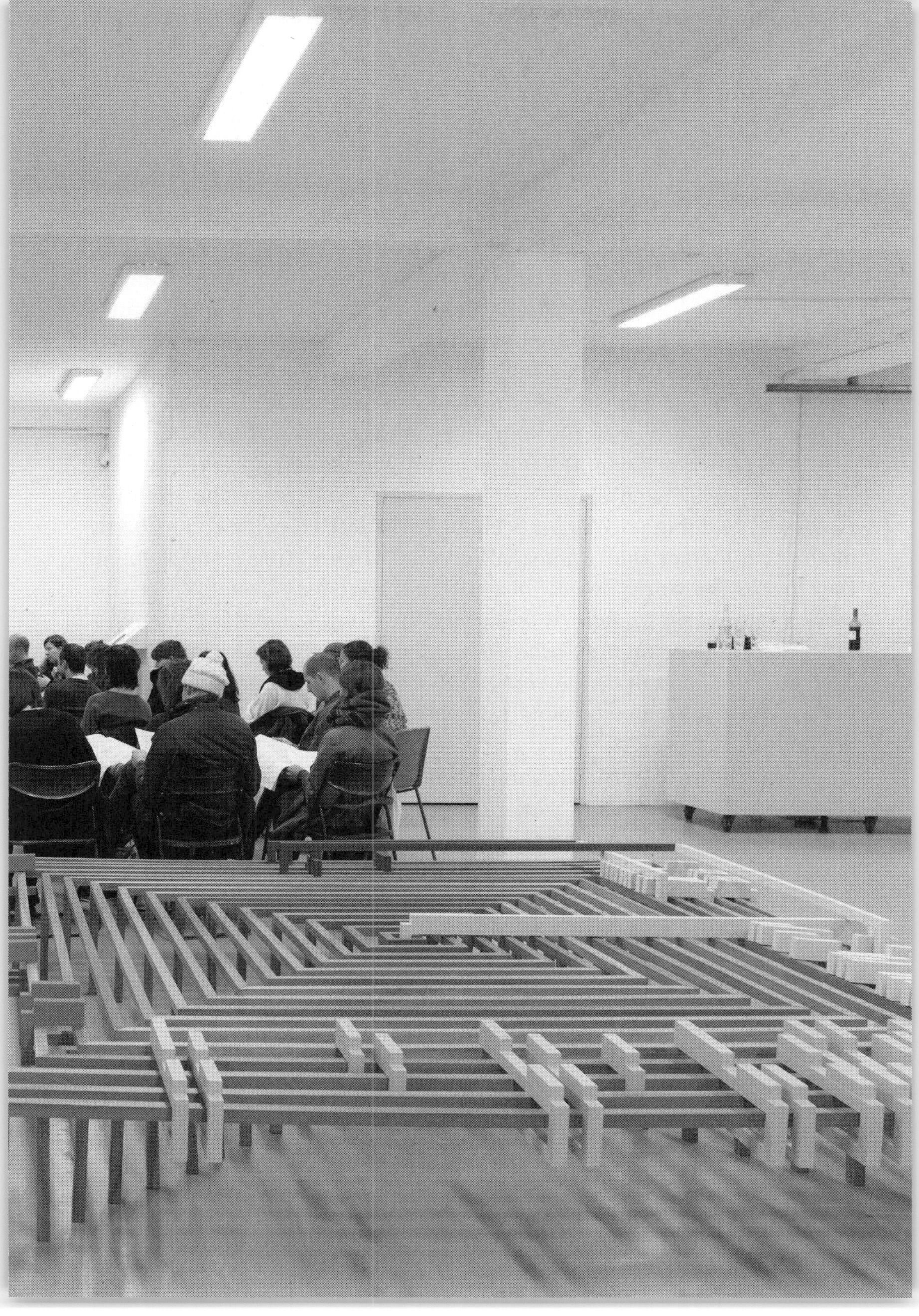

relevant that Moss was variously described as a drag king, a lesbian, and a pseudo-man? In *Conversation Six*, Wijnen has Moss describe the risks of wearing male clothes on the streets of interwar Paris. The "Conversations" restore and amplify some of the chatter, the exchanges and conflicts, the social mutations and new sexual lifestyles, the trans-cultural migrations, the actual encounters and missed moments from which abstract art emerges. Jameson's evocation of metropolitan life and its new thrills rings true here, and one could indeed oppose Moss the modernist to Wijnen the contemporary (or postmodernist).

Wijnen's work can be seen as a cultural mining operation in the era of financial capitalism: surplus is extracted from the archive. However, in doing so Wijnen perhaps articulates a central tension in modernism better than Jameson's account. In creating a supplement that makes the work "speak" in a different register, she addresses the work's muteness, its failure to signify. In *Conversation Six*, Wijnen's Moss also reflects on Mondrian: "He didn't accept the diagonal line; I used it. His horizontal line represents the reclining woman and the vertical line, the man who penetrates her. My horizontals and verticals are ends in themselves."[15]

This refers to a crucial conflict in De Stijl circles. In the mid-1920s, Theo van Doesburg and several artists in his wake broke with Mondrian's "Neoplastic" aesthetic of equilibrium, which was indeed based on an essentialist opposition between vertical (male) and horizontal (female). While Mondrian argued that the right angle was more fundamental to Neoplasticism than the question of whether those angles produced horizontal and vertical or diagonal lines, Van Doesburg ideologized the diagonal as a rejection of the latent naturalism in Mondrian's abstraction, and for the embrace of a dynamic, time-based approach to art.[16] It also meant that the easel painting was no longer necessarily the preferred medium.

In Van Doesburg's design for the *ciné-dancing* at the Aubette, in Strasbourg (1926–28), abstraction becomes a transforming force of daily (nocturnal) life, and the diagonals join the film image in celebrating dynamic urban life as the *real* new reality, over and beyond artistic dogma. The point was to go beyond an idealist form of abstraction to concrete social situations. The term "abstract" was on its way out.

Modern "abstract" art and its discourse were a problematization of abstraction. Mondrian always called his Neoplastic work "abstract-real" art, and his works could be said to derive much of their power from siding with the concrete: his brittle coatings of paint on canvas, exhibit their all too human imperfections and pentimenti.[17] As for Van Doesburg, by the time of his 1927 Elementarist manifesto, he stated that the terms "abstract" and "concrete" were nothing but (empty) phrases, and by 1930, he was advocating *art concret*, or Concrete art.[18] While Kandinsky was, like Mondrian, inspired by Theosophy, he too came to think of his work as a practice of concretion. Spiritualism itself underwent a material turn. This growing preference among artists for the term "concrete" around 1930 reflects the fact that art, as aesthetic practice, concretizes abstraction by addressing the senses in some manner. As Liam Gillick suggests, modernism is marked by a constitutive "failure of the abstract," promising an abstraction that it cannot deliver:

> By making the abstract concrete, art no longer retains any abstract quality, it merely announces a constant striving for a state of abstraction and in turn produces more abstraction to pursue. It is this failure of the abstract that lures and hypnotizes—forcing itself onto artists and demanding repeated attention. [...] It is the concretization of the abstract into a series of failed forms that lures the artist into repeated attempts to "create" the abstract—fully aware that this very act produces things that are the representation of impossibilities.

Art as the concretion of the abstract into a series of failed forms—a more succinct characterization of the logic of modern art can scarcely be imagined. Modern art is marked by an ongoing and uneasy dialectic of movements between abstraction and concretion, creating potent yet failed forms.[19]

A 1928 photograph by the abstract painter César Domela shows his wife Ruth in front of one of his paintings: a Van Doesburg–like "counter composition" with diagonal lines.[20] With this photograph, Domela stages a small-scale version of the dialectic that marks the Aubette: far from remaining an autonomous entity, the painting enters into a dialogue with the woman. The way in which this happens could not be further removed from the total design schemes of Henry van de Velde, who made his wife wear dresses that harmonized with the drapery and furniture. Without being in any way "formalized," Ruth Domela—her head in profile—exists on equal terms with the composition that is behind her, but which is more than a mere backdrop. A painting such as this, the image seems to say, is only complete when it is integrated into social situations. Mondrian's studio and the artist's life surrounded by his art proved highly fascinating to critics and photographers, yet Mondrian could only conceive of his praxis as anticipating a future life that was, as yet, impossible. With Van Doesburg and Domela, the future is now.

The discussions in the late 1920s and early 1930s about abstraction versus concretion were perhaps never more succinctly encapsulated than in Domela's photograph, which reframes the idealist utopia of abstract art as concrete lived reality. In this period, Domela also joined the ranks of those abstract and Constructivist artists who applied their photo-typography to advertising by working for companies in the avant-garde of capitalist technoscience, such as AEG. Around 1910, the architect Peter Behrens had designed actual products such as electric fans for AEG, as well as the stylish posters advertising

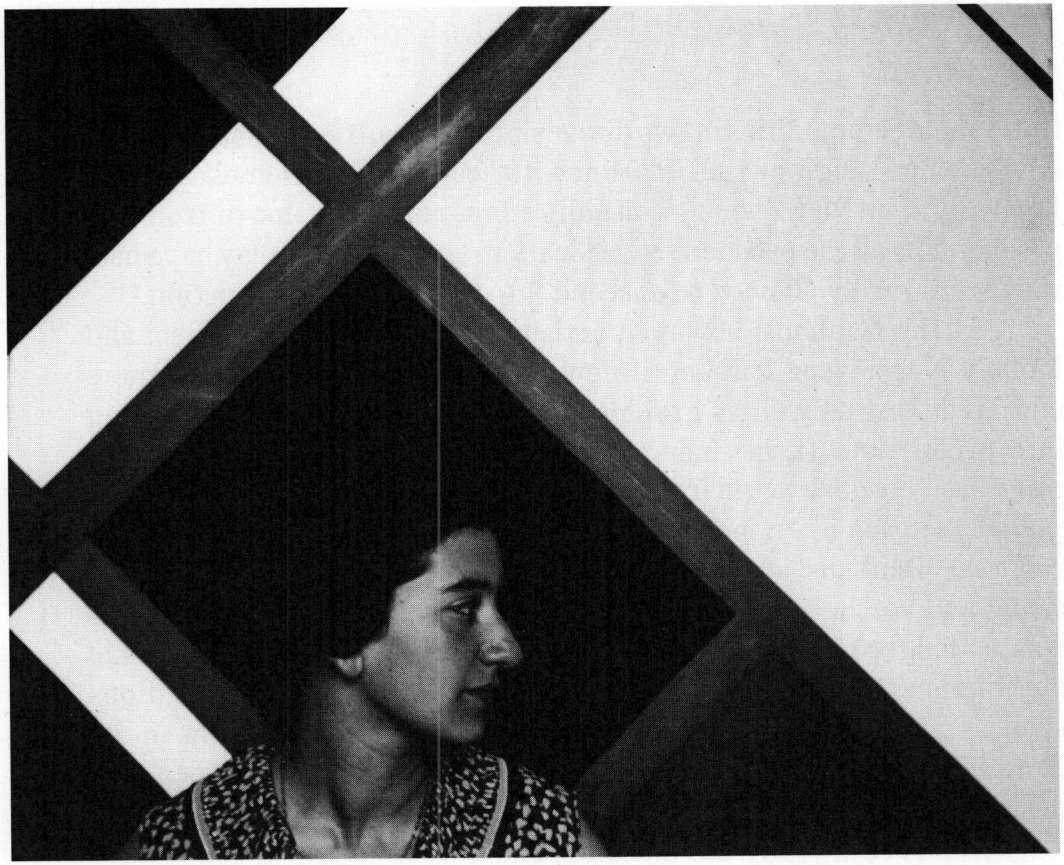

César Domela, *Ruth*, 1928

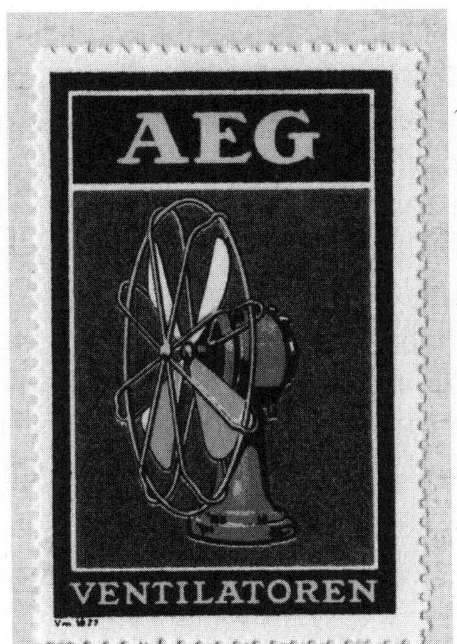

AEG stamp by Peter Behrens, ca. 1910

these same commodities in two dimensions. By contrast, Constructivist advertising design of the 1920s and 1930s—such as Domela's, or El Lissitzky's, or Piet Zwart's—usually remained at a remove from the product. For all the productivist inclinations the designers may have had, they were rarely allowed to descend into the abode of production.[21]

At the Bauhaus, however, artists such as Kandinsky, Klee, and Moholy-Nagy were training a new generation of product designers and architects as well as graphic designers; art, indeed, was moving into production. If, in their early work, artists such as Kandinsky progressively abstracted from material reality, with their art becoming *gegenstandslos* or "nonobjective," the Bauhaus effected a dialectical reversal. Bauhaus ideology and practice revolved around the functional and aesthetic design of industrial objects, which is to say: this was no longer an idealist abstraction *from* objects but an operational abstraction that (in)forms products. After World War II, institutions such as Max Bill's Hochschule für Gestaltung (HfG) in Ulm or its American counterparts helped the triumph of Bauhausian "good design" on a mass scale.

Abstract art may have been marked by a failure of the "truly" abstract, but a more positive take on the matter might emphasize its implication in the formation of industrial and graphic design as vehicles of concrete abstraction. In design, modernist abstraction transmuted its glorious failure into pragmatic productivism. In the process, its nonidentical muteness and elusive suggestions of new forms of life became normed proposals for living. I want to suggest that it is design that will allow us to get a better grasp of the transition from modernist to contemporary abstraction. Rather than positing an abstract break, I will analyze—in regrettably but unavoidably synoptic terms—how the discipline of design made the fundamental tension between abstraction and concretion (between abstraction and its failure) operative and productive in modernism and beyond, in our era of total design.

Abstraction Moves into Production

The process Marx termed original or primitive accumulation is not limited to any particular region or period. Not only did it have a crucial colonial dimension, as discussed in the last chapter; it also has to be permanent, since capitalism critically depends on the existence of a noneconomic outside to the market. As Nancy Fraser has put it, the capitalist economy needs a "non-economic background" that is both external to it and potentially open to incorporation, to appropriation and expropriation—to abstraction.[22]

In their collaborative works of the 1970s and 1980s, Oskar Negt and Alexander Kluge already suggested that a process equivalent to primitive accumulation was affecting intellectual workers, as the human brain becomes the most important raw material—a process that may also generate psychic resistances.[23] More generally, the psychological and behavioral "retooling" of laborers is crucial to twentieth- and twenty-first-century capitalism. The expropriated workers have to appropriate new skills and characteristics. New demands are made on the worker, demands that become interiorized and reshape the subject, finding ways of diverting libidinal flows.[24]

Capitalist expropriation and extraction are processes of abstraction. The commons are made productive by being abstracted from their status outside the capitalist *Wertschöpfungskette* (value-creation chain). As Negt and Kluge note, "Throughout history, progress above all seems to be made in the development of the principle of abstraction. Whenever it intervenes, a new dynamic is likely to emerge."[25] In *History and Obstinacy*, Negt and Kluge engage in a wide-ranging analysis of history on the basis of an evolutionary-anthropological notion of labor-power. They study the expropriation and instrumentalization of this labor-power (*Arbeitskraft*) in the form of specific labor capacities (*Arbeitsvermögen*) by successive economic regimes, as well as the resistances to such capture that are inherent in the subject's somatic memory.

Differentiating between a transhistorical "principle of abstraction" (associated with nomads and expropriation) and a "principle of concretion" (associated with agriculturists and production), they assert that "capitalism rests on the principle, that—for the first time in history—its abstractions break through into the productive sector."[26] Production had always been chained to the concrete, but capitalism unchains production through abstraction. This can be traced back even to merchant capitalism in the sixteenth and seventeenth centuries, in which a newly capitalized and centralized textile sector absorbed the "liberated" labor-power of commoners driven from the land. But it was in industrial capitalism that the reduction of workers to wage laborers was coupled with a progressive mechanization and "rationalization" of the production process—culminating in Fordism and Taylorism.

In a number of science-fiction films from 1969–70, including *Der große Verhau* (*The Big Mess*) and *Willi Tobler und der Untergang der 6. Flotte* (*Willi Tobler and the Decline of the 6th Fleet*), Kluge developed a kind of essayistic and fragmentary space opera of intergalactic colonization and extraction. He would continue to rework this body of work, reediting the films several times over the decades. He also published the related book *Lernprozesse mit tödlichem Ausgang* (Learning Processes with a Deadly Outcome, 1973).[27] Kluge's sci-fi complex chronicles the future destruction of Earth and a history of galactic conquest and interplanetary colonial extractivism, performed by a space fleet whose leadership (partly composed of old Nazis) is in cahoots with corporations such as the Suez Canal Company. Unpacking this potential history through a multitude of compacted stories, Kluge's science fiction is not plot-driven but speculative and essayistic, appropriating the tropes of space opera to ask whether another sci-fi cinema is possible.

Making this possible was Kluge's access to the facilities of the HfG Ulm—West Germany's "New Bauhaus." The state closed the school on December 31, 1968, but Kluge's Institut für Filmgestaltung, which by then was an independent foundation, retained access to the premises, where former students had installed a kind of commune.[28] Kluge and his crew shot the films between January 1969 and April 1970, under circumstances he characterizes, with characteristic understatement, as "relatively lively."[29] Similar to Kluge's institute, which survived the HfG's demise, his fictional version of the Suez Canal Company survives the loss of the canal in 1956 (due to postcolonial nationalization) and even the destruction of Earth: "The Suez Canal Company has survived the Black War as a mere idea, since neither its files nor its personnel have been evacuated into outer space; in 1956, it had already been dispossessed of its original capital object, the Suez Canal."[30]

Free from earthly entanglements, the corporation goes on to mine minerals and labor-power from other planets. Following Jameson, we can perhaps speak of a transition to a galactic financial capitalism with the loss of the original investment—but this causes the process of accumulation to hop from host to host, from the Isthmus of Suez to the metal planet of Dubna (via Russia), as the value-form colonizes countries and then alien planets. The company, having become a Platonic entity, a juridico-financial idea, can go on to extract materials and value from different contexts. Thus, Kluge's Suez Canal Company seems like a premonition of the likes of Apple: minerals are extracted in Africa by subcontractors, phones produced in China; what remains in Apple is the "idea." This idea, however, is an operational one. Accumulation as abstraction liquidates or liquefies concrete particularities through monetary equivalence. In this sense, it is a real rather than a conceptual abstraction.

Marx had criticized Hegel's philosophical notions because they remained mere philosophical concepts, in spite of their claim to concretion.[31]

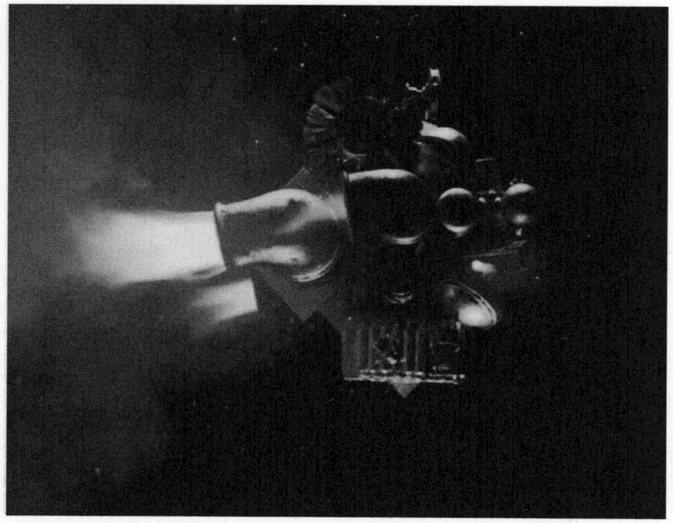

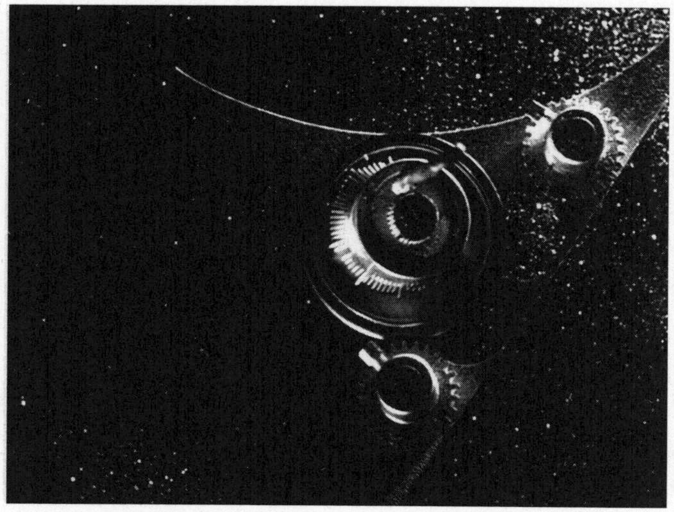

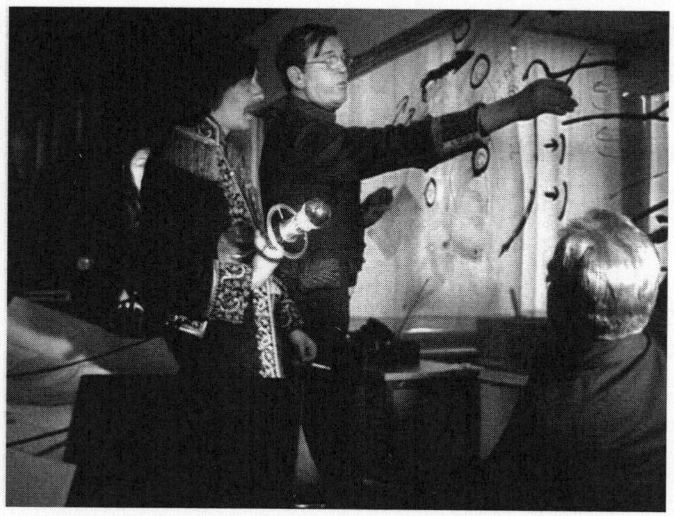

Frame enlargements from Alexander Kluge, *Willi Tobler und der Untergang der 6. Flotte*, 1969–70

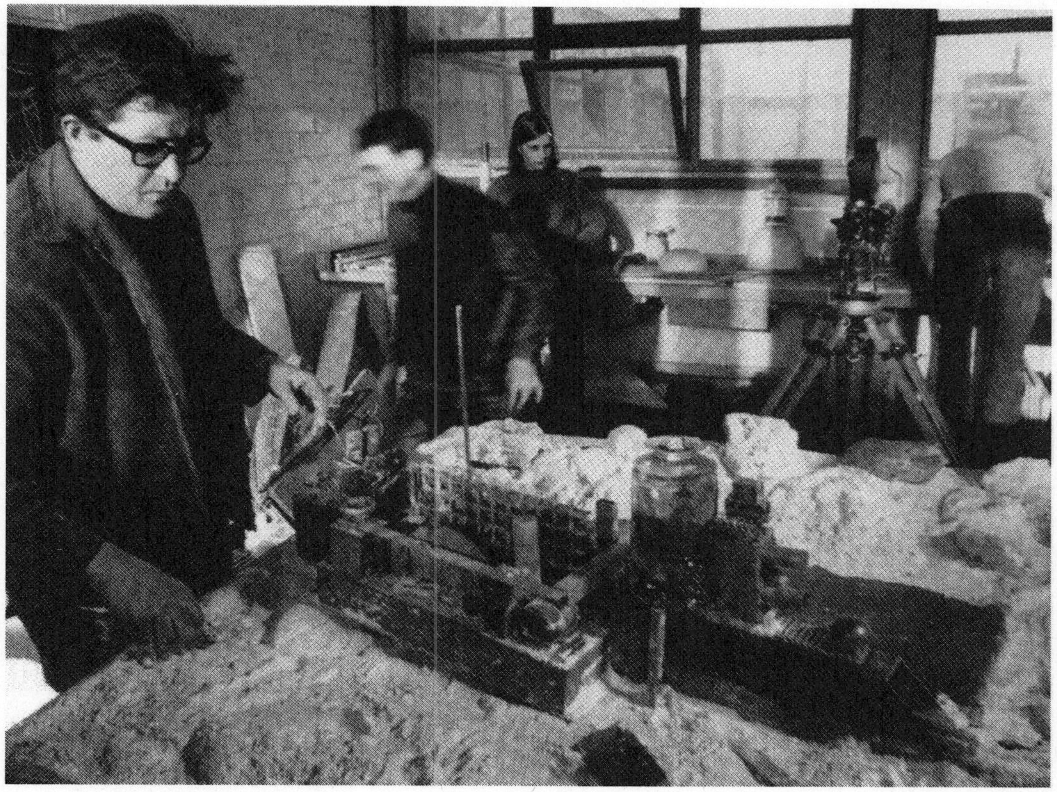

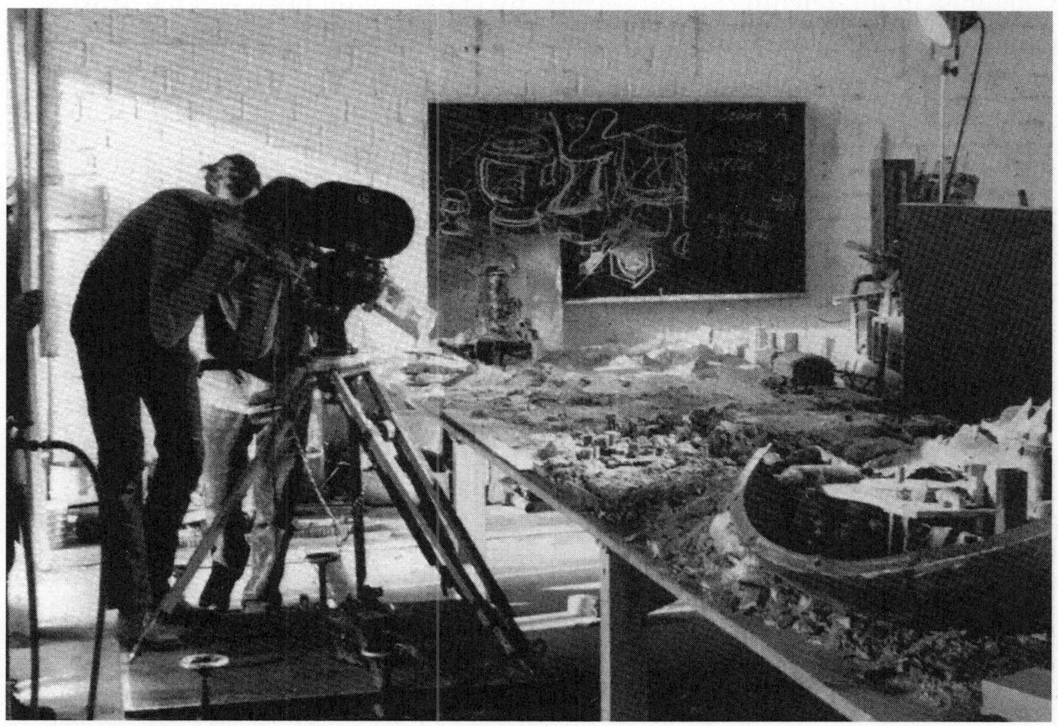

Production of Alexander Kluge's science-fiction films at the Hochschule für Gestaltung Ulm, 1969–70

When Marx analyzes the fundamental role of abstract labor in capitalism, or when Sohn-Rethel takes pointers from Marx in analyzing money as a real abstraction, something else is at stake: the social and economic reality of abstractions, as opposed to Hegel's philosophical abstract concepts.[32] In marked contrast to complaints about the increasingly abstract nature of the economy, of technology, of society as a whole, Marxists insist that the issue is not one of increasing abstraction, nor one of the failure of the abstract, but of the *becoming-real, becoming-concrete, becoming-productive of abstraction itself.* Labor itself becomes abstract labor-power, sold like any other commodity—a real abstraction. The becoming-productive of abstraction in capitalism is a becoming-concrete of the abstract itself.

Vectors of Real Abstraction

The opposition between art and science, as grounded in an opposition between concretion and abstraction, was repeated within the domain of science itself, within the university, by the division between natural science and the humanities, with the former being marked by "geometric formality," as Michel Serres calls it, and the latter by personal relativity.[33] But in reality, as Serres also acknowledges, the situation was more complex. Serres notes that the French university was traditionally split between humanities, science, and medicine and law. Serres argues that a "third subject besides that of science and humanities is born in those medical and law faculties."[34] In this sphere of thirdness, forms of operational rationality set to remake reality.

In medicine, science abstracts from the minutiae, and accidental details of sense data are used to create a feedback loop, to make incisions, to make cuts, in order to heal the body. Abstraction saves lives, even as it destroys other lives (or sometimes those same lives). In recent decades, medical and biological research has, of course, penetrated increasingly fundamental mechanisms, with genetic cures becoming a real possibility. Medicine, in short, stands for the erosion of the divide between fundamental and applied research, between science and technology. The resulting continuum is often termed technoscience: the becoming-operational and becoming-productive of scientific rationality. Law, as yet another strand of real abstraction, provides the protocols that regulate the procedures of technoscience (intellectual property) as well as those of finance (with the "liberalization" of financial markets being, of course, itself a form of regulation). Today's financial sector is, in turn, also crucially dependent on technoscience in the form of high-frequency trading algorithms whose autonomous actions far outrun the human capacity to react. I call this concrete abstraction: an ever-tighter integration of different vectors of "real abstraction"—monetary, technoscientific, and juridical real abstraction.[35]

In Sohn-Rethel's opposition between real abstraction and thought abstraction, the latter covers not only idealist philosophy but also science—or at least the ruling epistemology of modern science.[36] But have the "thought abstractions" of technoscience not also demonstrated their operational potential? Scientific rationality has long been implicated in the productive sector—as Sohn-Rethel acknowledges in remarks on science and technology in the service of production capital. We can again trace this back to merchant capitalism, or "print capitalism," in Benedict Anderson's words.[37] Peter Burke has opposed the "bureaucratic organization of knowledge" in China with the "entrepreneurial organization of knowledge" in early modern Europe—noting that, in the latter, "cognition was linked ever more closely to production via printing."[38] Industrial capitalism only intensified this process. While Sohn-Rethel considered the degree to which postwar production was shaped by "scientific intelligence" to be the first step toward a socialist reappropriation of the production process, the intensifying technoscientific becoming-operational and becoming-productive of science has given capitalism a new boost.[39]

The forms of real abstraction are anchored in institutional infrastructures. Marx had famously posited a "legal, political, religious, artistic or philosophic" superstructure in which economic and social conflicts are articulated and fought out.[40] In the twentieth century, sociologists and philosophers from Weber to Habermas and Bourdieu stressed the progressive autonomization of the different parts of this superstructure, such as art. Weber argued that in the process of modern rationalization, several distinct "value-spheres" emerge, which he identified as religion, the economy, politics, aesthetics, the erotic, and the intellectual.[41] Reworking and reducing this list, Habermas would later claim that Weber "characterized cultural modernity as the separation of the substantive reason expressed in religion and metaphysics into three autonomous spheres. They are: science, morality and art."[42] This is the sociological complement to Cassirer's pluralist epistemology.

For present purposes, I limit myself to economic, juridical, and technoscientific forms and their institutional infrastructure. These three vectors of real abstraction are the key preformations that shape capitalist modernity: this is form not as morphological Gestalt, but as operational structure. Modern reason is productivist, and its real abstractions become all the more operative as various vectors of real abstraction enter into a productive exchange. What I have termed a regime of "concrete abstraction" is produced by the ever-tighter integration of the vectors of real abstraction.[43]

Sohn-Rethel's key criterion for exchange being a "real abstraction" is that "in the exchange process, doing and thinking diverge on the part of the participants."[44] He clearly needs to maintain that this abstraction is not *just* conceptual but also actually takes a real social form. However, he also seems to make a logical slip in suggesting that it is a lack of awareness that makes it real rather than "intellectual." Real abstraction certainly remakes the world—it is not some ontological "deep structure" disconnected from appearance, but a constant pre-forming and in-forming. But does awareness—for instance, an awareness fostered by reading Marx—make capitalist market relations any less "real"?

Brenna Bhandar and Alberto Toscano have argued that "greater attention to the *legal* forms of property" problematizes "the unconscious character ascribed to commodity-exchange as a form of practical abstraction," as legal forms are, of course, consciously elaborated while still being real abstractions that are operative in the social world.[45] Meanwhile, Christoph Menke has proposed an ambitious critique of the modern conception of rights as a *form* that needs to be understood historically.[46] Indeed, I would argue that we need to conceive of legal abstraction as a consciously elaborated form of real abstraction. The value-form under capitalism is deeply dependent on the supposedly universal rights accorded to the abstract person, especially the right to own property.[47] Of course, some persons have always been more equal than others—and artificial juridical persons increasingly outstrip and outperform natural persons, who sign away rights by agreeing with any and all Terms & Conditions. The value-form thus needs the legal form or the *rights-form* as its counterpart.[48] The latter should not be thought of as mere superstructural reflections of the value-form; as Bhandar insists, "conceptions of legal subjectivity and juridical forms of property" are not reducible to economic exchange.[49]

The "vectorial" conception of concrete abstraction acknowledges that examples of integration, or at least collaboration and complicity, could already be found during the heyday of industrial capitalism: the very period marked by a progressive functional differentiation between, and relative autonomy of, different social spheres such as science, law, and art—as posited by Weber, Habermas, and Bourdieu.[50] Habermas's work is marked by the dialectic of specialization and publicness. The public sphere was the counterpart of the differentiated value-spheres: in the press, as the crucial medium of publicness, a supposedly "reasoning public" could argue over issues that could not be relegated to various cadres of specialists.[51] Politics itself—one of Weber's value-spheres—was a public matter par excellence; art, another. The tension between parliamentary party politics and the political in a more general and fundamental sense is mirrored by that between institutionalized art and the aesthetic. Just as representative politics is an enactment and a containment and neutralization of political antagonism, art is a fulfillment and a betrayal of the aesthetic promise.

Modern functional differentiation was productive in its own way. Autonomous science and an independent judiciary served a purpose—the former by producing fundamental research that could be translated into technological breakthroughs, and the latter by ensuring a stable legal framework for corporate and natural persons alike. With its premium on information and brands, post-Fordist semiocapitalism is marked by a market- and technology-driven reintegration of those semiautonomous spheres. Such vectorial integration is, in turn, never complete, and it produces interferences and contradictions that can be exploited—for instance, between the "enclosures" of intellectual property law and the deterritorializations of technology. However, what it means to own a book is being redefined by the agreements one signs when purchasing e-books. Ownership is becoming ever more partial and temporary and contradictory as juridical abstraction takes on the challenges of digital technology.

Both the value-form and the rights-form abstract from the material and sensory world. Sohn-Rethel quotes Marx to the effect that "not an atom of matter [*Naturstoff*]" enters into the composition of value, and the legal person is also abstracted from all particulars, at least in theory.[52] In practice, ever since nineteenth-century (racist) phrenology, psychology, and criminology, a variety of sciences were at the ready to determine which persons were more equal than others. Today, facial and voice recognition software, for instance, can be used for racial profiling or rejecting asylum claims. Still, the fundamental Hegelian notion of persons as interchangeable "units of freedom" (to which I shall return in chapter six, and in the next volume) stands as the ideological basis of the juridical apparatus, and the concretization (identification) of the person is farmed out precisely to technoscience.

The real abstraction of technoscience can be termed the *information-form*, to coin a pleonasm. If the basic operation of technoscience is a mathematical *Vermessung der Welt*, this quantification becomes the basis for computation. This was analog computation at first: the term "computers" famously referring to human, mostly female calculators working in observatories and laboratories, before becoming identified with machines in the 1950s. The first generation of electronic computers in the 1940s emerged in the military-industrial-academic complex of World War II. John von Neumann and others translated mathematical operations into electronic signals. Computers such as the ENIAC and the MANIAC, or IBM's SSEC, ran weather forecasts or simulated nuclear explosions—parsing and processing data to turn them into actionable information.[53]

As Alexander Galloway has stressed, taking cues from Flusser, data are "things having been given," while information means giving form or bringing out into form.[54] However, technoscientific datafication is always designed to become informed. Matteo Pasquinelli has noted that the term "digital code" refers to three different layers: binary digits encoding everything as zeros and ones; the programming language in which software is written; and scripts in such software that "[translate] the logic form of an algorithm," the latter constituting "the inner machinic logic of the code."[55] Digital algorithms, Pasquinelli avers, fundamentally come in two types: "algorithms to translate *information into other formats of information*" (like a text editing program or photo software) and algorithms that "accumulate information and extract metadata, that is, *information about information*" (like the software used by Google, Facebook, and sundry companies to map our habits and predict our preferences, or financial algorithms).[56]

Technoscience has culminated in an informational and networked paradigm in which life is to be (re)designed and managed.[57] Like automated Kantian categories, algorithms trawl vast quantities of data to identify patterns (consumer trends, suspicious behavior) that may not be apparent to any human eye or ear. [58] Informed data can be rematerialized in any number of production processes—3-D printing being today's phantasmagorico-real hylomorphism. Life itself has been de- and recoded by the information form: we can see the progression of the information form in the arc leading from Linnaeus's binomial taxonomy in the *Systema Naturae* (1735) to the publication of the double helix structure of DNA (1953). Genetics has reconfigured life in informatic terms: in terms of coded DNA sequences and the cellular protocols that regulate replication. That the informational paradigm in the life sciences is reductive is a just but not necessarily effective criticism; *it is productive because it is reductive.* It is the nature of this "productiveness" that needs to be questioned.

It is not only cellular depths that are mined for information; the same happens on the surface. Facial and voice recognition software, for instance, can be used for racial profiling or to reject asylum claims, while fitness trackers influence health insurance rates. Technoscience has culminated in an informational and networked paradigm in which life itself and its contingency are subject to constant (re)design and management. Algorithms trawl vast quantities of data to predict

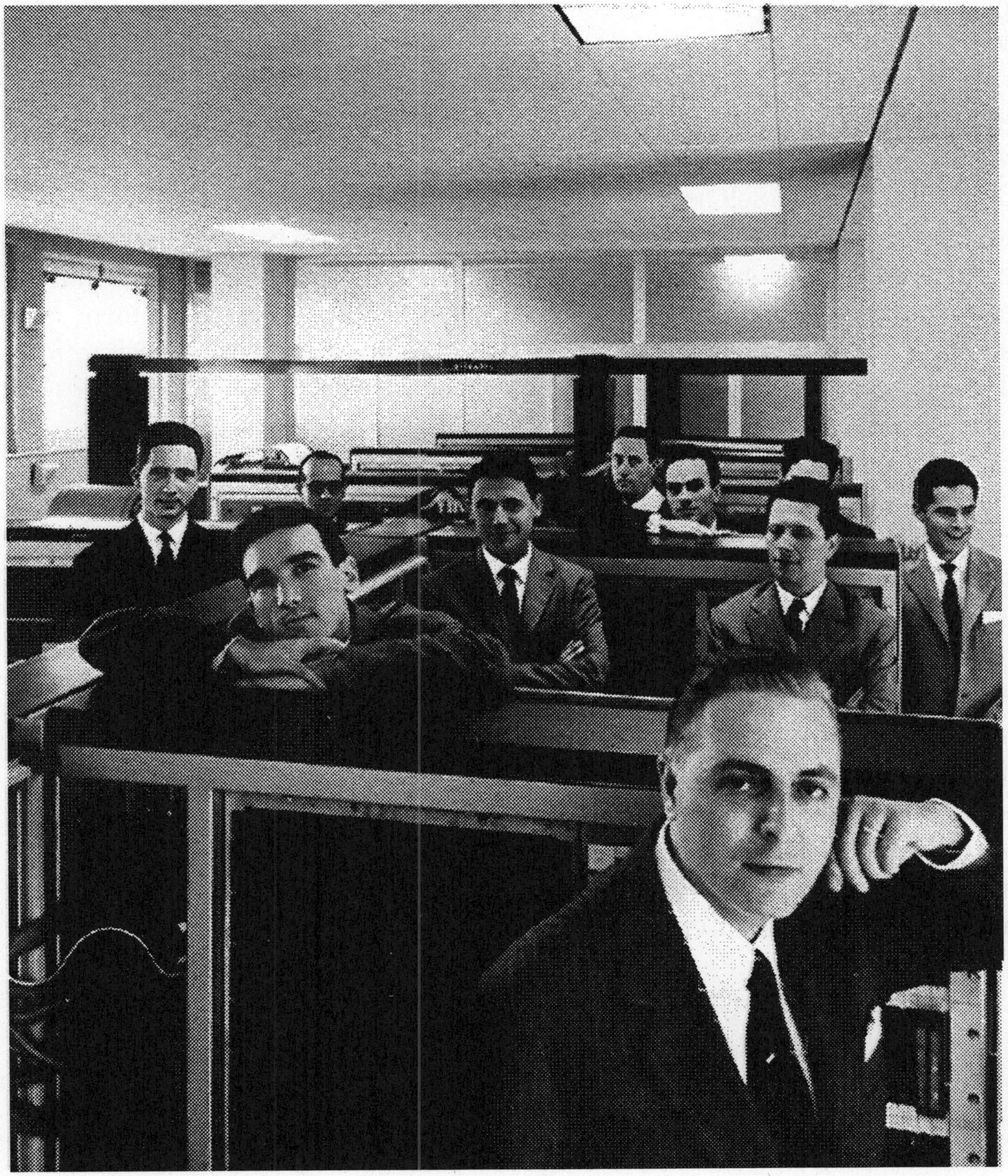

The Elea 9003 computer installed at the Monte dei Paschi bank, early 1960s

potential movements or occurrences that break the known patterns—whether they are fatal or profitable deviations from the norm.

If today's financialized capitalism both depends on and fuels techno-science, it is of course equally unthinkable without the juridical framework. In the register of the rights-form, the dialectic of subject and object manifests itself as that of person and property. In turn, both the legal person and property as real abstractions have concretized counterparts. In the economic register, property is translated as (potential) commodity—and for Marx, as noted, the commodity has a value-form and a physical form (*Naturalform*).[59] It is the latter that we perceive. The same, on the side of the subject, with labor: abstract and concrete labor. Similarly, the person can be a natural person who has certain basic rights merely by virtue of being recognizably a human being. On the other hand, the rights of intangible artificial persons may trump those of humans, while property loses its "natural form" of physical object in someone's possession and becomes subject to digital protocols and license agreements.

This produces, if not monsters, at least Monsanto; if not fascism, at least Facebook, or indeed the much-mooted Chinese "social credit" system. However, the ever-tighter integration also generates contradictions and conflicts between these forms of abstraction. Aesthetic and political strategies within concrete abstraction need to engage with the fault lines and contradictions created by ongoing processes of accumulation and expropriation. Crucial for both of these processes and for such critical interventions are design strategies.

Designing Information (Loss)

When abstraction becomes concrete, it takes the form of design. Informing matter so the value-form can take on an efficient, attractive "natural form," design is also shaped to the core by affordances of patented materials and technical solutions, and by the possibilities to copyright or trademark specific shapes, and by legal loopholes in corporate and tax law. Modern art, specialized in the failure of abstraction, frequently allied itself with design as the discipline that concretizes the abstract into form, that synthesizes the preformations into condensed concretion.

In 1962, Bruno Munari curated an exhibition titled "Arte programmata" (Programmed Art) that toured the showrooms of Olivetti, the Italian office machine company.[60] One artists' group that Munari involved, Gruppo N, had contact with the editors of *Quaderni Rossi*, which served as an incubator for Operaist Marxism.[61] Much later, *Quaderni* editor Antonio Negri would write that with their programmed art, Gruppo N had participated in an "orgiastic Taylorization of art."[62] This diagnosis makes a certain degree of intuitive sense, as Gruppo N's modus operandi came out of prewar Concrete art and seemed to be predicated on the efficiency of rational procedures. However, if, as Armin Medosch suggests, practices such as these "contributed to the fetishization of intellectual labor" and modeled the artist after "the planning department [...] of cybernetic society," the moment and movement of programmed art comes into focus as a tipping point between Fordism and post-Fordism, and between the modern and the contemporary.[63]

On *Quaderni*'s pages, Romano Alquati kept a watchful eye on Olivetti, where he was doing "co-research" with Socialist Party militants embedded in the company.[64] Alquati looked for forms of self-organized resistance by the "mass workers" populating Olivetti's seemingly perfectly run cybernetic factory.[65] He notes that Olivetti is in the business of selling "machines that run on programs," and that its own conveyor-belt production process makes use of "robots."[66] Ultimately, all this needs to be seen in the context of "the global logic of neo-capitalism connected to the phase of automation, of decentralization, of delegated planning, of enterprise-wide integrated planning, etc."[67]

One prominent "machine running on programs" sold by Olivetti in the early 1960s was the Elea 9003—one of the first fully transistorized mainframe computers, engineered in the late 1950s by Mario Tchou and designed by Ettore Sottsass. Sottsass sought to both humanize and flexibilize the room-size mainframe computers of the era. The Elea 9003 was designed in the form of an open series of modules that could be rearranged in any number of ways. Sottsass's design is based on hinged "wings" that are combined in larger units named "threes" in a system that allows for extension and customization. The "boxes" are connected to each other with beams that can hold cables, and the entire constellation is, in turn, connected to units that run magnetic tapes (for mass data storage) and perforated tape (for input and output), as well as with the operating console.[68] Work on this interface was farmed out to the information-design specialists of the "New Bauhaus" in Ulm: Tomás Maldonado and his assistants and students Gui Bonsiepe, Hans von Klier, and Andries van Onck.[69] With the Elea 9003, Olivetti participated in a push for automation that was also very much designed to undermine workers' organization. With the immaterial labor of the planning department getting ever more emphasis, physical production could be partly automated and also more easily outsourced—developments that the Operaists were among the first to seriously analyze.

Intriguingly, as has been briefly hinted in the last chapter, Alquati combines orthodox Marxist tropes with a focus on information as "the most important variable" of the industrial economy: "Information is the essence of labor-power, which the worker, with the help of constant capital [the machinery] and on the basis of judgments, measurements and elaborations transfers to the means of production so as to imprint the object with all those changes in form that will give it the desired use-value."[70] This is rather remarkable. As Pasquinelli has pointed out, Alquati seems to develop an account of cognitive capitalism and immaterial labor long before Maurizio Lazzarato et al.[71] However, his notion of information is strangely polyvalent. If Alquati "calls information precisely all the innovative micro-decisions that workers have to take along the production process" both to "give *form* to the machinic apparatus" and the production process as a whole, and to "give *form* to the product," a certain *information loss* would, nonetheless, seem to occur in this very product.[72] The commodity is, after all, a broken index; the fetish disavows its fetishized condition.

In theorizing labor in informational terms, Alquati suggests that information about the various decisions taken during the production process is embedded in the commodity as a "qualitative index of the socially necessary labor-time," allowing the product to be judged as the "vessel" of a specific amount of information.[73] From the decisions embedded in the final product, we can thus deduce the famous socially necessary labor-time, which, according to Marx, determines the true value of the commodity, hidden behind the fetishistic appearance. Alquati essentially *redefines this appearance as information*. But can we actually "read" this information? Labor may be "encrypted in the commodity," but does anybody have the key to decode it?[74] If Marx's version of the labor theory of value never posited that the labor invested in the production process could be calculated directly, without recourse to exchange value, the commodity's becoming-informational has only severed the indexical link with labor more fully.

An ad for Sottsass's 1969 Valentine typewriter in a neo–Art Deco style shows a woman almost straddling the elegant portable typewriter, with a man right next to her, looking on. Here, we get information not about the production *of* the typewriters but about the intended production *with* the typewriters—a supposedly affective and non-alienated production, in which one could dash off love poetry or theory on one's Valentine in between fishing and hunting. The design departments of most self-respecting museums own a copy of the Valentine, just as the art departments would own work by Marcel Duchamp. It may be instructive to return to two of Barnett Newman's two "bad objects" from the first chapter: the hypothetical Bauhaus screwdriver and the Duchampian readymade. One could slightly recast them with Sottsass's Valentine and Duchamp's *Traveler's Folding Item* (1916), a cover for an Underwood typewriter. As Jaleh Mansoor has suggested, these make for an instructive comparison. Not only did Olivetti acquire Underwood in 1959; beyond such anecdotes, Sottsass's sleek red Valentine indicates that "the opacity and mystery once reserved for the auratic art object [...] had moved into the domain of the anonymously generated commodity generated of collective socially necessary labor time."[75]

This, of course, was already acknowledged—or polemically posited—by the Duchampian readymade, although the latter added its own layers of references in order to reclaim functional objects for art by adding conceptual in-jokes. The value of the mythical Bauhaus screwdriver is supposed to lie in its functional yet beautiful form and in its mass replicability; without fully breaking with modernist design, the Valentine adds a libidinal element and an aura of boho exclusivity. With the readymade, functional form is folded into Duchampian linguistic and geometric games. In contrast to the topological blob that is *Traveler's Folding Item*, the urinal of *Fountain* has more pleasing forms, and Duchamp may not have been as indifferent to these properties of the "Madonna of the Bathroom" as he sometimes claimed; nonetheless, as an artwork *Fountain* is not valorized qua good design.[76]

In the course of the twentieth century, both types of object—the designed item and its readymade appropriation—came to be eligible for copyright protection. In her analysis of French intellectual property legislation and jurisprudence, Judith Ickowicz has analyzed how

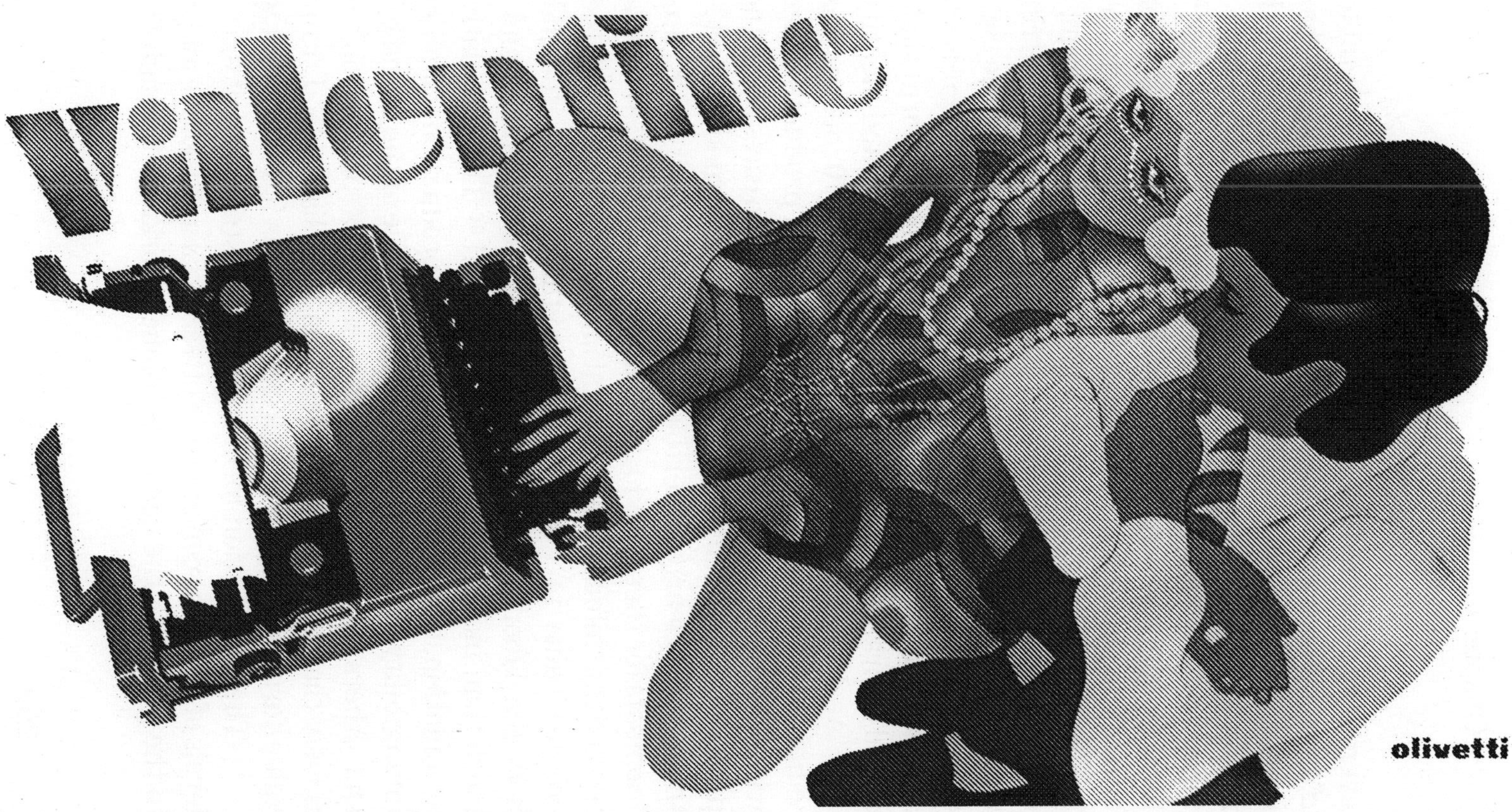

Advertisement for Olivetti's Valentine typewriter

even very basic industrial design came to be protectable as *oeuvres d'esprit* comparable to novels or paintings, while Duchamp's ready-mades, too, were eventually deemed copyrightable.[77] In this case, the notion of form (what is protected by copyright is not an idea but its formal articulation) had to be stretched to denote the "intellectual form [*forme intellectuelle*]" of the piece.[78] Duchamp's recontextualization of the object has not (or barely) transformed its natural form, but it has produced a specific information-form, value-form, and rights-form. The work of critics, curators, and viewers contributes to the market value, but only Duchamp or his estate have the right to market copies of this urinal as *Fountain*. Here, then, design is charged with additional meanings to result in an information-form that amounts to a kind of branding: the object as carrier of a brand identity.

As Jean Baudrillard argued around 1970, design produces sign-value.[79] It invites decryption in terms of a product's coded difference with other commodities. To put it bluntly: Who cares about the production process of the Valentine, or any Sottsass-designed artifact? The objects themselves clearly advertise the fact that they don't care; the *advertisements* for these products certainly advertise it. What Lazzarato has termed the "informational content and cultural content" of the commodity creates value in ways that, if anything, severs the indexical cord between labor and appearance, between substance and form, even more than industrial capitalism ever did.[80] The cumulative effects of automation, outsourcing, and offshore production, combined with the intangibility of "labor" invested in the value of the brand by consumers and others, obscure the "hidden abode of production" more efficaciously than ever.[81] The information-form has indeed transformed the value-form—severing the already tenuous indexical link with labor.

The information-form is stacked or staggered: it exists at various levels of sensuous concretion. Sottsass's Elea structure and casing relate to the design of the computer's inner workings through the operating console—the interface between the two. Even disregarding the design of the physical casing, data are not necessarily informed in ways that are compatible with human senses. As Trevor Paglen notes apropos of Harun Farocki's concept of operational images, which the latter had started using the context of works such as *Eye/Machine III* (2003): "Machines don't need funny animated yellow arrows and green boxes in grainy video footage to calculate trajectories or recognize moving bodies and objects. Those marks are for the benefit of humans—they're meant to show humans how a machine is seeing."[82] To invoke examples used by Pasquinelli, the information-form does not become sensible in algorithms tracking our behavior in the same way that it does in a word-processing or photo-editing program. Even so, we get brief glimpses of our role as providers of data for a sprawling informational hyperobject when we get personalized ads, or when we sign up to some kind of social media platform. As Paul Chan put it, in his analysis of such digital forms: "Now, as then, a form is something we fill out with what matters in our lives. And the principal substance that motivates and underwrites this operation is every bit as valuable, vital, and immaterial as what was once called the soul. Today, we call this substance data."[83]

The information-form interacts with the other vectors of real abstraction to mutate subjects, objects, and their concatenations. Design produces commodified objects as well as subjects, and quasi-subjects and quasi-objects, in ever new varieties. Instagram influencers, who gain followers by "endorsing" fashion and other design products and turning their lifestyle into a business model, are one striking mutation to occur in recent years. Here, consumption is made directly productive—at least on the micro level—and the self-objectification of their lifestyle makes influencers aspirational role models. The influencer, of course, is a creature of networked platform capitalism: a self-objectifying subject. Others become informational objects against their will.

Formerly ideologized as autonomous, art is now seen as being at the forefront of the "creative industries," as design-ified commodities have increasingly mimicked the artwork—particularly in economic terms, as discussed in the previous chapter. Art itself has been turned into a financial product, one speculative tool among others in one's portfolio. Even before the advent of NFTs, the art market was becoming increasingly software-based. While some major collectors have their own custom-built algorithms, websites such as ArtFacts and ArtRank offer help to a larger group. The latter site identifies "prime emerging artists based on qualitatively weighted metrics including web presence (verified social media counts, inbound links), studio capacity and output, market maker contracts and acquisitions, major collector and museum support, gallery representation and auction results."[84]

Natascha Sadr Haghighian, an artist who has long worked with heteronyms and deployed various strategies that counter the commodification of the artist-author as bankable genius, found herself confronted with a website that aggregates data and translates them into a "career curve"—a person's information-form on the art market. Sadr Haghighian's curve did not look great. Playing on the sexist, objectifying overtones of "curves," the artist wrote an open letter titled *Dear Artfukts, Look at My Curve: A Report to An Academy*, with a title page graced by a redesigned, abstracted version of her career graph. In the text, the artist disputes the site's logic, according to which a lack of high-profile solo shows can only mean that you're failing as embodied value-form, as a self-entrepreneurial subject in today's dynamic, disruptive, networked capitalism.[85] Her piece can be read an attempt to retake control of the process of losing control:

> I don't identify with what the image represents but I participate in it as much as it participates in me, drawing on its character and power as it draws on my character and power. The curve and I are entangled

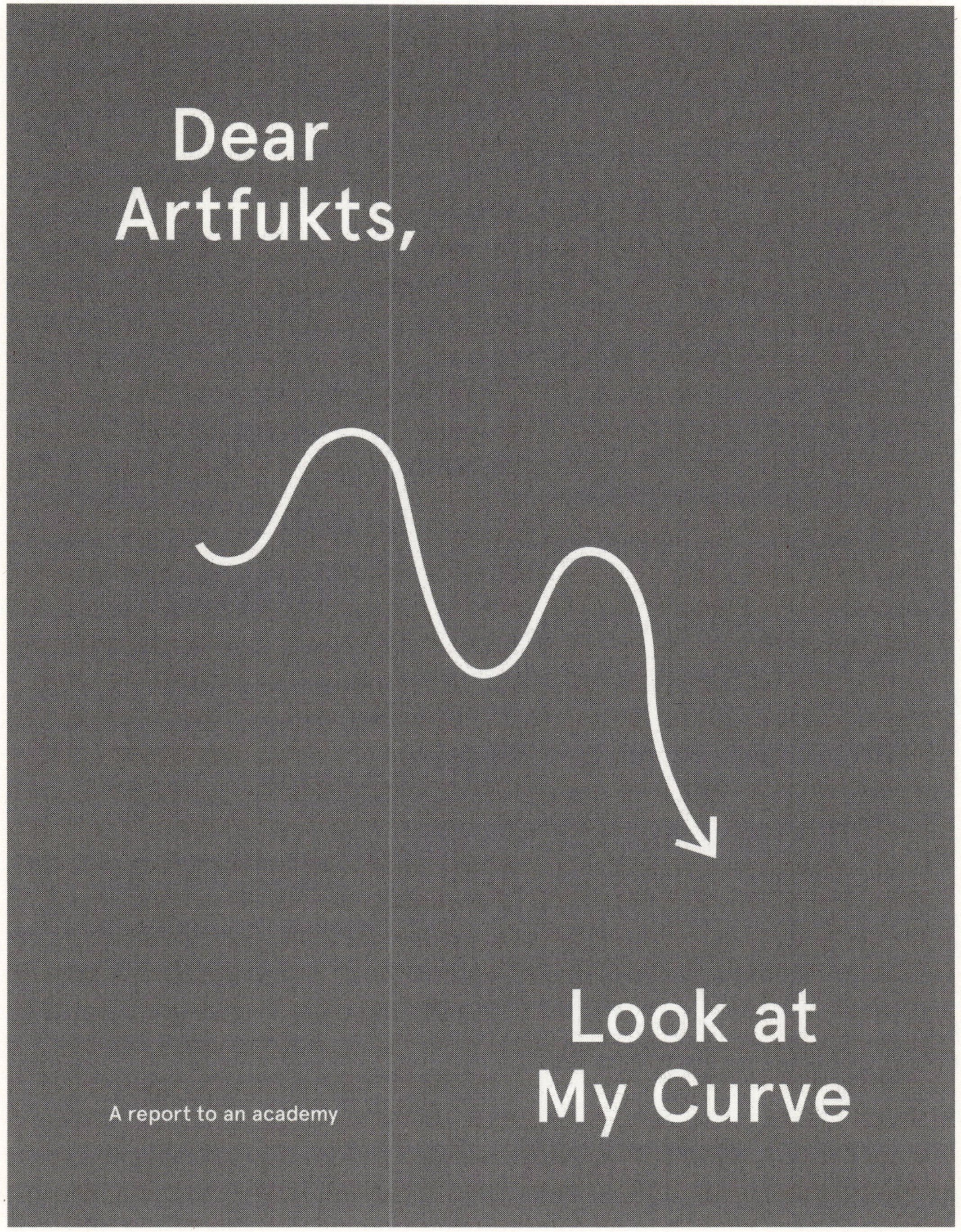
Dear Artfukts,

Look at My Curve

A report to an academy

Title page of Natascha Sadr Haghighian, *Dear Artfukts, Look at My Curve: A Report to an Academy*, 2013

> in a mimetic dance, imitating and becoming one another. Our shapes submerge into one amorphous thing as we interact, and in this process of participation I am not a subject looking at an object that represents me.[86]

In the essay, Sadr Haghighian responds to Nairy Baghramian's concern that in some art discourse, artworks "are sometimes treated like quasi-subjects capable of their own autonomous thinking," and that this could result in once more treating artists like quasi-mute objects (something that institutional critique had fought against).[87] However, Sadr Haghighian's curve shows that objectivation can and will take different forms—such as a designed objectivation of a career on the basis of networked data aggregation. This is both (almost by accident) a form of "social credit" that can impact an artist's life and (first and foremost) an investment tool.

In either case, the artist's data double functions as an online digital object composed of data and metadata, providing information for investors/collectors. How to get rid of oneself, of one's financialized and expropriated data body? In writing on "becoming a curve," Sadr Haghighian attempts to reclaim some degree of agency, fighting against her uncanny data-design doppelgänger. The graph clearly does not do justice to her life and practice in any way, yet its abstract-concrete representation of her career threatens to usurp her place. The stylized, elegant version of the graph on the essay's title page turns it from an investment tool into something much less functional: something closer to the real abstractions of modernist art, sensuously concrete but far from "productive."

Enmeshed in Networks

Sohn-Rethel's value-form, once constituted, seems to allow for no further development until it meets its dialectical demise in the transition to communism. By contrast, in recent times, the debate between Luc Boltanski/Arnaud Esquerre and Nancy Fraser concerning the "standard form" of value and the "asset form" and "collection form" suggests that differentiation is needed to understand the mutations of contemporary capitalism.[88] While I agree with Fraser that Boltanski and Esquerre overprivilege the collection form (neglecting, for instance, the use of art collections as asset), I would also insist that contemporary assets and collections are different instantiations of the *network-form of value*, which is the fundamental structuring principle of value in the realm of concrete abstraction. Collections and assets, for all their specificities, are also manifestations of the network-form: their value depends on data management and information politics between nodes in a network.

The regime of concrete abstraction amounts to a networked enmeshing of platforms, products, and lifestyles that is as dependent on neoliberal "deregulation" as it is on high-frequency trading algorithms. Design today is fundamentally the design of networks and of networked applications, services, products, and lifestyles. Design forges fragile and temporary syntheses of the networked forms of value, rights, and information. Under the onslaught of creative disruptions that might as well be called creative deformations of the old order, everything that is solid melts into Airbnb.

The dissolution of old juridical obstacles that hindered the total mobilization of equivalence enables disruptive design solutions just as it generates forms of entropy that are so many opportunities for further disaster-capitalist accumulation. Crises give rise to tailor-made fixes waiting to be marketed. During the COVID-19 pandemic, information-forms proper to Big Pharma and Big Tech merged in various (failed) virus tracking apps. The operational hylomorphism of networked design solutions—which had long promised (some of) us an ever-smoother life—turned out to be perfectly compatible with a state of emergency. Being stuck in an Airbnb at the other end of the world as one's cheap airline tickets have been canceled and everything goes into lockdown—this situation, too, is a product of operational abstraction, and a boon for social media giants. The state of exception is a state of product development.

Caroline Levine historicizes the network in her analysis of novels such as Dickens's *Bleak House*. While the tendency to equate form with a whole—with a Gestalt standing out against a ground—has always been strong, Levine understands the network as a specific type of form, "defined patterns of interconnection and exchange that organize social and aesthetic experience."[89] In a rather brilliant analysis, she argues that *Bleak House* "does for character something like what Marx did for commodities: casting narrative persons less as powerful and symbolic agents in their own right than as moments in which complex and invisible forces cross."[90] However, one can wonder if Levine does not underestimate the disruptive effects of the digital network, if her historical formalism does not end up suggesting that 'twas ever thus.

By contrast, Galloway and Eugene Thacker insist that "in recent decades the processes of globalization have mutated from a system of control houses in a relatively small number of power hubs to a system of control infused into the material fabric of distributed networks."[91] Today's Empire, then, would be a different beast from Dickens's British Empire. Breaking with 1990s net utopianism and its "tired of trees" rhetoric, Galloway and Thacker maintain that networks, even distributed networks, are not intrinsically liberating but impose new forms of control. Recently, Galloway has also attacked Bruno

Latour, the doyen of "actor-network theory," for his belief that "systems are disruptive of hierarchies, that bazaars are better than cathedrals, that networks corrode the power of the sovereign, that markets are the most natural, most democratic, and most scientifically accurate heuristic for redistributing and indeed defining knowledge," and for being unable to "acknowledge the historicity of networks. Such a step requires a number of things, but most importantly it requires an acknowledgement of the special relationship between networks and the industrial infrastructure, a relationship that began in the middle twentieth century and has become dominant now after the turn of the millennium."[92]

Latourian "networkism" risks being complicit in technolibertarian forms of net utopianism in the service of corporate interests. One could argue that the value-form has always been a network-form; one only need recall Marx's insistence that "the money-form is but the reflex, thrown upon one single commodity, of the value relations between all the rest."[93] The "social relations" between commodities and their value were, in fact, a distortion of the *real* relations, the productive relations. Insofar as "content is not a key issue for a digital object; what really matters are relations," networked (platform) capitalism sees the ultimate triumph of the value-form.[94] This networked iteration of the value-form is as dependent on digital technology as it is on a legal framework that cannily uses the free-trade agreements, competition between nation-states, and legal loopholes that characterize the Empire of globalization. Platform capitalism enmeshes users in the network-form in such a way as to generate a new kind of behavioral surplus.[95] Every little chat or shared meme produces information, and hence value—on the basis of rights that have been signed away.

Lacking activity on social networks may increasingly become a career risk and relational hazard. You have to keep moving, to keep producing traces. In the words of Geert Lovink and Ned Rossiter,

"The corporate assumption is that no matter how small, there is always an event in our lives that we can talk about. And it is especially the small talk that marketing experts are interested in." Noting that what we have today are "unstable networks with weak ties among their members, in which "we pass around status updates," Lovink and Rossiter theorize *organized* networks. On the one hand, "organized networks have existed for centuries. Just think of the Jesuits."[96] On the other hand, digital organized networks of the kind the authors propose (networks with strong links that enable organizational work over long durations) are said to not yet exist; hence, their text is propositional rather than descriptive.

Meanwhile, art-based anti-capitalist, anti-racist, feminist, or queer practices have continued to use the dominant social media platforms—in conjunction with physical assemblies such as workshops, reading groups, training sessions, or cookouts. Such meetings are networks physically manifested, and transformed in the process. As Werker Collective has put it, social media has a great potential to "mobilize the collective body [...] especially when online and offline collectivities invigorate each other to demand equal rights, equal pay, and respect."[97] But what if the dialectic between online and offline is brutally interrupted? In the early days of the COVID-19 crisis and lockdown, Kader Attia wrote a great rant (on Facebook) about the dire consequences of events being canceled, not just at La Colonie, but across the board of emancipatory practice; as much as the cancellation of gatherings was necessary, it was hard not to sympathize with Attia's outcry. Black Lives Matter protests went on to underline the necessity—with precautions being taken and a degree of risk being accepted—of physical protests that take the outrage found on Twitter to the streets, channeling it into transformative social forms. Meanwhile, the Far Right uses social media to reframe those protests and instill fear of "Marxists" and "antifa" in the minds of suburban voters; using social media to organize in real space and take to the streets is not enough if others are allowed to create the subsequent narrative.[98]

Surviving Unlivable Forms, or Performing Preformations Otherwise

In physical assemblies, the network takes on a reassuringly concrete form. The people you're having endless circular discussions and destructive ad hominem arguments with may be impossible, but they're *people*. In the digital network, who is to say if there is a living person behind an avatar—or if it is, in fact, a bot? For Aristotle, the true form of the human person was not their physical body, but the soul that animates it. Thus the *morphe* is not always the visible form. A human being and its sculptural representation do not have the same form; nor do a living person and a dead body, for the soul has departed from the latter.[99] Does the morphe of an entity posting propaganda on Facebook matter? What kinds of relations and assemblages between human and technical entities are possible, and are desirable?

One dystopian answer to such questions emerged in 2016, as Steve Bannon and others unleashed the potential of the troll army that had emerged on message boards in the last few years. In 2018, artist Jonas Staal organized an exhibition about Bannon as a "propaganda artist" that focused not only on the films he directed but also on his involvement with the online alt-right. If Staal tends to focus on physical assemblies—for instance, with his New World Summit assemblies, which bring together representatives of stateless peoples and blacklisted political organizations—it is not to naturalize the physical gathering as universal or transhistorical form. Rather, this is a tactical use of this form in and against contemporary conditions. Both online networks and physical gatherings are "natural forms" taken by the networked value-, rights-, and information-forms. Or rather: they will be natural(ized) forms as long as we resist engaging with the sometimes conflicting and contradictory ways in which they have been preformed, and the ways in which these preformations are performed.

For March 26, 2020, Staal and lawyer Jan Fermon had planned the "pre-trial" launch event for their Collectivize Facebook lawsuit—also announced on Facebook, of course—at Hebbel am Ufer (HAU) in Berlin. In the end, under the state of exception, this had to take the form of a website launch and an online video, in which Staal and Fermon explain the key points of the indictment (available on the site), which takes aim at Facebook (and Google, and the other tech giants) as "new feudal overlords" appropriating people's (informational) labor.[100] If capitalist technoscience is an operational hylomorphism that remakes matter and humans and social relations, then to work against such preformations and toward different technosocial formalizations may involve the seemingly impossible dream of a collectivization of Facebook (which, its reputation in tatters, has since renamed its holding company Meta), as well as the development and use of open-source alternatives to the dominant platforms.

Modern reason is productive and productivist. Its real abstractions have concrete effects—all the more so because various strands of real abstraction become increasingly integrated, enmeshed in the network. This productive reason creates facts—scientific, legal, social, historical facts. More often than not, forced synthesis by design creates forms that are impossible to live with and in. As Kerstin Stakemeier puts it, the "subject of capitalism inhabits an unlivable form."[101] The question then becomes how to live, how to form differently—under adverse and indeed impossible conditions?

Forms are frozen antinomies. In their manifesto *Now*, the Invisible Committee quotes Lukács to the effect that two mutually excluding principles that don't cancel each other out *become form.*[102] One could rephrase this in terms of the dialectical tensions between, for instance, modern ideas of emancipation and self-realization and the matrixes of economic, juridical, and technological real abstraction that channel and reroute desires and practices, resulting in forms of survival rather than forms of life. How to redesign concrete abstraction? How to perform its preformations otherwise? How to organize networks differently? When institutions and corporations post black squares on social media as part of the "Blackout Tuesday" campaign action against racist police violence, this digital black square no longer stands for a colonial-era joke about Blackness, but for progressive protest against anti-Black violence—without necessitating any actual change for the organizations that post the squares, or for the social media platforms they use.[103] On the other hand, Staal and Fermon's Facebook campaign opens up a vista for radically transforming actually existing platforms, for redesigning networks and the forms of subjectivity they foster.

More often than not, the antinomies of productive produce impossible and unlivable forms. How to live and act within those formal constraints? As deformed subjects attempting to attain a degree of self-organization by intensifying self-exploitation, we cultivate an art of breakdown in precarious affinity groups, coalitions, and alliances. When Sadr Haghighian works collectively as part of the Society of Friends of Halit and the NSU-Komplex Auflösen tribunal, which addresses the German state apparatus' complicity in the neo-Nazi NSU murders, this is exactly the kind of networking that will not contribute to her art-market "curve."[104] Grand (re)designs à la Collectivize Facebook may come out of such practices, but it remains a frequently unglamorous slog, a long march amid chaotic events. In the accelerating storm of history, today's historical formalists try to construct the necessary out of the impossible.

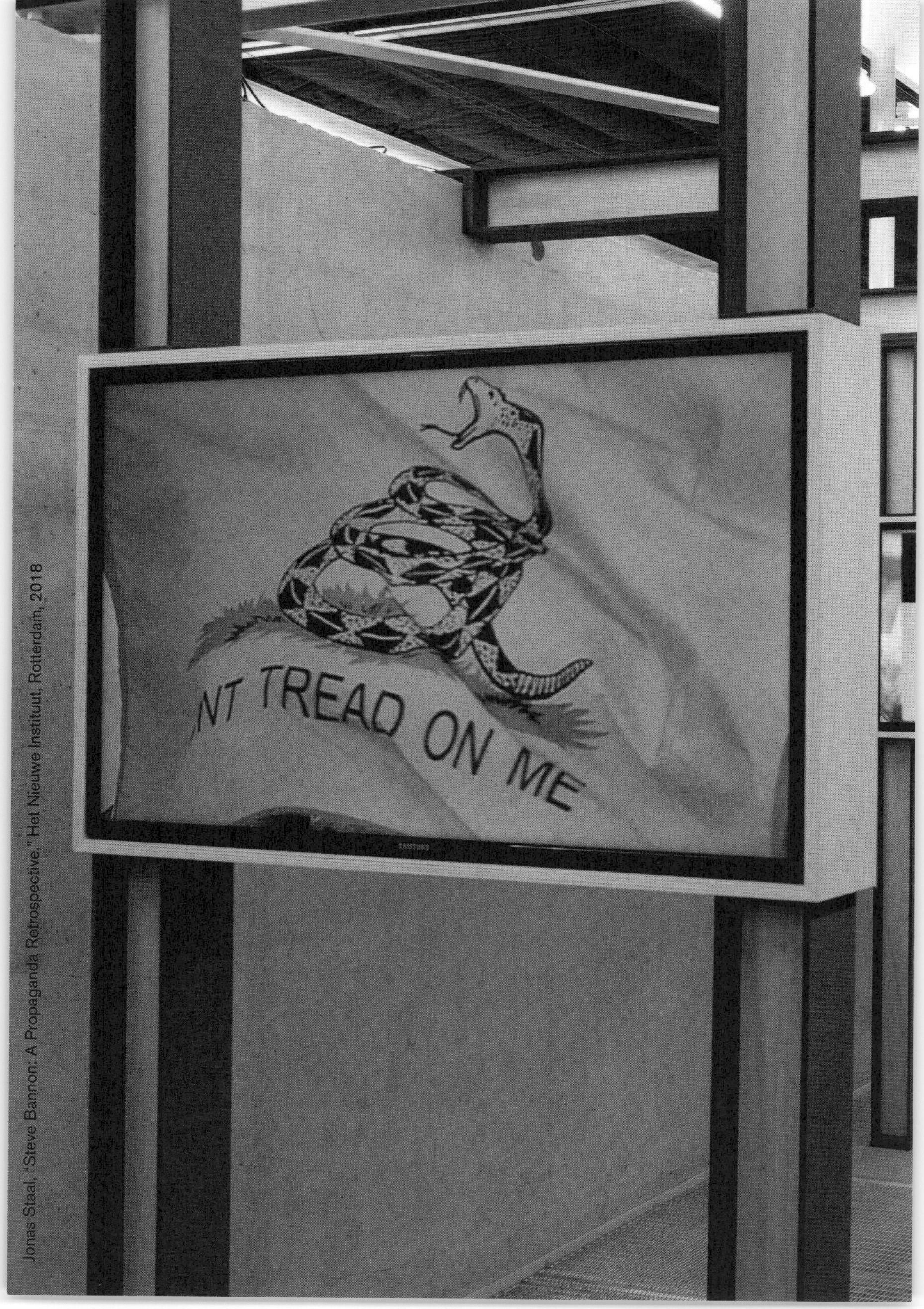

Jonas Staal, "Steve Bannon: A Propaganda Retrospective," Het Nieuwe Instituut, Rotterdam, 2018

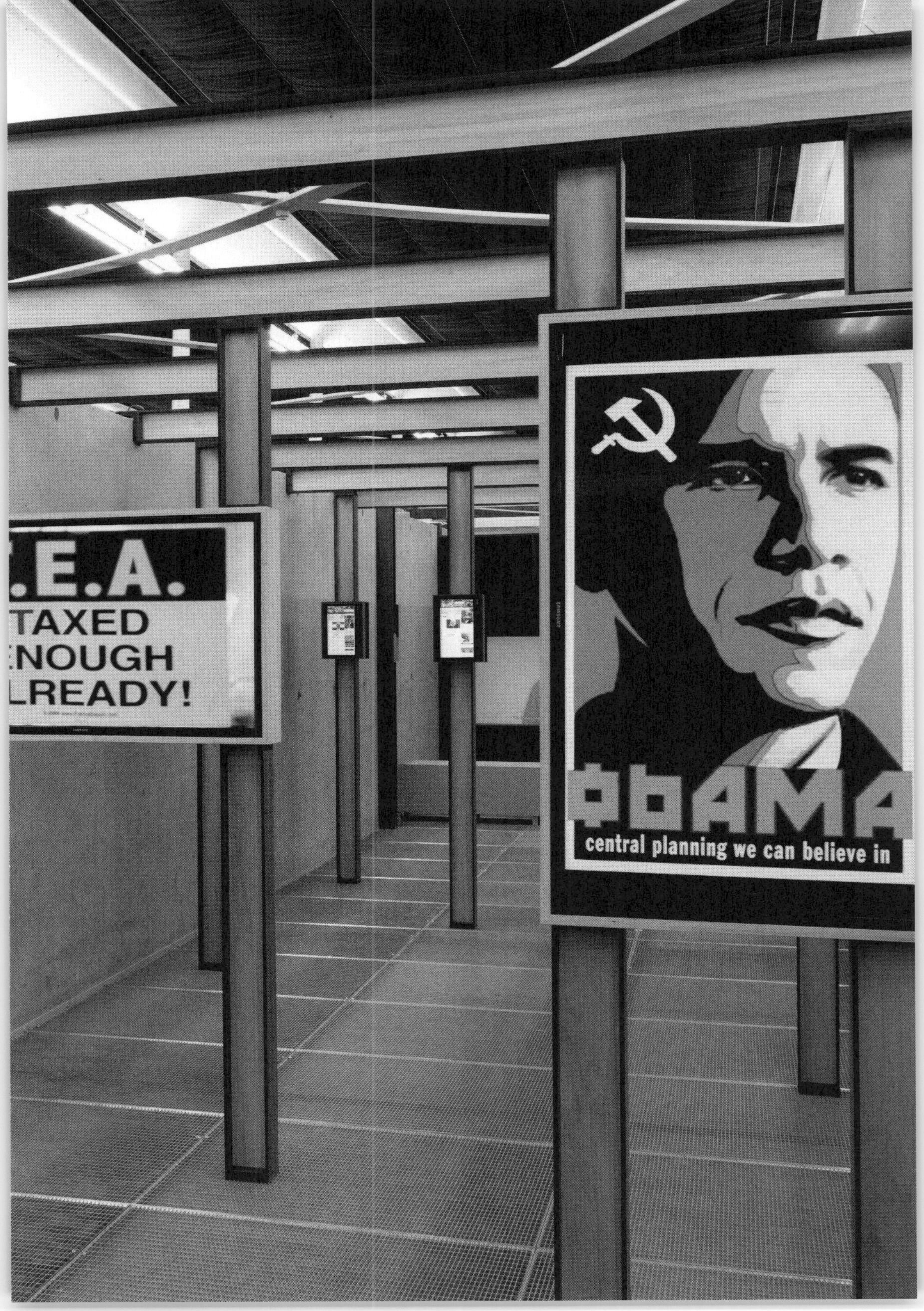
.E.A.
TAXED
ENOUGH
LREADY!
OBAMA
central planning we can believe in

Condensing Concretion

Beatriz Colomina and Mark Wigley have noted that the human "radiates design in all directions," and that this leaves its imprint on "the land, the oceans, the atmosphere, the plants, animals, organisms of every kind, chemicals, genetic makeup, and all frequencies of the mainly invisible electromagnetic spectrum."[105] The planet and its (former) commons have been remade by design, which manifests itself less in specific "traditional" objects but rather in scattered hyperobjects—to use Timothy Morton's term—that do not fully manifest themselves to our senses and our understanding.[106] Having been over-designed by too many cooks, the planet is acting up: total design breeds planetary chaos. If "the human is permanently suspended between being the cause and the effect, between designing living systems and being designed by them," then another wave of forceful redesign is already underway.[107]

For the time being, it is the fascists who reap the benefits of this, precisely by denying all complexity and offering simple Darwinian solutions for those who fear the loss of their privileges. In the false concretions of fascism, complex conditions get reduced to a single entity that explains everything away: a snowball held aloft on the US Senate floor shows that global warming is a hoax; a criminal asylum seeker shows that immigration (by brown people) is the mother of all evils. Reports that there are far fewer Muslims in Europe than most people think are immediately challenged by right-wing sites: "There are fewer 'fewer Muslims' than you'd think"![108] A conspiracist worldview could be said to be at the root of fascism: the *Volk* has to be defended against the (Jewish, Muslim, liberal, feminist, queer) Others that are undermining it for their own gain. It's not just that refugees coming to Europe and the US are "economic refugees"; they are really only the foot soldiers of a sinister program of "population exchange" and "white genocide." COVID-19 was a conspiracy by Bill Gates or George Soros, and Donald Trump is secretly fighting a cabal of murderous liberal pedophiles.

If migrants and minorities as well as the "hoax" of global warming and "cancel culture" are attacked, this is because they all are seen as gnawing away at historical privilege—even the relative privilege of the white underclass in the West. The implied message of today's fascist demagogues is that everything needs to change so that everything can remain the same—only worse. The pressures will only intensify. As the artist Franz Wilhelm Seiwert put it in 1929, when historical fascism was in the ascendant: all stabilization is a con.[109]

The political and aesthetic challenge is to provide concretions that effectively condense but do not negate complexity, and that counter the deadly fascist logic of scapegoating. Paul Chan has reminisced about his local McDonald's in the crisis of the early 1990s: "The McDonald's where I went now and then closed toward the tail end of the '91 recession; so did other businesses in the area. At the time I didn't think much of it, and if I did, I thought it strange."[110] The place seemed to do good business, since the neighborhood didn't have a grocery store or any kind of community center, so it doubled as those. Chan remarks that he was "too young and naive to know" much about the causes of the depression, and economic lingo was

> as abstract and remote to [him] as the actual reasons behind the appearance of a recession are in reality. [...] Survival had nothing to do with measuring the rise and fall of economic indicators, but the cunning of living between these inhuman quantifications, and finding novel ways to be unmoved and unmoored by their movements, in any direction. Progress was not chasing profit, but standing firm where you happened to have found yourself, against the forces that bull or bear either way.[111]

But how do these inhuman quantifications actually shape the in-between spaces that we traverse or doggedly occupy? It is both necessary and potentially dangerous to *condense* the distributed condition of concrete abstraction. As the case of Chan's local McDonald's shows, abstract quantifications *can* take on concrete qualities without isolating the concrete as a disconnected bad object or good fetish. Critical fetishization must counter these false concretions in its attempts to make sensate the distributed condition of concrete abstraction.

NOTES

1 Hal Foster, *Design and Crime (and Other Diatribes)* (London: Verso, 2002), 17–18, 19.

2 Jacques-Eugène Armengaud et al., *The Practical Draughtsman's Book of Industrial Design, and Machinist's and Engineer's Drawing Companion*, trans. William Johnson (London: Longman, Brown, Green and Longmans, 1853), iii.

3 For the latter, see https://www.iso.org/standard/71885.html.

4 See https://mnemosynedrone.info/ (site discontinued).

5 For a critical analysis, see Aleksandra Shatskikh, "Inscribed Vandalism: The Black Square at One Hundred," *e-flux journal*, no. 85 (October 2017), https://www.e-flux.com/journal/85/155475/inscribed-vandalism-the-black-square-at-one-hundred/.

6 Fredric Jameson, "Culture and Finance Capital," in *The Cultural Turn: Selected Writings on the Postmodern, 1983–1998* (London: Verso, 1998), 136–61.

7 Ferdinand Lion, "Der Geist des Kapitalismus in aestheticis," in *Synopsis: Festgabe für Alfred Weber*, ed. Edgar Salin (Heidelberg: Lambert Schneider, 1948), 247–48.

8 Jameson, "Culture and Finance Capital," 151.

9 Jameson, 151.

10 Fredric Jameson, "The Aesthetics of Singularity," *New Left Review*, no. 92 (March–April 2015): 116.

11 Carl Einstein, *Die Fabrikation der Fiktionen* (late 1930s), ed. Sibylle Penkert (Reinbek: Rowohlt, 1973), 311; translation from Kerstin Stakemeier, "Breaks with the Future: A Halt? Confessions, Some Notes," in *Futurity Report*, ed. Eric C. H. de Bruyn and Sven Lütticken (Berlin: Sternberg Press, 2020), 54–55.

12 Stakemeier, 55.

13 Jameson, "Culture and Finance Capital," 154.

14 Riet Wijnen, *Marlow Moss* (Amsterdam: Kunstverein Publishing, 2013).

15 Riet Wijnen, *Conversation Six: Double-Lines*, booklet (self-pub., 2018), 9.

16 See, for instance, Carel Blotkamp, *Mondrian: The Art of Destruction*

(London: Reaktion Books, 2001), 190–94.

17 This effect has, of course, become more pronounced over time as the paintings age.

18 See Theo van Doesburg, "Schilderkunst en plastiek: Elementarisme (Manifest-fragment)," *De Stijl* 7, no. 7 (1926–27): 85; the first and only issue of Van Doesburg's magazine *Art Concret* (containing the Concrete art manifesto) came out in 1930, but the term was discussed and used widely in the years to come.

19 Liam Gillick, "Abstract," written for "Abstract Possible," Museo Tamayo, Mexico City, 2011, https://www.on-curating.org/issue-20-reader/abstract.html#.YfGBq_XMJs8.

20 A similar photograph by Raoul Hausmann shows both Ruth Domela and her husband in front of the same painting.

21 See, for instance, Matthew Teitelbaum, *Montage and Modern Life, 1919–1942* (Cambridge, MA: MIT Press, 1994).

22 Nancy Fraser, "Behind Marx's Hidden Abode," *New Left Review*, no. 86 (2014): 66.

23 Oskar Negt and Alexander Kluge, *Öffentlichkeit und Erfahrung: Zur Organisationsanalyse von bürgerlicher und proletarischer Öffentlichkeit* (Frankfurt am Main: Suhrkamp, 1972), 304–5. Published in English as *Public Sphere and Experience: Analysis of the Bourgeois and Proletarian Public Sphere*, trans. Peter Labanyi et al. (Minneapolis: University of Minnesota Press, 1993). The "proletarian counterpublic" theorized by Negt and Kluge is a manifestation of such resistance. More recently, Michael Hardt and Antonio Negri have argued that the original accumulation is ongoing in the form of a "postmodern primitive accumulation" that is largely informational: "Informational accumulation (like the primitive accumulation Marx analyzed) destroys or at least destructs previously existing productive processes, but (differently than Marx's primitive accumulation) it immediately integrates those productive processes in its own networks." Hardt and Negri, *Empire* (Cambridge, MA: Harvard University Press, 2000), 258 (italics removed). David Moore has rightfully criticized Hardt and Negri for privileging "informational" accumulation over other forms of contemporary primitive accumulation, meaning that they effectively become complicit in the

systemic obfuscation of these forms of labor: "Presto, we have globalised information workers. One wonders if the coltan diggers in the eastern Congo shovelling the essential mineral for cell-phones, Sony play-stations and NASA space-stations under the guns of Rwandan-backed warlords, are 'conscious' of their new power, and whether their subjectivity was the force behind this constellation of extraction, production and consumption." David Moore, "Hardt and Negri's *Empire* and Real Empire: The Terrors of 9-11 and After," *ACME* 2, no. 2 (2003): 112–31.

24 See Oskar Negt and Alexander Kluge, *Geschichte und Eigensinn* (Frankfurt am Main: Zweitausendeins, 1981), 87–220, 414–88, 541–709. Published in English as *History and Obstinacy*, ed. Devin Fore, trans. Richard Langston et al. (New York: Zone Books, 2014). Not all the passages I cite or refer to here can be found in the English translation, which is a condensation of the sprawling original.

25 Negt and Kluge, *Geschichte und Eigensinn*, 553 (my translation).

26 Negt and Kluge, 522 (my translation).

27 Alexander Kluge, *Lernprozesse mit tödlichem Ausgang* (Frankfurt am Main: Suhrkamp, 1973). A selection of the original films and 1990s remixes can be found in discs 5 and 6 of the DVD collection/edition *Alexander Kluge: Sämtliche Kinofilme* (Frankfurt am Main: Zweitausendeins, 2007).

28 Peter C. Lutze, *Alexander Kluge: The Last Modernist* (Detroit, MI: Wayne State University Press, 1998), 225n9. On the state of the HfG Ulm at the time, see Christiane Wachsmann, *Vom Bauhaus beflügelt: Menschen und Ideen an der Hochschule für Gestaltung Ulm* (Stuttgart: av edition, 2018), 228–34. See also Kluge's comments in *Neonröhren des Himmels*, the accompanying booklet to *Sämtliche Kinofilme*, 28–29.

29 Alexander Kluge, email to the author, March 28, 2019.

30 Kluge, *Lernprozesse mit tödlichem Ausgang*, 312.

31 Karl Marx, *Grundrisse: Foundations of the Critique of Political Economy*, trans. Martin Nicolaus (London: Penguin, 1993), 100–102.

32 Alfred Sohn-Rethel, *Geistige und körperliche Arbeit: Zur Theorie der gesellschaftlichen Synthesis*, rev. ed. (Frankfurt am Main:

Suhrkamp, 1972); and the English translation, *Intellectual and Manual Labour: A Critique of Epistemology* (London: Macmillan, 1978). For an explanation of my use of German and English editions of Sohn-Rethel's book, see chapter 3, note 18, in this volume.

33 Michel Serres, *Petite Poucette* (Paris: Le Pommier, 2012), 75; translated by Daniel W. Smith as *Thumbelina: The Culture and Technology of Millennials* (Washington, DC: Rowman & Littlefield, 2014). Unfortunately, Serres's perceptive analysis of the structural transformations of contemporary society is marred by an at times grotesque unwillingness to also see the information society as a society of control. In Serres's world, the Edward Snowden revelations are proof that everything is going swimmingly since they demonstrate that a single man can "take on" the NSA and Silicon Valley. See Michel Serres, interviews by Martin Legros and Sven Ortoli, *Pantopie: De Hermès à Petite Poucette* (Paris: Le Pommier, 2014), 347.

34 Serres, *Petite Poucette*, 72.

35 See also Sven Lütticken, "Living with Abstraction," in *Idols of the Market: Modern Iconoclasm and the Fundamentalist Spectacle* (Berlin: Sternberg Press, 2009), 125–56; and Lütticken, "Inside Abstraction," *e-flux journal*, no. 38 (2012), https://www.e-flux.com/journal/38/61196/inside-abstraction/. In a usage that differs from mine, Falke Pisano employs the term "concrete abstraction" to refer to the failed abstractions (in Gillick's sense; see note 19) of modernism; see Pisano, "Concrete Abstractions," *Metropolis M*, no. 5 (2005): 72–75. For another application of the term to modernist "abstract" art, in relation to developments in late nineteenth- and early twentieth-century science, see Peter Galison, "Concrete Abstraction," in *Inventing Abstraction 1919–1925: How a Radical Idea Changed Modern Art* (New York: Museum of Modern Art, 2012), 350–57. Then there is Lefebvre's notion of (socially produced) space as a concrete abstraction; see Łukasz Stanek, *Henri Lefebvre on Space: Architecture, Urban Research, and the Production of Theory* (Minneapolis: University of Minnesota Press, 2011), 133–164.

36 The more general German phrase "Begriffe der Naturerkenntnis"

becomes "the concepts of natural science" Sohn-Rethel, *Geistige und körperliche Arbeit*, 42; and in the English edition, *Intellectual and Manual Labour*, 20.

37 See Benedict Anderson, *Imagined Communities: Reflections on the Origin and Spread of Nationalism* (London: Verso, 1983).

38 Peter Burke, *A Social History of Knowledge: From Gutenberg to Diderot* (Cambridge: Polity, 2000), 176.

39 Sohn-Rethel, *Geistige und körperliche Arbeit*, 167–72, 179–82.

40 Karl Marx, *A Contribution to the Critique of Political Economy* (1857), in *Marx and Engels Collected Works*, vol. 29 (New York: International Publishers, 1987), 263.

41 The fullest discussion of value-spheres can be found in Max Weber, "Religious Rejections of the World and Their Rejections" (1915), in *From Max Weber: Essays in Sociology*, trans. and ed. Hans H. Gerth and Charles Wright Mills (New York: Oxford University Press, 1946), 323–59.

42 Jürgen Habermas, "Modernity: An Incomplete Project" (1980), in *The Anti-aesthetic*, ed. Hal Foster (Port Townsend, WA: Bay Press, 1983), 9.

43 See also Lütticken, "Living with Abstraction," 125–56; and Lütticken, "Inside Abstraction."

44 Sohn-Rethel, *Geistige und körperliche Arbeit*, 57.

45 Brenna Bhandar and Alberto Toscano, "Race, Real Estate and Real Abstraction," *Radical Philosophy*, no. 194 (November/December 2015): 9.

46 Christoph Menke, *Kritik der Rechte* (Berlin: Suhrkamp, 2015), esp. pt. 2.

47 See also Sven Lütticken, "The Juridical Economy: Notes on Legal Form and Aesthetic Form," *New Left Review*, no. 106 (2017): 105–23.

48 I use rights-form as an analogue of the German *Rechtsform*, the complement of *Wertform*. In translation of and debate about Evgeny Pashukanis's critique of international law, "legal form" is commonly used. See China Miéville, *Between Equal Rights: A Marxist Theory of International Law* (Leiden: Brill, 2005), 84–115.

49 Brenna Bhandar, *Colonial Lives of Property: Law, Land, and Racial*

Regimes of Ownership (Durham, NC: Duke University Press, 2018), 12.

50 Habermas and Bourdieu have arguably developed the most influential late twentieth-century elaborations on Weber's analysis of the differentiation between social spheres in modern society. Habermas stayed closer to Weber, and Bourdieu created his own complex account of semiautonomous fields.

51 Jürgen Habermas, *Strukturwandel der Öffentlichkeit: Untersuchungen zu einer Kategorie der bürgerlichen Gesellschaft* (Neuwied: Luchterhand, 1962).

52 Sohn-Rethel, *Geistige und körperliche Arbeit*, 48.

53 James Bridle, *New Dark Age: Technology and the End of the Future* (London: Verso, 2018), 26–33.

54 Alexander R. Galloway, *The Interface Effect* (Cambridge: Polity, 2012), 81–82.

55 Matteo Pasquinelli, "Italian *Operaismo* and the Information Machine," *Theory, Culture & Society* 32, no. 3 (2015): 62.

56 Pasquinelli, 62.

57 Alexander R. Galloway and Eugene Thacker, *The Exploit: A Theory of Networks* (Minneapolis: University of Minnesota Press, 2007), 47–57.

58 Yuk Hui has argued that in the digital realm, protocols and metadata schemes function as quasi-Kantian schemata that are used to arrange, navigate, and mine data, creating value in the process. See Hui, *On the Existence of Digital Objects* (Minneapolis: University of Minnesota Press, 2016), 52.

59 Karl Marx, *Capital*, vol. 1, chap. 1, sec. 3, https://www.marxists.org/archive/marx/works/1867-c1/ch01.htm#S3.

60 See the exhibition catalogue *Programmare l'arte: Olivetti e la neoavanguardie cinetiche*, ed. Marco Meneguzzo et al. (Monza: Johan & Levi, 2012), which covers both Munari's exhibition and Sottsass's work on the Elea 9003.

61 Armin Medosch, *New Tendencies: Art at the Threshold of the Information Revolution (1961–1978)* (Cambridge, MA: MIT Press, 2016), 92.

62 Antonio Negri, *Art and Multitude* (Cambridge: Polity, 2011), 33.

63 Medosch, *New Tendencies*, 92.

64 Steve Wright, *Storming Heaven: Class Composition and Struggle in Italian Autonomist Marxism* (London: Pluto Press, 2003), 21–22, 53–58.

65 Medosch, *New Tendencies*, 90–91.

66 Romano Alquati, "Composizione organica del capitale e forza-lavoro alla Olivetti," pt. 1, *Quaderni Rossi*, no. 2 (April 1962): 81. English translation by Steve Wright, "Organic Composition of Capital and Labor-Power at Olivetti (1961)," *Viewpoint Magazine*, August 27, 2013, https://www.viewpointmag.com/2013/09/27/organic-composition-of-capital-and-labor-power-at-olivetti-1961/.

67 Alquati, 81 (Wright's translation).

68 See the typescript by Sottsass, with Hans von Klier and Andries van Onck, labeled "Industrial Design" (1959), Archivio Storico Olivetti, Fondo Zorzi, faldone 1, fascicolo 8; see also "L'elaboratore elettronico Olivetti Elea classe 9000," *Stile Industria*, no. 31 (March 1961): 3–13.

69 Maldonado attempted to use information theory to give a scientific basis to design; this is Bauhaus functionalism morphing into a postwar cybernetic paradigm. For the Elea 9003, Maldonado and Bonsiepe designed a graphic code from scratch. In this visual Esperanto, every symbol stood for a command, which, in theory, made the console universal and independent of the operator's natural language. Von Klier and Van Onck were sent to Italy to work with Sottsass on the console and implement Maldonado's system; however, possibly due to the shakeup at the company after Adriano Olivetti's death, Maldonado and Bonsiepe's system was not implemented. All documentation of the built consoles shows a more conventional panel with alphanumeric characters. See Wachsmann, *Vom Bauhaus beflügelt*, 146; and Elisabetta Mori, "Ettore Sottsass Jr. e il design dei primi computer Olivetti," *A/I/S Design: Storia e Ricerche* 1, no. 1 (March 2013), http://www.aisdesign.org/aisd/ettore-sottsass-jr-e-il-design-dei-primi-computer-olivetti.

70 Romano Alquati, "Composizione organica del capitale e forza-lavoro alla Olivetti," pt. 2, *Quaderni Rossi*, no. 3 (June 1962): 121.

71 Pasquinelli, "Italian *Operaismo* and the Information Machine," 55.

72 Pasquinelli, 54–55.

73 Alquati, "Composizione organica del capitale," pt. 2, 121.

74 Max Haiven, *Art after Money, Money after Art: Creative Strategies against Financialization* (London: Pluto Press, 2018), 37.

75 Jaleh Mansoor, "My Bloody Valentine: Ettore Sottsass and Readymade Subsumption," in *Ettore Sottsass and the Social Factory*, ed. Gean Moreno (Munich: Prestel, 2020), 97.

76 See William Camfield, "Marcel Duchamp's Fountain: Aesthetic Object, Icon, or Anti-art?," in *The Definitively Unfinished Marcel Duchamp*, ed. Thierry de Duve (Cambridge, MA: MIT Press, 1991), 133–78.

77 Judith Ickowicz, *Le droit après la dématerialisation de l'oeuvre d'art* (Dijon: Les presses du réel, 2013), 134–37.

78 Ickowicz, 324–44.

79 Jean Baudrillard, *Pour une critique de l'économie politique du signe* (Paris: Gallimard, 1972).

80 Maurizio Lazzarato, "Immaterial Labor" (1997), trans. Paul Colilli and Ed Emery, http://www.generation-online.org/c/fcimmateriallabour3.htm.

81 See the previous chapter in this volume, and Anselm Jappe, *Die Abenteuer der Ware: Für eine neue Wertkritik* (Münster: Unrast Verlag, 2005), 126.

82 Trevor Paglen, "Operational Images," *e-flux journal*, no. 59 (November 2014), https://www.e-flux.com/journal/59/61130/operational-images/.

83 Paul Chan, "Our Data, Our Selves," *Los Angeles Review of Books*, September 19, 2019, https://lareviewofbooks.org/article/our-data-our-selves/. In *Eye/Machine III*, Farocki focused on cruise missiles and other forms of machine vision. Farocki's notion has informed my own understanding of real abstraction as operational.

84 See ArtRank FAQ, accessed 2015, http://artrank.com.

85 Natascha Sadr Haghighian, *Dear Artfukts, Look at My Curve: A Report to an Academy*, in *9 Artists* (Minneapolis: Walker Art Center, 2013), 4–18.

86 Sadr Haghighian, 9.

87 Sadr Haghighian, 11.

88 See Luc Boltanski and Arnaud Esquerre, "The Economic Life of Things: Commodities, Collectibles, Assets," *New Left Review*, no. 98 (March/April 2016): 31–54; Nancy Fraser, "A New Form

of Capitalism? A Reply to Boltanski and Esquerre," *New Left Review*, no. 106 (July/August 2017): 57–65; and Boltanski and Esquerre, "Enrichment, Profit, Critique: A Rejoinder to Nancy Fraser," *New Left Review*, no. 106 (July/August 2017): 67–76.

89 Caroline Levine, *Forms: Whole, Rhythm, Hierarchy, Network* (Princeton, NJ: Princeton University Press, 2015), 126.

90 Levine, 126.

91 Galloway and Thacker, *The Exploit*, 3.

92 Alexander R. Galloway, "Theory Hot and Cold," October 28, 2018, http://cultureandcommunication.org/galloway/theory-hot-and-cold/.

93 Marx, *Capital*, vol. 1, chap. 2, https://www.marxists.org/archive/marx/works/1867-c1/ch02.htm.

94 Hui, *On the Existence of Digital Objects*, 140.

95 Shoshana Zuboff, *The Age of Surveillance Capitalism: The Fight for a Human Future at the New Frontier of Power* (London: Profile Books, 2019).

96 Geert Lovink and Ned Rossiter, *Organization after Social Media* (Colchester: Minor Compositions, 2018), 34.

97 Werker Collective, "Imaging Dissent: Towards Becoming a Collective Subject," *Art & Education*, January 15, 2020, https://www.artandeducation.net/classroom/310806/imaging-dissent-towards-becoming-a-common-subject/.

98 See Kevin Roose, "What If Facebook Is the Real 'Silent Majority'?," *New York Times*, August 27, 2020, https://www.nytimes. com/2020/08/27/technology/what-if-facebook-is-the-real-silent-majority.html; and Nora Noll, "Wie rechte Gruppe 'Black Lives Matter' diffamieren," *Süddeutsche Zeitung*, August 29, 2020, https://www.sueddeutsche.de/kultur/black-lives-matter-rechte-propaganda-1.5011836.

99 Christopher Shields, "A Fundamental Problem about Hylomorphism," Stanford Encyclopedia of Philosophy, https://plato.stanford.edu/entries/aristotle-psychology/suppl1.html.

100 The indictment can be downloaded from https://collectivize.org/.

101 Stakemeier, "Breaks with the Future," in De Bruyn and Lütticken, *Futurity Report*, 50. See also Stakemeier, *Entgrenzter Formalismus. Verfahren einer antimodernen Ästhetik* (Berlin: b_books, 2017).

102 Comité Invisible, *Maintenant* (Paris: La Fabrique, 2017), 149.

103 “Blackout Tuesday” took place on June 2, 2020.

104 See “The Society of Friends of Halit,” documenta 14, https://www.documenta14.de/en/public-programs/22411/the-society-of-friends-of-halit; and “The Tribunal,” NSU Tribunal, http://www.nsu-tribunal.de/en/.

105 Beatriz Colomina and Mark Wigley, *Are We Human? Notes on an Archaeology of Design* (Zurich: Lars Müller Publishers, 2016), 12.

106 Timothy Morton, *Hyperobjects: Philosophy and Ecology after the End of the World* (Minneapolis: University of Minnesota Press, 2013); see also the next chapter in this volume.

107 Colomina and Wigley, *Are We Human?*, 56–57.

108 See “Er zijn minder minder minder moslims dan u denkt,” *Geenstijl*, December 14, 2016, https://www.geenstijl.nl/5061992/moslimoverschatting/.

109 “Alle stabilisierung ist schwindel.” Franz W. Seiwert, “Es ist noch nicht aller Tage Abend,” *a bis z*, no. 1 (1929): 1.

110 Paul Chan, “The Spirit of Recession,” *October*, no. 129 (Summer 2009): 3.

111 Chan, 3.

Chapter 5

SHATTERED MATTER, TRANSFORMED FORMS

NOTES ON NUCLEAR AESTHETICS

> "Those who today limit themselves to the perception of whatever happens to be visible at the given moment miss reality."
> —Günther Anders, "Hiroshima Diary," 1958[1]

If total design can be said to include "everything from jeans to genes," it is clear that the informing of matter can entail the redesign of molecular structures.[2] Indeed, we can go further and argue that the fundamental design achievement of the twentieth century has been the development of nuclear reactors and atomic bombs. "Design" here should not be limited to the designing of the vessels (reactors or bombs); these are prosthetic devices that aid in the central design project on the subatomic level: "prompt critical" fission chains for nuclear weapons, and "delayed critical" fission chains for nuclear reactors. Such subatomic design has had drastic repercussions on the global scale, sealing Earth's transformation into a (botched) planetary design object.

The human senses have been increasingly confronted with their limits since the late nineteenth century, as technologies such as film and high-speed photography reveal an optical unconscious beyond human eyesight. X-rays, discovered by Wilhelm Röntgen in 1895, suggest that reality is traversed by invisible rays that can be revealed through media, even while transforming those media in the process.[3] The radioactivity of uranium, too, was revealed through photography in 1896: Henri Becquerel exposed photo paper to uranium, and a form of radiation invisible to the human eye manifested itself in the dark.[4] Together, Röntgen's X-rays and Becquerel's discovery of radioactivity suggested to artists that reality, as it had hitherto existed, had been abrogated. As Kandinsky wrote in 1913: "The collapse of the atom was equated, in my soul, with the collapse of the whole world. Suddenly, the stoutest walls crumbled. Everything became uncertain, precarious and insubstantial. I would not have been surprised had a stone dissolved into thin air before my eyes and become invisible."[5]

Thus, the operational abstraction of technoscience at first suggested an artistic abstraction from visible reality, a flight into the nonobjective. Yet, as noted in the last chapter, this art was irredeemably concrete in its appeal to the human sensorium. Not having access to the technology, modern artists found themselves in the position of outsiders, amateurs with little more than their obsolete senses to work with. And in the postwar nuclear regime, as the anthropologist Joseph Masco has argued, the disjunction between human perception and technical media only continued to widen: "While the prosthetic devices that populate nuclear physics laboratories enable scientists [that is, scientist-designers] to enter the subatomic realm and measure the material effects of plutonium and other radionuclides, most people in the nuclear age remain literally senseless to radiation, dependent in everyday life on biological, not machinic, insights."[6]

The literal invisibility of harmful ionizing radiation is coated in political invisibility that is broken only intermittently, at moments of spectacular disaster: Harrisburg, Chernobyl, Fukushima. The problem, as aesthetic as it is social, remains—and would remain even after an improbable global abandonment of nuclear technology in the form of vast quantities of radioactive waste. The Copernican decentering of human vision owing to particle physics' descent into the fabric of matter itself is matched by dizzying timespans that appear to cast doubt on the possibility of meaningful social and political action, which tends to think in shorter terms. The nuclear regime, then, exacerbates a certain modern crisis of aesthetics—driving home the point that the aesthetic is a practice and theory of crisis, of lack, of petrifying sublime expanses and decisions to work with whatever form or degree of concretion can be attained.[7]

This chapter will focus on artistic responses to the nuclear regime since 1945—responses, that is, to a regime of nuclear total design courtesy of the military-industrial complex. I obviously do not aim to give an encyclopedic overview, and I cannot do justice to the work of Japanese artists—whose country and lives were immediately affected by the 1945 bombings—nor to that of Aboriginal artists responding to the nuclear tests at Maralinga.[8] In engaging with a limited set of entangled genealogies revolving around artists active in some of the centers of postwar capitalism, I aim to show how such practices developed immanent (aesthetic and political) critiques of the regime they profited from.

Atomic Aisthesis: Hyperobjects and Infra-objects

"Correlationism" is a loaded, problematic framing of philosophy since Kant, which is said to have willfully reduced ontological questions to matters of epistemology—the "correlation" between object and subject. Kant's insistence that what we perceive as reality is the product of our mind's innate thought-forms has led to an abandonment of ontology in favor of epistemology and the mind-world "correlation."[9] The world, henceforth, was to be filtered through the human; the categories and schematisms of the mind structure reality as we perceive and know it, and the *Ding an sich* remains outside the purview of thought.

No matter that post-Kantian idealist and materialist philosophy goes from correlation to a dialectic of subject and object. This is still unacceptable for neo-ontologists such as Graham Harman, who seek to define objects not in relation to any shared reality with human perception and life, as "sensual objects," but "by their autonomous reality. They must be autonomous in two separate directions: emerging as something over and above their pieces, while also partly withholding themselves from relations with other entities."[10] These objects of thought are strangely like fetishized artworks. They recall Rainer Maria Rilke's insistence, in his essay on Rodin, on a quintessential ontological thingness of objects that would remove them from commodified relations, and from relationality as such. As the philosopher Günther Anders put it in his critical reading of Rilke's Rodin essay, "By taking things out of their 'alienating context' he alienated them anew; and this time for good. True, he saw the jug no longer as commodity; but he did not see it either as pitcher for beer but as a thing deprived of all relations."[11]

As alienated as they may be, artworks do, however, entertain relations with other artworks in a structural game of signification through difference—and with the viewers who accept the challenge to join the game. The modern "autonomous artwork" always complicated any neat distinction between object and subject by presenting the viewer (or listener, or reader) with an external entity possessed with an oneiric logic whose grasp lies forever behind the next corner of the aesthetic experience. Hegel famously defined the beautiful as "das sinnliche Scheinen der Idee"—the sensuous appearance or "shining" of the idea.[12] For idealist aesthetics, the artwork was a challenge and promise precisely because it was here, in an externalized or alienated form, that subjectivity could truly manifest itself. Later, materialist aesthetics homed in on the artwork's materiality or thingness precisely because it could serve as a corrective to the lordship of the idealist subject. With Harman, none of this seems to matter much.

Some proselytizers of object-oriented speculation try to "rescue" art from the aesthetic. Since "contemporary art as the aesthetic experience of sense and value-making, as the co-constitution of the art object and subject, assumes correlationism and reproduces it," art must become post-contemporary by becoming post-aesthetic and poetic.[13] The aesthetic, which is conveniently defined in narrow Kantian terms, is said to remain correlationist by limiting experience to "the conditions of the possibility of our thinking," whereas poetics "refers to a making of something in which the boundary from non-being to being is crossed."[14] Such meme-ified theory takes away all tools for cognitive mapping, for navigating the networked real abstractions and their overdetermined articulations. On the other hand, there are some positions within the speculato-objective field that provide pointers for such an orientation.

While Timothy Morton goes along with the critique of correlationism, he proposes what one might term a *disjunctivist* rather than a correlationist reading of Kant. Morton stresses that Kant, in positing that the "thing in itself" is unknowable and all we can access is what has been produced by our own mind, opened up a "phenomenon-thing gap" that foreshadows his own account of what he terms "hyperobjects." The Kantian gap becomes "the rift between weather, which I can feel falling on my head, and global climate, not the older idea of local patterns of weather, but the entire system."[15] Hyperobjects are "massively distributed in time and space" and could be anything from a black hole to an oil field, the Everglades, the biosphere, or "the sum total of all the nuclear materials on Earth; or just the plutonium, or the uranium."[16] They are so distributed that they are never fully concrete, fully sensate. However, in keeping with object-oriented ontology, Morton stresses that hyperobjects are not necessarily "hyper" only or primarily in relation to humans, for "a thing is just a rift between what it is and how it appears, for any entity whatsoever, not just for that special entity called the (human) subject."[17] His relative focus on "hyperobjects as they pertain to humans" is presented as a concession of sorts.[18] Since Morton notes that he writes as "one of the entities caught in the hyperobject […] global warming," this is clearly a more pressing hyperobject for him than black holes.[19]

However, does climate change actualize the Kantian *gap* between phenomenon and thing-in-itself, or rather the Kantian *correlation* between mind and world, of which the thing-in-itself is the irrelevant remainder? As Déborah Danowski and Eduardo Viveiros de Castro have argued, "We can see the irony of our predicament as that of a catastrophic *terrestrial objectivation of the correlation*."[20] In other words, "human thought, materialized as a giant technological machine of planetary impact, effectively and destructively *correlates the world*."[21] If the productive abstractions of modern technoscience—this weaponized, transformative, operative logos—have remade the world, they have done so through GDPs and CO_2 levels.

A refrain throughout Morton's work, especially when it comes to the nonlocal nature of hyperobjects, is radiation: "Nuclear radiation is not visible to humans. The nuclear accidents at Chernobyl and Fukushima bathed beings thousands of miles away in unseen alpha, beta, and gamma particles, as radioactive specks floated in air currents across Europe and the Pacific. Days, weeks, months, or years later, some humans die of radiation sickness. Strange mutagenic flowers grow."[22] Morton is the latest in a number of theorists, writers, and artists to address the crisis of the human sensory apparatus in the age of nuclear technology—in a frequently mystificatory register, and without acknowledging the connection to a very different strand of theory. His dictum that "locality is always a false immediacy" recalls the Marxian critique of pseudo-concretion.[23] In fact, Marxian theory has long analyzed capitalism as a hyperobject without Morton's mystifications. For Marx, there is a sensory void at the heart of capitalism as an economy of real abstraction, in which the productive relations do not "show themselves" in the commodity fetish. Whereas Morton concocts a Lovecraftian post-Kantianism in which the mystique of hyperobject generates a "speculative" version of the sublime, Marxists such as Fredric Jameson have cogently theorized the representational challenges posed by capitalism, and the form of "cognitive mapping" that go some way in addressing them.[24]

The post-Situationist polemicist Jaime Semprun has offered one of the most acerbic critiques of the nuclear regime from a Marxian perspective. In his tract *La nucléarisation du monde*, written in the guise of an ironic, Swiftian defense of nuclear technology, Semprun notes that "nothing is more discreet than radiation."[25] As an infra-sensible phenomenon that can, however, result in very visible physical consequences, the nuclear is an aesthetico-political problem of the first order. Semprun, whose 1980 text was republished after the Chernobyl disaster at Guy Debord's behest, stresses that in this respect the nuclear should be seen as an exacerbation of commodity fetishism. Capitalist commodities already claim an "autonomy" from the human and relegate the labor and the productive relations that brought them forth to invisibility:

> Because nuclear fission acts on the very structure of inorganic matter (just as genetic engineering—the indispensable complement for the construction of a nuclearized human being—acts on the very structure of organic matter), from now on there is no longer anything to see.
>
> We understand that this might be somewhat disconcerting in a world where sight is the sense that instructs all the other senses; what is not so easy to understand, however, is the fact that while people rebel against a power that escapes their senses, they none-theless do not seem to have noticed that all of their activities are

> subjected to a power that is just as impalpable and invisible as nuclear power, a power whose reach is so generalized that nuclearization itself is merely one of its consequences, among others. It was undoubtedly necessary for the boundless social power constituted by the existence of market relations to boldly proclaim its autonomy in the form of nuclear power, so that people should become aware of the necessity of submitting to its imperatives. In this sense, nuclear power is, for the social question, a discovery that is just as important as the discovery of the unconscious was for individual psychology.[26]

Tongue firmly in cheek, Semprun asks: "What person with even the least degree of respect for materialism would deny that our environment is much less aquatic than social"?[27] Today, the rhetoric of such a takedown would have to be different, as much anthropocenic discourse is predicated precisely on the realization that our environment is natural as well as cultural and social—a realization triggered by the drastic effects of human activity on the planetary ecosystem. Critics of the notion of the Anthropocene such as Christophe Bonneuil and Jean-Baptiste Fressoz have argued that its promotors falsely assume that "becoming conscious" of the situation would lead to swift political action. One can only maintain this by conveniently forgetting that concern over the ecological and climatic consequences of human activity goes back to the decades around 1800, and by turning a blind eye to massive interests that stand in the way of climate action.[28] The influence of the Koch brothers and their money on US politics would be a case in point.

The anthropocenologists (as Bonneuil and Fressoz call them) naturalize the new geological era and the catastrophic symptoms it generates by ascribing it to the "anthropos," the human race as such. Should we not rather use the term "Capitalocene," for instance? And should an analysis of hyperobjects (such as global warming or radiation) not include economic hyperobjects like the financial system and capitalism? One popular date for the beginning of the Anthropocene is 1945, with the explosions at Trinity Site, in Hiroshima, and in Nagasaki. Such dating is convenient in that it puts all the blame on a single technology, rather than deeper causes. More commonly, the year 1945 is seen as the start of the "Great Acceleration" phase of the Anthropocene, whose origins can be dated back to the Industrial Revolution or even the "discovery" and colonization of the Americas.[29] Both of these possible starting points suggest very strongly that the relevant actor is not some undifferentiated anthropos, but the capitalism that emerged in Europe in a number of successive phases—from merchant to industrial capitalism.

The latter was hooked on coal and oil, and still is; by and large, nuclear power has not been a substitute, but an *addition*. Owing to their reliance on imported oil and minerals as well as on nuclear power, the developed countries of the postwar era began to outstrip their local biocapacity—which is essentially an ecosystem's maximum capacity for sustainable and regenerative consumption of resources—to a staggering degree: according to one calculation, in 1973 the United States had consumed 176 percent, West Germany 292 percent, and Japan 576 percent of its biocapacity.[30] As the strikingly precise outcome of impenetrable calculations, such numbers can themselves become false concretions. Yet concretize we must, without turning a single object (or number) into a static and disconnected fetish.

We can never *see* capitalism as such. All commodities are mere epiphenomena of the hyperobject; as are our own experiences as workers, as unemployed, or as refugees; as are signs of ecological and social destruction we may witness. How to use personal experience—or the failure of experience, the missed encounter with the hyperobject—as a point of departure for critical fetishizations?

Ontological, Scientific, and Monetary Atomism

Intriguingly, Karl Marx's 1841 doctoral dissertation was on an atomic subject: the difference between Democritus's and Epicurus's philosophy of nature, both of which were atomistic. Greek atomism had been rediscovered in the Renaissance, largely through the Roman poet Lucretius's *De rerum natura*. With its denial of the creation and of a divine plan, its assertion of infinite time and space, and its insistence that everything consists of minute particles, as well as its ethical privileging of pleasure over self-abnegation and suffering, atomism was anathema to a Catholic Church that could make peace with various elements from Platonism and Aristotelianism. As a seventeenth-century Latin prayer for young Jesuits quoted by Stephen Greenblatt stresses, atomism denied the divine *form* of creation:

> Nothing comes from atoms.
> All the bodies of the world shine with the beauty of their forms.
> Without these the globe would only be an intense chaos.[31]

Marx, who makes extensive use of Lucretius, notes that for Democritus, the atomistic principle can be "percieved only through reason, since they are inaccessible to the sensuous eye if only because of their smallness. For this reason they are even called ideas. The sensuous appearance is, on the other hand, the only true object, and the aisthesis [sensuous perception] is the phronesis [that which is rational]; this true thing however is the changing, the unstable, the phenomenon."[32]

In Democritus's philosophy, "the concept of the atom and sensuous perception face each other as enemies," with sensuous reality playing the role of "subjective semblance" vis-à-vis the philosophical concept (of the atom).[33] By contrast, Marx argues, Epicurus stresses the objectivity of sense appearances: "While Democritus turns the sensuous world into *subjective semblance, Epicurus* turns it into *objective* appearance. And here he differs quite consciously, since he claims that he shares *the same principles but* that he does not reduce the sensuous qualities to things *of mere opinion*."[34]

Here, we begin to see why these seemingly arcane philosophical issues would be of interest to the young Marx, who was working his way through Hegel and who was already moving beyond idealism. Concerning the actual theory of the atom, both thinkers assume that atoms share two types of motion: falling in a straight line in the void, and mutual repulsion among atoms. However, Epicurus adds an extra element, which is the atom's ability to deviate from the straight line: "The atoms are purely self-sufficient bodies or rather bodies conceived in absolute self-sufficiency, like the heavenly bodies. Hence, again like the heavenly bodies, they move not in straight, but in oblique lines. The motion of failing is the motion of non-self-sufficiency."[35]

The "declination" from the straight line introduced by Epicurus was said by Lucretius to have broken "the fati foedera [bonds of fate]."[36] In a further approving reference to Lucretius, Marx notes that "if the atoms were not to decline, neither their repulsion nor their meeting would have taken place, and the world would never have been created."[37] Epicurus, then, comes to be identified for Marx with materialism—a materialism that is not ahistorical and deterministic but places emphasis on development and on contingency. Whereas for Democritus the atom remains "a pure and abstract category, a hypothesis, the result of experience, not its active [*energisches*] principle," in Epicurus "atomistics with all its contradictions has been carried through and completed as the natural science of self-consciousness. This self-consciousness under the form of abstract individuality is an absolute principle."[38] Such abstract individuality is the limit of Epicureanism:

> The purpose of action is to be found therefore in abstracting, swerving away from pain and confusion, in ataraxy. Hence the good is the flight from evil, pleasure the swerving away from suffering. Finally, where abstract individuality appears in its highest freedom and independence, in its totality, there it follows that the being which is swerved away from, is all being, for this reason, the gods swerve away from the world, do not bother with it and live outside it.[39]

Thus Marx, steeped in idealist aesthetic theory, almost accidentally provides an atomistic basis for classical Greek art, as these gods who "are unconcerned with us and the world, are honoured because of their beauty, their majesty and their superior nature, [...] are no fiction of Epicurus. They did exist. They are the Elastic gods of Greek art."[40]

This represents progress against an earlier moment in which the gods were held in awe. Marx cites a line from Aeschylus's *Prometheus Bound* that he associates with Epicurus: "Better be the servant of this rock/Than to be faithful boy to father Zeus."[41] This familiar Young Hegelian critique of religion remains Feuerbachian: Marx here theorizes the emancipation from superstition as an aestheticization of the gods. However, in a patrician/slave society, this only results in a form of aristocratic critique and personal ethics of aloofness; the move from such a contemplative critique to a collective and revolutionary praxis lies in the future.

Marx produced his dissertation at a moment when atomism in modern science was still largely a theoretical school, even if increasingly buttressed by experimental results such as the chemical decomposition of water into oxygen and hydrogen. Speculative ontology was in the process of becoming operational science. The social dialectic becomes inextricably entangled with the metabolisms of nature. The paradoxical triumph of scientific atomism would come around 1900 with the realization that atoms were *not* the smallest, indivisible building blocks of reality. Though the notion of social *atomization*, of modern society being composed of "atomized individuals," became a common concept in twentieth-century (pop) psychology, science moved beyond atomism around 1900; it moved on to *nuclearize* the world.

With Becquerel's discovery of the radioactivity of uranium in 1896, it became evident that the fabric of material reality was not as solid as eighteenth-century materialism or nineteenth-century positivism had assumed. Frantic research into the inner structure of the atom culminated in the 1911 "planetary" Rutherford model of the atom, with a small nucleus around which electrons circle at a distance. This signaled the transition from *atomic physics* to *nuclear physics*, which was accompanied by the quantum-mechanical problematization of the fundamental distinction between particles and energy waves—subatomic particles and light could register as either. The discovery of the neutron and of nuclear fission and chain reactions during the 1930s laid the basis for the development of nuclear weapons during World War II. Hiroshima spelled the death of atomism and the triumph of nuclearism.[42]

Nonetheless, as military and "peaceful" nuclear power transformed the planet in the 1950s and 1960s, Greek atomism was revisited both in popular and more highbrow attempts to come to terms with the new (un)reality. As the creator of a new breed of "elastic gods," Walt Disney produced a mass-market paperback (1956) and a TV film (1957), both called *Our Friend the Atom.*[43] In this teleological history, Democritus—but not Epicurus—is praised for his "prophetic" atomic theory, which was, however, soon lost and forgotten.[44] Old qualms about the atomists' alleged atheism and hedonism, and about the "formlessness" of their worldview, were put aside. The Disney staff and their hired expert Heinz Haber gave the distinctly nonclassical and orientalist form of a genie in a bottle to nuclear energy; a fisherman opens the vessel and unleashes the genie. However, so the lesson of this dialectical image goes, "man" can make the genie do his bidding and harness its power.[45]

In the 1960s, the German writer and activist Heinrich Schirmbeck claimed that "our era reaps what the Greek atomists have sown," as they started a process of *Entsinnlichung* (desensualization) that ends with nuclear and biological science.[46] In the register of political economy, this diagnosis was mirrored by Sohn-Rethel's emphasis on the "atomicity" of money, but this concerned mathematical divisibility rather than physical atomicity; the "real abstraction" that is money must be "divisible in order to leave the commodities undivided."[47] Sohn-Rethel quotes from *Capital* to the effect that "not an atom of matter enters into the objectivity of commodities as values; in this it is the direct opposite of the coarsely sensuous objectivity of commodities as physical bodies."[48]

We have seen that for Sohn-Rethel, Kant's categories were the foundational blueprint of the modern scientific method and its quantification of all that is "qualitatively sensuous."[49] Morton, for his part, notes that between Kant and today's anthropocenic theory lies the moment of 1900, when "quantum theory blew a huge hole in the idea of particles as little ping-pong balls," and "relativity theory destroyed the idea of consistent objects." All of this amounted to a confirmation of the Kantian gap, and a prefiguration of hyperobjects. "What did the 'discoveries' have in common? Water, quanta, spacetime began to be seen. They were autonomous entities that had all kinds of strange, unexpected properties."[50] For his part, Sohn-Rethel likewise notes the break with the modern-bourgeois scientific conception of material substance as consisting of minute, permanent particles.[51] Quantum physics insisted that events, and not particles, are the stuff of physics, and that a particle can appear as either matter or as energy. For Sohn-Rethel, this was one indication of an impending breakthrough to socialism: as bourgeois science reflected the reign of the value-form under technocratic capitalism, so the revolutions in modern physics seemed to presage a social revolution.

Such crude and direct parallelism of the politico-economic and the scientific has its counterpart in popular parallels between modern science and modern art. Some moments in art's aesthetic revolution were indeed informed by breakthroughs in physics, but this involved a complex process of translation—a translation at times sloppy and hasty, riddled with projections and misconceptions, but producing unprecedented forms in the process.

Reality after Realism

The avant-garde of the 1920s and 1930s had a profound investment in realities below the threshold of visibility—and with technical operations that would introduce them into the visual by changing the nature of the image. László Moholy-Nagy's "new vision" and Walter Benjamin's "optical unconscious" are cases in point. X-rays, which had so shaken Kandinsky, feature prominently in his Bauhaus colleague Moholy-Nagy's book *Malerei, Fotografie, Film* (1925).[52] Akira Mizuta Lippit has argued that psychoanalysis, X-rays, and cinema, all developed or discovered around the same time, were the essential techniques of "avisuality" of the early twentieth century, promising to make things and the mind transparent.[53] Film and photography were credited with the power to make the world manifest itself in unprecedented ways, beyond nineteenth-century realism, and beyond the capabilities of the human eye. One might say that "vision and visuality have come to be culturally supervalued," but one also needs to acknowledge the coexistence of different visualities and their mutual critique.[54]

With Moholy-Nagy and some of his followers, the artistic avant-garde aspired to become (a participant in) operational design, and the use of scientific images made with lab equipment to which the artists

Illustration in Heinz Haber, *The Walt Disney Story of Our Friend the Atom* (1956)

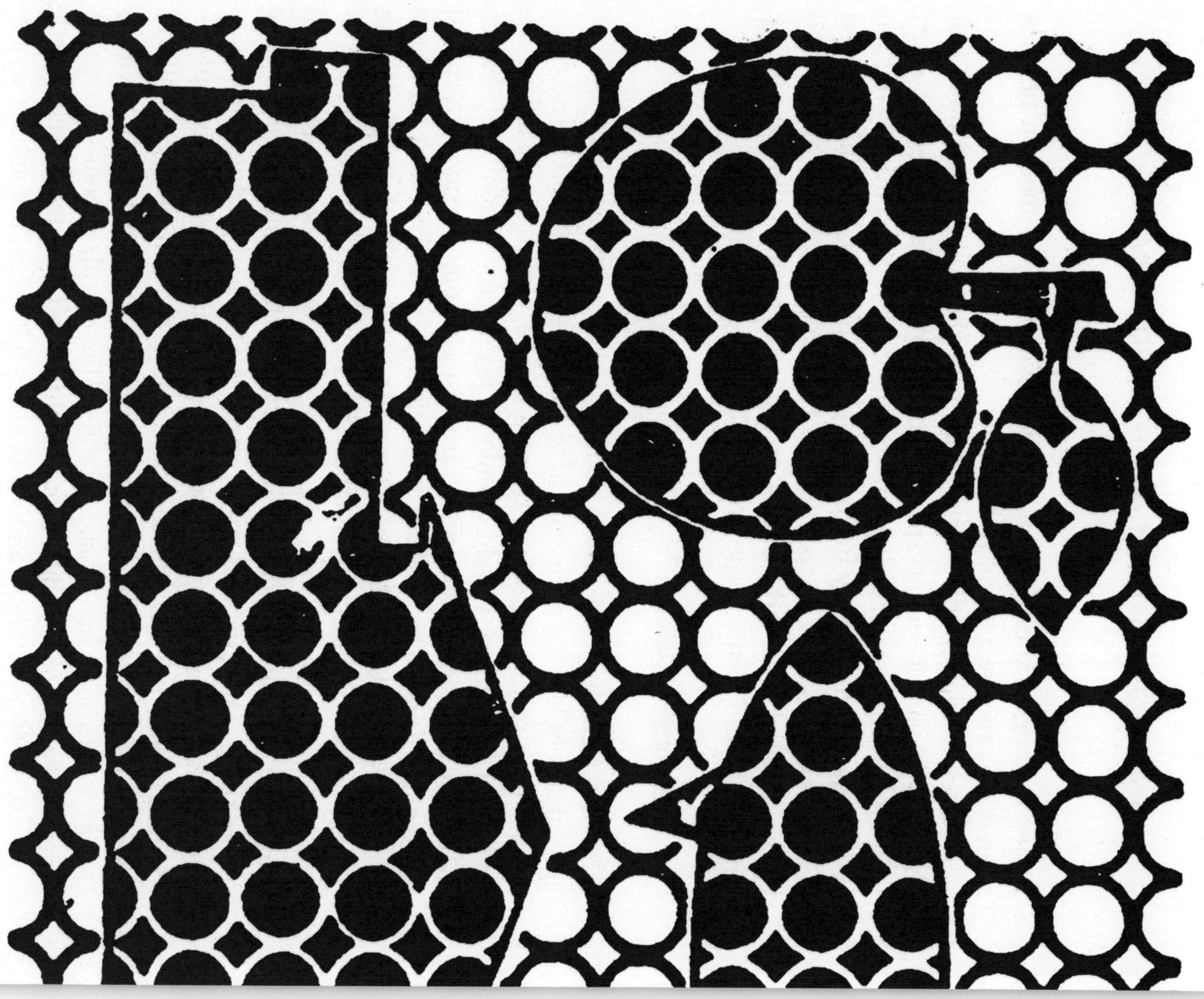

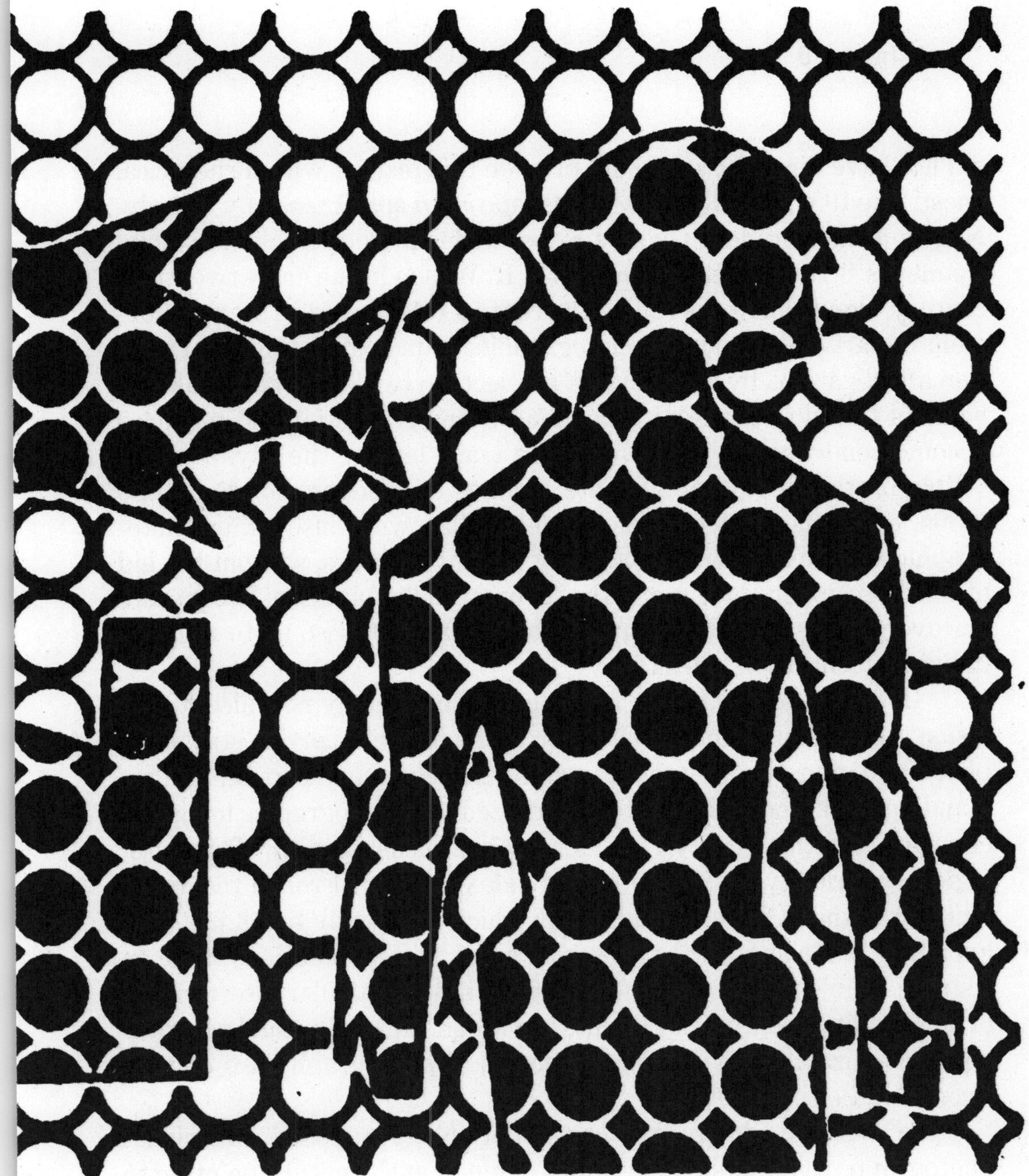

did not have direct access could provide this project with a rhetorical boost. The 1954 book *The New Landscape in Art and Science* by Moholy-Nagy's former student György Kepes includes photos taken in cloud chambers.[55] Developed by Charles T. R. Wilson in the early twentieth century, cloud chambers reflect the central role played in the development of particle physics by photographic technologies. Ionizing radiation affects atoms by knocking off an electron (which is what makes it harmful to living tissue); in the cloud chamber, the ionized particles become condensation points, and the trails left by the rays become visible on the photographic plate as lines of condensation.[56] By the 1930s, experimenters such as Marietta Blau were also using photographic emulsion to directly register radiation tracks, without the aid of a cloud chamber—a return to the "photogram" approach of Becquerel's discovery, but with the setup now being calibrated so as to register individual ionization tracks.[57]

If, for Moholy-Nagy as for Kepes, photography revealed a new vision that had to be retranslated into human terms, certain strands of photo and film theory (and certainly the common, popular understanding of photography) have naturalized the photographic image by equating it with a reality that viewers are accustomed to. This ontological superiority of the photo is an indexical one: "From a real body, which was there, proceed radiations which ultimately touch me, who am here," in Roland Barthes's words.[58] But these "radiations" take on a stable visible form in the photograph, whose particular intertwining of indexicality and iconicity results in a unique aura of "visual accuracy and recognizability."[59] But not all forms of photography are equally "iconic" in Peircean terms.

In *Malerei, Fotografie, Film*, Moholy-Nagy opposed pictorialist photographs that mimic conventions of nineteenth-century painting to "new vision" images that are not as instantly readable. Kepes's cloud chamber picture is as indexical as a photo of your grandmother, yet it needs more instructions to become "readable" as an image of radiation. An index is a sign that operates through physical contact; this could be photons affecting the emulsion in analog photography, or being translated into pixels in digital photography. It could be X-rays or gamma radiation revealing an "avisual" visuality. No wonder that the index is easily interpreted as a "natural sign," as pure causality. Thus conceived, the index is a *proto-sign* at best. However, for Kepes, cloud chamber photos intimated a subatomic "preformation" of reality that suggested ways of structuring reality on the human level: atomic design.

Spending the years before and during World War II at Moholy-Nagy's New Bauhaus in Chicago, Kepes moved on to MIT at the end of the war to develop an interdisciplinary program. If Kepes was here in the belly of the military-industrial beast, collaborating with MIT scientists, he still mostly had to be content with working with materials and technologies developed by others. Nonetheless, as with Moholy-Nagy's X-rays, his appropriated cloud chamber photos presented a new vision, and supposedly provided pointers for constructing a new world—perhaps still capitalist, but transcending nineteenth-century bricks and mortar.[60]

The Surrealists agreed that atomic and nuclear science—which was both materialist and surreal—shattered the old worldview and promised new ways of understanding and altering reality. Not, of course, within the design regimes of Bauhaus or MIT. Rather, the revolutions of science necessitated a fundamental break with the society that technoscience and industrial design tried to optimize. Wolfgang Paalen, who lived and worked in Mexico during World War II after having broken with André Breton's group, claimed in a 1944 interview: "It seems to me that we have to reach a *potential* concept of reality, based as much on the new directives of physics as on those of art."[61] Freed from Breton's tutelage, Paalen embarked on a crusade against dialectics, reserving special scorn for Engels's notion of a *dialectics of nature*, which made the mistake of applying logical categories

Cloud chamber photographs in Gÿorgy Kepes, *The New Landscape in Art and Science* (1956)

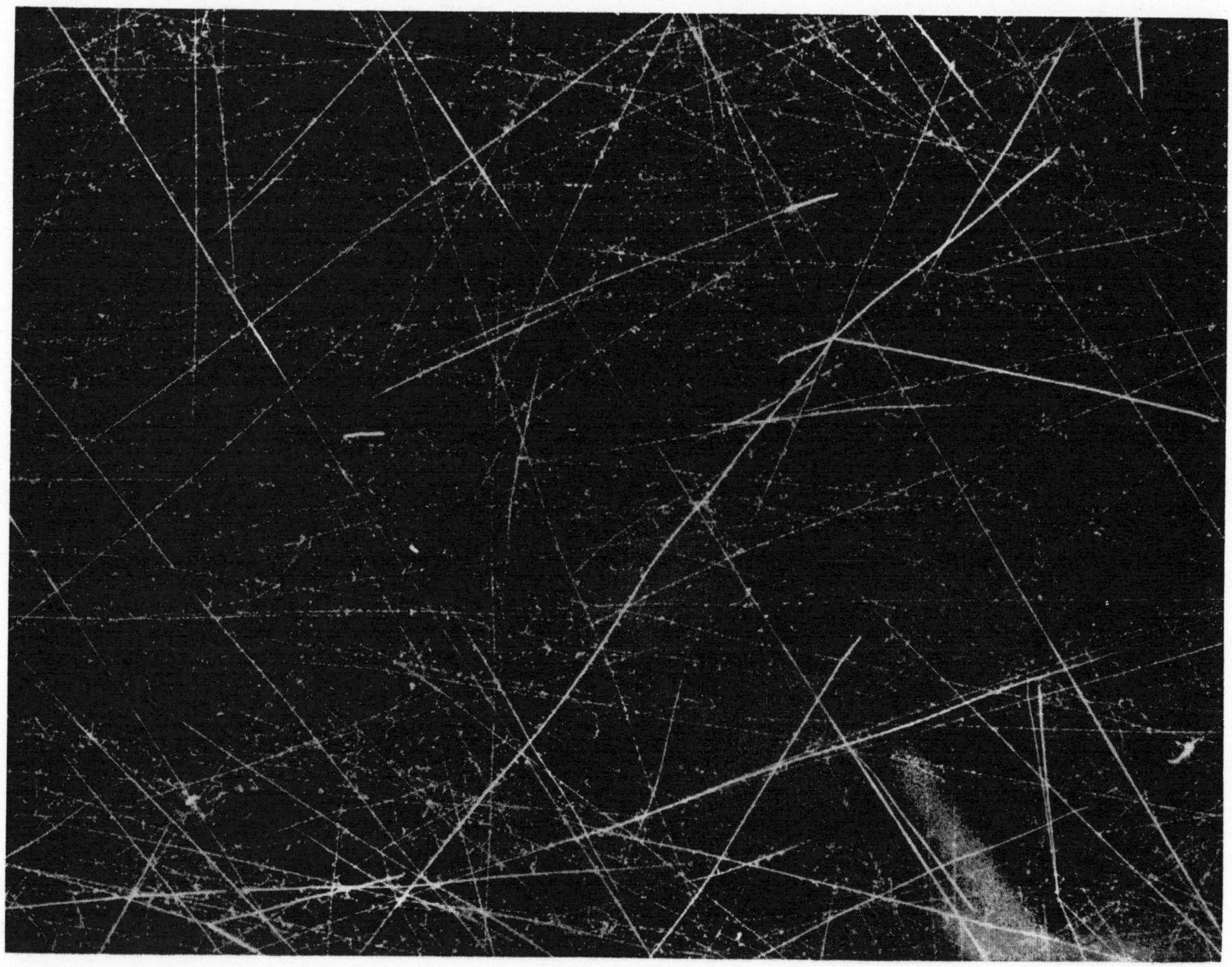

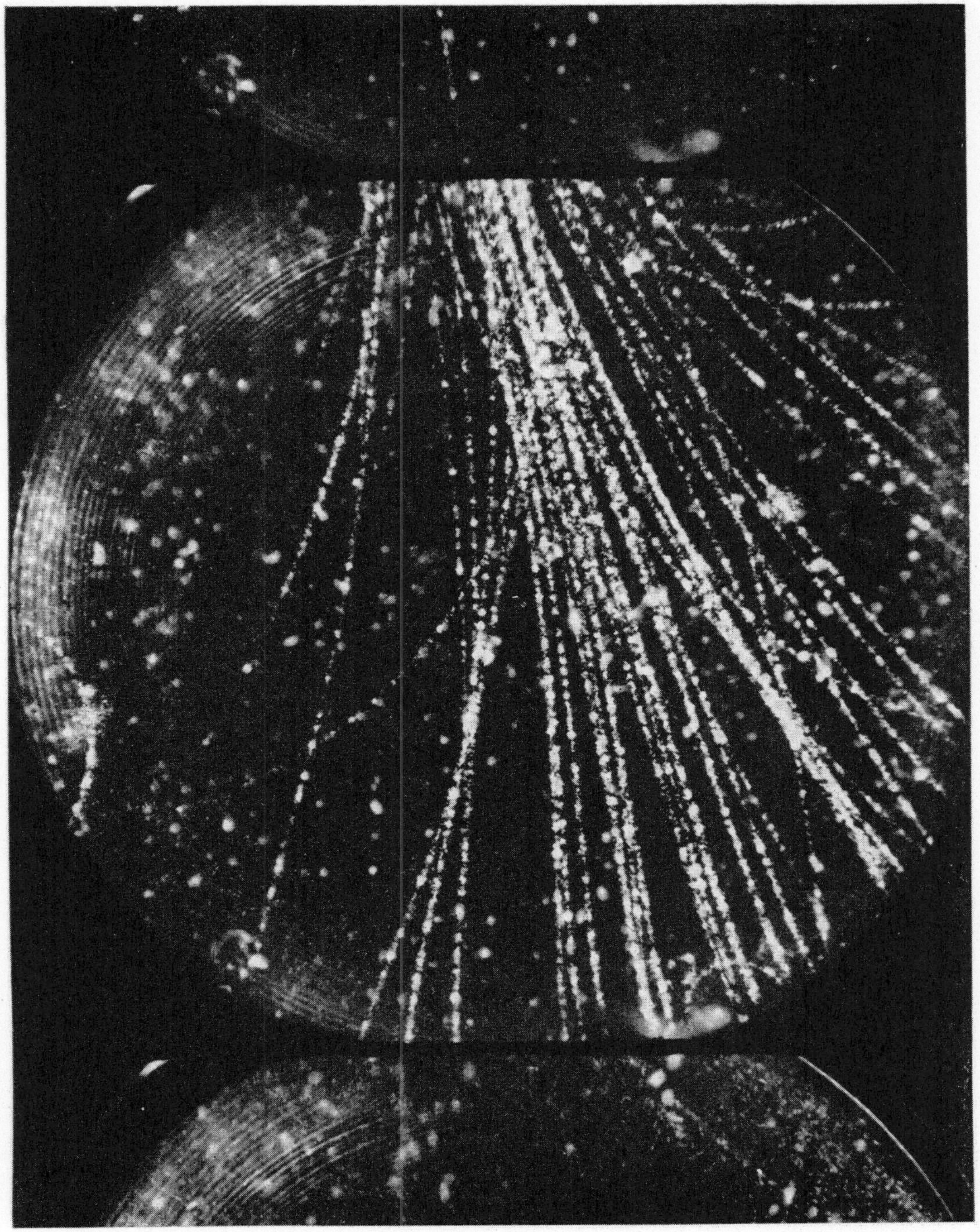

not only to history but even to the natural world.[62] If Sohn-Rethel attempted to dialecticize natural science, for Paalen, science sealed the bankruptcy of dialectical materialism.

However, while Paalen attacked Engels's famous law of the transformation of quantity into quality as nonsense, he effectively presented his own version of Surrealist dialectics by arguing that "the new Quantum Physics is compelled to abandon the rigorous determinism that until now was held to be the very foundation of physics," and, therefore, compelled to question physics' "pretension of offering us a purely quantitative and yet satisfying interpretation."[63] This, in turn, had to have consequences for art as the domain of *qualitative* experience, albeit one that had often been made subject to pictorial rules and "laws."

As Paalen phrased the relation between advanced science and advanced art: "Quantitative physics, in perceiving that the causal concept becomes inapplicable in the microscopic domain—and painting, in abandoning the causal development of plastic relations—is the same revolution."[64] With the "new physics" having abandoned causality and certitude for potentiality and possibility, Paalen adopted the Greek term *dynaton* (the possible) for his art. Abbreviated to *Dyn*, this became the name of the journal he published from Mexico—in part to retain a foothold in the New York art world.

Roberto Matta's characterization of Paalen as "the first painter of the Atomic Age" irked the latter, who complained about it in a letter written a few weeks after the Hiroshima and Nagasaki bombings.[65] To Paalen, it seemed that Matta was compromising his work with his "first painter of the Atomic Age" comment—placing it in an illustrative relation with Hiroshima and Nagasaki.[66] In fact, Paalen did respond quite directly to the double nuclear event of August 1946 with a play he completed the following year, *The Beam of the Balance.* In a post-Hiroshima counterpoint to his earlier praise for the new physics, Paalen's play is a sci-fi allegory on the dangers of nuclear power in the hands of all-too-human scientists and barely human politicians. As Paalen notes in the "Brief Outline" for his play: "Reality has, at last, become big enough to do away with realism. [...] The incommensurable explosions of 1945 have not only smashed cities but also shattered consciences. The same men who have been able to release forces beyond the dreams of yesterday, have proved inadequate to tell us what to do with these forces."[67]

Convinced that only an artistic "liberation of the imagination" can result in the "broadening of vision: necessary to deal with the new (un) reality," Paalen opens his three-act play with a cosmic vision set among the stars. "Cosmogons," great cosmic forces, watch stars and/or planets (Paalen seems not to care about the distinction) blow up one after another, as civilizations develop technologies they cannot control. Earth, we hear, still hangs in the balance—there is a "decisive struggle" going on, and in the three acts that follow, we witness that struggle, involving a scientist (Prometheus/Faust), an apelike, brutish dictator whose name (Gori) is a reference to Stalin's birthplace, and a stand-in for Paalen himself (Frank).

The first two acts are set in a post office that is crumbling under the unleashed power of "anagravity," which has been unlocked by Prometheus/Faust and stolen by Gori—and which is Paalen's stand-in for nuclear power. In the third act, Prometheus and Frank return to a postapocalyptic Earth, having absconded with a spaceship when things went really wrong. They find a wasteland, but Gori is still alive and unchanged. Disappointed with Marxism and with Surrealism, Paalen retreats to a position of bourgeois humanism; his critique of human folly is prevented from being truly withering by its general and abstract nature.

A reading of *The Beam of the Balance* took place at Robert Motherwell's house. The year before, Motherwell had published a collection of Paalen's writings, *Form and Sense*.[68] Motherwell's fellow post-Surrealist, Barnett Newman, saw in Hiroshima the need for a new tragic culture. In his essay "The New Sense of Fate" (1948),

Newman praised Greek tragic poetry to the detriment of Greek visual art (sculpture), which had no real sense of tragedy and was focused on physical beauty. Newman noted that after World War II, the artist "has more feeling and consequently more understanding for a Marquesas islands fetish than for the Greek figure."[69] The war was the gruesome realization of Surrealism, making much Surrealist art look very recherché and aesthetic in the process:

> The war the Surrealists predicted has robbed us of our hidden terror, as terror can exist only if the forces of tragedy are unknown. We now know the terror to expect. Hiroshima showed it to us. We are no longer, then, in the face of a mystery. After all, wasn't it an American boy who did it? The terror has indeed become as real as life. What we have now is a tragic rather than a terrifying situation.[70]

In his conclusion, Newman asks whether modern artists will "make the same error as the Greek sculptors" and create an art of overrefined beauty, and exhorts his contemporaries to take cues from the Greek *writers* instead, and "tear the tragedy to shreds."[71] In practice, such tragic shredding could itself easily become an exercise in angsty aestheticism. While there are notable exceptions, especially in literature and the cinema, on the whole, the art of the "first responders" of the late 1940s and 1950s tended to stage the postwar nuclear age *as existential tragedy* rather than as political issue.[72] In much 1950s art, the possibility of a total and remainderless destruction of culture and of life is evoked yet at the same time symbolically conquered through the proliferation of tattered, ravaged, or starkly simplified and thereby sublime and existential forms.[73]

In 1958, during an antinuclear conference in Tokyo, Günther Anders visited the memorial of the nuclear bombardment in Hiroshima. Its abstract arch, which only appeared symbolic "because the non-functional always suggests symbolism," reminded him of Abstract Expressionism and its endorsement by the United States, even by the War Department itself:[74]

> It is no coincidence that this belated official preference for the destruction of figurative forms in art (the propaganda for enjoyment of this destruction and the mocking of those who did not go along with this artistic progress) occurred simultaneously with the actual destruction of the world; nor is it a coincidence that the dress rehearsal for this destruction, which occurred in Hiroshima, found its memorial in a "non-objective object."[75]

Anders's unwillingness to see in Abstract Expressionism anything but a politically motivated rip-off of prewar European modernism is obviously problematic, but his suspicions of the open, noncommittal nature of the pseudo-symbolism of such art are worth pondering.[76] In Europe, certainly, Lucio Fontana and other artists of the Spatialism movement courted "nuclear" connotations with certain of their forms (swirls comparable to the patterns of electrons, and so on). More explicit, and moving beyond such abstract symbolism, was the post-Surrealist movement of Arte Nucleare, launched in 1951–52 by Enrico Baj and others.[77]

In 1952, Baj painted the *Manifesto Bum* (Boom Manifesto), featuring a black mushroom-cloud-shaped head against an acid-lemon background overlaid with nuclear slogans and formulas. At the center, the text says: "People's heads are charged with explosives. Every atom is about to explode. The blind, which is to say the non-nuclears, ignore the situation." While this seems to sound a note of warning, the text on the left picks up on the utopian dimension: "Forms disintegrate. Man's new forms are those of the atomic universe." Once again, dreams of a new vision: Arte Nucleare was a profoundly ambiguous undertaking.

In 1953, the critic Beniamino Dal Fabbro asked:

> Was not matter, exactly like painting, disintegrating under the dangerous bombardments of physics and chemistry? So we should allow the Nuclearists to say that they imitate, that they represent the dances of the nuclei, the battle of the atoms, the molecular whirlings, the encounters of ions with electrons. In origin, after all, the Nuclearists are romantics in revolt, against the academic classicism of the Abstractionists.[78]

This revolt, however, increasingly took the movement beyond even more expressionist evocations of "molecular whirlings." The art underwent a figurative turn, showing bloblike disfigured beings in a primitivist style. Rather than dancing nuclei, some of the work appeared to evoke nuclear blasts and fallout-riddled wastelands. Still, the lure of micro/macro analogies remained strong, as a text by Asger Jorn shows:

> I have noticed a tremendous desire to fathom blots, whirls and all kinds of dripping, to mould forms, images and symbols, as if out of a primitive chaos; little by little to reduce every possible chance-event; to condense a clot of phosphorous enamel around the symbols that change themselves from "nuclear" into "natural." In these symbols is stored the nucleus of the artistic language necessary for the expression of this new world that we feel is creating itself about us day after day.[79]

Protesting Mutants

Jorn participated in the Arte Nucleare movement later in the decade, and Baj was involved in Jorn's International Movement for an Imaginist Bauhaus (which attacked the functionalist HfG Ulm). In

1960, Breton and Marcel Duchamp included work by Baj in the last major Surrealist exhibition, "Surrealist Intrusion in the Enchanters' Domain." Two years later, Breton wrote an essay on the artist that would be included in the definitive edition of *Surrealism and Painting*—in which he notes that Baj illustrated Lucretius's *De rerum natura* as "a first celebration of an atomic vision of the universe."[80] Arte Nucleare, then, belongs to the postwar afterlife of Surrealism and to the prehistory of the Situationist International; it is the historical avant-garde morphing into the neo-avant-garde.

Shortly after World War II, Matta illustrated Denis de Rougemont's *Lettres sur la bombe atomique*, published by Brentano's in New York. As the introduction states, Matta "was always drawn to modern physicists' work on wave propagation and radiation, and to the huge transformations that scientists had imposed on matter"—with drawings of emaciated beings in some non-Euclidian forcefield.[81] However, his illustrations for de Rougemont's book reflect an anthropomorphic turn in his work, characterized by emaciated figures Matta often referred to with the term *vitreur*. These vitreurs appear to inhabit the universe of the "Grands Transparents"—Breton's "new myth," which had been launched in "Prolegomena to a Third Surrealist Manifesto or Not," published in *VVV* in 1942. That same year, Breton's speculative fiction was also included in the "New Myths" section of the *First Papers of Surrealism* exhibition catalogue.[82]

The "Great Invisibles" or "Great Transparent Ones" were supposedly giant invisible creatures. What if we were surrounded by higher beings that our senses cannot perceive? What if we are nothing but the pets or parasites of these invisible beings? In *VVV*, Breton's text was illustrated by Matta, who always maintained that he had provided Breton with the idea for the Grands Transparents.[83] Whereas Breton interpreted them more literally as enormous invisible beings, for Matta they were waveforms.[84]

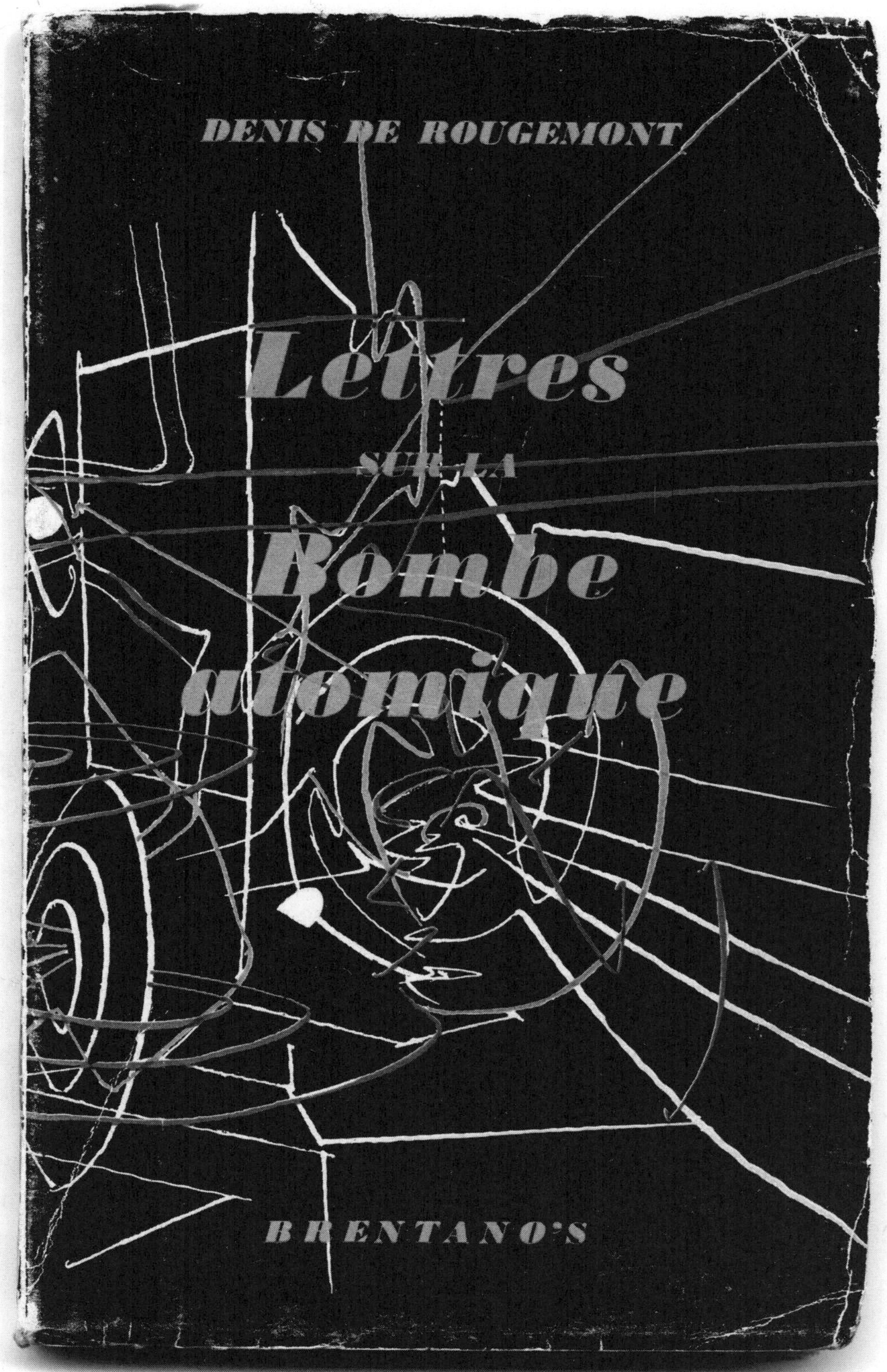

Cover of Denis de Rougemont, *Lettres sur la bombe atomique* (1946), artwork by Matta

Breton's myth of the Grands Transperants would be revived by Jacques Bergier and Louis Pauwels in "Reverie on Mutants," the final section of their 1960 bestseller *The Morning of the Magicians* (*Le matin des magiciens*). They merged Breton's myth with the sci-fi trope of super-/posthuman mutants that are among us, unobserved. Referencing Alfred E. van Vogt's *Slan*, the duo freely indulges in suggestive speculation: "As Andre Breton said, when imagining the presence among us of 'Great Transparent Beings,' it is possible that they escape our observation thanks to some form of camouflage of the kind adopted by mimetic animals."[85]

While Breton had noted that these putative beings are above us "on the animal scale," suggesting that they have evolved beyond the human, there is no suggestion that these beings are posthuman mutants. In a manner that must have been profoundly offensive to Breton, Pauwels and Bergier continue: "'The New Man is living amongst us! He is there! What more do you want? I will tell you a secret: I have seen the New Man. He is intrepid and cruel! I was afraid in his presence!' Thus spake a trembling Hitler."[86] Obviously, there is no source for this grotesque assertion, which is one among many in a work of esoteric pseudo-history that is suffused with an odious fascination for the "secret knowledge" supposedly possessed by the Nazis.

In 1961, Pauwels and Bergier went on to found the magazine *Planète*, in which they continued to present a hodgepodge of suggestive exercises in historical fiction or mythologizing history under the name of "fantastic realism." Zapping between ancient civilizations and impending future mutations, their publication again, had a particular fascination for supposed occult Nazi knowledge and practices. The first issue alone contains an introduction by Pauwels on "a changed world in which humans begin to suspect that they may be in the process of mutating," notes on a book on the Third Reich that dwells on the "fascination" Nazism exerts on the "people of the 1960s"—with an image caption characterizing Himmler as "the incredible Himmler"—as well as texts on Lovecraft, Pierre Teilhard de Chardin, and more of Pauwels's speculations on a "new Renaissance." The latter is marked both by a quest for the lost or disappearing knowledge of ancient and aboriginal cultures and by the search for life in outer space, with "intelligence undergoing a mutation."[87]

In the same inaugural issue, Pierre Guérin speculates on extraterrestrial life while challenging traditional views of man as the end point of evolution. The editors made sure to include subheadings lifted more or less straight from *The Morning of the Magicians*: "A Species beyond Man," "The Problem of Mutations," and "If Mutants Were among Us…"[88] Pierre Restany, meanwhile, presented Nouveau Réalisme as a potential first step toward the new Renaissance.[89] As Gavin Parkinson notes, after Yves Klein's death in 1962, Restany would unabashedly write about Klein as a prophetic mutation of the human species.[90]

Speculative theory seeks to purify philosophy of the element of praxis while donning it in some of the aura of speculative fiction. Tellingly, a blurb on one of Graham Harman's books claims his style "evokes that of a William James merged with the spirit of H. P. Lovecraft."[91] It turns out that the *Ding an sich* is Cthulhu. It is telling that the reference here is not to, say, a figure like Alexander Bogdanov, but to a proto-fascist mythmaker who already played an extremely problematic role in *The Morning of the Magicians* and *Planète*. As Parkinson's admirable reconstruction shows, Pauwels and Bergier were known among the avant-garde as reactionaries who supported French colonialism in Algeria. In 1960, Pauwels conducted a fawning TV interview with former Vichy war criminal and then-current Paris police prefect Maurice Papon, who would become responsible for the notorious police massacre of Algerians in Paris on October 17, 1961. Breton's late-Surrealist group and the Situationists rejected Pauwels and Bergier's stance on colonialism as much as their mutational rhetoric, which can be regarded as a mystifying response to widespread concerns over the consequences of nuclear testing and a potential nuclear war.[92]

Mutants abound in 1950s and 1960s culture, from B movies and comics such as *The Incredible Hulk* and *X-Men* to Leslie Fiedler's notorious 1965 essay "The New Mutants," which analyzes the changing habitus of young Americans in the age of counterculture and sexual revolution in mutational terms.[93] By the end of the decade, Henry Flynt's 1969 manifesto "Overthrow the Human Race!" presents nuclear mutation as a pseudo-Nietzschean tool to overcome "man," proposing to induce a thermonuclear war to cause mutations and thereby go beyond the human race.[94] The trope, of course, also plays a significant role in Japanese popular culture (*Godzilla*), and in the sculptures and installations of Tetsumi Kudo, who worked in Paris from 1962 on.

Mutation, strictly speaking, is a form of genetic recombination that affects individuals; through successful reproduction, such mutants can lead to new species or subspecies. Its proliferation in twentieth-century art and culture suggests that the aesthetic regime always bred speculations—but, then as now, such proposals have ambiguous and sometimes troubling overtones. With its speculative-suggestive subheadings of "If Mutants Were among Us" and "An Invisible Society of Mutants?" Pauwels and Bergier's *Morning of the Magicians*, like *Planète*, suggested a superhuman mutation in progress. This (r)evolution was linked, in obscure ways, to Nazism and its scientific experiments. The mythmaking duo liked to ruminate on concentration camps as experimental labs, and they often appeared to intimate that the mutants among us were a secret sect of "cosmonazis."[95] In equally obscure and contradictory ways, the mutation motif was also linked to the advent of nuclear weapons at the end of the war. On the pages of *Planète*, the reader encountered references to J. Robert Oppenheimer, the "father of the atomic bomb," as well as to Teilhard de Chardin's eschatological interpretation of the "liberation of energy from the atom."[96]

Meanwhile, Robert Jungk more grimly noted the "poisoning of the atmosphere with radioactive isotopes" as a particularly dramatic manifestation of the changes imposed by humans on their environment—such radiation presumably inducing mutations and, thus, inaugurating a next step in evolution.[97] Jungk introduces a degree of seriousness and concern in the context of *Planète*. With *Brighter Than a Thousand Suns* (first published in 1956 in German), he had published the classic account of the Manhattan Project.[98] The book became important in the context of the early Campaign for Nuclear Disarmament (CND) in the United Kingdom, founded in 1957, and Jungk himself became active in the CND.

More on the margins, in 1958, Breton penned an antinuclear manifesto in Paris, *Démasquez les physiciens, videz les laboratoires*, which was cosigned mostly by younger Surrealists and attacked the "theology of the bomb" and science's status as the new "opium of the people."[99] While the text exhorts the reader to support a Comité de Lutte Anti-nucléaire, possibly modeled after the CND, this does not appear to have gained any traction. Nonetheless, this tract is a sign of things to come: the neo-avant-garde would go on to desublimate the nuclear aesthetics of the postwar era. The Surrealists responded to *The Morning of the Magicians* and *Planète* with several screeds, collected in the booklet *Les fausses cartes transparentes de planète*, whose main authors, José Pierre and Robert Benayoun, were also cosignatories of Breton's antinuclear tract.[100]

As for the Situationists: in 1962, Debord and Jorn planned a journal titled *Mutant*, which never saw the light of day. In the announcement/manifesto, they lambast atomic shelters and "the new aristocracy of the caves."[101] The proposed journal's title is undoubtedly a dig at

Pauwels and Bergier's mutational rhetoric: an attempt to desublimate their numinous intimations about a "Renaissance" through mutation and an evolutionary leap. For Debord and Jorn, the powers that be were speculating on a life reduced to survival, as embodied by the nuclear fallout shelter. These shelters, the Situationists note, will obviously not offer real protection in the case of nuclear war, but protection was only a pretext used to integrate people ever more tightly into a socioeconomic order that depends on the renouncing of their real desires and channeling them into artificial needs:[102]

> Survival as the opposite of life, if rarely voted for so clearly as by the buyers of shelters in 1961, can be found at all levels of the struggle against alienation. It is found in the old conception of art, which stressed survival through one's works, an admission of a renunciation of life—art as excuse and consolation (especially since the bourgeois era of aesthetics, that secular substitute for the religious otherworld).[103]

Art, then, had been a de facto fallout shelter of the bourgeois soul long before Hiroshima.

With the ecological movement gaining momentum toward the end of the 1960s, concerns over mutation increasingly also related to other species—not just to us (post)humans. In Holland, for instance, the Kabouter movement that emerged from the ashes of Provo in the late 1960s painted a grim picture of impending monstrous mutations. Protagonist Roel van Duijn argued that the mere collectivization of the means of production was insufficient; they needed to be *transformed*, beginning with energy—not nuclear energy, but high-tech windmills.[104]

In 1971, Van Duijn and Co. rang the alarm bell over the production of nerve gas by Philips-Duphar in the sleepy Dutch town of Weesp,

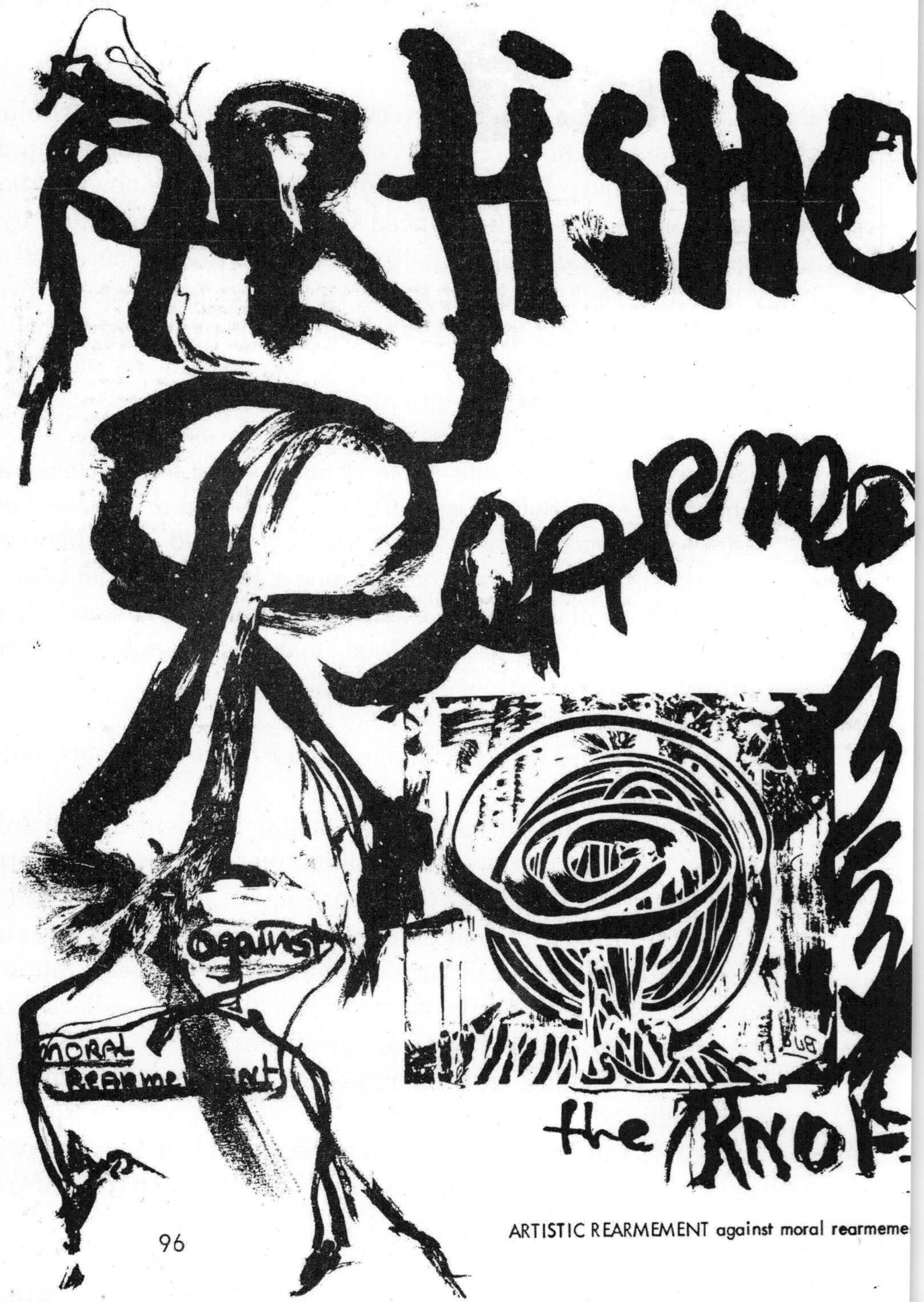

ARTISTIC REARMEMENT against moral rearmeme

MUTANT 1962

European critique of the inadequate programme which has just been presented to President Kennedy and Governor Rockefeller by the academic staff of Universities, Colleges, and Research Institutes for New York City and the Cambridge-Boston Area, with the aim of overthrowing the absurd procedures of "civil defense" in the United States.

We should like to point out the absurdity and complete emptiness of the decalration made by you as the "Civil Defense Letter Commettee" in the "New York Times" of Saturday December 30, 1961 (International Edition), unless one considers it onlyas a pure declaration of personal conscience against the new American defense policy. We regret the fact that there cannot be found a single element of real importance in all your opposition, and we propose that you join us in a concrete attitude towards our common aim. We therefore suggest that you adopt the positive programme of the "Comité European pour une Relance de l'Expansion Humaine" (European Committee for the Persuit of Human Expamsion) which proposes to create a new cultural Renaissance, a new practical liberty.
For this, it is necessary to subscribe to our three fundamental demands.

1. I promise that I shall never, personnally, under any circumstances, set foot in an atomic shelter.
   It is better to die standing with all the cultural heritage of humanity, the perpetual modification of which must remain our task.
2. I refuse to have anyhing whatsoever to do with the new aristocracy of the caves, and never to drink in the company of an owner or builder of an atomic shelter; for this subterranean aristocracy, even if it manages to survive the disaster, will be of the quality of sewer rats, and could in no case be considered a continuation of the human race.
3. At this point in our present situation it is not so much the thermonuclear war, but rather the threat of this was, which shows the absolute bankruptcy of all the politicians in the world. The capitalist or bureaucratic leaders of both East and West, already make use of their bombs every day, in order to secure power for themselves. Only if one realizes that they have placedthemselvesbeyond the law can one establisha new legality
   I therefore pledge myself not to expect the necessary upheavals of society by any of the existing formations of specialised politics.

In the first stages one can demanda nautralisation of the defense program of states by their transference into anArmed Force controlled by the United Nations. At the same time military programme of conquest could be submitted to a world organization like U.N.E.S.C.O. though radically transformed and divested of its dependecy upon state bureaucracies. This organization would coordinate the development of spacial-interplanetary activites of different groups intoa perspective of human solidarity. Only the unification of our military traditions in the whole world towards a spacial expansion can guarnatee world peace, the alternative of peace and atomic war beeing false, because in fact there is no choice. The choice which imposes itself upon modern man is the continuation of imperialis competition of human destruction or the Renaissance of humanity on a spacial scale.
But the new frontier of mankind is not only in Outer Space; it is in the radical transformation of life on this planet. If the nations can come to an agreement to maintain peace in transforming it into spacial expansion, on the question of total expansion of mankindwe cannot come to an understandingwiththe "nations". Weare not unconditional partisansof peace: the profound error of the intellectual Americans in their defense, devoid of imagination, of the actual peace which they wish to preserve. Nobody really likes this peace, which nourishes not only the menace of such a was, but also the total alienation of actual daily life, and the absolut boredom of a society on the road to cybernitisation. Peace remains, like this life itself, without importance; and what is important is human expansion: the creation of events that suit us.
We are going to inform you ingreater detail in our reviewMUTANT, which will appear in the spring, of your underdeveloped attitudes, as well as those of the Russians. We hope that many of the subscribers to your manifest will join us in this perspective, which can give a future to your direction.

Guy Debord and Asger Jorn, "Mutant" manifesto (1962) in Jacqueline de Jong's *Situationist Times*, no 3 (January 1963)

which—they feared—messed with the genetic makeup of the insects in the region. In a Kabouter publication, Hans Korteweg and Van Duijn referenced an anonymous Philips-Duphar employee who sketches a possible scenario for the near future:

> This means that most insects in the area are sterilized—and according to someone from the PR department, Philips-Duphar will use this as a selling point in its advertising—but what is hidden from the public is the fear that many insects will undergo mutations. Just imagine! Wasps with a diameter of 40 cm who will attack little children in the streets! Butterflies who will only feed on blood protoplasm![105]

Here countercultural ecologists use provocative pulp horror imagery, seeking to marshal fears about humans falling prey to mutant insects. Ultimately, then, this scenario of animal mutation is highly anthropocentric. But what if we *are* the animals? In his *La nucléarisation du monde*, Semprun hints at coming mutations that will make humans feel "like a fish in the water of Minimata [*sic*]," a reference to bioaccumulated mercury in fish in Minamata Bay, causing mercury poisoning.[106] Infra-sensible phenomena can result in very visible physical consequences—bodily symptoms indexing an intractable aesthetico-political problem.

Indexical Conceptualism

Starting in the 1960s and throughout his career, Sigmar Polke showed an interest in radiation. His library contains books from the period when the German *Umweltbewegung* and Green Party took off, such as the volume *Strahlung in Umwelt, Medizin und Technik* (1983), but also earlier literature that is more purely technical or historical in nature—ranging from an introduction to X-rays dating to 1930 via

Hermann Römpp's *Atom-Lexikon* (1945) to Hellmut Droscha's *Kernreaktoren* (1958) and Franz Kirchheimer's *Das Uran und seine Geschichte* (1963).[107] Uranium, in particular, held a fascination for Polke. His collection contains examples of "uranium glass"—items made from glass containing uranium, which is fluorescent under UV light—and from 1982 to 2000, he produced several series of *Uranografien*, autoradiographs of uranium samples.[108] This is a link back to the early days of radiation enthusiasm.

When seen in conjunction with Polke's paintings such as *Höhere Wesen befahlen: Rechte obere Ecke schwarz malen* (1969)—with its implication that the abstract composition was determined by "higher beings" using the artist as medium—Polke's take on autoradiography also seems to revive the spiritualist and occultist overtones that the discovery of radioactivity had for Kandinsky (a theosophist with a firm belief in auras and "thought-forms"). At the same time, Polke's Uranografien take their place in the mythology of Polke as "alchemist," handling and exposing himself (and perhaps also the viewers) to dangerous and toxic materials. The index of radiation here becomes a sign for the grandeur of the artist-magus.

While there is a tendency to interpret indexicality in crudely causal terms, the index only starts to signify when it is interpreted *as a sign*. When, in a discussion of the implications of quantum mechanics, Karen Barad (in tellingly "photographic" language) writes that "images or representations are not snapshots or depictions [...] but rather condensations of multiple practices of engagement," this evokes both physical experiment (as in cloud chambers) and "conceptual experiments" in the form of quantum physicists' *Gedankenexperimente*.[109] In the context of quantum physics, Barad argues that the measured value is attributable neither to an independent object/reality nor to the act of measurement as such, and that the *referent* should be thought of not as an independent object but as a phenomenon, with phenomena including "all relevant features of the experimental arrangement." This can be taken as the point of departure for a general reconsideration of indexicality.

Barad can be seen as continuing Latour's critique of scientific objectivity as being "supposed to be *acheiropoieta*, that is *not* made by any human hand."[110] The index has often been cast as an acheiropoetic sign, but again: insofar as it signifies, insofar as it *matters*, it is the product of interpretation as well as physical causality, and the feedback between the two. A watch that stopped running during the Hiroshima blast can be read as an index of that moment; a photograph of such a watch is a second-degree index that can enter into circuits of curatorial and critical practice. Video footage recorded by automated cameras in Fukushima can become part of a video by Philippe Rouy, in which the disturbances in the image caused by radiation become not only evidence of contamination, but also a reflection on visibility and (a)visuality.[111] More dramatically, bodies exposed to radiation become indices through symptoms that emerge sooner or later. This is itself part of an "experimental arrangement" in which the risk of accidents is not avoided but managed in more or less successful ways—and diagnosis and treatment may be subject to all kinds of economic and political constraints.

A number of artistic practices of the 1960s have used the exhibition space as an experimental setup: the white cube as a camera lined with photographic paper or a cloud chamber in which, through aesthetic Gedankenexperimente, radiation could become sensate, sensible. Precisely because such practices took the modernist critique of representation to its limit, the zone of abstraction that is the white cube could become a radiation-sensitive device.

The work of Yves Klein—Restany's mutant—contains explicit references to the advent of the nuclear age, such as an "anthropométrie" titled *Hiroshima* (ca. 1961), in which the blue imprints evoke the "atomic shadows" created by the bomb blast. However, Klein's white *vide* spaces, those absolutely purified white cubes, may constitute the next step, as is suggested by a Klein quotation that reads like a Cold War version of Kandinsky's much earlier statement: "One must—and this is not an exaggeration—keep in mind that we are living in the atomic age, where everything physical and material could disappear from one day to another, to be replaced by nothing but the ultimate abstraction imaginable."[112]

With the well-known photos of Klein in his vide in Krefeld's Haus Lange suggesting that the even light here eliminates shadows, the vides can be interpreted as zones in which all that is solid evaporates into energy; particles reveal themselves to be waves.[113] Such a reading is strengthened by two pieces that resonate with Klein's vides. For his contribution to René Block's series of installations titled "Blockade '69," Polke turned an empty white gallery space into a podium in which he could "imagine that a particle [*ein Teilchen*] circulates around this space."[114] Here, the white cube becomes a kind of zone of meditation in which a (presumably) subatomic particle outside the space is imagined. The reference to Klein is highly probable given the latter's prominence in the Rhineland in the 1960s.

However, a project by Stanley Brouwn from the subsequent year, which, in turn, appears to respond to Polke, moves the premise back to something closer to Klein's, but without the privileging of the artist as seer that Polke shares (albeit in a frequently ironic mode) with Klein. In Brouwn's piece, everybody can be a visionary. Brouwn's 1970 exhibition in the Museum Abteiberg in Mönchengladbach consisted of empty spaces with the instruction "gehen sie sehr bewusst durch die kosmischen strahlen in den museumsräumen" (walk very deliberately through the cosmic rays in the museum spaces). Rather than using technology to reveal cosmic background radiation, Brouwn tries to create a kind of imaginary awareness of indexical affectedness.

Yves Klein in the *Immaterial Pictorial Sensibility* room at Museum Haus Lange, Krefeld, January 1961

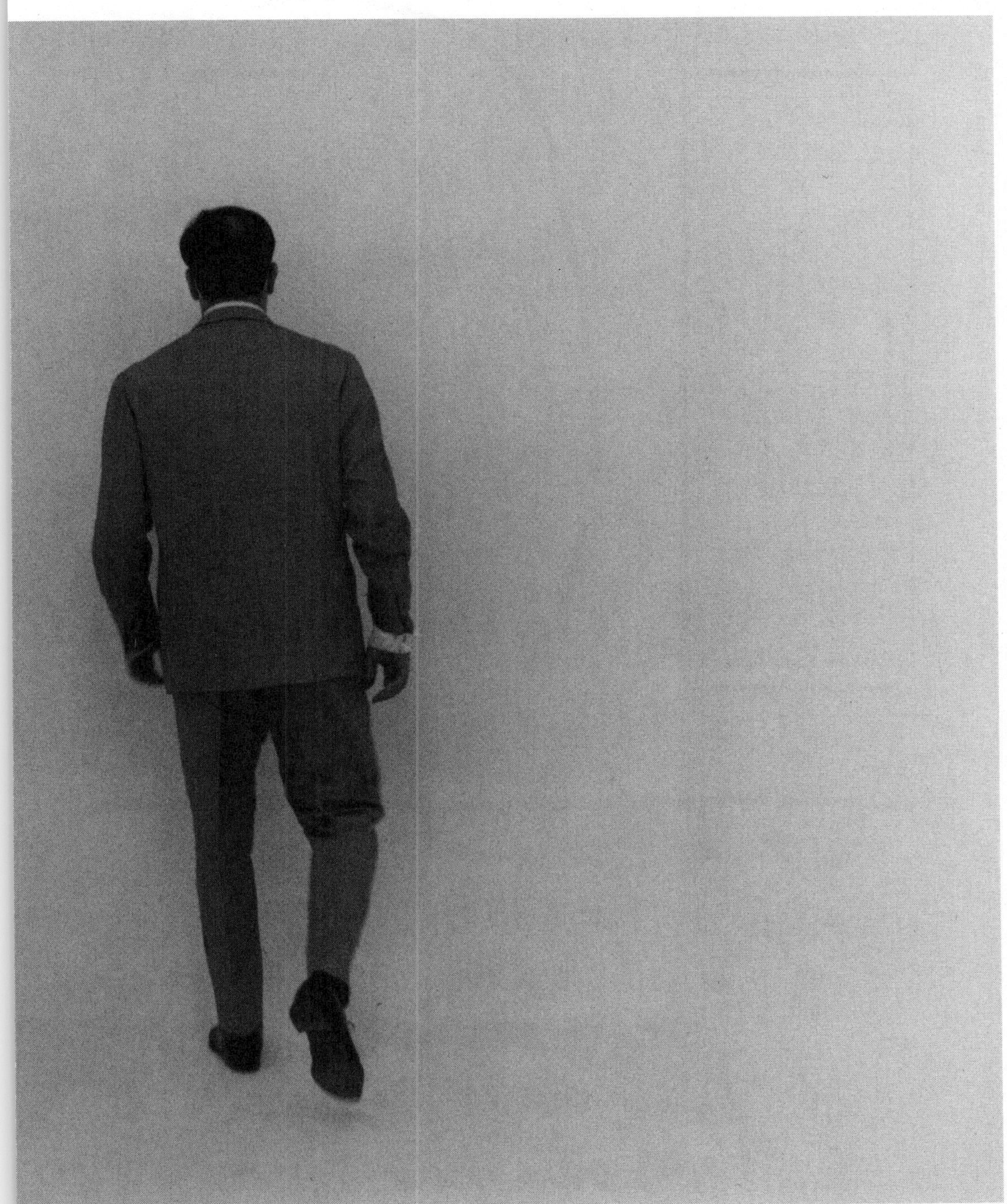

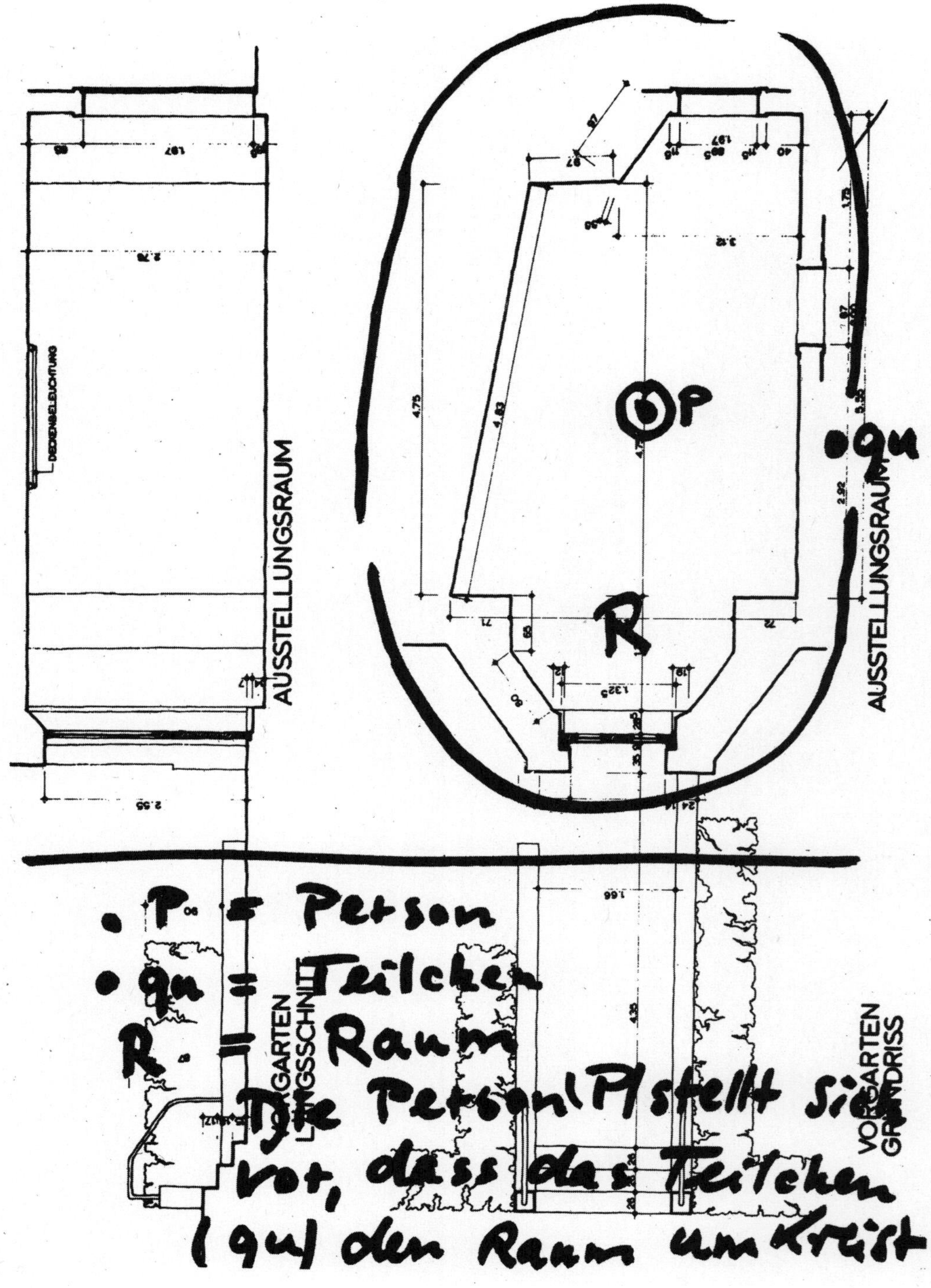

Sigmar Polke's project for "Blockade '69," Galerie René Block, Berlin, 1969

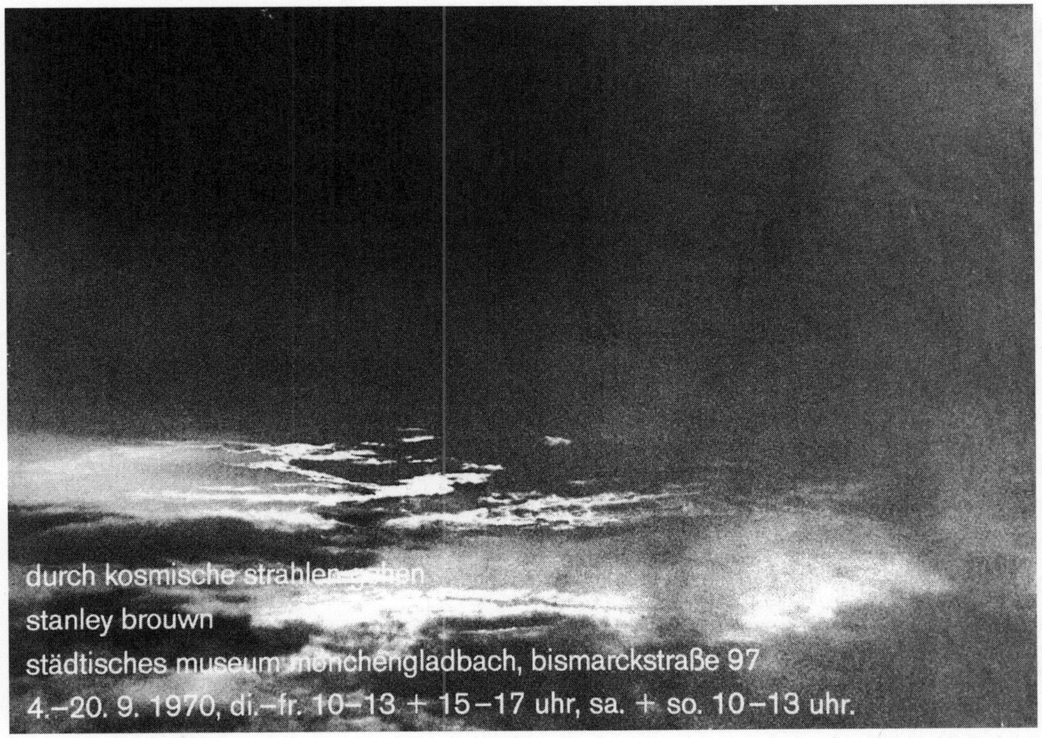

Exhibition poster for Stanley Brouwn, "durch kosmische strahlen gehen," Museum Abteiberg, Mönchengladbach, 1970

Even so, the very notion of cosmic rays is, of course, dependent on a mass of physical research—particularly 1930s and 1940s research with photographic plates showing the tracks of particles that exploded due to cosmic rays.

Some of Robert Barry's Conceptual pieces from this period do involve the presentation of photographic documentation in addition to texts, but the photos are conventional landscapes that Moholy-Nagy would have rejected as reactionary. Barry's *Radiation Installation (Central Park)*, also known as *0.5 Microcurie Radiation Installation* (1969), involved the artist burying a capsule containing barium-133, a stable isotope that would give off low-level, non-harmful, non-iodizing radiation for ten years in Central Park, behind the Metropolitan Museum of Art. As shown in exhibitions, the piece comprises a text as well as black-and-white photos of (supposedly) the spot where the capsule was buried, but, of course, nothing "shows." Barry leaves the political implications of such opacity unstated. As in his work with radio transmitters, the focus is on invisible forces and invisible information that are rendered here through photos but ultimately mostly through language.[115] At the same time, Polke was, in fact, beginning to make autoradiographs with uranium, but Barry's piece seems to be about exploiting conventional photography for its poverty (even as the black-and-white prints are tonally rich), its blind spots.

To jump to the present: in her recent project "Pechblende" (2014–16) and related works, Susanne Kriemann has engaged with the nuclear-photographic archive, exhibiting historical autoradiographs produced by exposing marine creatures after Operation Crossroads in the Bikini Atoll, as well as cloud chamber photographs and other archival images, in conjunction with her own autoradiographs of uraninite, or pitchblende, exposing the material for different amounts of time (three days, seven days, ten days, etc.).[116] Kriemann also photographed and gathered plants from the terrain of a former East

German uranium mine. Some of her photo prints show the plants in situ, printed in dye extracted from those very plants—dye that contains traces of toxic heavy metals, and potentially of radiation, even while it fades over time.[117]

This is a socialization and historicization of Polkean alchemy. Kriemann engages with and intervenes in the nuclear archive, taking snapshots of the ongoing process of planetary nuclearization. In contrast to conventional photography, of which Barthes said that "the duration of the transmission is insignificant," evoking Susan Sontag in claiming that "the photograph of the missing being [...] will touch me like the delayed rays of a star," here duration matters a great deal. Radiation is an index that keeps on shouting.[118]

Compared to Barry's ten years of non-ionizing radiation, some recent pieces emphasize the staggering half-life of radioactive waste generated by the nuclear industry—and its disasters. Taryn Simon's *Black Square* (2006–ongoing) at the Garage Museum in Moscow is, for the time being, an empty square depression in a concrete wall. Simon collaborated with Russia's State Atomic Energy Corporation Rosatom, to produce a vitrified piece of nuclear waste from Chernobyl. Vitrification converts radioactive waste from a volatile liquid to a stable solid mass, which resembles polished black glass. In addition to the highly explicit reference of Malevich's *Black Square* (1915), the work could also be seen as referencing Matta's vitreurs. The piece of glass will supposedly be installed in a void (alcove) at the museum in 3015.

An artist "tirelessly pursuing the creation of monumental, 'critically' grounded images for art-world patriarchs/validators," Simon seems to bank on the continuous existence of a Moscow museum run by an oligarch's ex-partner.[119] This is a reversal of "nuclear semiotics" à la Thomas Sebeok, whose idea for an atomic priesthood presupposed a collapse of most social structures; in the new dark ages, this priesthood would warn people of the danger associated with certain nuclear

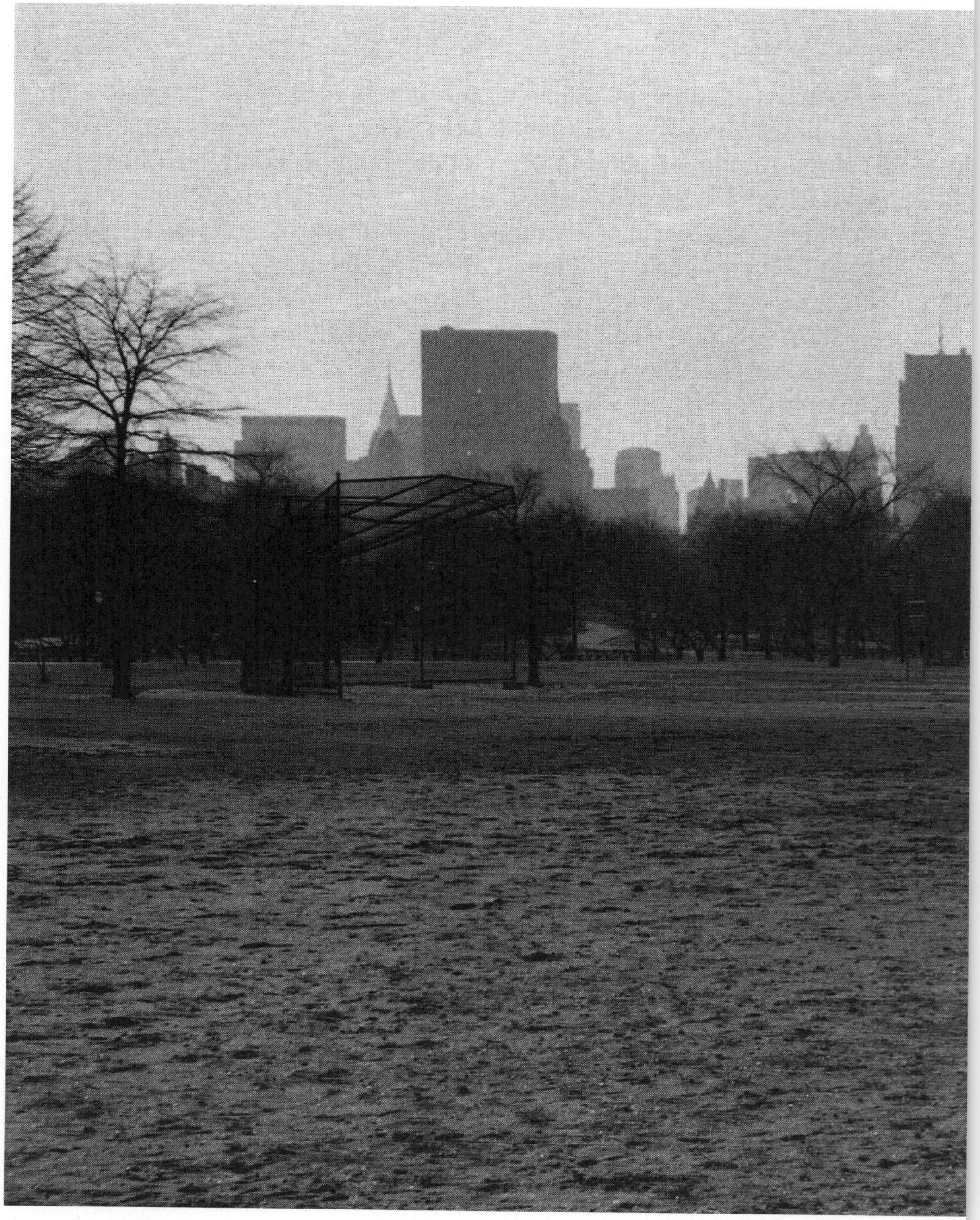

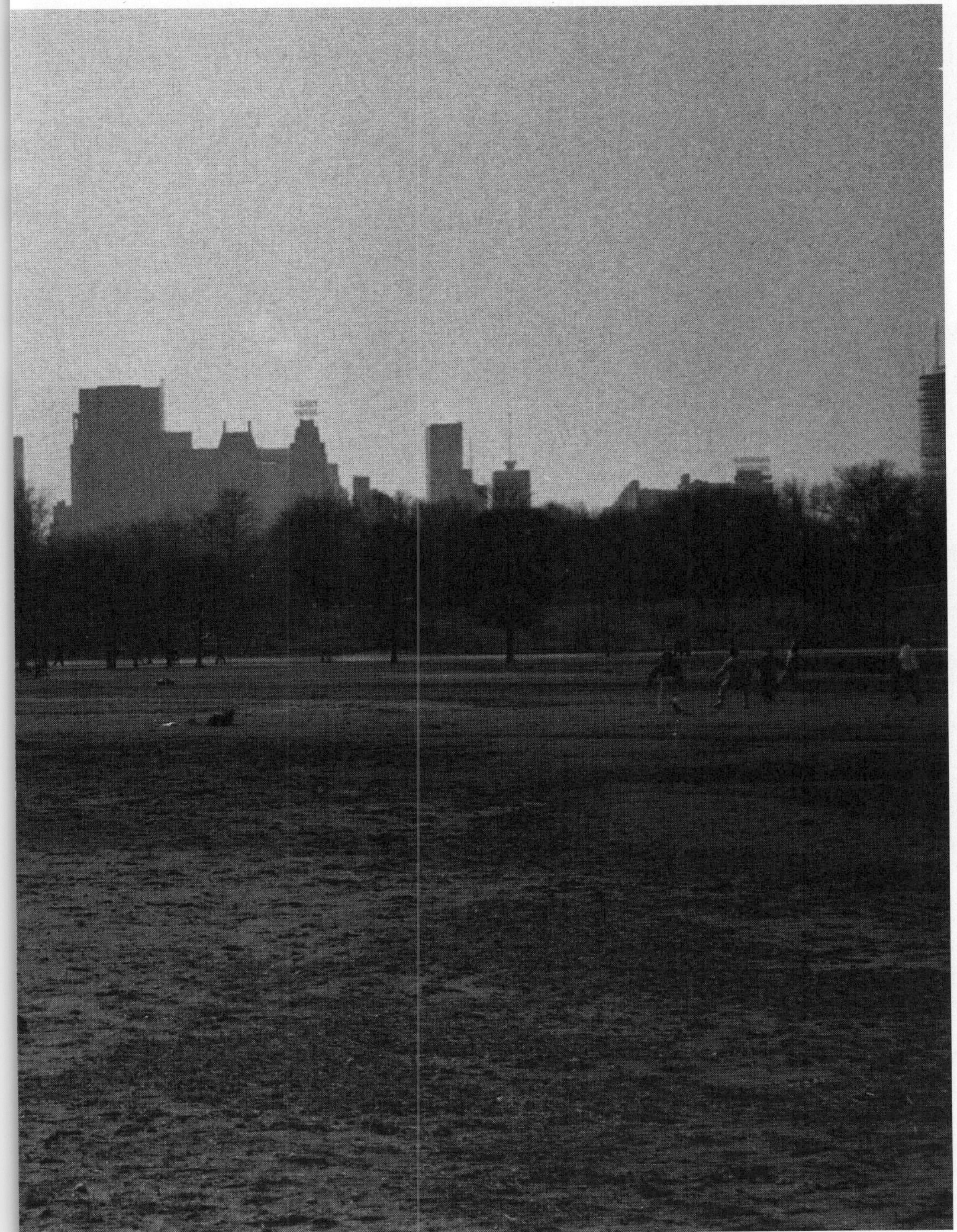

Robert Barry, *Radiation Installation (Central Park)*, 1969

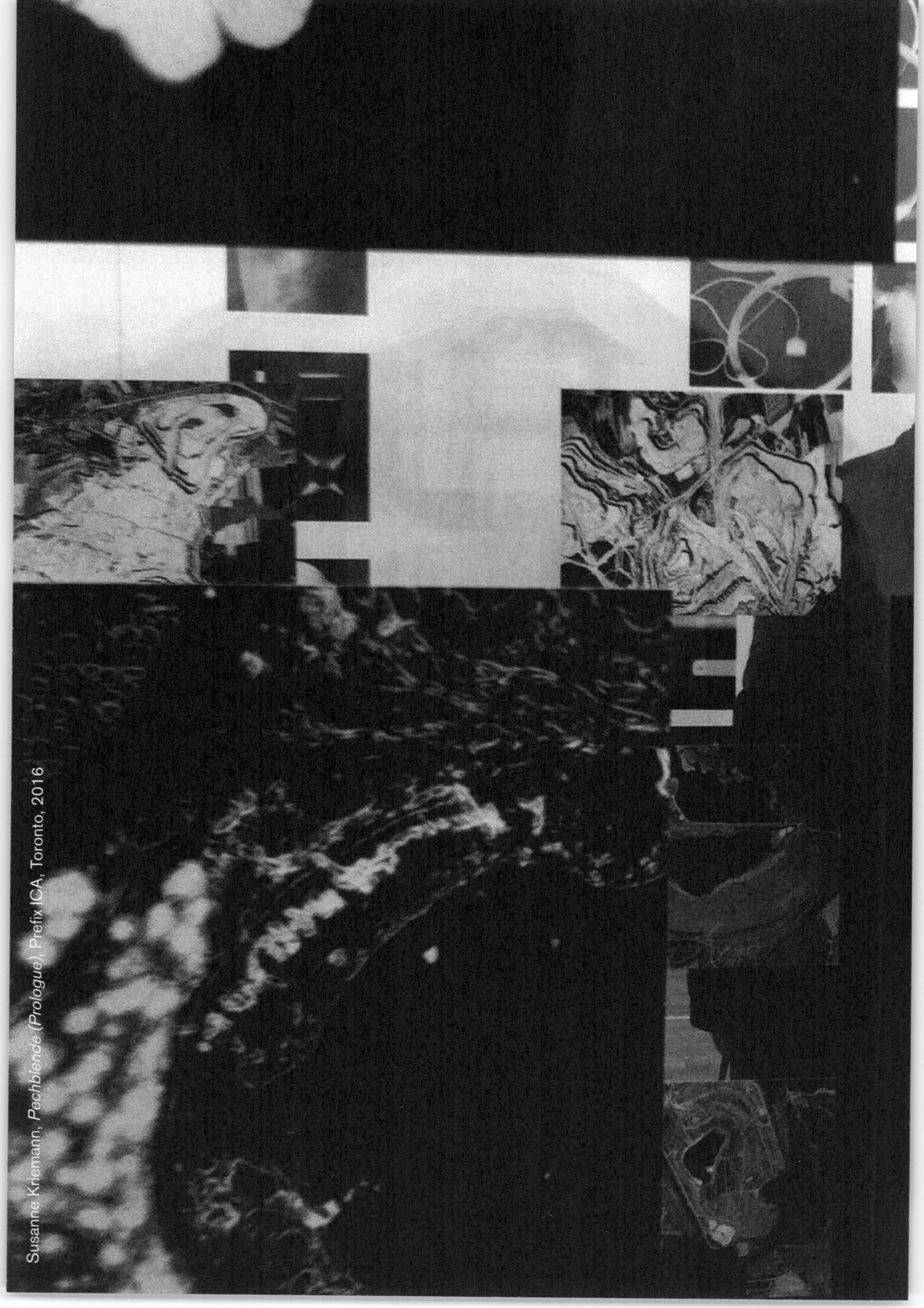

Susanne Kriemann, *Pechblende (Prologue)*, Prefix ICA, Toronto, 2016

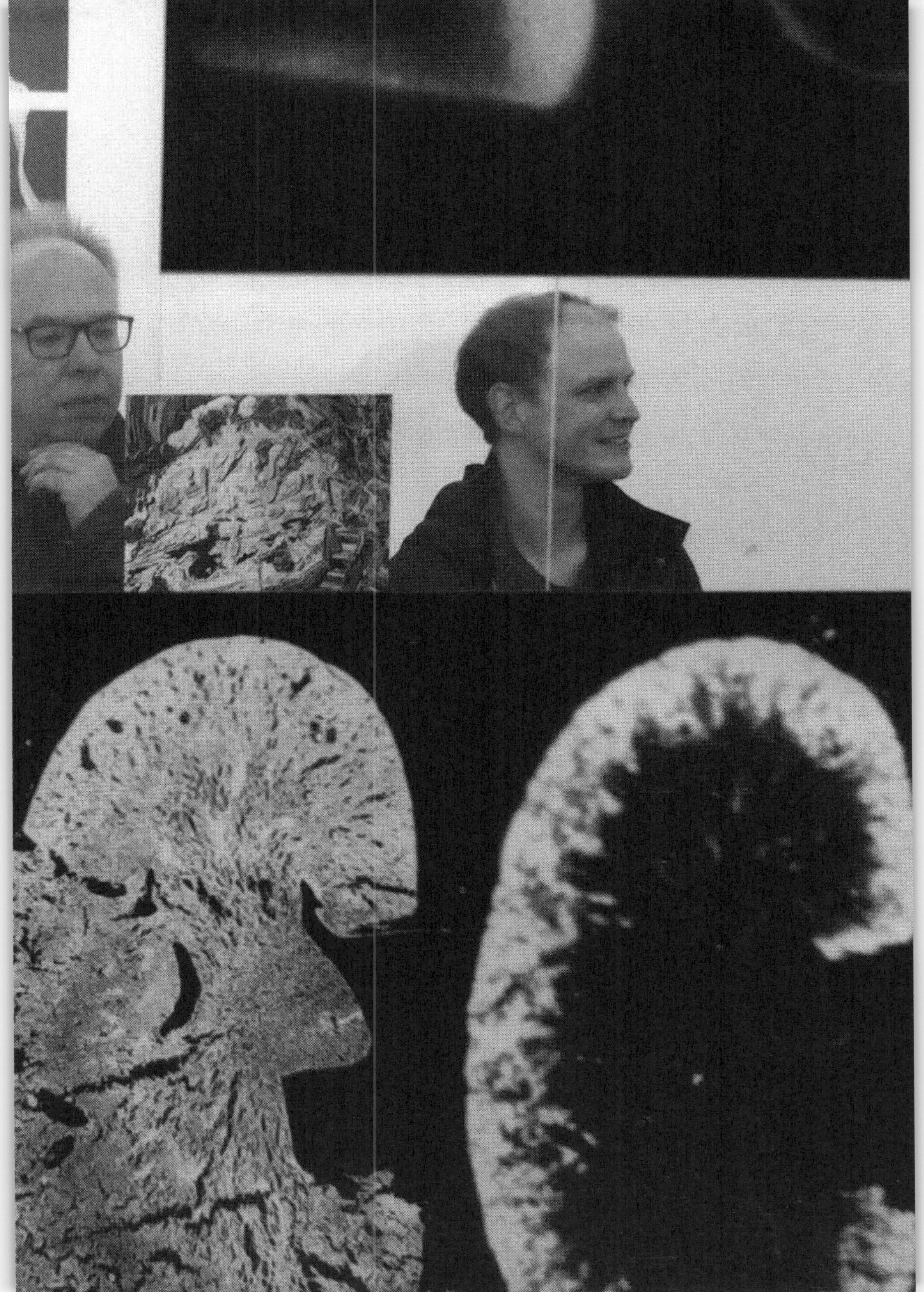

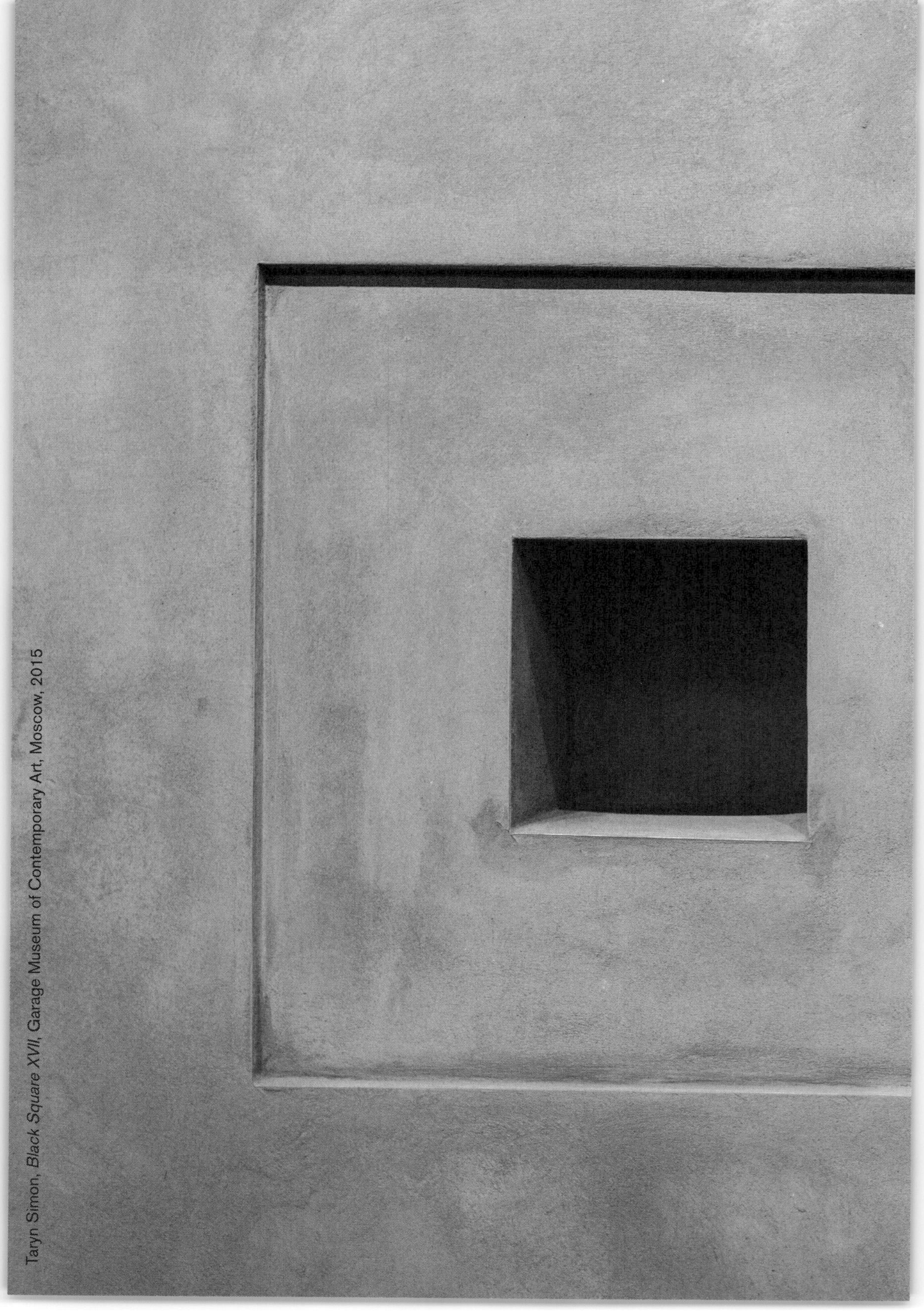

Taryn Simon, *Black Square XVII*, Garage Museum of Contemporary Art, Moscow, 2015

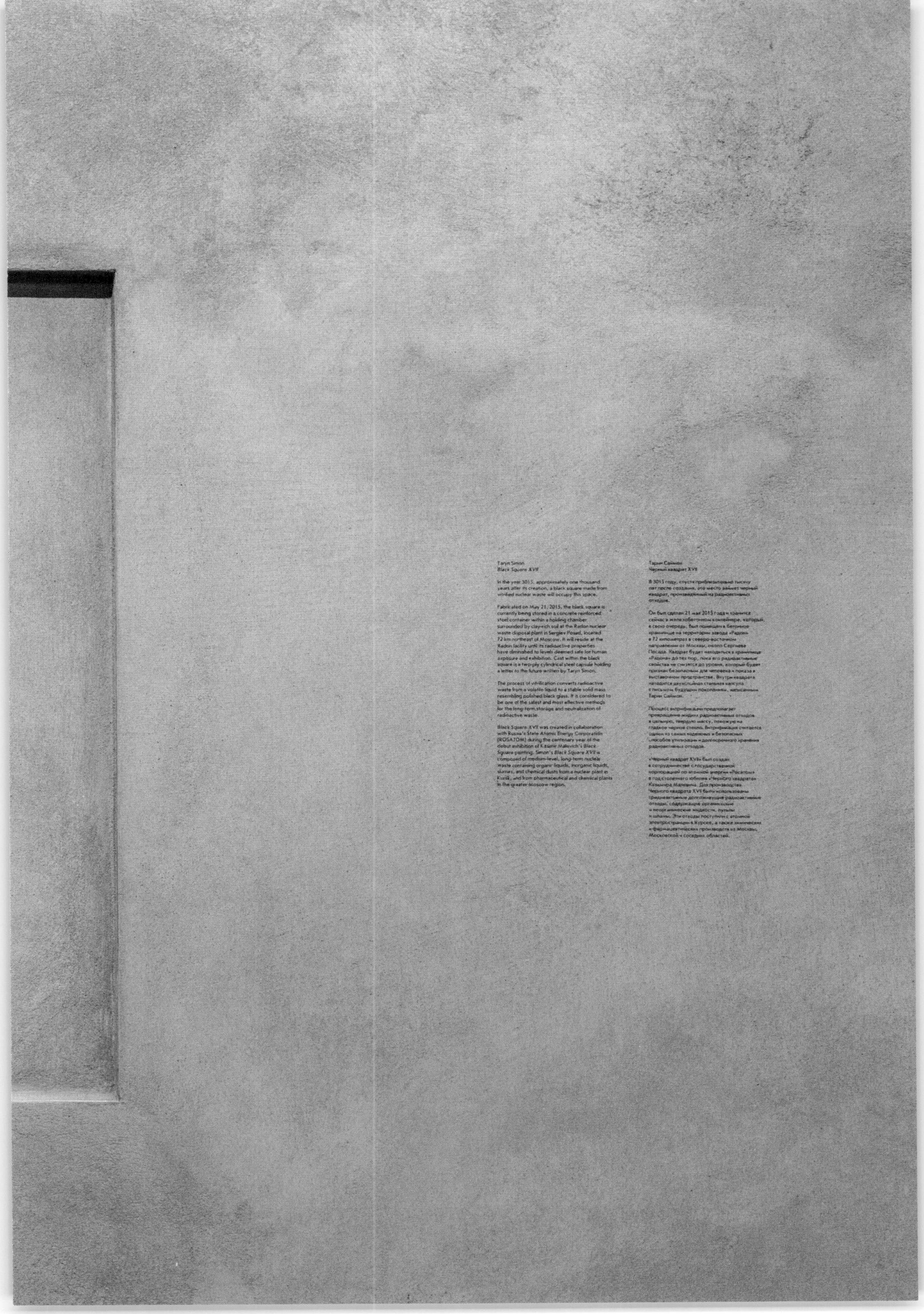
Taryn Simon
Black Square XVII
In the year 3015, approximately one thousand years after its creation, a black square made from vitrified nuclear waste will occupy this space.
Fabricated on May 21, 2015, the black square is currently being stored in a concrete reinforced steel container within a holding chamber surrounded by clay-rich soil at the Radon nuclear waste disposal plant in Sergiev Posad, located 72 km northeast of Moscow. It will reside at the Radon facility until its radioactive properties have diminished to levels deemed safe for human exposure and exhibition. Cast within the black square is a two-ply cylindrical steel capsule holding a letter to the future written by Taryn Simon.
The process of vitrification converts radioactive waste from a volatile liquid to a stable solid mass resembling polished black glass. It is considered to be one of the safest and most effective methods for the long-term storage and neutralization of radioactive waste.
Black Square XVII was created in collaboration with Russia's State Atomic Energy Corporation (ROSATOM) during the centenary year of the debut exhibition of Kazimir Malevich's Black Square painting. Simon's Black Square XVII is composed of medium-level, long-term nuclear waste containing organic liquids, inorganic liquids, slurries, and chemical dusts from a nuclear plant in Kursk, and from pharmaceutical and chemical plants in the greater Moscow region.

sites.[120] With Simon, the new dark ages take the form of the perpetuation of the structures of an autocratic state and its resident kleptocracy. Malevich's zero of form, his quivering stand-in for the infinite, becomes a receptacle for an object that, most of all, seems to perpetuate and celebrate the opacity of the art-industrial complex of Putin's autocratic Russia.

Meanwhile, in the context of the "Don't Follow the Wind" project, Trevor Paglen has installed his *Trinity Cube* (2015) in the Fukushima Exclusion Zone. This small minimalist cube combines an outer layer composed of irradiated broken glass from the zone, with a core made of trinitite—the greenish glass that was created at Trinity Site in Nevada during the first atomic blast on July 16, 1945. The project description states that "the artwork will be viewable by the public when the Exclusion Zone opens again, anytime between 3 and 30,000 years from the present."[121] Even more than Simon, Paglen exploits the "mathematical sublime" of long time spans. While Paglen tends to go for a data-sublime aesthetic that stands at odds with his critical pretensions, the *Trinity Cube* text's rather grotesque oscillation between three and thirty thousand years can be read as an acknowledgment of the vagaries of decontamination. Could the zone be declared safe(ish) sooner rather than later due to political and economic motives? Slow violence (to use Rob Nixon's term) affects people differently based on class, as well as ethnicity and other factors.[122] The Japanese government is massively promoting a "return to normal" for (parts of) the zone. Will it be resettled by a vanguard of "expendables"?

Such questions drive home the point that nuclear indexicality is not a purely "natural" question reducible to the half-life of this or that isotope. The political economy of the nuclear has to be factored in. In *La nucléarisation du monde*, Semprun's persona asks if the invisibility on which the nuclear regime depends is not the ultimate, "autonomous" manifestation of "this limitless social power that is the existence of commodified relations."[123] If the commodity fetish depends on the concealment of labor, then does it not now also depend on a concealment of the dead, anorganic labor of nuclear power?

World-Laboratory and World-Object

Peter Galison has argued that modern physics was marked by a tension between an "image tradition" and a "logic tradition." The former is associated with cloud chambers and bubble chambers producing unique visual events and documentation, whereas the latter can be associated with the Geiger counter and its nonvisual registration of multiple events (the Geiger counter is not about individual clicks but about accumulation).[124] It is still an indexical device that registers particles, with ionization producing an electric charge rather than registering visually. The logic tradition took a step beyond indexicality when, in Galison's account, its focus on statistics and probability took it into the realm of simulation. Since the late 1940s, the development of nuclear weapons has been closely linked with digital computation. Los Alamos scientists used computers such as the ENIAC, the MANIAC, and IBM's SSEC, and deployed "Monte Carlo" simulations to predict the behavior of particles and the chain reactions in (thermo-) nuclear devices—a "new method for extracting information from physical measurements and equations."[125] The measuring of the world becomes its codification, its in-formation.

There is no linear, Baudrillardian progression from "the real" to a "simulation" that marks the loss of this real. Rather, these simulations—from the late-1940s Monte Carlo calculations to the first three-dimensional VR simulation of a thermonuclear explosion at Los Alamos in 2001—are always designed to feed back into reality.[126] This is an operational modeling of reality; the simulated explosion has real-world agency *either* when it is successfully implemented in the real world, producing physical indices, *or* through the logic of deterrence, as a spectral possibility, affecting minds. As event horizon, the big bang of nuclear Armageddon infiltrates subjectivities as surreptitiously as radiation may infiltrate people's lives and bodies—producing indexical effects when it's too late. Simulation, then, contributes to the experimental transformation of the world into a laboratory. In their book *Catastrophism*, Semprun and René Riesel take up a remark by Anders: "Günther Anders' theory of the 'world-laboratory,' according to which the 'laboratory' became co-extensive with the planet at the time of the first nuclear tests, has been positively recuperated, without any rebellious or critical intention whatsoever: as bland confirmation of our confinement in the experimental protocol of industrial society."[127] Anders had been a student of Heidegger's, and his account of the world becoming a laboratory can be seen as a postwar variation on Heidegger's famous notion of the *Weltbild*, or world-picture, according to which modern science objectified the world into a picture.[128] The proliferation of world maps and globes, and their role in colonization and imperial expansion, would be a concretization of that point. But what if we are now *in the picture*, part of the object, part of the global lab?

Michel Serres has termed the atom bomb the first "world-object," defining world-objects as "tools with a dimension that is commensurable with one of the dimensions of the world. A satellite for speed, an atomic bomb for energy, the Internet for space, and nuclear waste for time [...] these are four examples of world-objects."[129] Noting that an object is literally (etymologically) "that which has been thrown or which one throws in front," Serres questions whether such world-objects are still facing us as *obiecta*: "The global dimension that characterizes them eliminates the distance between us and them which in the past defined objects. We now live *in* those world-objects as we live in the world."[130] However, it is precisely this sense of living in a world-object—a global hyperobject—that has generated attempts to objectify the Earth as one object in shared use.

Around 1970, moon landings and photographs taken from space made visible the Earth as a single, unified system: the "Whole Earth." The "Earthrise" photo became an icon, and the demand for NASA to release a photo of the whole Earth was marshaled by Stewart Brand and others into a movement and a business (*The Whole Earth Catalog*).[131] The fascination was felt far outside of Californian techno-libertarian hippie circles. In a 1969 video produced by René Block in Berlin, *Bildnis Stanley Brouwn*, Brouwn walks through the city accompanied by a voice-over that announces that space missions had shown the Earth sitting "like an object in space" at a distance of four hundred thousand kilometers. The conclusion to be drawn from this is that "we can now move on Earth in a very spatially conscious manner," becoming aware of "what space is: i.e., time."[132] The ultimate world-picture, the objectification of Earth in the form of a blue marble, was supposed to have radically altered the mental horizon.

At the end of World War II, the nuclear bomb had already functioned as a kind of anticipatory mockery of the Whole Earth image—for example, in de Rougemont's aforementioned book, in which the Swiss author argued that the "planetary weapon" contained "possibilities for a global union," for a "universal community."[133] As many science-fiction films would reiterate, it takes a planetary threat to create global unity. It's not the Whole Earth but the bomb that will bring us together; or rather, the former becomes a promise due to the threat of the latter: "Well before the images of the Earth seen from the moon, the atom bomb appeared as the event that unified the human condition and the planet."[134] De Rougemont's manifesto stands as one compromised attempt to think global unity not through the Earth but through its otherworldly double, the bomb.

If the Cold War period saw much anguish over the potential end of the world due to a nuclear Armageddon, a collapse due to overpopulation and the exhaustion of natural resources—as predicted in the projections of the Club of Rome's world model—seemed a best-case scenario. What was needed, then, was a Plan B, or a Planet B. For Brand, the lesson of the Whole Earth image was emphatically *not* that this blue planet is all we have. In the 1970s, he became an ardent proponent of space colonization, using designs and strategies proposed by Gerard K. O'Neill, and working in tandem with California governor Jerry Brown.[135] While gently mocking techno-utopians who claimed that space colonization could solve all problems on Earth, Brand was, in fact, far more derisive of environmentalists who rejected the idea out of hand, suggesting that the Earth did indeed have to be left behind by a new breed of pioneers.

Like O'Neill, who came up with proposals for gigantic tubelike space colonies that would provide habitats mimicking California and the South of France, Brand embraced the term "space colony" (which NASA rejected), but argued that this would be a good form of colonization, as "no Space natives are being colonized."[136] Brand's book on the subject contained a quote from *Star Trek* actress Nichelle Nichols on the need for Black people to get in on the act.[137] In general, Brand, like O'Neill, seemed all too willing to sweep questions of social organization and selection (Who gets to go? Who decides?) under the technocratic carpet. In the early twenty-first century, space colonization fantasies returned, with films such as *Interstellar* and *The Martian*, and Jeff Bezos's and Elon Musk's private space programs.

In contrast to O'Neill's and Brand's traveling space colonies, today's space colonization is usually conceived of in terms of settling (and mining) planets, first and foremost Mars. In Kim Stanley Robinson's *Mars* trilogy, nuclear detonations play a crucial part in terraforming Mars (a project that is hugely contested among the protagonists of Robinson's novels): the very technology that threatens to make the Earth uninhabitable helps to make Mars inhabitable.[138] Thus the same logic of design fixes is applied both to Earth (geoengineering) and to other planets (terraforming as another type of planetary engineering). And in case geoengineering just makes things worse because the complexity of the global hyperobject keeps producing unintended consequences, we can start from scratch elsewhere.

Eyal Weizman reminds us that the term "climate change" emerged during late eighteenth-century debates involving David Hume and Thomas Jefferson about the human capacity to influence the climate—what we now would call geoengineering, climate design—long before it came to stand for the unintended consequences of industrialization. By the early nineteenth century, Charles Fourier was concerned about the climatic consequences of deforestation and the "material degradation of the planet," and argued that social change—the realization of "harmony"—would right things: Saint Petersburg would get the weather of the South of France.[139] These are early intimations of what I have elsewhere termed "third nature": the transformation of "first nature" through human "second nature."[140] In Teilhardian terms, the *noosphere* as "technological brain for the world" transforms the *biosphere*—the very biosphere that gave Earth its "blue marble" appearance is affected by the technology that allowed for the blue marble photo to be taken from space.[141] Here conscious design and unintended side effects are two sides of the same coin.

As a discipline of control, design also breeds a proliferation of overdetermined chaos. As more and more lines are drawn and volumes are defined, entropy accumulates all around. Delineating forms creates a formless outside where monsters live. Geoengineering or geodesign projects will exacerbate the issues they seek to address—which will cause the geoengineering lobby to intensify its PR. Affiliated with the push for geoengineering projects such as deflecting sunlight away from Earth and iron fertilization of oceans is the renewed push for nuclear energy—preferably a new, clean(er) nuclear technology that's always just around the corner. The basic presupposition in all of this is that energy demand will continue to rise and that alternative energy sources cannot meet this demand; the only alternative to CO_2-emitting fossil fuels, then, would be nuclear. What is unquestioned is the growth imperative—perhaps not so much a real growth in global GDP as a growth in energy consumption owing to technology such as the computer on which I'm writing this (though at least I'm not mining Bitcoin at the same time).

It is not an exercise in rearguard primitivism to argue that this is precisely where the problem lies. Why would it be a human right (for middle classes in developed countries) to take a cheap flight to a holiday destination once or several times a year? Why would it be a human right to use up more than a fair share of power each year, every day? So far, these questions are usually relegated to the consumer's individual ethics. They need to become properly political questions—questions about the consumption of energy underlying and informing the global distribution of the sensible. Atomization and nuclearization need to be countered by relational forms beyond and against the value-form. In Barad's words, "The world is not populated with things that are more or less the same or different from each other. Relations do not follow relata, but the other way around."[142]

But *how* to relate otherwise under the conditions of capitalist irrealism? How to transform the social if, for the time being, we continue to be shaped by the operational abstractions that have wrought the nuclear regime? There is obviously no single answer to this, no magic spell. Art constitutes a museum of more or less gloriously failed tactics, and there are many different ways of performing the constitutive contradictions of social form that make and break us. "Don't Follow the Wind" can be seen as a collection of artworks by relatively high-profile artists, some of which seem to auraticize the exclusion zone as a sublime void. On the other hand, it is also a curatorial project that involves ongoing exchanges with the members of a displaced community—relational work that takes the disruption of social relations in the region as its point of departure.

In 2013, Ei Arakawa and the Green Tea Gallery (with Stefan Tcherepnin and Hanna Törnudd) made a contribution to the Studium Generale of the Rietveld Academie in Amsterdam that amounted to an exercise in atomic cuisine.[143] For *Yum Yum Vibe* (2013), Arakawa and Co. passed around a parcel containing radishes his mother had sent him from the Fukushima region, where she lives. Subsequently, Arakawa and his associates prepared soup from these vegetables. In 2014, Arakawa repeated the exercise together with his brother in the context of Frieze Art Fair, now titled *Does This Soup Taste Ambivalent?* The imposition on the participants, who had to decide for themselves whether they wanted to eat this ambivalent soup, made it clear that there is no outside. In the wake of a spectacular meltdown, subtle and accumulating effects are everywhere.[144]

Yum Yum Vibe was no rousing call to action, but a sly experiment that created a sense of negative community. Everybody was in the same situation yet ultimately alone when it came to their decision—even as antinuclear activists in the auditorium debated the risks. Being part of this negative community made the need for collective political action as tangible as the sense of being atomized mutants inside the world laboratory—willing, but not necessarily able, to re-form themselves and relate differently.

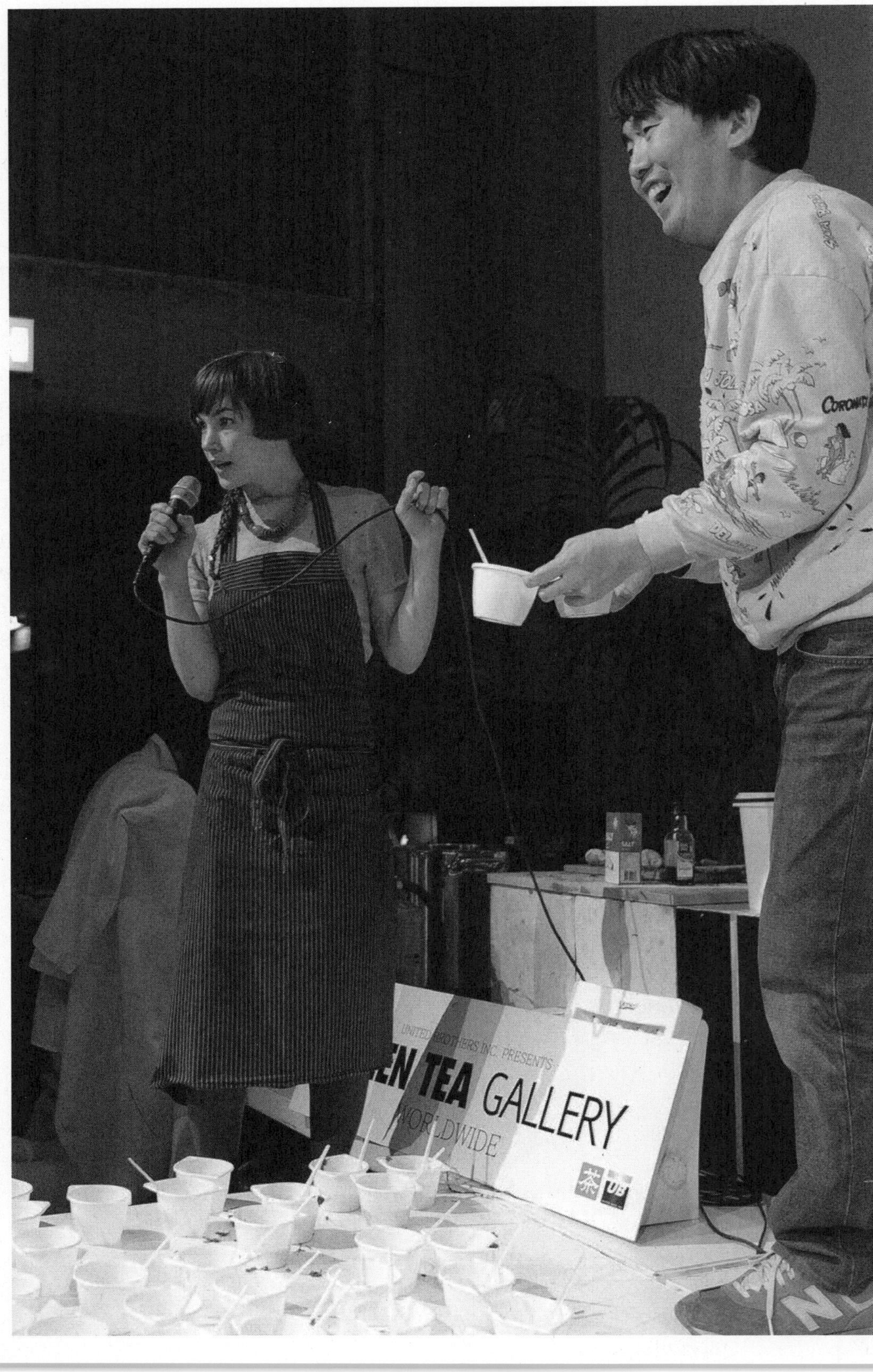

Ei Arakawa and Green Tea Gallery (with Stefan Tcherepnin and Hanna Törnudd), *Yum Yum Vibe*, 2013

NOTES

1 "Wer sich heute auf die Wahrnehmung dessen beschränkt, was der Augenblick gerade an Sichtbarem bietet, der verfehlt die Realität." Günther Anders, "Tagebuch aus Hiroshima und Nagasaki" (1958), in *Hiroshima ist überall* (Munich: C.H. Beck, 1982), 48.

2 Hal Foster, *Design and Crime (and Other Diatribes)* (Cambridge, MA: MIT Press, 2002), 17.

3 Akira Mizuta Lippit has insisted on the crucial importance of three interrelated "phenomenologies of the inside" that were launched in 1895: psychoanalysis, X-rays, and cinema; see Lippit, *Atomic Light (Shadow Optics)* (Minneapolis: University of Minnesota Press, 2005), 5.

4 See, for instance, Susan Schuppli, "Radical Contact Prints," in *Camera Atomica*, ed. John O'Brian (London: Black Dog Publishing, 2015), 284–87.

5 Wassily Kandinsky, "Rückblicke" (1913), in *Theories of Art 3: From the Impressionists to Kandinsky*, ed. Moshe Barasch (New York: Routledge, 2000), 296.

6 Joseph Masco, *The Nuclear Borderlands: The Manhattan Project in Post–Cold War New Mexico* (Princeton, NJ: Princeton University Press, 2006), 31.

7 Among those working on nuclear aesthetics, Ele Carpenter needs to be mentioned. Although she tends to frame her research on artistic responses to the nuclear in terms of "nuclear culture," in at least one essay she uses the notion of nuclear aesthetics; see Carpenter, "Shifting the Nuclear Imaginary: Art and the Flight from Nuclear Modernity," in *Cold War Legacies: Systems, Theories, Aesthetics*, ed. John Beck and Ryan Bishop (Edinburgh: Edinburgh University Press, 2016). 116–33.

8 For Japanese artistic responses, see Gabrielle Decamous, *Invisible Colors: The Arts of the Atomic Age* (Cambridge, MA: MIT Press, 2019). Capitalist empires have always depended on the extraction of value from and the consequent economic spoliation of their colonial holdings, so it makes sense that the risk of irradiation has been

outsourced as much as possible to internal or external colonies: native lands in the United States (New Mexico), Australia (Maralinga), and the Pacific (Bikini Atoll and Moruroa); in Japan, Fukushima sits in an area that has been described as "Japan's internal colony." See Nathan Hopson, "Systems of Irresponsibility and Japan's Internal Colony," *Asia-Pacific Journal: Japan Focus* 11, no. 52 (2013), https://apjjf.org/2013/11/52/Nathan-Hopson/4053/article.html.

9 The notion was introduced by Quentin Meillassoux, who is critiqued by Graham Harman for remaining in thrall to correlationism; see Harman, *The Quadruple Object* (Winchester: Zero Books, 2011), 136–37.

10 Harman, 19.

11 Günther Stern [Günther Anders], "Homeless Sculpture," *Philosophy and Phenomenological Research* 5, no. 2 (December 1944): 294.

12 G. W. F. Hegel, *Vorlesungen über die Ästhetik I* (Frankfurt am Main: Suhrkamp, 1970), 151.

13 Armen Avanessian, "The Speculative End of the Aesthetic Regime," *Texte zur Kunst*, no. 93 (March 2014), https://www.textezurkunst.de/93/speculative-end-aesthetic-regime/.

14 Avanessian, "The Speculative End of the Aesthetic Regime."

15 Timothy Morton, *Hyperobjects: Philosophy and Ecology after the End of the World* (Minneapolis: University of Minnesota Press, 2013), 12–13.

16 Morton, 1.

17 Morton, 18.

18 Morton, 23, 81.

19 Morton, 3.

20 Déborah Danowski and Eduardo Viveiros de Castro, *The Ends of the World*, trans. Rodrigo Nunes (Cambridge: Polity, 2017), 36.

21 Danowski and Viveiros de Castro, 36.

22 Morton, *Hyperobjects*, 38.

23 Morton, 48.

24 Jameson proposed the notion of cognitive mapping in the context of his work on postmodernism in the mid-1980s; see *Postmodernism; or, The Cultural Logic of Late Capitalism* (Durham, NC: Duke University Press, 1991), i.a., 52–54. He has returned to it several

times since, most recently in *Representing "Capital": A Reading of Volume One* (London: Verso, 2011), 6. See also chapter 3, note 117, in this volume.

25 Jaime Semprun, *La nucléarisation du monde* (Paris: Gérard Lebovici, 1986), 30. This and the following quotations of Semprun are from the English translation, "The Nuclearization of the World," *libcom.org*, January 7, 2016, https://libcom.org/library/nuclearization-world-jaime-semprun.

26 Semprun, 39.

27 Semprun, 75.

28 Christophe Bonneuil and Jean-Baptiste Fressoz, *The Shock of the Anthropocene: The Earth, History and Us*, trans. David Fernbach (London: Verso: 2017), 72–83, 253–87.

29 Bonneuil and Fressoz, 222–52.

30 Bonneuil and Fressoz, 203.

31 Anonymous, "Exercitatio de formis substantialibus et de qualitatibus physicis," quoted in Stephen Greenblatt, *The Swerve: How the World Became Modern* (New York: W. W. Norton, 2011), 250.

32 Karl Marx, "The Difference between the Democritean and Epicurean Philosophy of Nature" (1841), pt. 1, chap. 3, https://marxists.architexturez.net/archive/marx/works/1841/dr-theses/ch03.htm

33 Marx, pt. 1, chap. 3.

34 Marx, pt. 1, chap. 3.

35 Marx, pt. 2, chap. 1, https://marxists.architexturez.net/archive/marx/works/1841/dr-theses/ch04.htm.

36 Marx, pt. 2, chap. 1.

37 Marx, pt. 2, chap. 1.

38 Marx, pt. 2, chap. 5, https://marxists.architexturez.net/archive/marx/works/1841/dr-theses/ch08.htm.

39 Marx, pt. 2, chap. 1.

40 Marx, pt. 2, chap. 1.

41 Karl Marx, "Draft of New Preface," in "The Difference between the Democritean and Epicurean Philosophy of Nature" (1841–42), https://marxists.architexturez.net/archive/marx/works/1841/dr-theses/pref_new.htm.

42 With Peter Galison's *Image & Logic: A Material Culture of*

Microphysics (Chicago: University of Chicago Press, 1997), one can add a third phase after atomic and nuclear physics: postwar particle physics, dedicated to the study of ever more arcane subatomic particles. Since I focus on technoscience that fundamentally derives from the nuclear physics of the 1930s and 1940s, this distinction is less relevant here.

43 The TV version of *Our Friend the Atom* was broadcast on January 23, 1957, as part of the Disney anthology series. In the show, a lavishly illustrated mock-up book of that title is shown that bears little relation to the actual paperback of the previous year: Heinz Haber, *The Walt Disney Story of Our Friend the Atom* (New York: Dell, 1956).

44 Haber, 20–23.

45 Haber, 9–13.

46 Heinrich Schirmbeck, *Die Formel und die Sinnlichkeit: Bausteine zu einer Poetik im Atomzeitalter* (Munich: Paul List, 1964), 61, 9.

47 Alfred Sohn-Rethel, *Intellectual and Manual Labour: A Critique of Epistemology* (London: Macmillan, 1978), 54. For the equivalent passage in German, see *Geistige und körperliche Arbeit: Zur Theorie der gesellschaftlichen Synthesis*, rev. ed. (Frankfurt am Main: Suhrkamp, 1972), 82. For an explanation of my use of German and English editions of Sohn-Rethel's book, see chapter 3, note 18, in this volume.

48 Marx, quoted in Sohn-Rethel, *Intellectual and Manual Labour*, 27; *Geistige und körperliche Arbeit*, 47–48.

49 "Diese abstrakte Natur beschreibt sich in reinen, alles Wahrgenommene, qualitative Sinnliche der Quantifizierung unterwerfenden Begriffen und Prinzipien." Sohn-Rethel, *Geistige und Körperliche Arbeit*, 89.

50 Morton, *Hyperobjects*, 11.

51 Sohn-Rethel, *Geistige und körperliche Arbeit*, 208–10.

52 László Moholy-Nagy, *Malerei, Fotografie, Film* (Munich: Albert Langen, 1927), 66–68, 70.

53 Lippit, *Atomic Light (Shadow Optics)*, 30–60.

54 Galison, *Image & Logic*, 464.

55 Gÿorgy Kepes, *The New Landscape in Art and Science* (Chicago: Paul Theobald, 1956), 200–203.

56 Galison, *Image & Logic*, 65–141.

57 Galison, 143–60.

58 Roland Barthes, *Camera Lucida: Reflections on Photography* (1980), trans. Richard Howard (New York: Hill and Wang, 1981), 80.

59 Tom Gunning, "What's the Point of an Index? or, Faking Photographs," in *Still Moving: Between Cinema and Photography*, ed. Karen Beckman and Jean Ma (Durham, NC: Duke University Press, 2008), 26.

60 On Kepes's trajectory, see also John R. Blakinger, *Gyorgy Kepes: Undreaming the Bauhaus* (Cambridge, MA: MIT Press, 2019).

61 Carter Stone and Wolfgang Paalen, "During the Eclipse," in *Form and Sense*, Problems of Contemporary Art, no. 1, ed. Wolfgang Paalen (New York: Wittenborn, 1945), 21.

62 See Wolfgang Paalen, "The Dialectical Gospel," *Dyn*, no. 2 (July/August 1942): 54–59. This issue also contains Paalen's famous "Inquiry on Dialectical Materialism" (49–54).

63 Paalen, "Art and Science" (1942), in *Form and Sense*, 64.

64 Paalen. "On the Meaning of Cubism Today" (1944), in *Form and Sense*, 30.

65 Wolfgang Paalen to Gordon Onslow Ford, August 26, 1945, quoted in Annette Leddy, "The Painting Aesthetic of *Dyn*," in *Farewell to Surrealism: The "Dyn" Circle in Mexico*, ed. Annette Leddy and Donna Conwell (Los Angeles: Getty Research Institute, 2012), 33.

66 As Andreas Neufert puts it in his biography of Paalen: "Paalen wiederum schlug sich mit Einwänden und Skrupeln gegen Matta herum, der von Hiroshima und Nagasaki einfach gestrickte Rückschlüsse auf seine Malerei ziehen wollte." Neufert, *Auf Liebe und Tod: Das Leben des Surrealisten Wolfgang Paalen* (Berlin: Parthas Verlag, 2015), 527.

67 Wolfgang Paalen, "Brief Outline," in the unpublished typescript of *The Beam of the Balance* (1946). I am grateful to Andreas Neufert for making this script available to me.

68 Paalen, *Form and Sense*.

69 Barnett Newman, "The New Sense of Fate" (1948), in *Selected Writings and Interviews*, ed. John P. O'Neill (Berkeley: University of California Press, 1990), 165.

70 Newman, 169.

71 Newman, 169.

72 Kurosawa's *I Live in Fear* (1955) is an example of a film that addresses the social and psychological fallout of the threat (and, for Japan, the memory) of nuclear war.

73 See also Stephen Petersen, "Explosive Propositions: Artists React to the Atomic Age," *Science in Context* 17, no. 4 (2004): 579–609.

74 Anders, "Tagebuch aus Hiroshima und Nagasaki," 64.

75 Anders, 65.

76 It should be noted that Anders could be a highly perceptive art critic and art theorist. A case in point is his essay on Rodin's sculptures as homeless things; see Stern, "Homeless Sculpture," 293–307.

77 On both movements, see Petersen, "Explosive Propositions."

78 Beniamino Dal Fabbro, "Definition of the Nuclearists" (1953), in *Arte nucléaire*, ed. Tristan Sauvage [Arturo Schwarz] (Paris: Éditions Villa, 1962), 207.

79 Asger Jorn, unpublished article, quoted in Sauvage, *Arte nucléaire*, 36.

80 *Surrealist Intrusion in the Enchanters' Domain*, ed. André Breton and Marcel Duchamp (New York: D'Arcy Galleries, 1960), 40–41; and André Breton, "Enrico Baj" (1963), in *Le surréalisme et la peinture* (Paris: Gallimard, 1965), 395–400; the comment on Baj's Lucretius illustrations (a portfolio of thirty-six prints published in 1958) is on 398.

81 "À toujours été attiré par les travaux des physiciens modernes sur la propagation des ondes et les radiations, et par les transformations gigantesques que les savants viennent de faire subir à la matière." Robert Tenger, "Note de l'éditeur," in Denis de Rougemont, *Lettres sur la bombe atomique* (New York: Brentano's, 1946), 11. Translations of de Rougemont are by Michael Andrews, in Sven Lütticken, "World History and Earth Art," *e-flux journal*, no. 49 (November 2013), https://www.e-flux.com/journal/49/59999/world-history-and-earth-art/, on which this discussion is based.

82 See the last page of "On the Survival of Certain Myths and on Some Other Myths in Growth or Formation," in *First Papers of Surrealism*, ed. André Breton and Marcel Duchamp (New York: Coordinating Council of French Relief Societies, 1942), n.p.

83 André Breton, "Prolegomena to a Third Manifesto of Surrealism or Else [*sic*]," *VVV*, no. 1 (1942): 18–26. Matta selected preexisting images but also used one of his own drawings of the Grands Transparents. On Breton, Matta, and the cultural context in which the Grands Transparents emerged, with a focus on fantasy and science fiction, see also Gavin Parkinson, *Futures of Surrealism: Myth, Science Fiction, and Fantastic Art in France 1966–1969* (New Haven, CT: Yale University Press, 2015), 19–36.

84 Matta, "Mythomattaque: Entretien avec Matta," interview by Christian de Maussion, *L'Autre Journal* 9 (1986): 39.

85 Louis Pauwels and Jacques Bergier, *The Morning of the Magicians: Secret Societies, Conspiracies, and Vanished Civilizations* (1960), trans. Rollo Myers (Rochester, VT: Destiny Books, 2009), 393.

86 Pauwels and Bergier, 393.

87 *Planète*, no. 1 (n.d. [1961]), 8, 131, 75.

88 Pierre Guérin, "Hypothèses sur les mondes habités," *Planète*, no. 1, 30, 32.

89 Pierre Restany, "Notre actuelle avant-garde," *Planète*, no. 1, 87–93.

90 Parkinson, *Futures of Surrealism*, 167.

91 Olivier Surel, blurb on the back cover of Harman, *The Quadruple Object*.

92 *Internationale Situationniste*, no. 7 (April 1962), which opened with an attack on nuclear bunkers and the "geopolitics of hibernation," also contains a kind of attack ad about *Planète*, on 46, with the header "Si vous lisez 'Planète' à haute voix, vous sentirez mauvais de la bouche!" (If you read *Planète* out loud, your breath will smell!). Further down, there is a reference to the mutation motif in the style of a Pauwels/Bergier subheading: "Et s'il le faut, mutons ensemble!" (Let's mutate together, if that's what it takes!).

93 Leslie A. Fiedler, "The New Mutants," *Partisan Review* 43, no. 4 (Fall 1965): 505–25.

94 The Realists [Henry Flynt], "Overthrow the Human Race!," in *Happening & Fluxus*, ed. H. Sohm (Cologne: Kölnischer Kunstverein, 1970), n.p.; see also Branden W. Joseph, *Beyond the Dream Syndicate: Tony Conrad and the Arts after Cage* (New York: Zone Books, 2008), 210, 419n135. Joseph notes that Flynt founded his

"party," the Realists, in 1968, and dates the "Overthrow" manifesto as "ca. 1969."

95 In the third issue of *Planète*, we encounter speculations on Nazis founding a secret order after the war—a "cosmonazism" (helpfully illustrated with a photo of a rocket) that would allow them to subject not just Earth but also other planets to their regime, with subtler methods than the crude means used the first time around. *Planète*, no. 3 (n.d.): 124.

96 Teilhard de Chardin and Oppenheimer are already conjoined in Pauwels's editorial in the first issue, Louis Pauwels, "Pour saluer la Planète," *Planète*, no. 1, 10. The reference to the liberation of the atom's energy is from George Magloire, "Le genie que j'ai vu vivre en liberté," *Planète*, no. 3, 29.

97 Robert Jungk, "L'intelligence prend le pouvoir," *Planète*, no. 1, 15–17.

98 Oddly enough, in a move that no doubt will have delighted Pauwels and Bergier, in a footnote, Jungk gives credence to the "Nazi UFO" myth still beloved by esoteric (and neofascist) conspiracy theorists. Robert Jungk, *Brighter Than a Thousand Suns: A Personal History of the Atomic Scientists* (1958), trans. James Cleugh (San Diego, CA: Harcourt, 1986), 87.

99 As is evident from the title, Breton presents science as a lost cause altogether, rather than defending it against its instrumentalization, against its reduction to *Zweckvernunft*. This is a symptom of Breton's progressive withdrawal into esotericism. See André Breton, *Démasquez les physiciens, videz les laboratoires!* (1958), http://www.andrebreton.fr/work/56600100719690.

100 José Pierre et al., *Les fausses cartes transparentes de "Planète,"* Le Petit Écrasons 3 (Paris: Éditions Le Terrain Vague, 1965). See also Parkinson, *Futures of Surrealism*, 171.

101 Guy Debord and Asger Jorn, "Mutant" (January 1962), in *Cosmonauts of the Future: Texts from the Situationist Movement in Scandinavia and Elsewhere*, ed. Mikkel Bolt Rasmussen and Jakob Jakobsen (Copenhagen: Nebula; Brooklyn, NY: Autonomedia, 2015), 65.

102 This critical motif plays an important role in both the anonymous/collective text "Géopolitique de l'hibernation" and in Raoul Vaneigem's "Banalités de base" in the aforementioned *Internationale*

Situationniste, no. 7, which can be regarded as part of the Situationists' anti-*Planète* offensive; see note 92, above.

103 "Géopolitique de l'hibernation," *Internationale Situationniste*, no. 7, 6; translation by Ken Knabb, "Geopolitics of Hibernation," Bureau of Public Secrets, http://www.bopsecrets.org/SI/7.hibernation.htm.

104 Roel van Duijn, *Energieboekje: Over de energie-krisis en de oplossing daarvan door een alternatieve technologie* (The Hague: Bert Bakker, 1972).

105 "Weesp testgebied voor Philips-Duphars Zenuwgassen," *De Paniekzaaier*, no. 1 (November 1971), 6.

106 Semprun, *La nucléarisation du monde*, 14, 38 (my translation).

107 These volumes are represented in the artist's library, kept in the Sigmar Polke Archiv, Cologne.

108 Kathrin Rottmann, "Urangestein im Atelier," in *Alibis: Sigmar Polke 1963–2010*, ed. Kathy Halbreich (Munich: Prestel, 2015), 60–61.

109 Karen Barad, *Meeting the Universe Halfway: Quantum Physics and the Entanglement of Matter and Meaning* (Durham, NC: Duke University Press, 2007), 53.

110 Bruno Latour, "What Is Iconoclash? or Is There a World beyond the Image Wars?," in *Iconoclash: Beyond the Image Wars in Science, Religion, and Art*, ed. Bruno Latour and Peter Weibel (Cambridge, MA: MIT Press, 2002), 16.

111 In his Fukushima trilogy (2012–14), Philippe Rouy makes use of livecam and robot footage from the Fukushima plant.

112 Yves Klein, quoted in Petersen, "Explosive Propositions," 599.

113 As Petersen puts it, "*The Void*, in its emptiness and its use of strategic annihilation, also made metaphorical reference to the emptiness of nuclear obliteration" (599).

114 One key difference is that Polke's piece was about a mental exercise by the artist ("Polke stellt sich vor, dass ein Teilchen diesen Raum umkreist"), whereas Brouwn's exhibition invited the viewer to experience walking through cosmic rays.

115 On Robert Barry, see also the discussion of his use of a different kind of "invisible waves" with his *Telepathic Piece* of the same year, in Eric C. H. de Bruyn, "Vanishing Acts: Notes on a Genealogy of Dematerialisation," in *DeMaterialisations in Art and Art-Historical*

Discourse in the Twentieth Century, ed. Wojciech Bałus and Magdalena Kunińska (Kraków: Artibus et Historiae, 2018), 107–25.

116 See Susanne Kriemann, *P(ech) B(lende): Library for Radioactive Afterlife* (Leipzig: Spector Books, 2016). It also contains a version of Susan Schuppli's essay "Radical Contact Prints" (see note 4, above) which discusses the Bikini Atoll autoradiographs of fish on p. 133.

117 See *Supplement 2: Exclusion Zones* (Vancouver: Fillip, 2017), a booklet with text by Eva Wilson and images by Kriemann.

118 Barthes, *Camera Lucida*, 80–81.

119 For a general critical assessment of Simon's work, see Robert Kulisek and David Lieske, "Husbands Have Got to Die!," *Texte zur Kunst*, no. 100 (December 2015): 172–97.

120 See Thomas A. Sebeok, "Communication Measures to Bridge Ten Millennia," *Technical Report for the Office of Nuclear Waste Isolation* (April 1984), https://static1.squarespace.com/static/5668df83cbced6c419064be1/t/568b587dc21b86066ae9b121/1451972733768/Communication+Measures+to+Bridge+Ten+Millenia.pdf.

121 Trevor Paglen, "Trinity Cube," 2015, https://paglen.studio/2020/01/21/trinity-cube/.

122 Rob Nixon, *Slow Violence and the Environmentalism of the Poor* (Cambridge, MA: Harvard University Press, 2011).

123 Semprun, *La nucléarisation du monde*, 39 (my translation).

124 Galison, *Image & Logic*, 433–88.

125 Galison, 692. In addition, see also Thomas Haigh, Mark Priestley, and Crispin Rope, "Los Alamos Bets on ENIAC: Nuclear Monte Carlo Simulations, 1947–1948," *IEEE Annals of the History of Computing* 36, no. 3 (July–September 2014): 42–63, who fill in gaps in Galison's account; and James Bridle, *New Dark Age: Technology, Knowledge and the End of the Future* (London: Verso, 2018), 25–32.

126 Masco, *Nuclear Borderlands*, 90–96.

127 René Riesel and Jaime Semprun, *Catastrophism, Disaster Management and Sustainable Submission* (n.p.: Roofdruk, 2014), 12. The reference appears to be to a passage in Günther Anders, *Die Antiquiertheit des Menschen*, Bd. 1 (1956; Munich: C.H. Beck, 2010), 150.

128 Martin Heidegger, "The Age of the World Picture" (1938), in *The Question Concerning Technology, and Other Essays*, trans. William

Lovitt (New York: Garland, 1977), 115–54.

129 Michel Serres, *Times of Crisis: What the Financial Crisis Revealed and How to Reinvent Our Lives and Future* (New York: Bloomsbury, 2014), 14; and Serres, "Revisiting *The Natural Contract*," *CTheory*, November 5, 2006, https://journals.uvic.ca/index.php/ctheory/article/view/14482/5325.

130 Serres, "Revisiting *The Natural Contract*."

131 See *The Whole Earth: California and the Disappearance of the Outside*, ed. Diedrich Diederichsen and Anselm Franke (Berlin: Sternberg Press, 2013).

132 The video was shown in a cabinet adjacent to the exhibition "Hanne Darboven: Korrespondenzen."

133 De Rougemont, *Lettres sur la bombe atomique*, 90, 110 (Andrews's translation).

134 Bonneuil and Fressoz, *The Shock of the Anthropocene*, 76. This observation on the whole Earth and the bomb was first published (in French) in 2013, the same year as my essay "World History and Earth Art," on which this passage of the present chapter is based.

135 See Stewart Brand, ed., *Space Colonies: A CoEvolution Book* (Harmondsworth: Penguin, 1977).

136 Stewart Brand, "The Sky Starts at Your Feet," in Brand, *Space Colonies*, 5.

137 Brand, *Space Colonies*, 129.

138 See in particular the first volume, Kim Stanley Robinson, *Red Mars* (London: HarperCollins, 1992).

139 Eyal Weizman, *Forensic Architecture: Violence at the Threshold of Detectability* (New York: Zone Books, 2018), 255; see also Bonneuil and Fressoz, *The Shock of the Anthropocene*, 76.

140 Sven Lütticken, *History in Motion: Time in the Age of the Moving Image* (Berlin: Sternberg Press, 2013), 255–94.

141 Marshall McLuhan, *The Gutenberg Galaxy: The Making of Typographic Man* (Toronto: University of Toronto Press, 1962), 32.

142 Barad, *Meeting the Universe Halfway*, 136–37.

143 Their contribution also had other components, notably the screening of a Japanese film set near a nuclear power plant.

144 In "Muddling Through Wicked Complexity: Why We Should Look

at Art When We Talk about Nuclear Power" (PhD diss., University of Leiden, 2021), Anna Volkmar references Aya Hirata Kimura's discussion of food as a focal point for fears about radiation; however, such a "radicalization through food politics" did not occur in post-Fukushima Japan.

Chapter 6

ABSTRACT HABITATS

ON COEXISTENCE AND COEVOLUTION IN ART

"Atomization" has long been code for alienation, for modernity and capitalism rendering asunder what should be an organic whole. In the early nineteenth century, the German legal theorist Adam Müller railed against what he termed "the newfangled French representation of heads and souls," that is, representative democracy. He argued that a political system should be based on "the living limbs of the state, and not its dead atoms."[1] Müller was a reactionary Romantic, and Romanticism more broadly was united in its rejection of social atomism and its embrace of "the organic." This Romantic critique of modern society and social atomism was indebted to a more general organicist turn in philosophy, which would feed into Bergsonian and Deleuzian vitalisms, and into various forms of systems theory after the Second World War.[2] In her early book on metaphors of organicism in twentieth-century biology, Donna Haraway quotes the biologist Paul Weiss:

> If nature were atomized and inherently chaotic, only creative mind could see and carve into it and from it those patterns of higher order to which we concede consistency and beauty. But nature is not atomized. Its patterning is inherent and primary, and the order underlying beauty is demonstrably there; what is more, human mind can perceive it only because it is itself part and parcel of that order.[3]

If both natural science and social theory thus opposed the atomized to the organic, this opposition was called into question by twentieth-century nuclearization. Nuclear technology works in tandem with biotech to de- and recompose the organic. In 1964, the French humanist Pierre Bertaux published a book that was very much of its time; *La mutation humaine* argued that humankind was "acquiring the power to act on the destiny of the species" in two different ways: through either the *destruction* or the *modification* of the human race. The first could take the form of nuclear Armageddon or a "catastrophic modification of the climate" and soil depletion, while the second was identified with a form of genetic modification—not involuntarily, through radioactive contamination, but as a matter of planning and design. As Bertaux rightly notes, this was a qualitative leap from old techniques of cross-breeding horses, dogs, cows, sheep, and pigs.[4] In the world laboratory, the designing of life becomes possible—and possibly even imperative. At the same time, age-old forms of coexisting and using animals that have themselves been transformed and perverted through industrialization are being questioned and attacked.

In this chapter, I will examine a number of installations by contemporary artists that function as artificial and aesthetic habitats for animals, and for humans. My interest in this context is in installations that alter or readjust the relations between organisms—that abstract them from their regular environment or form of life and, in doing so, foreground the historical nature of these organisms and their habitats. Of course, such readjustments may involve genetic modifications, but my focus is not so much on those as on the "mutation" of the global biosystem that has become world laboratory. Through genetic as well as nuclear technology, technoscience is altering life on earth in conjunction with financial and juridical real abstraction, producing both symptoms of collapse and tentative harbingers of other ways of living. What, then, are the vicissitudes of the organic in the framework of concrete abstraction, and what are its challenges to this framework?

Birds before Swine

If cognitive capitalism and biopolitics "must be understood as the exploitation and control of the power of abstraction of our being," to quote Matteo Pasquinelli, this degree of exploitation and control—of design—marks the leap from the animal to the human.[5] There is no point in smoothing over historical antinomies and the existence of asymmetries and hierarchies with vitalist homilies. What matters biopolitically as well as bio-aesthetically is a willingness to engage critically with abstraction as a real force in today's technoscience—abstraction not as airy theoretical or artistic exercise but as an operation with profound consequences, as in the case of genetic engineering. But not every property of every living organism has "a gene" to account for it, as early (and current) forms of genetic reductionism would have it. Furthermore, as Haraway stresses, the human genome is found in only 10 percent of the cells that make up our bodies, the rest being accounted for by a host of microorganisms with which each of us cohabits.[6]

In 2005, artist duo Bik Van der Pol installed their piece *Birds Must Be Eliminated (Bird Shot)* in an exhibition space in the lobby of the main building of the Vrije Universiteit in Amsterdam. *Birds Must Be Eliminated* consists of a large cage with live birds, accompanied by a window with a blue film and a quotation by Yves Klein, in which the artist demands that all birds be shot so they can no longer pollute the boundless azure of the sky with their annoying presence. The piece was first realized in a simpler version in 2000 in New York, sans birds but with a gun leaning against the wall. It references the "Chelsea Hotel Manifesto," written by Klein in 1961, in which he recalls lying on the beach in Nice as an adolescent, feeling "hatred for birds which flew back and forth across my blue, cloudless sky because they tried to bore holes in my greatest and most beautiful work."[7]

Carsten Höller and Rosemarie Trockel, *A House for Pigs and People*, documenta X, Kassel, 1997

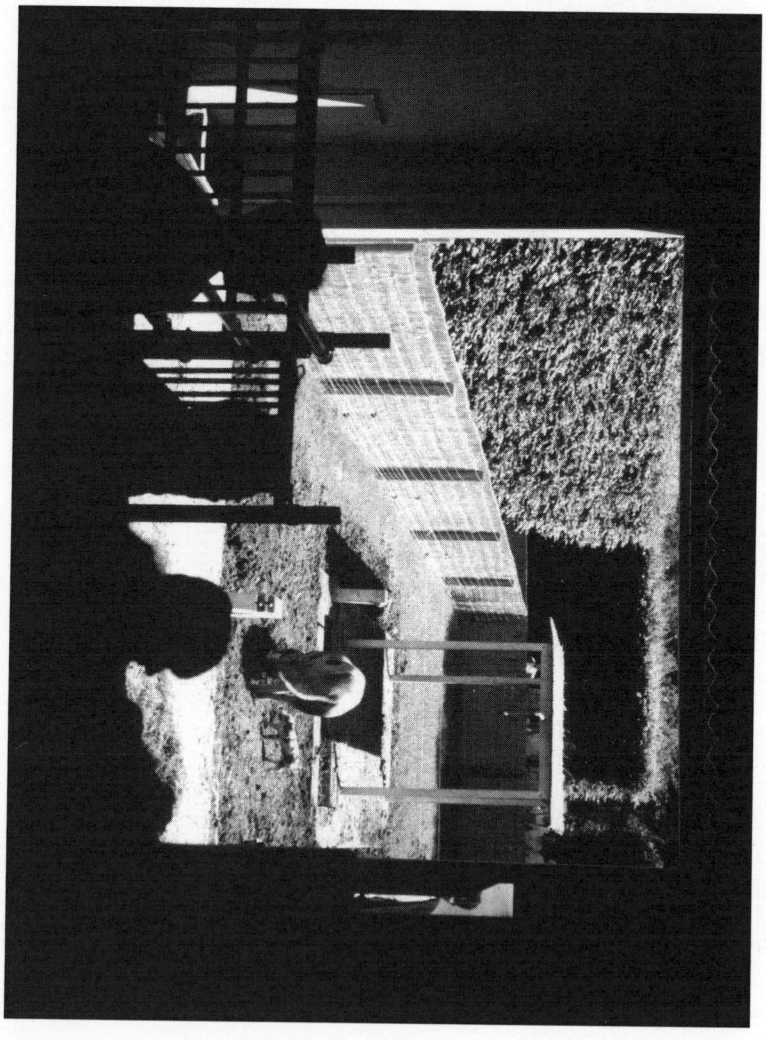

Bik Van der Pol, *Birds Must Be Eliminated (Bird Shot)*, 2000, Vrije Universiteit, Amsterdam, 2005

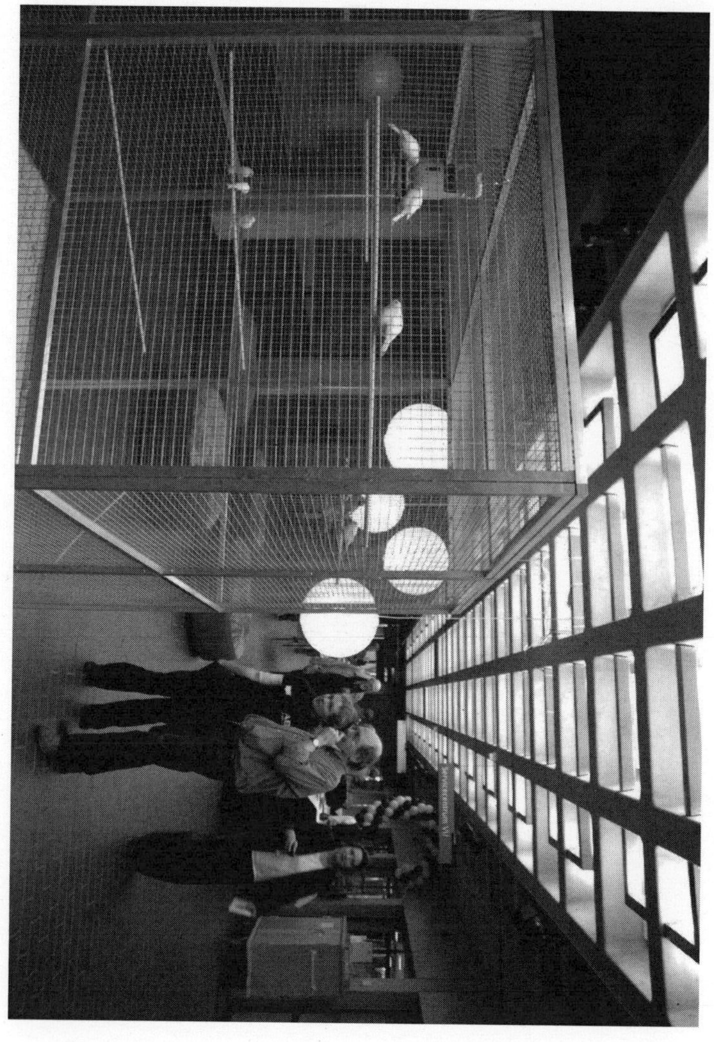

The quotation can be seen as an extreme instance of modern aestheticism, pitting an art purified and abstracted from all too earthly concerns against nature. The caged birds were not, of course, shot, but neither were they free as a bird; they were songbirds bred by humans.[8] During the exhibition at the university, animal rights activists decorated the door of the curator's office with threatening slogans and demands: "Free the birds," and "We know where to find you!" The protest seemed not inspired by concrete complaints about the manner in which these particular birds were held, but against the birds having been abstracted from the state of "nature" and kept as pets at all.[9]

If the Cartesian subject relegated animals to the sphere of objecthood, the artist in Klein's exterminatory reverie appears as a cartoon version of such a subject, determined to purify teeming, unpredictable nature, to replace living multiplicity with an airy abstraction that mirrors his sublime mind. Klein takes the verb "to abstract" in its most literal sense: to take away or remove—in this case, to remove the birds from the picture (the sky). The birds in Bik Van der Pol's cage, however, are the products of abstraction in a different sense. The songbirds are products of crossbreeding and, thus, products of human thought intervening in natural processes and effecting a transformation, a mutation. This operation is only possible because of certain processes that long predate human activity; DNA and the whole biochemical factory inherent in cells are machines of abstraction in that they reduce specific qualities to general programs.

At documenta X in 1997, Carsten Höller and Rosemarie Trockel's *A House for Pigs and People* constituted a site for encounters between members of two species. The concrete construction contained two spaces divided by a large one-way mirror window through which documenta visitors could see the pigs, while the latter only saw their own reflection. The communication between the two species was thus reduced to a one-sided scopic relation, with the senses other than sight being largely canceled out. Höller and Trockel, thus, seemed to duplicate the objectification of animals—their reduction to image-objects studied and manipulated by a gazing human subject. However, the "human" half of the installation contained a concrete incline on which people could recline and watch the pigs more or less from the same height; the vertical biped became horizontal, or at least diagonal. Furthermore, these were Bentheim Black Pied pigs—an archaic breed no longer in vogue in today's bio-industry. Yet these impressive, speckled swine were clearly not "nature"; rather, they were an ancient hybrid, a relic of a historical stage of the human-animal dialectic.[10]

Höller's solo work, particularly in the early to mid-1990s, has often been marked by a crude behaviorism and a disturbingly reductivist biologism, objectifying humans as little more than Darwinian vessels for "selfish genes."[11] By contrast, his collaboration with Trockel between 1996 and 1999 led to far more open works that sound out histories and well as possibilities of cohabitation—and coevolution. In their introductory text, the artists questioned the legitimacy of "all talk of an 'objective' limit (animal as object)," asking an extended series of questions about whether or not it is permissible to kill Scottish sheep that have some human genes, about different degrees and kinds of consciousness, and about the interconnections between the subjugation of nonhumans and of nonruling classes in various societies.[12]

Such questions are properly historical and materialistic—in the Marxian sense of materialism, which focused on material social practice, on "sensuous human activity," in contrast to older ontological or epistemological materialisms. By now, of course, the dialectical transformation has wrecked the planet in ways that make the "metabolic rift" discussed by Marx in relation to nineteenth-century agriculture look like child's play. John Bellamy Foster stresses that "from the start, Marx's notion of the alienation of human labor was connected to an understanding of the alienation of human beings from nature."[13]

However, Engels's not terribly convincing attempts to apply Marxian dialectics to nature, and the positivistic drift in the work of some Marxists during the early twentieth century, generated a countermovement after World War I. Georg Lukács and Karl Korsch led a revolt against undialectical positivism and against any attempt to turn the dialectic into something resembling a set of natural laws. While there were good reasons for this critique, Foster has compellingly argued that it led to an unfortunate narrowing of the scope of dialectical inquiry to "purely human" history.[14] Marx and Engels had insisted as early as the 1840s that natural and human history are two branches of the same science; this insight, or ambition, seems to have been lost.[15]

Marx never came up with a compelling brand name for his particular fusion of insights from ancient materialism (Lucretian atomism) and modern idealism (Hegelian dialectics).[16] Engels started using "historical materialism" during Marx's lifetime; soon after, "dialectical materialism" reared its head. The latter term would come to be associated with works by Engels such as *Anti-Dühring* and the (posthumously published) *Dialectics of Nature*, and in the end, none other than Stalin decreed the following:

> Dialectical materialism is the world outlook of the Marxist-Leninist party. It is called dialectical materialism because its approach to the phenomena of nature, its method of studying and apprehending them, is dialectical, while its interpretation of the phenomena of nature, its conception of these phenomena, its theory, is materialistic. Historical materialism is the extension of the principles of dialectical materialism to the study of social life, an application of the principles of dialectical materialism to the phenomena of the life of society, to the study of society and of its history.[17]

If the Western Marxism that hails from Lukács and Korsch—principally, the Frankfurt School—was a necessary critique of Engelsian scientism and Soviet "Diamat," it also constituted an impoverishment in that it neglected the "natural-physical aspects of material existence"—aspects that a "*strong historical materialism*," in Raymond Williams's words, would restore.[18] Such a strong historical materialism would be attentive to the ways in which ecological conditions shape social formations, and the ways in which the latter remake the former; it would entail a critique of exploitation and spoliation. In Marx's own words: "The view of nature which has grown up under the regime of private property and of money is an actual contempt for and practical degradation of nature. [...] In this sense Thomas Müntzer declares it intolerable that 'all creatures have been made into property, the fish in the water, the birds in the air, the plants on the earth—all living things must also become free.'"[19]

Herbert Marcuse has summarized this Marxian project of a joint emancipation of the human and the nonhuman by stating:

> Nature would become a Subject in its own right Nature would become a Subject in its own right and *Telos*: as the environment and soil of freedom, which is incompatible with the enslavement and violation of nature, its treatment as a mere object. In other words, the object would be experienced as subject to the degree to which the subject, man, makes the object world into a humane world. Realization of nature through the realization of man as "species being": for nature too, has become an object of destructive exploitation—nature too calls for liberation. [...] Exploitation is not really abolished, its heritage not really thrown off until man has established this new relationship to nature: the humanization of nature would also enable man to have the good conscience of his own nature, of himself as part of nature.[20]

In Marx's anthropological conception of labor as the self-creation and self-objectification of man, it was labor as a social relationship that set humankind apart from animals, resulting in properly *social* relationships (which animals cannot have).[21] We might want to argue that there is still too much of Hegel in this, too much self-aggrandizement of spirit over dumb nature; that animals *do*, in fact, form relationships; that "living things are singularities composed of relations and intensities," and that we need to "think of life beyond structure, substance, or constitutive subject-object relationships."[22] Marx certainly struck a precarious balance between Promethean productivism and his desire to liberate the object of that Promethean drive—the living beings that are subjected to it and, at times, produced by it.

Even if we clearly position ourselves against the Promethean colonization of the fabric of life, we need to acknowledge that the self-abstraction of humans from this fabric is a historical fact. To be precise, it is *the original historical event*; it is what produced history as something other than natural history. There is no shortage of theorizations of this leap, from Engels's and Freud's ruminations on the role played by labor in the becoming-human of apes—with Engels focusing on the emergence of the multifunctional human hand and the accompanying increase in brain size—to more recent theories about the importance of fire and cooking in decreasing the size of the digestive tract and increasing that of the brain.[23]

Critical modern accounts of hominization emphasize that to be(come) human is to *lack* something: from Freud's definition of the human as a "prosthetic god" to authors associated with German philosophic anthropology such as Helmuth Plessner, who defined the human being as "eccentric" (lacking a center), as a naked halfling.[24] In the same philosophical school, the politically far more dubious Arnold Gehlen coined the term *Mängelwesen*, a defective or lacking creature. Later, Alexander Kluge and Oskar Negt would riff off this with their notion of the human *Mangelmutant*—a mutant born from lack, from deprivation.[25] As naked, toiling apes, humans are enthusiastic house-builders while being radically homeless in the world in a way that animals are not. As Hegel put it, "Paradise is a park in which only animals can remain; humans cannot."[26] Acting in history and trying to gain some degree of agency amid portents of imminent global ecological and social cataclysm, it would be folly to try to wish away this *Urszene* of history—the decentering of the human animal, or post-animal.

The pigs in Höller and Trockel's *House* are examples of traditional (or archaic) breeding methods—yet the piece is not nostalgic. In literalizing an asymmetrical relationship while taking the humans down a notch, a site of abstraction, the house provides literal and metaphorical *Denkraum*. For Freud, humans' adoption of an upright posture took them out of an animal world of smells and into a visual, scopic regime that created the need for sublimation, for repression, for culture.[27] Höller and Trockel's *House for Pigs and People* acknowledges this precisely by temporarily and partially reversing the process—placing the humans on an incline while maintaining scopic asymmetry. The *House* suggests that this epochal shift cannot be canceled out by inserting a one-way mirror between the two species.

All Systems Go

Pierre Huyghe has characterized his 2017 Skulptur Projekte Münster installation *After ALife Ahead*—which featured, among other items, a beehive, an incubator with cancer cells, and an automated opening in the ceiling—as "a network of self-organizing systems" that "shift constantly," and an engagement with postwar systems thinking and aesthetics is evident from his work.[28] If Hans Haacke once made the switch from works dealing with "natural systems" to pieces addressing "social systems," Huyghe's practice is concerned with systems that foreground their hybridity, as assemblages of algorithms and organisms, of pre- and posthuman visions.

Haacke's effortless linking of the two realms via the notion of the system itself speaks to the universalist sway held by postwar systems theory. His work of the late 1960s and early 1970s developed in conjunction with the "systems aesthetics" developed by the art historian, critic, and curator Jack Burnham, whom the artist had first met in 1962.[29] Even though Burnham and his systems aesthetics had been ostracized in the early 1970s, Caroline A. Jones has noted that "systemic artworks had [re]emerged with a vengeance" in the 1990s, and that, in the early twenty-first century, "Burnham's concerns about everything from the consumption of natural resources to the implementation of machine technology seem tailor-made for the contemporary art world."[30] Still, certain shifts in emphasis can be detected.

In his 1968 book *Beyond Modern Sculpture*, Burnham argued that "an age which sought vitality in latent visual metaphor"—as in the works of Arp, Brancusi, and Moore—was coming to an end.[31] What this meant was a transition from sculpture as monolith to sculpture as *system*. Burnham followed Ludwig von Bertalanffy in regarding cybernetics—defined by Norbert Wiener as the science of control and communication "in the animal and the machine"—as one specific, albeit important form of "general systems theory."[32] Other sources or strands of general systems theory included information theory, operations research, Bertalanffy's biology, and Talcott Parsons's sociology. Systems theory, as Burnham put it, promised "a convergence of knowledge and activities," in which the Earth could be conceived as "a total organism with its own metabolism"—including the "metabolic information" produced by humans and their technological apparatus.[33]

Such a systems theory spelled the triumph of what Burnham termed *organicism*, as opposed to vitalism. In contrast to what he saw as the reactionary vitalism of Bergson, with its mystical *élan vital*, organicism abstracts from organic function to arrive at general principles: "As the machine takes over and translates organic function in principle," the difference between organisms and machines evaporates.[34] In his essay "Real Time Systems" (1969), Burnham noted:

> Some recent tendencies in Haacke's work intrigue me. One is a willingness to use all forms of organic life—from the most elementary to the most complicated. This seems a logical extension of his philosophy of natural systems. A work of last winter involved the incubation of chicks as an on-going process. Already Haacke is planning more complete animal "ecologies" where information is derived from the normal activities of animals in their environments. For a museum, he is planning a steady output of statistical information about visitors involving a small process-controlled computer and a display device. Two years ago Haacke would have balked at using this kind of technology; today, working more closely with events, it became necessary.[35]

It is breathtaking how quickly Burnham moves from hatching chickens to "more complete animal 'ecologies,'" under which he then appears to subsume Haacke's project for Burnham's own 1970 show "Software" at the Jewish Museum, in New York, for which the artist planned an automated *Visitors' Profile* piece.[36] Postwar systems theory has rightly been criticized for its "weakness for programmatic statements coupled with a scarcity of concrete results" and its "fundamental begging of questions that takes the form of an unstated and presumably invisible shift from concrete world 'systems' in their fullness and complexity to closed formal models based on convenient 'simplifying assumptions.'"[37] In a charmingly explicit way, a set of "simplifying assumptions" underlies another project in Burnham's "Software": *SEEK* by Nicholas

Negroponte and the Architecture Machine Group at MIT, which was an environment for gerbils, consisting of blocks that were moved around by robotic arms in response to the gerbils' "disrupting" of the configuration. This cybernetico-behaviorist system was clearly no proposal for the perfect gerbil habitat, but rather a demonstration of computerized real-time feedback with implications for human society. The question would seem to be what constitutes the difference between the human visitors responding to Haacke's questions and the gerbils tussling with the robotic arm.[38]

Burnham's show came at the high-water mark of artistic interest in systems theory and cybernetics. In part, it was precisely large shows such as "Software" and the 1971 "Art and Technology" show at Los Angeles County Museum of Art that spawned a critical backlash against what Max Kozloff called the "multimillion dollar art boondoggle."[39] What had seemed progressive to a fairly large number of practitioners in the 1960s—art abandoning the commodity-object in favor of an adaptation of new technologies and feedback mechanisms in the service of a kind of progressive, emancipatory social engineering—was now attacked for delivering art to the military-industrial complex hook, line, and sinker.

This critique, which was prefigured by the Situationists during the 1960s, won the day in the art world. Burnham fell from grace rather rapidly around 1970, as MIT-facilitated high-tech in art came to be eyed with suspicion. There were more continuities in the counterculture, especially in California. As Fred Turner and others have averred, one can trace a genealogy from the *Whole Earth Catalog* to Silicon Valley and the internet, and to neoliberal ideologies of self-organization as a substitute for state welfare or healthcare.[40] Attempting to introduce a greater degree of differentiation, Brian Holmes has noted:

> The so-called "hippie" version of cybernetics springs from an intense epistemological struggle over the uses of high-level technical, scientific and philosophical knowledge; and even if none of the cyberneticists was really a hippie, still it's to the counter-culture's credit that its participants recognized this struggle and tried to embody it in a more popular, daily-life sort of way.[41]

Haacke's artistic appropriation of systems theory and cybernetics was likewise part of this epistemological struggle—though at a remove from Californian "Whole Earth" hippie culture.

The success of systems theory in the 1960s and the rise of the ecological movement toward the end of the decade went hand in hand with the popularization of the term "ecosystem," which had been coined by Arthur Tansley.[42] This is a concept that puts a premium on stability and equilibrium; thus, like the notion of "nature," it was rather compatible with essentialist views of an unchanging, stable natural world. However, being involved with the push for a more reflexive "second-order cybernetics" around 1970, Gregory Bateson's systems ecology took a more critical turn. In his 1972 book, *Steps to an Ecology of Mind*, Bateson not only used the concept of a mental ecology but also stressed the role of technology in the ecosystem.[43]

Some of Haacke's pieces appear to deal straightforwardly with "natural" ecology, such as 1970's *Ten Turtles Set Free*, for which Haacke released ten tortoises, bought from a pet store, in the countryside of Saint-Paul-de-Vence, home to the Fondation Maeght. With its release of abstracted animals back into nature, *Ten Turtles* is, in a sense, the opposite of *All Systems Go!*, a project in which he trained a mynah bird to pronounce that phrase for his (canceled) show at the Solomon R. Guggenheim Museum. Here, a caged bird is made to parrot human language as an artwork, whereas with *Ten Turtles*, the animals have been "liberated" by being purchased as living commodities and then released in the vicinity of an art institution in the French countryside, with its Miro-designed garden evoking an ideal synthesis of nature and culture. The institution surreptitiously combined its not-for-profit status with the sale of prints published by Galerie Maeght, and in his other 1970 piece at this site, *En vente à la Fondation Maeght*, Haacke broadcast the prices of these prints over the PA system of the foundation's theater—interrupted by the latest news from the Agence France-Presse wire service.[44] Together, the pieces suggest a polemical analogy between the pet store and the Fondation Maeght, with the turtles—belonging to the species Herman's tortoise, which is indigenous to southern France—escaping the institution and left to amble off into the undergrowth.

With their focus on institutional constraints (which these turtles can escape, while the artist cannot), Haacke's two Fondation Maeght pieces do not amount to a "hippie" version of cybernetics or systems theory—but they don't represent the military-industrial version either. Something is set in motion, as the turtles are able to trace their own paths through a changing environment that may pose challenges to them. Like Burnham, Haacke was interested in technological as well as natural *real-time systems*, as opposed to the idealist duration of traditional art and its appreciation.[45] By 1972, his work had taken on an explicitly political dimension: *Rhine Water Purification Plant*, shown in Krefeld, was a fish tank filled with filtered water from the heavily polluted Rhine.

Rhine Water Purification Plant is, in fact, an open system whose attempt to restore homeostasis is itself dependent on electricity—and thus implicated in a political economy that destroys social and ecological fabrics in order to stabilize itself. The term "purification" may make some uncomfortable, but the German *Aufbereitung* (the original title being the rather wonderful compound word *Rheinwasseraufbereitungsanlage*) is rather more neutral in this regard. On the other hand, the

English version of the title could be seen as a dig at (late-)modernist ideologies of purity. In fact, the Haus Lange Museum, a house designed by Mies van der Rohe, inside which Haacke's piece was installed, also contains Yves Klein's white void.[46]

What is crucial is that Haacke homes in on intersections and interferences between systems—counteracting the tendency to fetishize the self-sufficient and autarkic system or structure.[47] Taking place in a public institution in Krefeld, the project spawned a press investigation into the city's part in the pollution of the river through its dumping of untreated household and industrial sewage: social feedback with potential environmental effects.[48] In terms used by Félix Guattari (in part on the basis of Bateson's work), one can see in this the forging of transversal connections "between ecosystems, the mechanosphere and the social and individual Universes of reference."[49]

For Haacke, as for Burnham, systems theory could be applied to social and natural systems. This made for parallels, but not necessarily a sense of dialectical and historical interaction. It was in the *Rhine Water* piece that Haacke really began to address the interdependencies between ecology and political economy—his works from the late 1960s do not necessarily have that degree of "second-order" reflexivity. One 1969 piece involved Haacke throwing one hundred plastic bottles into the North Saskatchewan River, each containing a message asking future finders to report the location.[50] The bottles here were used as neutral tools to study the river as natural system; there was not yet an acknowledgment of plastic bottles as agents that affect and transform the environment.

Another one of Haacke's systems pieces from the same year, *Chickens Hatching*, consists of serial minimalist incubators and chicks that give "feedback" to the system by hatching. The asymmetry between chicks and spectators is clear: while the latter are, of course, also part of a (social, art-world) system, they are on a higher level than the chickens, which are framed and looked at. This situation is turned around in Höller and Trockel's 1997 installation *Addina*, which was installed in a stable in Palermo. A large oval or egg-shaped space was demarcated by polyester walls made from panels with egg-shaped negative forms. One horizontal row near the top, however, had one-way mirrors instead of indentations. Visitors could enter the central space and eat eggs or wafers; the producers of the eggs could only be heard, as they were behind the polyester wall. The chickens, however, could see the visitors, as they could climb up a perch and look through the one-way window. This reverses the situation of *A House for Pigs and People*, where the one-way mirror worked the other way around.

Höller and Trockel's use of mirrored glass (in one direction in *A House for Pigs and People*, and the other in *Addina*) emphasizes the human spectator's own implication in the situation. Höller and Trockel's houses are abodes for montages of different species, including humans. When their "houses" were exhibited at the Musée d'Art Moderne de la Ville de Paris in 1999, they were all shown as models or partial or reduced reconstructions. The only one containing living animals was the home for urban silverfish: the single-species *Silverfish House*.[51] However, since they live everywhere, including the museum, there was an element of both species montage and site-specificity; the silverfish are at home in the museum anyway, where they cohabit with humans. Höller and Trockel turned their custom-built house within the museum into a technological spectacle by affixing it to an overhead projector that cast their moving shadows on the gallery wall—in *real time*, as Burnham would have put it. The silverfish become nonhuman labor-power, producing a shadow play.

Here, one may also think of further works by Bik Van der Pol. Their 2010 installation at the Museum of Contemporary Art of Rome (MACRO) can be seen as a contemporary engagement with systems ecology, but one that foregrounds the differences in the repetition. *Are you really sure that a floor can't also be a ceiling?* consisted of an

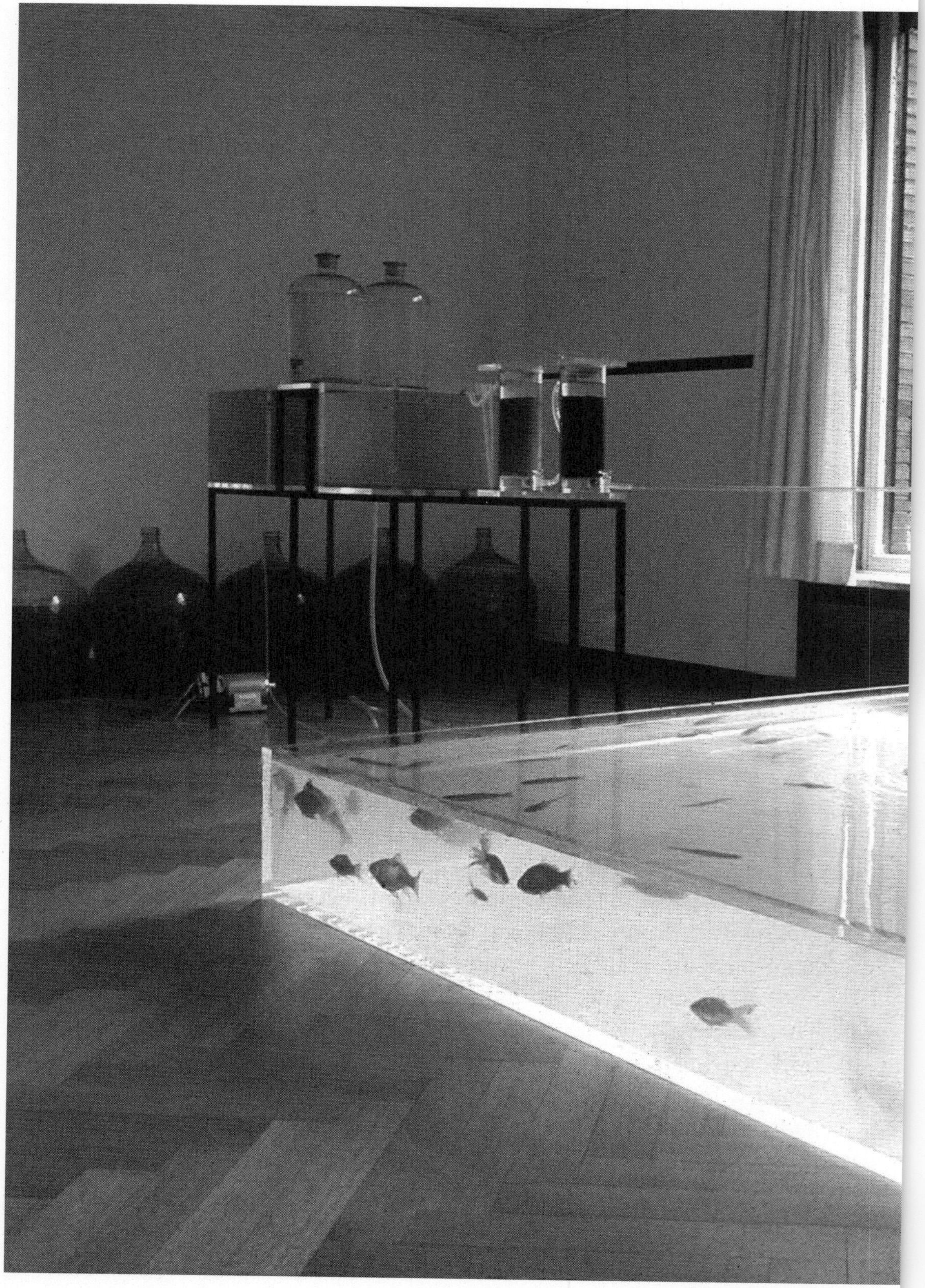

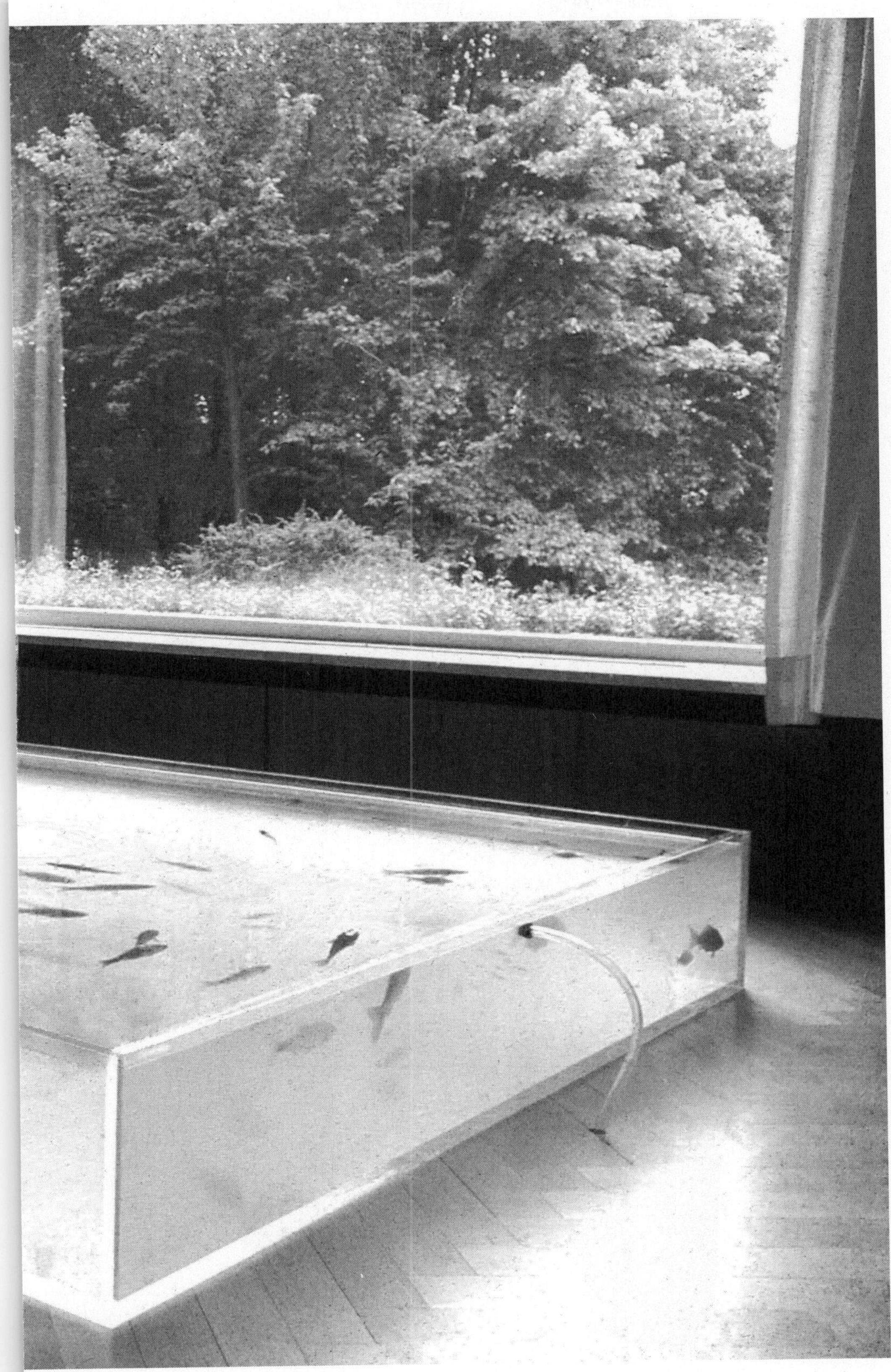

Hans Haacke, *Rhine Water Purification Plant*, Haus Lange Museum, Krefeld, 1972

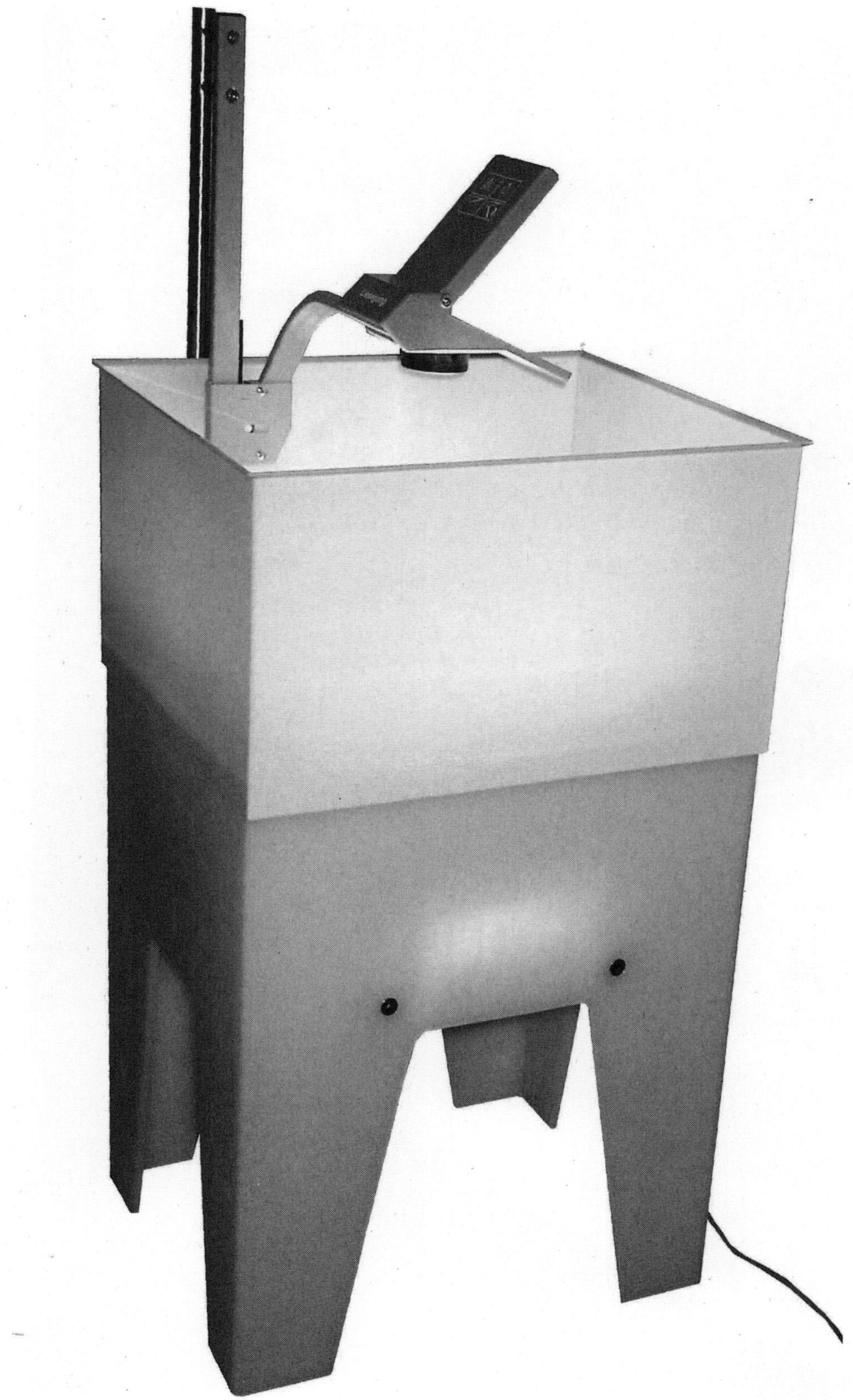

Carsten Höller and Rosemarie Trockel, *Silverfish House*, 1999, details

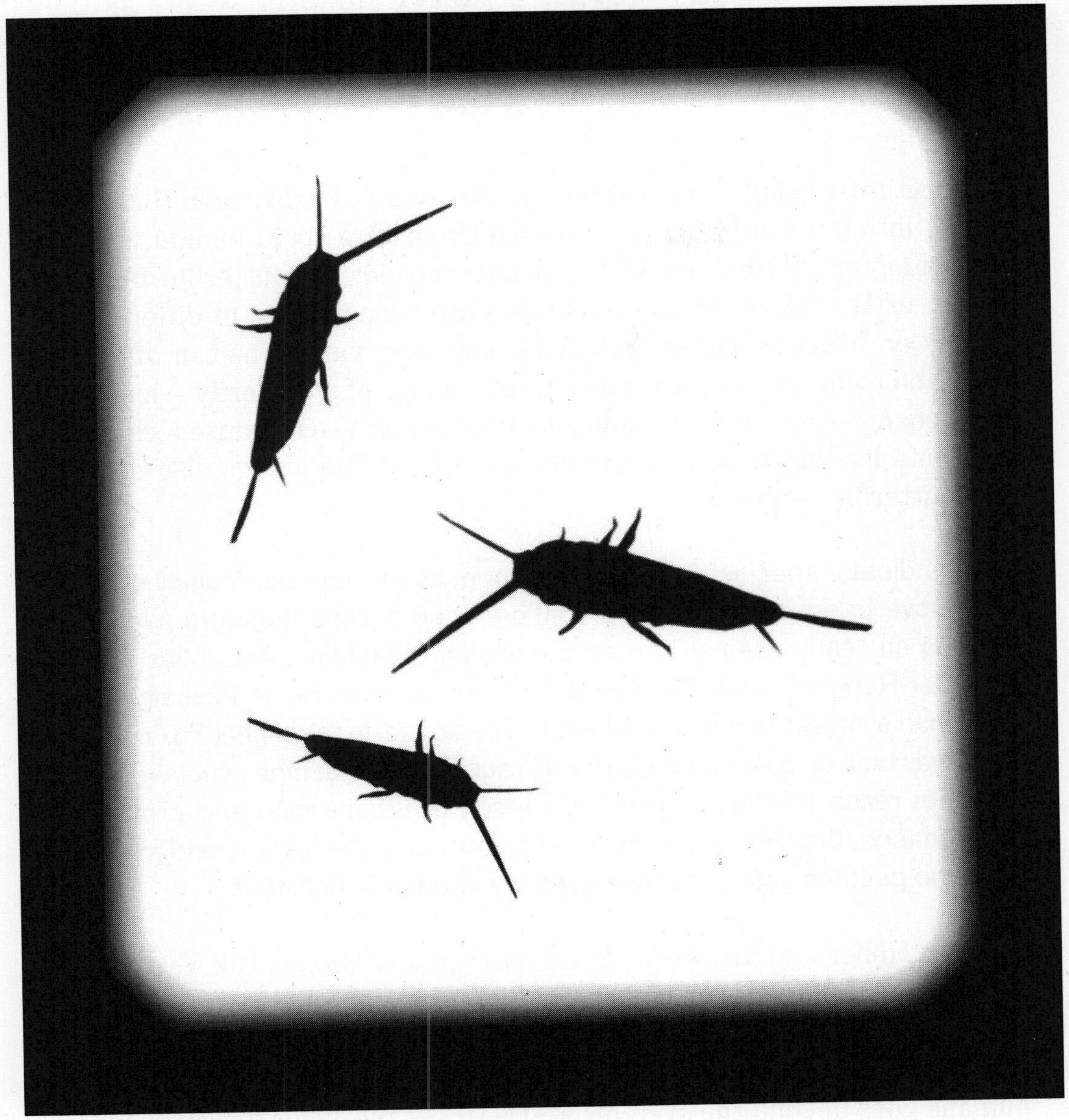

architectural model, based on Mies van der Rohe's Farnsworth House, turned into a butterfly habitat—in which visitors could mingle with the lepidoptera. With this work, the artists evoked: "the butterfly effect; a term used to describe the sensitive (inter)dependence of different actions on initial conditions, showing how tiny variations can affect giant and complex systems. The flapping wings of a butterfly—just a small change in the initial condition of the system—can cause a chain of events leading to large-scale alterations."[52] The artists also note that butterflies serve as

> "indicator species" for climate change, as they are particularly sensitive to environmental degradation. Their decline therefore serves as an "early warning" on environmental conditions. Also Mies van der Rohe's Farnsworth house [...] can be seen as an indicator of man's impact on the environment. The house, located near Fox river, was built on poles and designed in such a way that high water would not reach the house. But, as a result of urbanization and climate change, the river began to rise dramatically in the 1950s, and since the past ten years, the river regularly floods the house.[53]

As with Höller and Trockel's *House for Pigs and People*, Bik Van der Pol's installation stresses the specular. Functioning like a stage set, with the glass walls acting as membranes that are transparent to light while protecting the microclimate inside, this house for butterflies and humans goes beyond the systems aesthetics of the 1960s by stressing human implication in a highly visual and visceral manner. As evinced by their choice of an "ancient" pig breed, an acknowledgment of historical feedback between natural and socioeconomic systems is at the root of Höller and Trockel's short-lived collaboration in the late 1990s. This acknowledgment of interference undermines the purity of the models constructed by postwar systems theory. The focus in more recent practices is less on "whole systems" than on the specific forms of entanglement and coexistence that constitute the ecosystem. To this end, the artists treat the ecosystem as a social system.

They, in turn, run the risk of naturalizing the social system of a financialized art world, in what could be seen as a regression vis-à-vis institutional critique: the art world and its infrastructure are basically abstracted to the white cube as a theater for systems aesthetics. Bik Van der Pol's work was realized through the context of the ENEL Award, sponsored by the Italian energy company—an irony that reveals the work's embedded and compromised status as part of the destructive ecology of contemporary art.[54] Bik Van der Pol did not foreground or problematize this explicitly in the piece—and artists like Huyghe or Höller are certainly not interested in anything that could compromise their large-scale projects, being as comfortable in their milieu as peas in a pod. The step from an aestheticization of systems to a dialectics of self-implication may be a leap too far. Even so, these practices so often provide pointers in that direction.

Umwelt and Umgebung

Pieces by Huyghe titled *Umwelt* and *UUmwelt* indicate a theoretical reference that has entered neo-systems aesthetics via Deleuze and Guattari's *A Thousand Plateaus*, in which they use Jakob von Uexküll's notion of an animal's *Umwelt*. In one passage, they recall the "unforgettable associated world of the Tick, defined by its gravitational energy of falling, its olfactory characteristic of perceiving sweat, and its active characteristic of latching on."[55] The tick, thus, has an Umwelt or "associated world" that is limited to "three factors, and no more."[56]

The scion of a Baltic German noble family, and a German nationalist who lost much of his family fortune after World War I, Uexküll used crude biological metaphors to attack Germany's external enemies

Bik Van der Pol, *Are you really sure that a floor can't also be a ceiling?*, MACRO, Rome, 2010

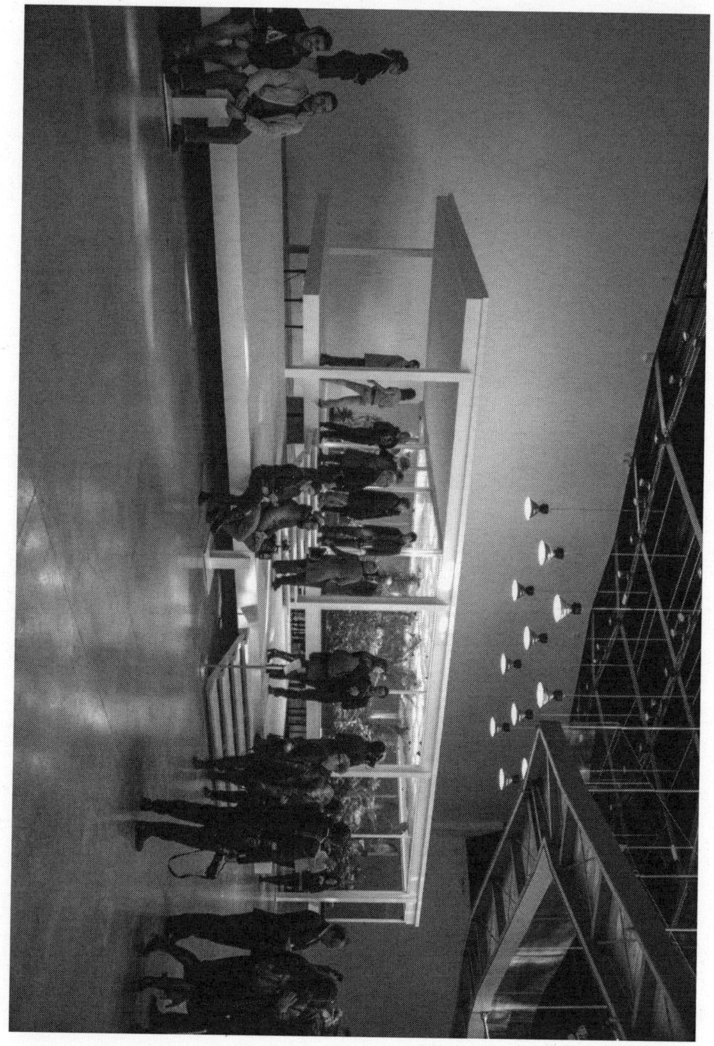

(the British), as well as its internal enemies (no prizes for guessing their identity).[57] In his more strictly scientific work, he contrasts the Umwelt with the *Umgebung*. The Umgebung (surroundings) is is the physical context of an organism, which it cannot access *as such*; what it inhabits is rather its behavioral environment or "milieu" (Umwelt). The Umwelt is an organism's subjective world, like the three-factor world of the tick.[58] Uexküll treats all organisms as subjects, no matter how primitive or advanced they are. These subjects are in a constant feedback loop with the Umgebung, which, thus, becomes their Umwelt—a feedback loop involving their sense organs (*Merkorgane*) and their acting organs (*Wirkorgane*). You may build a house for pigs and humans, but within this shared Umgebung, the pigs and humans still inhabit different Umwelten.

While Deleuze and Guattari's reading of Uexküll as a theorist of becoming has been dominant in recent years, it is important to note that Uexküll basically recast the Kantian dichotomy between the phenomenal world as it is perceived by the subject and the noumenal *Ding an sich* in biological terms. His ethology is the biological equivalent of Ernst Cassirer's philosophy of symbolic forms; Uexküll's son Thure would later be involved in the development of "biosemiotics" on the basis of his father's work. The drawings for Uexküll's book *Streifzüge durch die Umwelten von Tieren und Menschen* attempted to show different subjects' "symbolic" universes. The environment of a sea urchin, a primitive "reflex republic," is represented as an Yves Tanguy–like landscape in which what are for us distinct objects become formless blobs.[59] (Now that sea urchins are increasingly affected by the hyperobject of microplastics in the oceans, a new version of this drawing may be needed.)

Another sequence of illustrations shows three different meanings or "overtones" that a sea anemone can have for a hermit crab. A hermit crab will often have anemones on its shell in order to give it further protection; a crab with a "bare shell" will try to graft the anemone onto it. A crab without a shell will try (fruitlessly) to crawl into the anemone, whereas one outfitted with a shell that has anemones on it, and which has gone without food for a while, will now regard the anemone as a meal and eat it. In the illustrations, the sea anemone is given a different color in each case, representing the "tone" of the anemone for the crab in each case.[60] One of Huyghe's aquarium-based "Zoodram" installations (*Zoodram 4*, 2011) contains a hermit crab that has been offered a particular type of housing: rather than a shell, it drags around a bronze cast of a Brancusi head. For the crab, this object obviously has a very different "tone" than for a human observer.

Here the two (human-subject and crab-subject) have not only largely divergent Umwelten but also different Umgebungen. For the crab, the Umgebung is largely constituted by the contents of the aquarium, with movements outside it presumably registering as a kind of background noise. For the human spectator, the aquarium is part of an art space, one of the elements between which they can move back and forth—without, however, being able to immerse themselves in the tank. The aquarium is a second framing device within the framing device that is the art space; the human spectator is between the two frames.

By contrast, in an exhibition that explicitly referenced Uexküll's work in his exhibition "Influants," at Esther Schipper in 2011, Huyghe created a *copresence* of different Umwelten in the same Umgebung. Here, spiders and ants shared the gallery space with visitors in a piece that is actually titled *Umwelt*. Another element of the show, *Influenced*, consisted of a person with a flu virus that may or may not be passed on to the visitor. The installation was, in Huyghe's words, a choreography that staged "cohabitation and at the same time separation" between the spiders, ants, human beings, and flu virus—with visitors potentially stepping on ants or carefully avoiding them.[61]

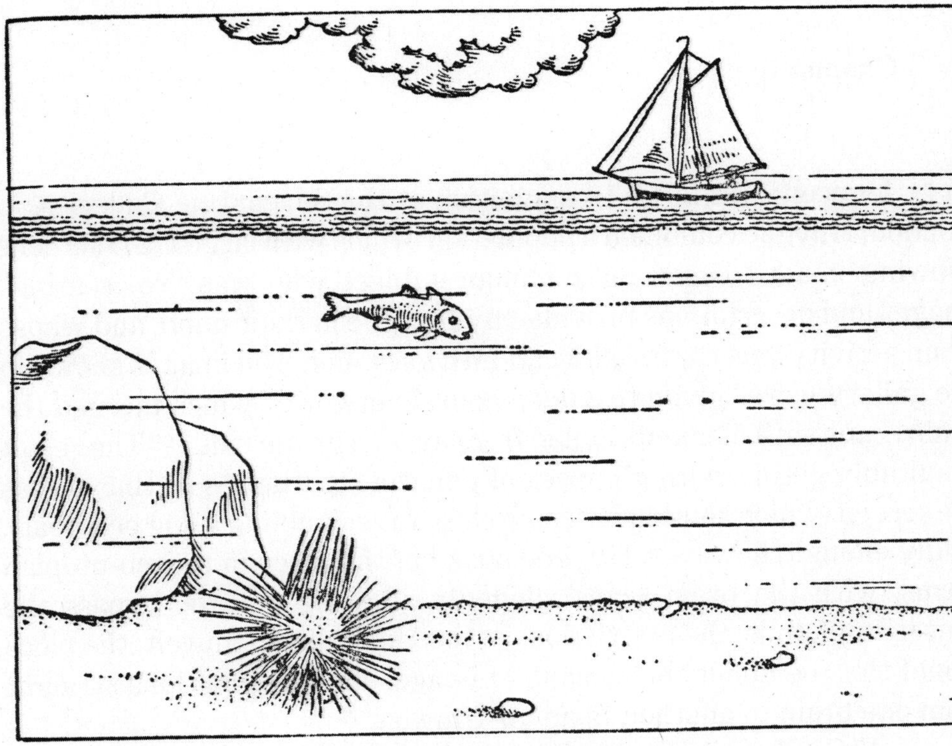

Abb. 19 a. Umgebung des Seeigels

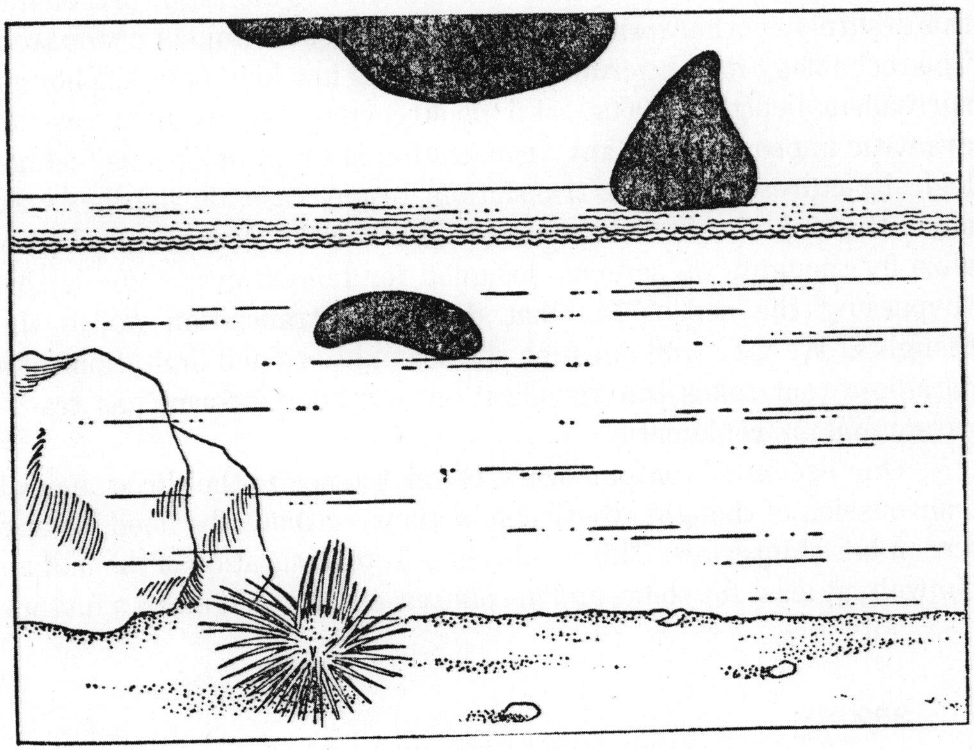

Abb. 19 b. Umwelt des Seeigels

The Umgebung and Umwelt of the sea urchin, illustrations in Jakob von Uexküll, *Streifzüge durch die Umwelten von Tieren und Menschen* (1934)

In "UUmwelt," his 2018–19 exhibition at the Serpentine Galleries, in London, Huyghe combined a population of flies with large LED screens showing images based on a human subject who was "re-creating" images and descriptions provided by Huyghe in their mind, and whose brain activity was captured by an fMRI scanner. The images shown in the gallery were "given to a deep neural network," which merged the brain scans with elements culled from its own image bank.[62] The result is suitably gothic, with glimpses of generic nightmares flitting across the screen (which sometimes come close to resembling a dog or a boat). Oddly enough, however, Huyghe spoke of the piece in techno-utopian terms, with the brain scans allegedly allowing one to "bypass the senses" and, thus, the restrictions of the Uexküllian Umwelt: the piece would thus be about the sharing of images and imaginations straight from one brain to another, in an un-Umwelt.[63]

While Huyghe is certainly correct that advanced technology is making strides in the automated vocalization or visualization of thought, this is surely another form of mediation, a different kind of *pharmakon*. The technology may be crude now, resulting in a kind of kitsch horror surrealism befitting 1960s sci-fi book covers, but even in case of dramatic improvements, any visualization of brain images as technological pictures involves a translation. In any case, do the flies care about the *look* of what flickers on the LED screen? And when we visualize fly thoughts on screens designed for human eyes (how is this "bypassing the senses"?), what does that translation *do* to the thoughts? We may well question the assumptions and limitations of a paradigm that takes the visualization of "thought-forms" as transparent and unproblematic.

One dream of contemporary technoscience is the direct neural transmission of thoughts (between humans) without the need for any screen-based interface. This would constitute a mutation of the human Umwelt, at least for some, and in some cases. It would mean a further diversification of Umwelten, in which old senses interact in complex ways with new devices. Rather than creating a posthistorical world of complete transparency, this would result in new relations that would, in all likelihood, be at least as complex and contradictory as anything we know.

Coevolution and Cohabitation

If there is a distinction to be made—as David Craven has argued, invoking d'Alembert—between an *esprit de système* that thinks "for the sake of the system" and an *esprit systématique* that involves the continual questioning of one's conceptual framework, then postwar systems theory unapologetically opted for the former.[64] The latter would have to involve a dialectical willingness to think about systemic and unresolvable contradictions, antinomies, and antagonisms, and their dynamic and open-ended unfolding.

For their 2000–2002 series of "library drawings," Bik Van der Pol hand-traced photos from magazines and catalogues, mostly pertaining to the neo-avant-garde of the 1960s and 1970s. However, the drawings also include a set photo from *Planet of the Apes*, a giant greenhouse labeled "artificial nature," a picture of Walt Disney "feeding" the audio-animatronic dinosaurs his company designed for the Ford pavilion at the 1964 World's Fair, as well as a drawing of Haacke's turtles.[65] Shown in an installation with an electric fan that puts the paper-covered walls in motion, the "library drawings" place systems aesthetics in a dialectical historical constellation with forms of simulated nature—mutations of the socioeconomico-ecological system.

Huyghe's unrealized 2000 project *Mies Cuba Gets Cold* aimed to engage with Disney's simulations more fully. Huyghe proposed turning the main floor of Mies van der Rohe's Neue Nationalgalerie in Berlin—a postwar temple to modernism—into a Cuban jungle. Mies van der Rohe's design is said to be a variation on an office building in Cuba he

Pierre Huyghe, *Umwelt*, Esther Schipper, Berlin, 2011

designed for Bacardi, which was never realized because of the revolution. The design was then repurposed for the *Frontstadt* of the Cold War, West Berlin.[66] Huyghe's jungle was supposed to have an artificial weather system based on the weather in Berlin between 1957 and 1968, and a film on actual insect life in the artificial jungles of Disney theme park attractions—where Americans and other tourists can get the sensation of "tropical adventure" without facing unpleasant social, political, and ecological conditions. If common house spiders are perfectly adapted to human habitations, could the proliferation of "artificial jungles" ultimately result in "artificial jungle life"?

Rather than presenting a scenario of artifice killing life, as in *A Rebours*, *Mies Cuba Gets Cold* fosters speculation on a new breed of insects in simulated jungles—on coevolution. In 1974, Stewart Brand's *Whole Earth Catalog* morphed into *CoEvolution Quarterly*, with the first issue explaining:

> The term [coevolution] was introduced in 1965 by Paul Ehrlich and Peter Raven in their study of the predator-prey relationship of caterpillars and plants. They found that the eaters and the eaten progressively evolved in close response to each other—coevolved. [...] It seems that all evolution is coevolution. The beauty of the term is what it adds to the concept of ecology. Language such as "preserving the ecology" suggests something quite perfect—static, knowable, oriented backward, unwelcoming to human foolishness, [...] unreal. Ecology is the whole system alright, but coevolution is the whole system in TIME. The health of it is forward—systemic self-education which feeds on constant imperfection.[67]

As fuzzy and neoliberal as Brand's rhetoric often was, the terms "cohabitation" and "coevolution" are both needed to understand the biosocial dialectic staged in recent art such as Huyghe's, which not only brings together different species but also understands their interrelations as historical and mutable.[68] If to abstract is to subtract irrelevant traits or noise, to reduce the number of stimuli until only the crucial information remains, then animals such as the tick are, in fact, masters of abstraction. With much more—too much, yet never enough—data at their disposal, humans can take abstraction to a higher degree, calculating or guesstimating the effects of various actions (and of inaction) on the Umgebung of various species, and on the global ecosystem.

In extracts from his then-upcoming book *Four Arguments for the Elimination of Television* published in the winter 1977/78 issue of *CoEvolution Quarterly*, Jerry Mander noted the extent to which the human environment—the human version of Uexküll's Umwelt—had become a media environment: "With natural environments having been replaced and remade into a new artificial form (cities, suburbs), environment itself had become media, an intervention between humans and direct personal experience and knowledge of natural process."[69] This means that "the environment has been reconstructed into an already abstracted, arbitrary form," and television adds another layer of abstraction, of filtering and editing.[70] Hence, "any attempt to instill a caring about natural environments or their destruction that is confined to TV cannot succeed. Most of the message is lost in translation. Most of the key information is not communicable."[71]

This is one of the problems the counterculture of the late 1960s sought to address and continued to struggle with—in Europe as in the United States. The Dutch Provo movement of 1965–67 was highly aware of the media, staging public happenings (initiated by Robert Jasper Grootveld) and protests that not only transformed the country but were also mediated internationally, inspiring countercultural and protest movements elsewhere.[72] The previous chapter already provided a brief glimpse into the Kabouter movement started by ex-Provo Roel

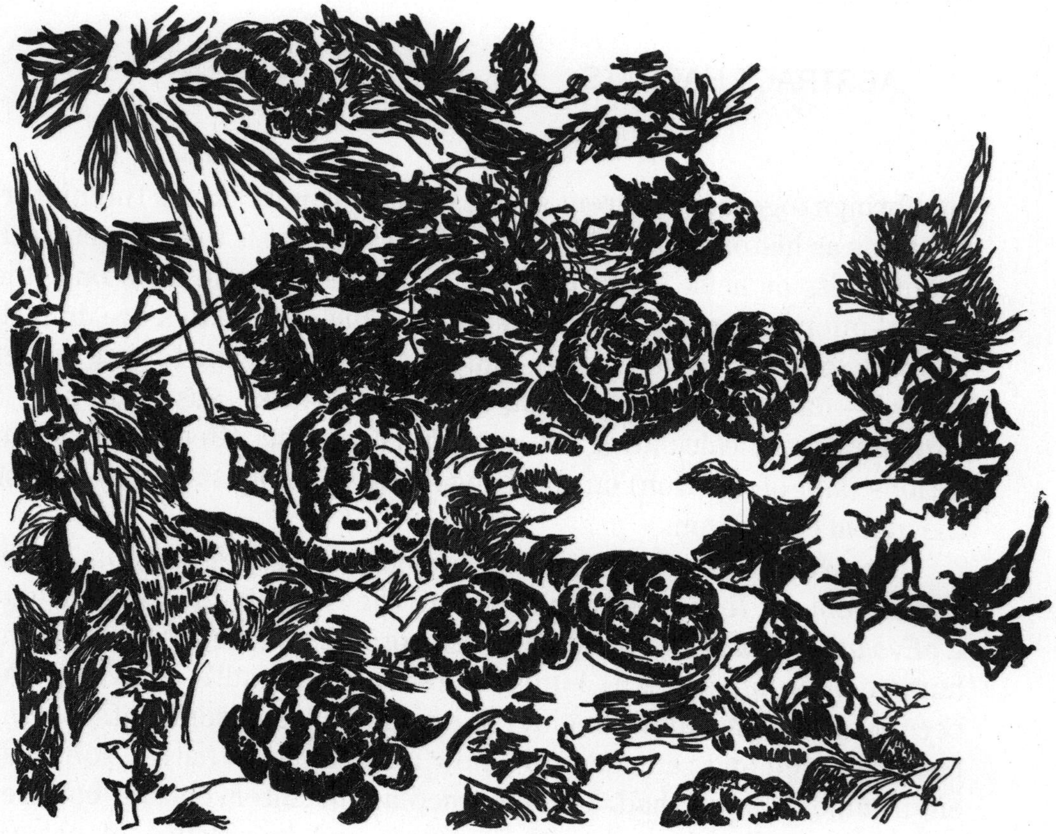

Bik Van der Pol, "library drawings" from *Catching Some Air*, 2000

Walt Disney
"feeding the dinosaurs in the ford Pavilion's "Magic Skyway"

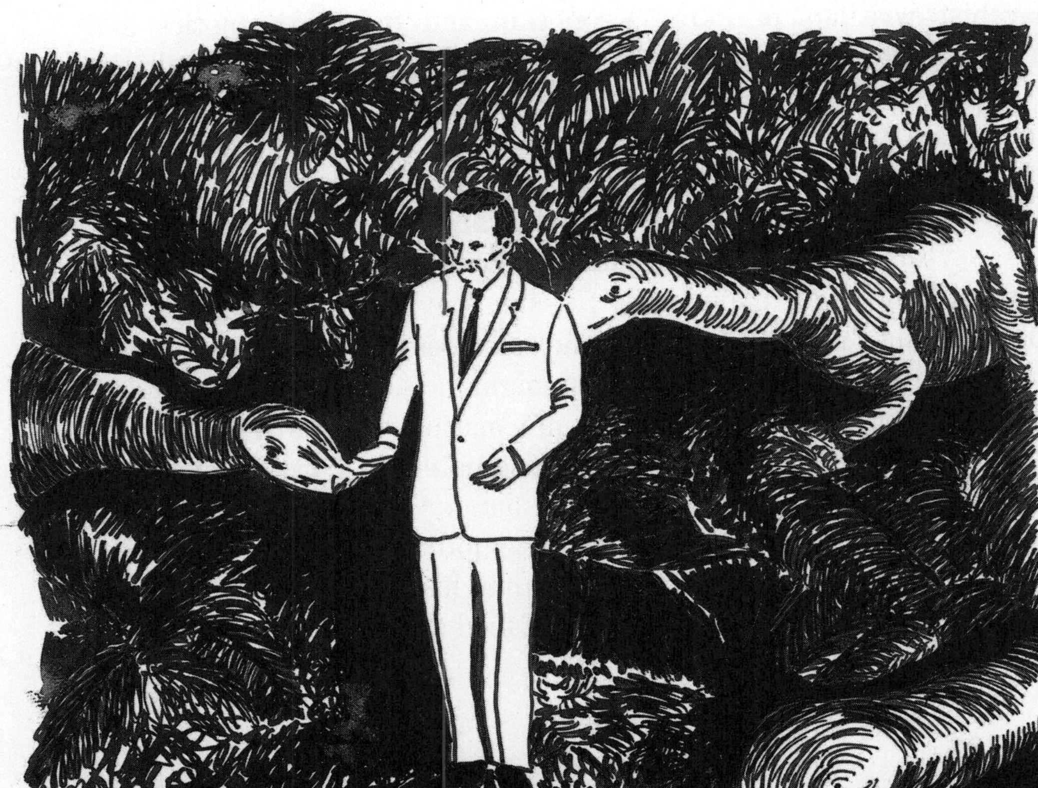

van Duijn in 1969 when he declared Amsterdam to be a *Kabouterstad*—a gnome city or hobgoblin city.[73] In 1970, the Kabouter movement proclaimed Amsterdam to be an *Oranjevrijstaat*—an anti-state freed from the House of Orange, governed in an anarchist-councilist manner.

Having inherited Provo's brand of depoliticized spontaneism, which had been roundly criticized by the Situationists, the Kabouters assumed that the old state and the capitalist economy would simply wither away while they were building up their own structures—though Van Duijn ran for city council to have a foot in the other camp, that of representative democracy. Predictably, given the fuzziness of Kabouter ideology and their reliance on the magical agency of their memelike slogans, the excitement and publicity generated by and for the Kabouters in 1970 proved short-lived. Nonetheless, the movement did help initiate a cultural and behavioral turn.

Drawing on fairytales and esoteric sources as well as from the anarchist writings of Peter Kropotkin and from cybernetics and systems theory, Van Duijn styled himself a "tegenkoppelende cultuurkabouter" (culture-gnome giving negative feedback). He declared cybernetics to be an extension of dialectics, with feedback mechanisms either tending toward stability/homeostasis or, eventually, creating upheaval, a dialectical tipping point. While first-order cybernetics—and 1960s systems theory in its wake—generally privileged homeostatic stability, Van Duijn analyzed the Russian Revolution with cybernetic tools, arguing that the czarist regime collapsed when it was no longer susceptible to negative feedback that might have modified its behavior; dependent on false or incomplete information, it could not prevent things from reaching a dialectical tipping point.[74] In order to prevent the *ecological* crisis from reaching a dangerous tipping point, Van Duijn and his Kabouter movement attempted to give critical sociopolitical feedback in order to effect an anarchist remodeling of society, with small-scale and local production of food and most goods.

A major enemy for the Kabouters was the car, and the idea was to make Amsterdam completely car free. Van Duijn launched a plan to equip cars with small roof gardens, turning them into mobile green lungs—which he presented on Dutch television on October 14, 1969, attempting to use the medium to his advantage.[75] Even while Van Duijn was well aware that such a TV appearance itself would not change anything, with "ecological problems" becoming "content" fodder, he endeavored to short-circuit the media ecology with "natural" ecology precisely by presenting a possible—though not entirely plausible—plan for action. Van Duijn's limit was his anarchist voluntarism, which assumed that capitalist structures would wither away in the face of a countercultural offensive, but he was clear-eyed when it came to the need to establish a feedback loop between the media Umwelt, social ecology, and natural ecology.

Organisms among Others

The protests and legal challenges against art projects that incorporate living animals are manifestations of the fight over personhood in contemporary culture.[76] Historically, there has been a struggle to extend full human rights to people partly or fully deprived of them—women, slaves, or colonized Others in general. Wendy Brown and Janet Halley have characterized as "left legalism" the set of practices that attempts to defend the rights and better the position of women and minorities through legal action, demanding for such groups to be included in the liberal order based on the abstract individualism of the person.[77] In some of her writings, Brown homes in on the paradoxes of universalism and particularism; claiming that women (Black people, queer people, etc.) have or should have equal access to universal rights creates as many problems as arguing that some rights are specific to them.[78] These paradoxes reassert themselves with a vengeance in the debate on (non)human rights for animals.

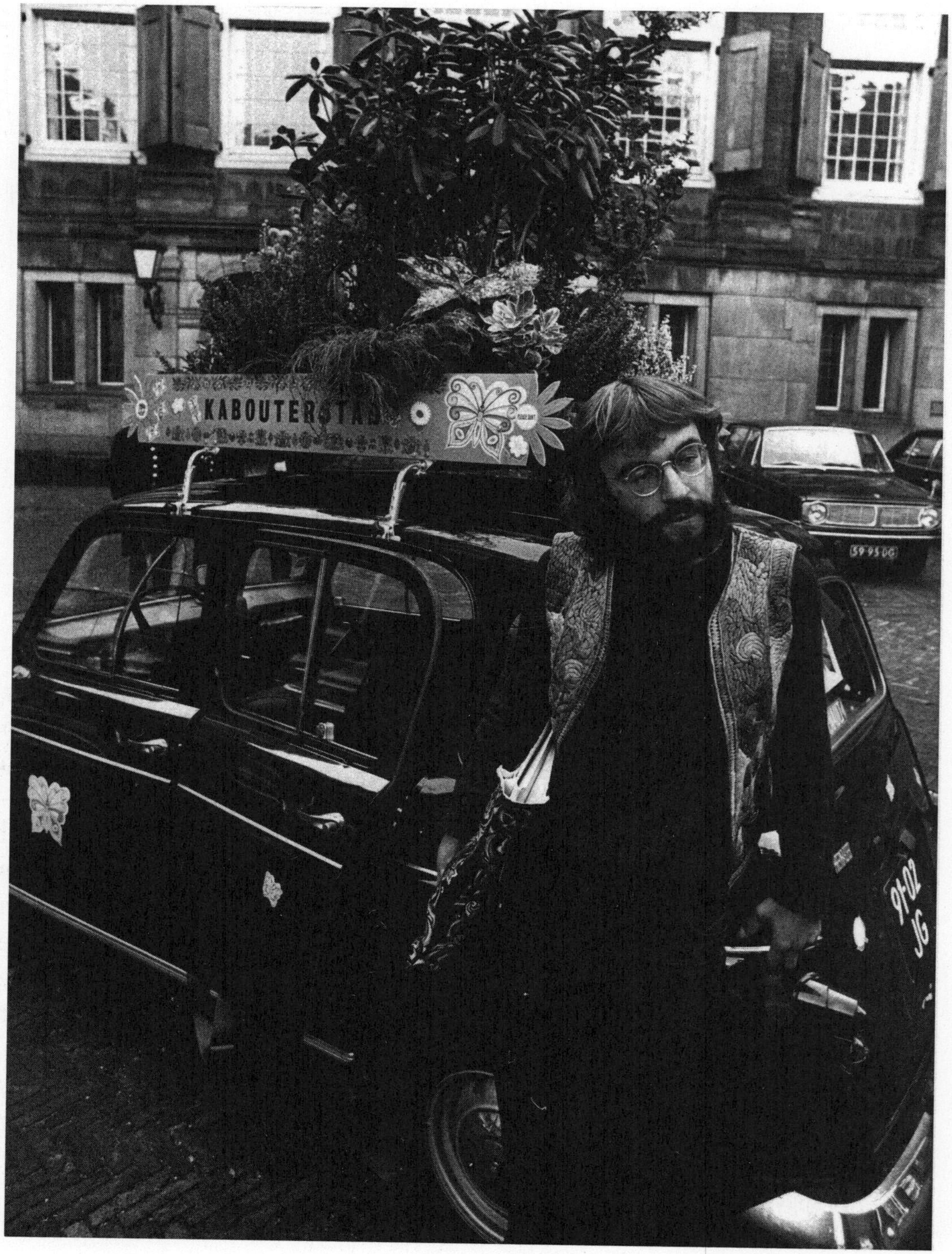

Roel van Duijn and car with roof garden, 1969

In the United States, for instance, the Nonhuman Rights Project has waged a legal campaign on behalf of the chimpanzees Tommy and Kiko. Applying categories designed for humans to apes makes sense given recent attempts to show a more gradual transition from the animal to the human in the case of the great apes—who have been shown to use tools and to have specific cultures. As Forensic Architecture's Eyal Weizman notes, "Given that apes, like orangutans, were considered to be part of a fuzzy definition of humanity until being 'expelled' at the end of the eighteenth century, current attempts at granting apes legal personhood and some form of nonhuman rights do not amount to a simple admission into an expanded humanity, but rather re-admission."[79] As Weizman also argues, this expulsion of the apes from humanity occurred in a context of colonial extractivism, when the planet itself "came to be approached from a managerial, technocratic, and profit-oriented perspective as a design object."[80]

Now that the productive rationality and operative abstraction of the global design project have wrecked the planet to such an extent that Silicon Valley gazillionaires are funding space colonization programs, treating life-forms as design objects is understandably extremely sensitive. In the context of a looming systemic ecological collapse, the notion of "humankind" will have to be given up altogether, as differences in access to good water and food, education, and, last but not least, medicine (including the latest advances in genetics) will make the posthuman condition one of a bifurcation into different species.[81] Thus, the posthuman future will be marked by asymmetries that are much stronger than current—already accelerating—class and race divisions. In the process, the divide between humans and nonhumans created by the Enlightenment may wither—and while some people may de facto be expelled from humanity, some apes may be readmitted (if it's not already too late).

Another symptomatic simian court case concerned the famous "monkey selfies" that had been taken by a macaque with photographer David Slater's camera. This monkey selfie case features as *Thing 001652* in the archive of Kobe Matthys's Agency. It was part of Agency's presentation at the 2017 Contour Biennial in Mechelen, Belgium—in the form of David Slater's photo book *Wildlife Personalities* and an accompanying text on a table surrounded by benches; this was also the setting for an assembly where the legal case was discussed with experts. Slater considered the pictures to be his photos, but Wikipedia and other sites claimed they were public domain, as the pictures were taken by a monkey, which is not a legal person and cannot hold copyright. PETA started a court case to make the case that monkeys *can* be legal persons and, hence, authors. They acted as "next friends of Naruto," with Naruto being the name of the alleged monkey photographer and the "next friend" principle allowing one to represent another person who is unable to do so and has no legal representative. This was rejected by the appeals court in 2018.[82]

In this case, the question of authorship comes to act as a stand-in for personhood. The current push for nonhuman personhood seems like a literalization of Uexküll's Kantian treatment of animals as subjects rather than objects. Uexküll radicalized Kant's "Copernican revolution"—and Deleuze, in turn, further decentered the animal, as Brett Buchanan has emphasized.[83] Is there really a "subject" called the tick, or is it rather a kind of assemblage of different triggers and responses, different affects? The latter step, however, is not taken by today's proponents of animal rights, who want to secure subjecthood for animals through the operative legal fiction of personhood—for, in the realm of juridical real abstraction, the subject is articulated as *person*. This is the fundamental juridical form, which constitutes its counterpart: property. Subject is to object as person is to property.

What *is* a person? It may be worthwhile to recall Hegel:

> "Person" is essentially different from "subject," since "subject" is only the possibility of personality; every living thing of any sort is a subject. A person, then, is a subject aware of this subjectivity, since in personality it is of myself alone that I am aware. A person is a unit of freedom aware of its sheer independence. As this person, I know myself to be free in myself. I can abstract from everything, since nothing confronts me save pure personality, and yet as this person I am something wholly determinate, e.g., I am of a certain age, a certain stature, I occupy this space, and so on through whatever other details you like.[84]

The person, then, is always already a manifestation of real abstraction: it is a self-objectification that turns the subject into one of many equivalent "units of freedom" able to sell their labor-power, own property, and enter into contractual relations.[85] While the subject-object dichotomy of Western philosophy is being critiqued by everyone and their aunt Hildegard, the subject qua person is becoming ever more firmly entrenched legally—though this entrenchment may, in fact, be another form of demolition or deconstruction, as nonhuman entities such as corporations lay claim to legal subjecthood, having long been treated as juridical persons. If Hegel's "units of freedom" need not be natural persons but can also be artificial, corporate entities, then why not create a different kind of legal fiction and award personhood and legal protection to entire ecosystems? If "corporations are people," then why not animals?

Thing 001652 is not the first "thing" with which Agency raised the question of whether nonhuman protagonists—such as animals, objects, or computer programs—can be considered creative and can lay claim to authorship and protect their work with the instruments of

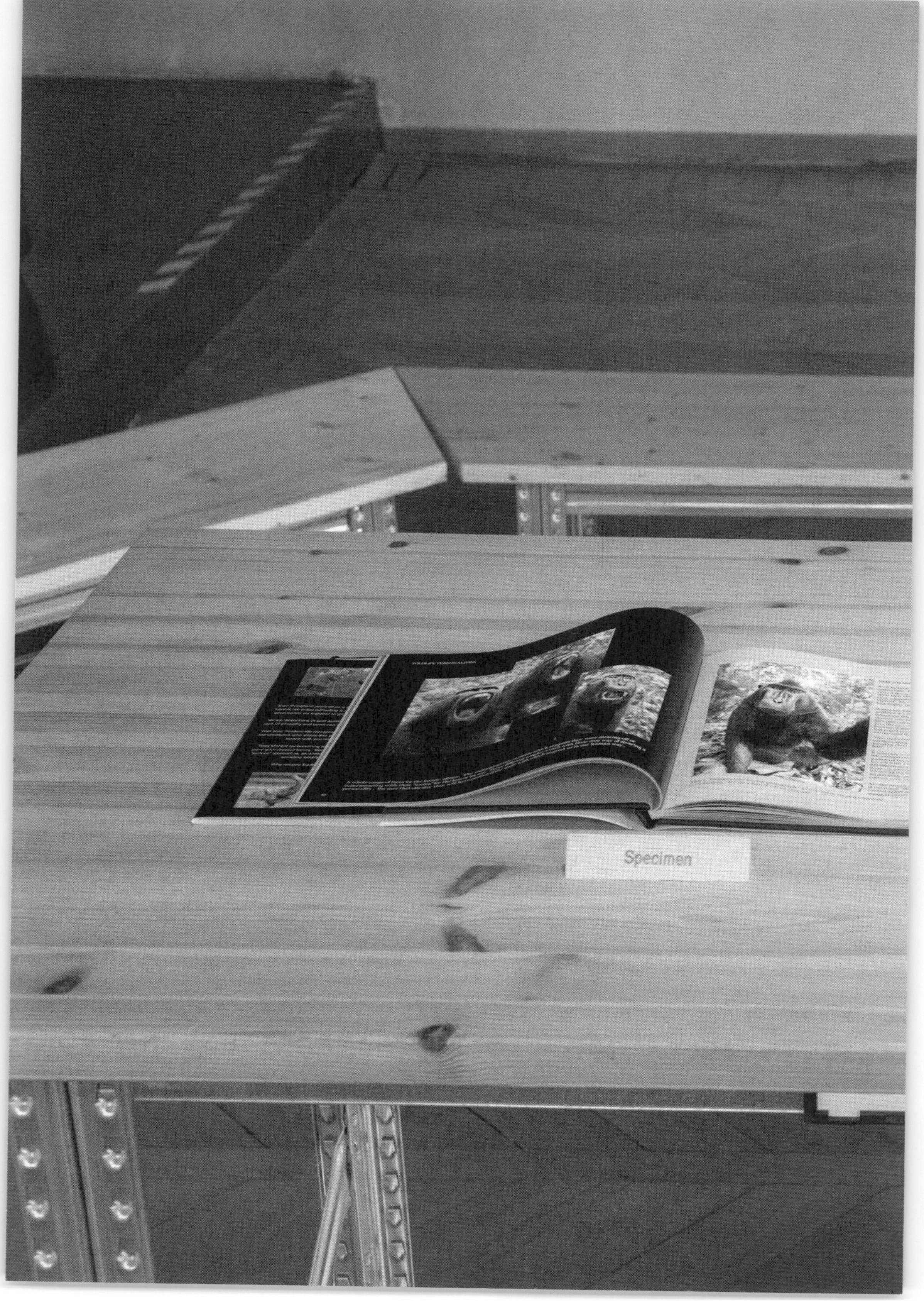
Specimen

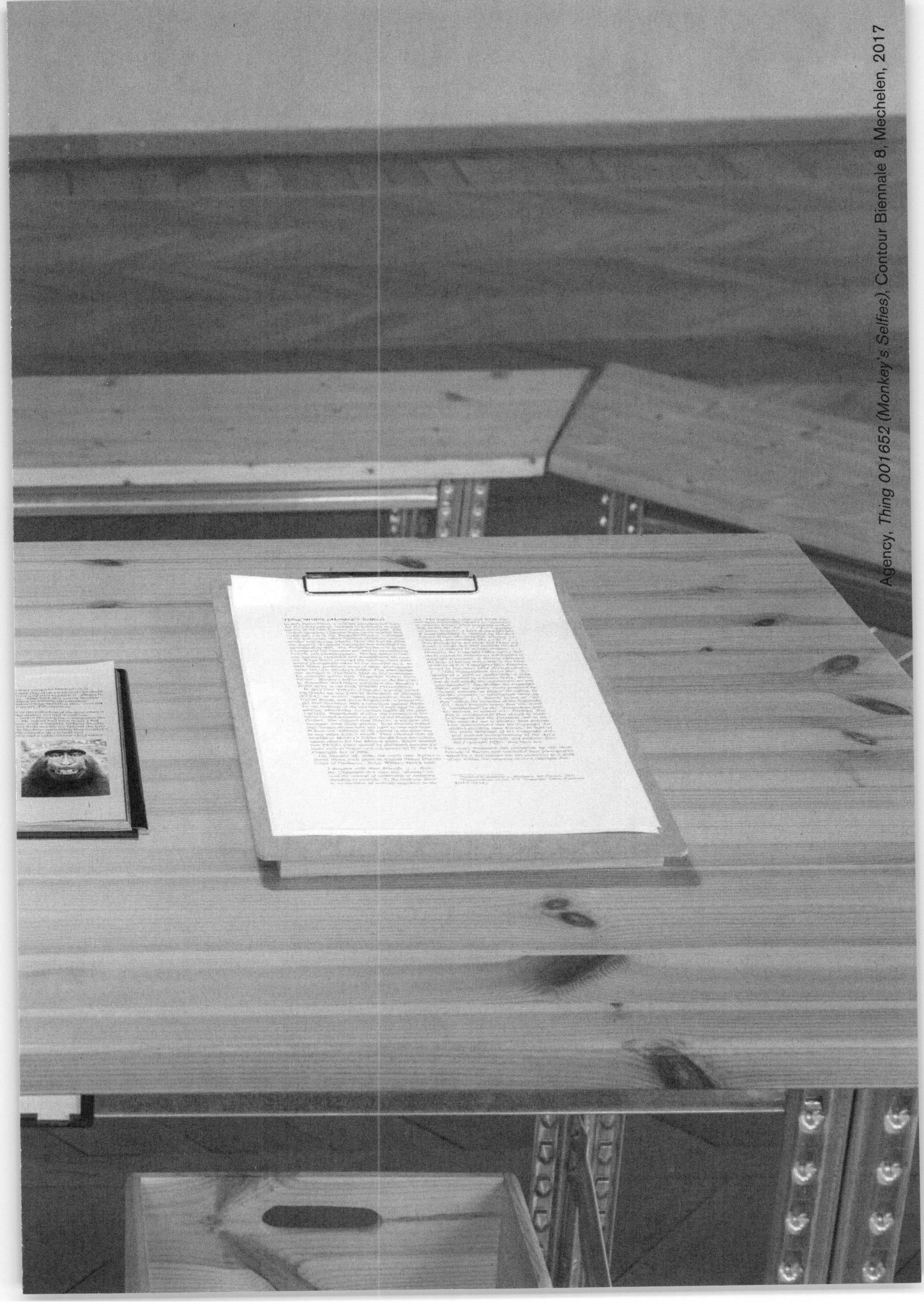

Agency, *Thing 001652 (Monkey's Selfies)*, Contour Biennale 8, Mechelen, 2017

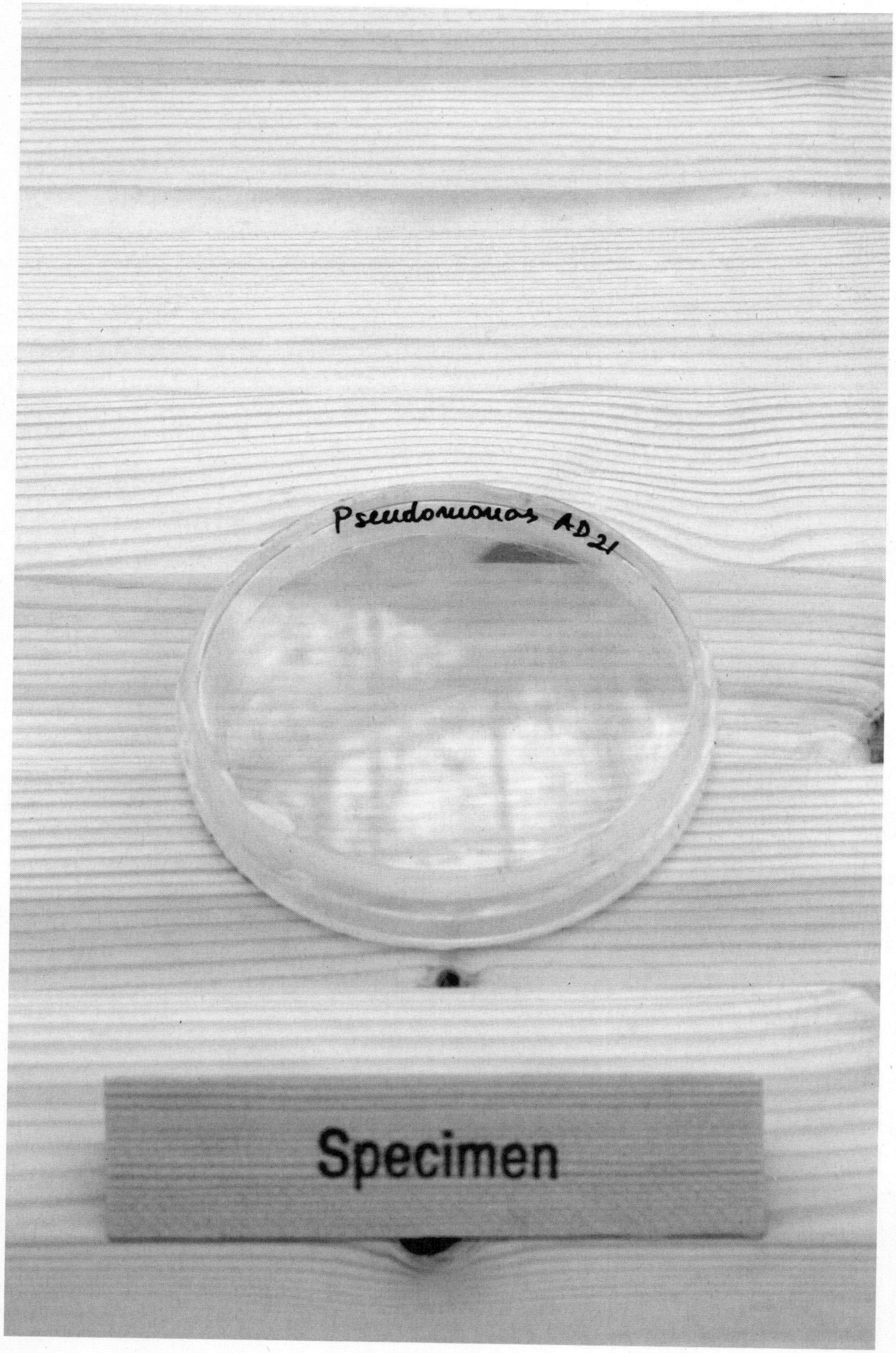

Agency, *Thing 000773 (Pseudomonas)*, 2013

intellectual property law.[86] Agency's *Thing 000773 (Pseudomonas)* revolves around a nonhuman organism *as protected work*, rather than as author: in this case, the genetic material of an organism (a bacteria) was at the center of a patent dispute. For millennia, bacteria in cow dung slurry had been used in India to detoxify waste:

> For example, when sprinkled over oil spillage, the bacteria living inside cow dung soak and degrade crude oil. In 1971, Ananda Chakrabarty, an Indian microbiologist at General Electric Company in Schenectady, New York, extracted deoxyribonucleic acid or DNA plasmids from four different bacteria from the pseudomonas family and inserted them into one single strain. By genetic transfer, Chakrabarty grew bacteria that he hoped would break down multiple components of crude oil. These bacteria were to be used to clean oil spills. In 1972, after conversations with his coworkers, Chakrabarty filed a patent application, assigned to General Electric.[87]

At first, the patent claim was rejected because living organisms were seen as "products of nature" and not patentable. Chakrabarty appealed, and won, making his Pseudomonas the first patented organism. As the Court of Customs and Patent Appeals put it: "The fact that microorganisms [...] are alive [... is] without legal significance [...] for purposes of the patent law."[88] Chakrabarty later stated: "I simply shuffled genes, changing bacteria that already existed [...] like teaching your pet cat a few new tricks."[89] In shuffling genes, the scientist teaches life new tricks. This is the organicism of technoscience, of concrete abstraction.

During an exhibition in 2013, Agency presented a Pseudomonas culture in a petri dish—a "house" that is the product of scientific abstraction. Such a culture has a life span of about a month, and therefore needed to be replaced after that period. More important than this simple display was the assembly with various experts and activists organized by Agency. One might argue that what is lacking in Agency's practice, in contrast to works by Höller/Trockel, Bik Van der Pol, or Huyghe, is the element of cohabitation in the same space. What we see in the exhibition space is a photo book or some other object—and the petri dish, while it supposedly contains Pseudomonas, has a rather different kind of presence from chickens or pigs. Nonetheless, as a quasi-object and potential quasi-subject, this petri dish exerted agency as an invitation to think through conflicting and colliding categories (microbiological life, intellectual property). Within a meta-juridical framework, the biological commodity fetish gives rise to a second-degree practice of fetishization.

Forms of Life, Assembling

In line with Agency's use of the term "thing" for its cases, the assemblies clearly evoke the Latourian notion of a *parliament of things*. Opposing the modern division between the parliament that represents humans and the scientific laboratory that represents nature (a "parliament of mutes"), Latour argues that a parliament of things is needed where "matters of concern" are addressed in a way that is not limited to human concerns.[90] In para-artistic and para-academic milieus, this has given rise to Pollyannaish projects such as the Embassy of the North Sea, in which Dutch culturati play at being "ambassadors" for North Sea "actors" such as fish and the wind.[91] Refusing to take such literalist shortcuts in its assemblies, Agency is less grand—but more precise in its ambitions and use of the assembly-form to unpack some of the preformations we labor and live under.

Jonas Staal's 2018 project *Interplanetary Species Society* took the form of a daylong assembly in the massive underground hall that used to house Sweden's first nuclear reactor during the 1950s and 1960s.[92] In this concrete cavern, twenty-five meters underground, Staal built a temporary structure that included a table with meteorites in the reactor pit, as well as pavilions with illustrations of "proletarian plantae" (from Maoist China) and with actual fossilized ammonites that he turned into the heads of constructivist, Lissitzkyesque "comrades." Politicizing Latour's ultimately technocratic conception of a hybrid parliament in the context of the ongoing wave of mass extinction and the revival of space colonization by the likes of Elon Musk, this assembly gathered underneath slogans declaring: "No to interplanetary colonization, yes to interplanetary cooperation." In a site redolent with anthropocenic Prometheanism, *Interplanetary Species Society* refused to pit an essentialized and externalized "nature" against "technology" as such; rather, the project proposed different bio-techno-social assemblages.

Jack Burnham, we might recall, opposed vitalism to organicism. The biomorphic works of vitalist sculptors such as Moore or Arp suggested a Bergsonian élan vital; on the other hand, scientists, engineers, and architects arrived at a functionalist understanding of organisms. If vitalism was "a preeminently poetic view of life," organicism amounted to "a beautiful view of the utilitarian evolution of systems, both biological and non-biological."[93] From the cast-iron architecture of nineteenth-century greenhouses to cybernetics and systems theory, organicism sought to capture and operationalize the essence of organic function. In the process, the difference between mechanism and organism became one of degree, as it emerged that "*the real destiny of the machine was to merge itself with natural organisms*."[94]

Reflecting on the resurgence of interest in cybernetics and systems theory, Yuk Hui has recently presented an account of the modern organism of incomparably greater depth. Drawing genealogies from Schelling to Lovelock and from Hegel to cybernetics, Hui argues that the organicist turn in modern thought can be traced back to Kant's third critique, the *Critique of Judgment*. In art history and aesthetics, Kant's third critique is usually identified with the judgment of taste, and the section on the teleological judgment of natural organisms is given short shrift. However, as Hui notes, "The aesthetic judgment is analogous to the teleological judgment in the sense that the natural end is an ideal of self-organization that conditions the process without pre-given rules, meaning that it is open to contingency."[95] Kant acknowledged that his a priori principles were insufficient to explain the self-organizing abilities of living organisms.[96] Faced with these capacities for self-organization, the philosopher must accord some purpose to these beings, yet this purpose falls outside the realm of science and can only be glossed over as a baffling *Zweckmäßigkeit ohne Zweck*, or purposiveness without purpose. This, of course, closely mirrors the artwork, or any object that is subject to disinterested aesthetic pleasure.

Here, Kant himself went beyond the "thought-form" and engaged with actual living forms that challenged a priori categories. On the one hand, we have Kant the epistemologist so despised by today's speculative theorists; on the other hand, there is an opening toward the organic. For Hui, drawing on Schelling and cybernetics in particular, the latter takes the form of a dialectic of contingency and recursiveness. Organisms self-organize by recursively folding contingent encounters with obstacles back into their evolving open system. However, as Joan Steigerwald has noted, "Schelling blurred the boundary between organic and inorganic processes, positing each natural object as an organized and dynamic whole."[97] Hui discusses Schelling's example of a stream of water meeting an obstacle and forming a whirlpool that keeps changing. This kind of Romantic/*naturfilosofische* organicism arrives at an abstracted model of process that can, in turn, be functionalized.

Concrete abstraction appears to be a form of operational hylomorphism, "stamping" its value-, information-, and rights-forms on raw matter. Vilém Flusser's example of the production of plastic ballpoint pens is the perfect encapsulation of this. However, with Gilbert

Simondon (whose critique of hylomorphism I discussed in chapter two), we can argue that Flusser's image can only attain such an appearance of perfection because it excludes much that is rather essential: human labor, and, indeed, the reduction of always already informed matter to cheap nature. As Simondon put it, "If the hylomorphic schema appears to emerge from technical experience, it is as a norm or as an ideal rather than as an experience of the real."[98] The operational hylomorphism of capitalist technoscience is a reductive, fetishized reflection of the functional organicism that allows capitalism to deal with contingency. It does so by minimizing contingency in day-to-day operations and exploiting it at moments of disruption.

For Hui, the task is to move from organism to an *organology*, in line with Simondon and Bernard Stiegler. Rather than abstracting schematics of the system/organism, which still privileges systemic integrity, such an organology gives much greater agency to contingency by tracing patterns and relations of individuation and individualization.[99] This is the shift from an *esprit de système* to an *esprit systématique*. But how to unpack and intervene in the operational hylomorphism of concrete abstraction? How to foreground the constitutive exclusions and elisions that result in the suggestion of some capitalist *logos* imprinting matter though the value-form, the rights-form, and the information-form? How to problematize the current conditions under which genes are "shuffled"?

The central importance of Kant's third critique for the philosophy of technology was already recognized in the 1920s by Friedrich Dessauer and his associate Karl August Meissinger. Dessauer argued that technical objects—being possessed with a Zweckmäßigkeit that transcended the boundaries of Kant's categories of understanding—belonged in the realm of the *Critique of Judgment*. In his 1928 *Philosophie der Technik*, Dessauer argued that the Kantian tripartition of the world is ultimately insufficient, and that Kant's "drittes Reich"—as Dessauer

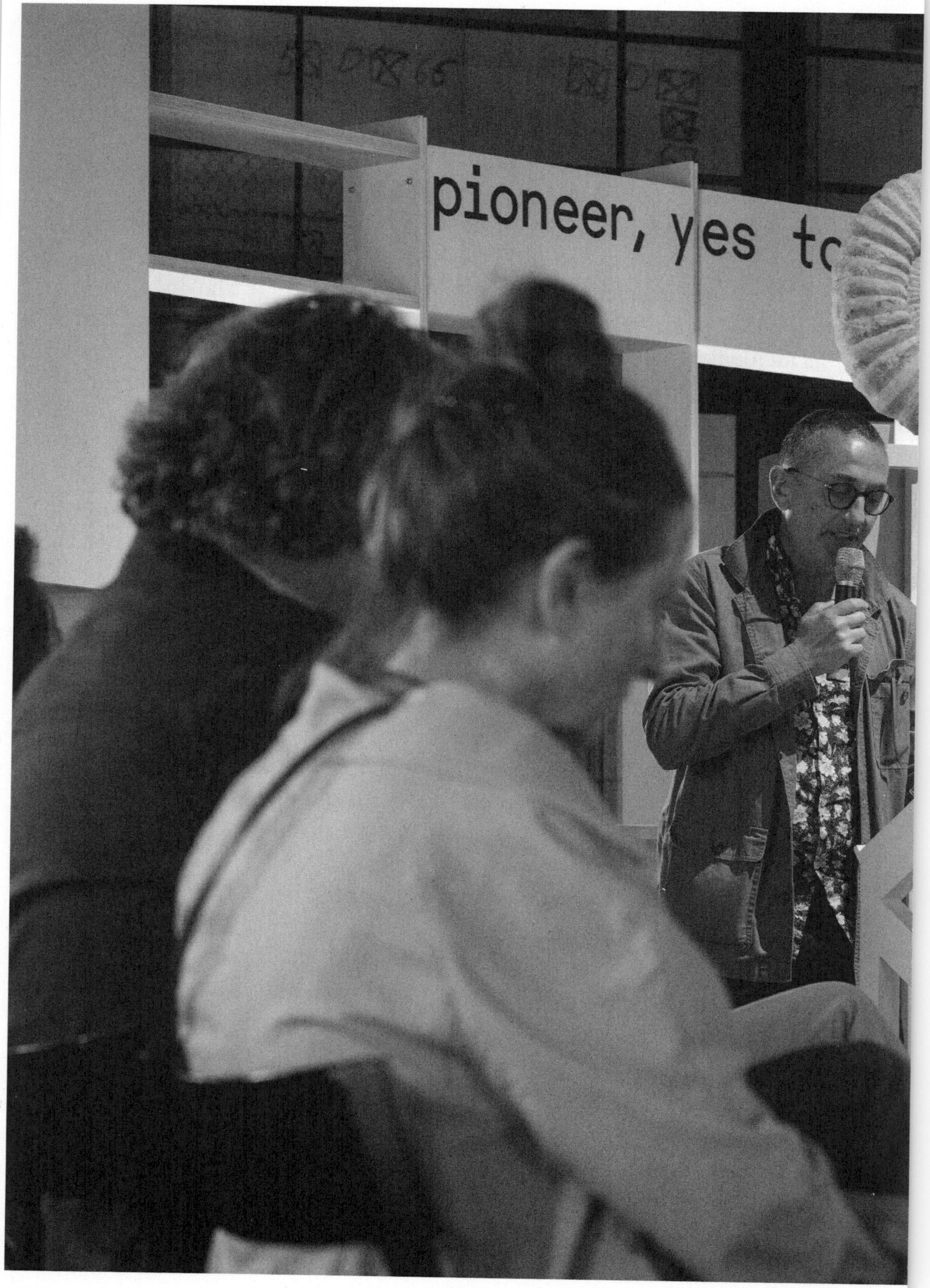
pioneer, yes to

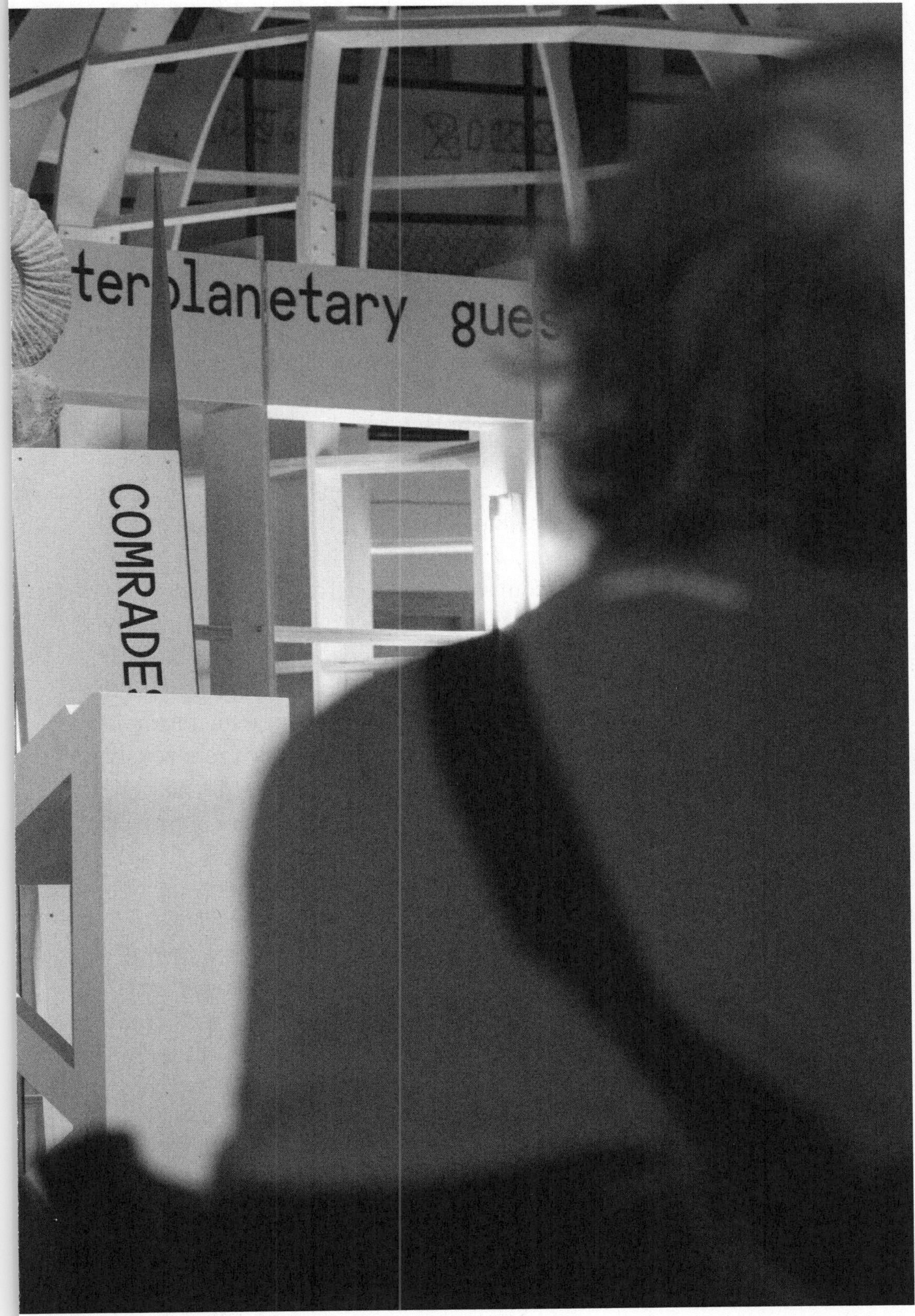

Jonas Staal, *Interplanetary Species Society*, Reaktorhallen, Stockholm, 2019

termed it, in a somewhat infelicitous phrase—needed to be complemented with a "viertes Reich" of *possible* things that emerge out of human activity.[100] In a later volume coauthored with Dessauer, *Befreiung der Technik*, Meissinger attempted to "insert" technology into the third *Critique*, as a third way between nature and the aesthetic.[101]

Dessauer and Meissinger took issue with the subservient place which Karl Eduard Spranger had accorded the technical in his book *Lebensformen*. Supplementing Spranger's catalogue of human character types, Dessauer posits a "technical type" as counterpart to Spranger's "theoretical type." For Spranger, technology could not be considered a distinct *Lebensform*, an autonomous *Wertgebiet*; it is purely instrumental and has no values of its own.[102] The notion of the *Lebensform* (life-form, or form of life) was everywhere in early twentieth-century German discourse; it graced the titles of serious philosophical tomes and etiquette books alike. It has its roots in early nineteenth-century biology. As Stefan Helmreich and Sophia Roosth have recently put it, the concept "bears an inheritance from Kant and Goethe (though this exact word was used by neither) in which form is aesthetic, self-determining, and teleological, as well as (generously assuming sufficient knowledge of the mechanism of its formation) deductively predictable (even if the favored apprehensional approach was often a combination of the intuitive and empirical)."[103]

While its biological meaning remained strong, thanks in part to Ernst Haeckel, it also came to be applied to social forms. In Plessner's philosophical anthropology, the specifically human Lebensform is precisely that which is decentered. To be human is to be "unrealized" in "artificial forms of action, in habits and customs." In Plessner's great phrase, artifice comes naturally to humans; human nature *is* culture.[104] One might say that humans can only live by *leading a life*, or by transmuting *zoē* into *bios*—to reference Agamben, one of the thinkers who have taken up the concept of the form of life in recent decades.[105]

In the present anthropogenic and anthropocenic emergency, the question is: How to create sustainable forms of life among the unlivable forms of real abstraction, inside the accelerating catastrophe of hypercapitalism, and against resurgent fascism? In line with Agency's and Staal's projects, one might concretize this as: How to assemble, as humans and nonhumans, as persons and as surplus populations, as mutants and fossils, in various forms of collaboration and organization? How to socialize otherwise—as human and nonhuman persons, as persons and nonpersons—so as to become a contingent obstacle and obstruction that cannot be reincorporated into business as usual?

These questions will be taken up in
Personafications: Forms of Abstraction, Vol. 2

NOTES

1 Adam Müller, "Vom Gedankenfrieden in Deutschland," in *Deutsche Staats-Anzeigen I* (Leipzig: Voss'sche Buchhandlung, 1816), 10.

2 See Joan Steigerwald, "Rethinking Organic Vitality in Germany at the Turn of the Nineteenth Century," in *Vitalism and the Scientific Image in Post-Enlightenment Life Science, 1800–2010*, ed. Sebastian Normandin and Charles T. Wolfe (Dordrecht: Springer, 2013), 51–75.

3 Donna J. Haraway, *Crystals, Fabrics, and Fields: Metaphors of Organicism in Twentieth-Century Developmental Biology* (New Haven, CT: Yale University Press, 1976), 147.

4 Pierre Bertaux, *La mutation humaine* (Paris: Payot, 1964), 55–57.

5 Matteo Pasquinelli, "Politics of Abstraction," *Open!*, October 1, 2013, http://www.onlineopen.org/columns/the-politics-of-abstraction/2.

6 Donna J. Haraway, *When Species Meet* (Minneapolis: University of Minnesota Press, 2008), 3.

7 Bik Van der Pol, "Birds Must Be Eliminated," http://m.bikvanderpol.net/468/birds_must_be_eliminated/.

8 As a kind of footnote to *Birds Must Be Eliminated*, in 2013 Bik Van der Pol invited a local bird breeders' club to participate in the performance *Not all those who wander are lost*, during which a number of local hobby societies and clubs demonstrated their activities in the Utrecht shopping center Hoog Catharijne, as part of the art project "Call of the Mall." It was performed on July 6 and September 21.

9 *Ad Valvas* (Vrije Universiteit weekly), February 24, 2005, 1, 3.

10 See Emily Martin, "Pigs as People; People as Pigs," in *A House for Pigs and People: Carsten Höller, Rosemarie Trockel* (Cologne: Verlag der Buchhandlung Walther König, 1997), 13–19.

11 See Sabeth Buchmann, "Von der High-Tech-Tauglichkeit der Kunst," *Die Beute*, no. 4 (1995): 68–77.

12 Carsten Höller and Rosemarie Trockel, "Introduction," in *A House for Pigs and People*, 7–12.

13 John Bellamy Foster, *Marx's Ecology: Materialism and Nature* (New York: Monthly Review Press, 2000), 9.

14 Foster, 7–9, 10.

15 Karl Marx and Friedrich Engels, crossed-out passage from the manuscript of *Die Deutsche Ideologie* (1845), in *Marx-Engels-Werke*, Bd. 3 (Berlin: Dietz, 1978), 18; for the English translation, see http://www.marxists.org/archive/marx/works/1845/german-ideology/ch01a.htm.

16 Foster, *Marx's Ecology*, 229–30.

17 Joseph V. Stalin, "Dialectical and Historical Materialism" (1938), https://www.marxists.org/reference/archive/stalin/works/1938/09.htm. See also David Craven, "Meyer Schapiro, Karl Korsch and the Emergence of Critical Theory," in *Art History as Social Praxis: The Collected Writings of David Craven*, ed. Brian Winkenweder (Chicago: Haymarket Books, 2017), 188–216.

18 Quoted in Foster, *Marx's Ecology*, 9.

19 Karl Marx, "On the Jewish Question" (1843), quoted in Foster, *Marx's Ecology*, 74.

20 Herbert Marcuse, "Cultural Revolution" (ca. 1970), in *Towards a Critical Theory of Society*, vol. 2 of *Collected Papers*, ed. Douglas Kellner (London: Routledge, 2001), 132.

21 Marx and Engels, *Die Deutsche Ideologie*, 30–31; for the English translation, see https://www.marxists.org/archive/marx/works/1845/german-ideology/ch01a.htm.

22 Jussi Parikka, *Insect Media: An Archaeology of Animals and Technology* (Minneapolis: University of Minnesota Press, 2010), 72.

23 Friedrich Engels, "Der Anteil der Arbeit an der Menschwerdung des Affen," an unfinished 1876 text that is part of the *Dialektik der Natur*, in *Marx-Engels-Werke*, Bd. 20 (Berlin: Dietz, 1990), 444–55; for the English translation, see http://www.marxists.org/archive/marx/works/1876/part-played-labour/index.htm. Haraway is mistaken when she states that it was Sherwood Washburn who "generated the theory of tool use as the motor of evolution of the human body," but her feminist critique of such theories remains pertinent. Donna J. Haraway, *Simians, Cyborgs, and Women: The Reinvention of Nature* (London: Free Association Books, 1991), 25. On recent theories about fire and cooking, see James C. Scott, *Against the Grain: A Deep History of the Earliest States* (New Haven, CT: Yale University Press, 2017), 17, 40–42.

24 Sigmund Freud, *Das Unbehagen in der Kultur* (1930), in *Das Unbehagen in der Kultur und andere Schriften* (Frankfurt am Main: Fischer, 1994), 57; in contrast to the dominant English translation of Freud's *ein Prothesengott* as "a prosthetic God," a lowercase "god" would seem to be called for here. Helmuth Plessner, *Die Stufen des Organischen und der Mensch: Einleitung in die philosophische Anthropologie* (1928; Berlin: De Gruyter, 1975), 316.

25 Devin Fiore discusses Gehlen's use of *Mängelwesen* in relation to Negt/Kluge's *Mangelmutant* in his introduction to Oskar Negt and Alexander Kluge, *History and Obstinacy*, trans. Richard Langston et al. (New York: Zone Books, 2014), 25. Having worked with Adorno, Kluge must have been well aware of the former's public postwar debates with Gehlen, a conservative and former Nazi. In a 2019 conversation, in response to a prompt by the interviewer, Kluge effectively uses Gehlen's Mängelwesen and Mangelmutant as synonyms. See Nils Markwardt, "Das Zwerchfell besitzt rebellische Fähigkeiten," *Philosophie Magazin*, no. 2 (2019), https://philomag.de/das-zwerchfell-besitzt-rebellische-faehigkeiten/.

26 G. W. F. Hegel, *Vorlesungen über die Philosophie der Geschichte* (Frankfurt am Main: Suhrkamp, 1970), 389.

27 Freud, *Das Unbehagen in der Kultur*, 64–65.

28 Andrew Russeth, "Constant Displacement: Pierre Huyghe on His Work at Skulptur Projekte Münster," *ArtNews*, June 26, 2017, http://www.artnews.com/2017/06/26/constant-displacement-pierre-huyghe-on-his-work-at-skulptur-projekte-munster-2017/.

29 Marga Bijvoet, *Art as Inquiry: Toward New Collaborations between Art, Science, and Technology* (New York: Peter Lang, 1997), 81. For Haacke, Burnham, and systems aesthetics in general, see Bijvoet as well as Luke Skrebowski, "All Systems Go: Recovering Hans Haacke's Systems Art," *Grey Room*, no. 30 (Winter 2008): 54–83; Caroline A. Jones, "Reconstituting 'Systems Art,'" in *Hans Haacke 1967* (Cambridge, MA: MIT List Visual Art Center, 2011), 4–27, http://listart.mit.edu/exhibitions/hans-haacke-1967; and Alexander Alberro and Nora M. Alter, "Systems, Dialectics, and Castles in the Sky," in *Hans Haacke: Castles in the Sky* (Madrid: Museo Nacional Centro de Arte Reina Sofía, 2012), 20–29.

30 Caroline A. Jones, "System Symptoms," *Artforum*, September 2012, 116.

31 Jack Burnham, *Beyond Modern Sculpture: The Effects of Science and Technology on the Sculpture of This Century* (New York: George Braziller, 1968), 16.

32 The great contribution of cybernetics, according to Bertalanffy, had been the model of feedback regulation in both technology and biology—in the latter, homeostasis can be explained by the feedback model. Like cybernetics, systems theory has an implicit ideal of equilibrium; the living organism manages to overcome entropy and achieve a "fantastically improbable state" of equilibrium because it is an open system that can regulate its relations with the environment through negative feedback. Ludwig von Bertalanffy, *General System Theory: Foundations, Development, Applications* (New York: George Braziller, 1969), 159, 161–63.

33 See Jack Burnham, "Real Time Systems" (1969), in *Great Western Salt Works: Essays on the Meaning of Post-formalist Art* (New York: George Braziller, 1974), 29–30.

34 Burnham, *Beyond Modern Sculpture*, 53.

35 Burnham, "Real Time Systems," 30.

36 Flow charts for the unrealized "Software" version of *Visitors' Poll*, Hans Haacke's personal archive.

37 Robert Lilienfeld, *The Rise of Systems Theory: An Ideological Analysis* (New York: Wiley, 1978), 227.

38 *SEEK* was deemed sufficiently emblematic of "Software" for it to be illustrated on the cover of the catalogue.

39 Max Kozloff, "The Multimillion Dollar Art Boondoggle," *Artforum*, October 1971, 72–76.

40 See Fred Turner, "The Politics of the Whole circa 1968—and Now," in Diederichsen and Franke, *The Whole Earth*, 43–48. See also (without direct reference to the *Whole Earth Catalog*) Luther Blisset, "Adam Curtis, Self-Organisation and UK Uncut: An Ecology of Weeds," *New Left Project*, May 30, 2011, http://www.newleftproject.org/index.php/site/blog_comments/adam_curtis_self_organisation_and_uk_uncut_an_ecology_of_weeds (site discontinued); and Mark Fisher, "After Networks: In Defense of Adam

Curtis," *New Left Project*, July 20, 2011, http://www.newleftproject.org/index.php/site/article_comments/after_networks_in_defence_of_adam_curtis (site discontinued).

41 Brian Holmes, "Cybernetics, Epistemological Struggles, Unwanted Consequences?," *Continental Drift* (blog), July 28, 2013, http://brianholmes.wordpress.com/2013/07/28/3215/.

42 Arthur G. Tansley, "The Use and Abuse of Vegetational Concepts and Terms," *Ecology* 16, no. 3 (July 1935): 284–307. A search of the *New York Times* archive shows that the term "ecosystem" starts being used in 1967 and 1968, but the frequency rises dramatically in 1969 and 1970.

43 Gregory Bateson, *Steps to an Ecology of Mind: Collected Essays in Anthropology, Psychiatry, Evolution, and Epistemology* (1972; Chicago: University of Chicago Press, 2000), 477–501.

44 *Hans Haacke: Unfinished Business*, ed. Rosalyn Deutsche and Brian Wallis (Cambridge, MA: MIT Press, 1986), 80–81.

45 See Burnham, "Real Time Systems," 27–38. Here Burnham discusses several projects by Haacke.

46 Klein's work was, of course, a crucial reference point for the Zero movement, which Haacke was associated with in the mid-1960s.

47 Haacke explicitly stated at the time that his work is about "interference in" systems. See Lucy Lippard, *Six Years: The Dematerialization of the Art Object from 1966 to 1962* (1973; Berkeley: University of California Press, 1997), 123.

48 Hans Haacke, "Rheinwasseraufbereitungsanlage, 1972," in *Hans Haacke: "Obra social"* (Barcelona: Fundació Antoni Tàpies, 1995), 76. See also T. J. Demos, "The Politics of Sustainability: Art and Ecology," in *Radical Nature: Art and Architecture for a Changing Planet, 1969–2009* (London: Koenig Books, 2009), 22.

49 Félix Guattari, *The Three Ecologies* (1989), trans. Ian Pindar and Paul Sutton (London: Athlone Press, 2000), 43.

50 See documentation of the piece (*Untitled*, 1969), in the CCCA Canadian Art Database, http://ccca.concordia.ca/traffic/artists/pages/haacke.html.

51 See the exhibition catalogue *Maisons/Häuser: Carsten Höller, Rosemarie Trockel* (Cologne: Oktagon, 1999). Curiously, the catalogue

published on the occasion of Trockel's 2015 exhibition at Kunsthaus Bregenz lists *Silberfischchenhaus* as a solo work by Trockel.

52 Bik Van der Pol, "are you really sure that a floor can't also be a ceiling?," https://bikvanderpol.net/168/are_you_really_sure_that_a_floor_cant_also_be_a_ceiling/.

53 Bik Van der Pol, "are you really sure that a floor can't also be a ceiling?"

54 Enel Contemporanea Award press release, March 9, 2010, https://www.enel.com/media/explore/search-press-releases/press/2010/03/enel-contemporanea-award-2010-and-the-winner-is-dutch-artist-duo-bik-van-der-pol-.

55 Gilles Deleuze and Félix Guattari, *A Thousand Plateaus: Capitalism and Schizophrenia* (1980), trans. Brian Massumi (London: Athlone Press, 1988), 51.

56 Deleuze and Guattari, 51.

57 On Uexküll's politics, see Torsten Rüting, "History and Significance of Jakob von Uexküll and of His Institute in Hamburg," *Sign Systems Studies* 32, nos. 1/2 (2004): 40–44.

58 Rüting, 50; and Jakob von Uexküll, *Streifzüge durch die Umwelten von Tiere und Menschen* (1934; Hamburg: Rowohlt, 1956), 30–31.

59 Uexküll, 53.

60 Uexküll, 66–67, 97.

61 Pierre Huyghe, interview by Timothee Chaillou, *Double*, no. 22 (Fall/Winter 2011), http://www.timotheechaillou.com/conversations/pierre-huyghe/. The protocol for "Influants," which used to be on the Esther Schipper website but has since been taken down, stated: "Prior to the exhibition, a person with the flu has to be found. It is best if the person is already associated with the space, and naturally encounters people entering the space. If this person cannot be found, find a person that will accept to be injected with the 'flu shot' or a small cold. For the exhibition 'Influants' in Berlin, Xanaflu was used." Xanaflu is an inactivated vaccine that is not infectious and does not normally produce flulike symptoms (or a "small cold") in the injected person. Given the health risks of an influenza infection, this is perhaps for the better. Huyghe's installations are obviously speculative propositions rather than scientific experiments, but the fuzzy rhetoric produced by the artist and his curatorial and institu-

tional collaborators can nonetheless be needlessly mystifying.

62 Pierre Huyghe, "UUmwelt," Serpentine Galleries, https://www.serpentinegalleries.org/exhibitions-events/pierre-huyghe-uumwelt.

63 See, for instance, "Pierre Huyghe in Conversation with Hans Ulrich Obrist," YouTube video, 1:12:33, October 3, 2018, https://www.youtube.com/watch?v=emYOOVRzG8E.

64 Craven, "Meyer Schapiro, Karl Korsch and the Emergence of Critical Theory," 188–89.

65 Bik Van der Pol, *Catching Some Air: Library Drawings* (Leeds: Henry Moore Institute, 2002), n.p.

66 *Pierre Huyghe*, ed. Emma Lavigne (Munich: Hirmer, 2013), 85.

67 Stewart Brand, "CoEvolution," *CoEvolution Quarterly*, no. 1 (Spring 1974), inside cover.

68 As seen in the previous chapter, Brand was willing to abandon the Earth as a traditional site of coevolution and, presumably, most species on it as he started to promote the idea of space colonization. His latest hobby horse is "deextinction": genetically reverse-engineering and reintroducing extinct species.

69 Jerry Mander, "Four Arguments for the Elimination of Television," *CoEvolution Quarterly*, no. 16 (Winter 1977/78): 40.

70 Mander, 45.

71 Mander, 49.

72 See also Sven Lütticken, *History in Motion: Time in the Age of the Moving Image* (Berlin: Sternberg Press, 2013), 192–95; and Lütticken, *Cultural Revolution: Aesthetic Practice after Autonomy* (Berlin: Sternberg Press, 2017), 29, 54n21, 60.

73 In the Netherlands, the *kabouter* is an iconic representative of the "little folk," donned with a pointy hat and (in male kabouters) a beard. The translation of kabouter into an equally recognizable and broadly equivalent English term proved difficult, however. Possibly owing to his Theosophical roots or Tolkien's popularity in the counterculture, Van Duijn, at first, opted for "elves"—even though the more uniquely Tolkienian "hobbit" would come closer to what the figure of the kabouter stands for (differences in size notwithstanding). See Roel van Duijn, "Message from Elfencity," *Aloha*, February 20, 1970, 1; and Van Duijn, "Orange Free State," *Aloha*, May 29, 1970, 4. For use

of the term "hobbit" in the context of the Kabouter movement, see "De hobbit," *Aloha*, July 24, 1970, 2.

74 Roel van Duijn, *De boodschap van een wijze kabouter* (Amsterdam: Meulenhoff, 1969), 89–90.

75 See the chronology in Coen Tasman, *Louter Kabouter: Kroniek van een beweging* (Amsterdam: Babylon-De Geus, 1996), 392.

76 Bik Van der Pol, whose *All Birds Must Be Eliminated* had been the target of animal rights activists, also received criticism when they exhibited their piece *Speechless* in Miami: in an aviary decorated with colorful letters that could be used to spell out "global warming," "climate change," and "sustainability" (contested terms in Republican-run Florida and also under Trump on the national level) sit four parrots that have been taught phrases from T. S. Eliot's *The Waste Land*. Like *All Birds Must Be Eliminated*, and like the 1974 Marcel Broodthaers installation with a parrot whose planned acquisition by the Musée d'Art Moderne de la Ville de Paris was canceled in 2002 after protests, this piece proved controversial. One critic noted that parrots have the intelligence of a four-year-old, and while admitting that the parrots seemed well cared for, asked: "Would you be OK with four-year-olds being held in a cage for seven months in the name of art?" Questioning "the use of intelligent animals as part of a display," the author was reminded of the case of "Ota Benga, a Congolese man who was part of an exhibit at the Bronx Zoo in 1906. At the time people presumed Benga's intelligence and cognition to be equal to that of monkeys. Mayor George B. McClellan, Jr. eventually released Benga, but he fell into a depression and committed suicide at the age of 32." While not claiming equivalence between a parrot and a Black man, the author still maintains that holding highly intelligent animals in captivity is problematic—in a text that wavers between attempts to make a cogent case and angry rhetoric. Scout McEachron, "Four Parrots in a Cage Isn't Art! Four Parrots in a Cage Isn't Art!," *Hyperallergic*, February 18, 2016, https://hyperallergic.com/276878/four-parrots-in-a-cage-isnt-art-four-parrots-in-a-cage-isnt-art/.

77 *Left Legalism / Left Critique*, ed. Wendy Brown and Janet Halley (Durham, NC: Duke University Press, 2002).

78 Wendy Brown, “Suffering the Paradoxes of Rights,” in Brown and Halley, *Left Legalism / Left Critique*, 420–34.

79 Eyal Weizman, “Are They Human?,” *e-flux Architecture*, October 10, 2016, https://www.e-flux.com/architecture/superhumanity/68645/are-they-human/.

80 Weizman, “Are They Human?”

81 See, for instance, Tony Fry, *Becoming Human by Design* (London: Berg, 2012), 205–9, 219.

82 Meagan Flynn, “Monkey Loses Selfie Copyright Case. Maybe Monkey Should Sue PETA, Appeals Court Suggests,” *Washington Post*, April 24, 2018, https://www.washingtonpost.com/news/morning-mix/wp/2018/04/24/monkey-loses-selfie-copyright-case-maybe-monkey-should-sue-peta-appeals-court-suggests/?utm_term=.706668bfb3ee.

83 Brett Buchanan, *Onto-ethologies: The Animal Environments of Uexküll, Heidegger, Merleau-Ponty, and Deleuze* (Albany, NY: SUNY Press, 2008), 13, 185.

84 G. W. F. Hegel, *Grundlinien der Philosophie des Rechts* (Frankfurt am Main: Suhrkamp, 1970), §35, p. 95.

85 I will discuss the person/property form of juridical abstraction more extensively in the second volume, *Personafications*.

86 See Agency, “Assembly (Animism),” in *Animism (Volume 1)*, ed. Anselm Franke (Berlin: Sternberg Press, 2010), 146.

87 Agency, *Thing 000773 (Pseudomonas)*, text as part of the presentation in context of Beelden op de Berg, Wageningen, 2013.

88 Agency, *Thing 000773 (Pseudomonas)*.

89 Agency, *Thing 000773 (Pseudomonas)*.

90 The “parliament of things” was first proposed in the conclusion of Bruno Latour, *We Have Never Been Modern*, trans. Catherine Porter (Cambridge, MA: Harvard University Press, 1993), 142–45. Karen Barad has rightly pointed out that Latour’s focus on overcoming the human/nonhuman divide means that he tends to essentialize the human and to disregard the work of feminist, queer, decolonial, and Marxist theorists; “Nonhumans are in, but the concerns of this motley crew of theorists and activists seem not to have been heard, let alone taken into account.” Barad, *Meeting the Universe Halfway: Quantum*

Physics and the Entanglement of Matter and Meaning (Durham, NC: Duke University Press, 2007), 58. It is only in his recent work that Latour acknowledges, again in rather broad and abstract terms, a split between (modern) humans and those he calls the "Earthbound." Latour, *Facing Gaia: Eight Lectures on the New Climate Regime*, trans. Catherine Porter (Cambridge: Polity, 2017), 246–54.

91 "Embassy of the North Sea," Parliament of Things, https://theparliamentofthings.org/case/embassy-of-the-north-sea/.

92 Jonas Staal, "Interplanetary Species Society," 2019, http://jonasstaal.nl/projects/interplanetary-species-society/. If the actual assembly did not live up to its potential, for reasons that need not be discussed here, Staal has nevertheless provided a crucial model.

93 Burnham, *Beyond Modern Sculpture*, 50. It should be noted that Burnham's account of vitalism, and particularly of Bergson, is highly reductive.

94 Burnham, 49.

95 Yuk Hui, *Recursivity and Contingency* (London: Rowan & Littlefield, 2019), 9.

96 Steigerwald, "Rethinking Organic Vitality," 55–56.

97 Steigerwald, 68.

98 Gilbert Simondon, *On the Mode of Existence of Technical Objects* (1958), trans. Cécile Malaspina and John Rogove (Minneapolis, MN: Univocal, 2017), 184; Hui, *Recursivity and Contingency*, 188–89.

99 Hui, 187–278.

100 Friedrich Dessauer, *Philosophie der Technik: Das Problem der Realisierung* (Bonn: Friedrich Cohen, 1928), 49–66.

101 Friedrich Dessauer and Karl August Meissinger, *Befreiung der Technik* (Stuttgart: Cotta, 1931), 54–67. The chapter in question was written by Meissinger.

102 Dessauer and Meissinger, 12–53. Eduard Spranger's *Lebensformen* (Halle: Niemeyer, 1914/1921) was a veritable bestseller during the 1920s.

103 Stefan Helmreich and Sophia Roosth, "Life Forms: A Keyword Entry," in Stefan Helmreich, *Sounding the Limits of Life: Essays in the Anthropology of Biology and Beyond* (Princeton, NJ: Princeton University Press, 2016) 24.

104 Plessner, *Die Stufen des Organischen und der Mensch*, 316.

105 Giorgo Agamben, *Homo Sacer: Sovereign Power and Bare Life*, trans. Daniel Heller-Roazen (Stanford, CA: Stanford University Press, 1998).

IMAGE CREDITS

Introduction

p. 13 — Graffiti written on a wall of the Scheringa Museum of Realist Art, Spanbroek, 2009. Photo: Michiel Eijsbouts.

p. 13 — "This is a form." Illustration in Paul Chan, "Our Data, Our Selves," *Los Angeles Review of Books*, September 19, 2019, https://lareviewofbooks.org/article/our-data-our-selves/.

p. 22 — Willem de Rooij, *Residual*, Bentheim Castle, 2012, installation view. Courtesy of the artist.

p. 23 — De Rijke / De Rooij, *Bouquet II*, 2003. Courtesy of Willem de Rooij.

pp. 28–29 — Louise Lawler, *Cabinet 2, Shelf 14*, 1997/1999. Silver dye bleach print, 48.3 × 93.3 cm. Courtesy of the artist and Metro Pictures.

Chapter 1

pp. 44, 45, 46 — Gert Jan Kocken, *Judenporzellan*, 2009, details and exhibition view. Courtesy of the artist.

p. 58 — "European colonial fetishes" on display in the exhibition "La vérité sur les colonies," 1931. Illustration in *Le Surréalisme au Service de la Révolution*, no. 4 (December 1931).

p. 65 — Willem de Rooij, "Intolerance," Neue Nationalgalerie, Berlin, 2010–11, exhibition view. Photo: Jens Ziehe. Courtesy of the artist.

p. 65 — "The Potosí Principle," Museo Nacional Centro de Arte Reina Sofía, Madrid, 2010–11, exhibition view. Photo: Andreas Siekmann.

pp. 68–69 — Museum of American Art, *Sites of Modernity (Collection of the Museum of Antiquities) (1502–2010)*, 2010. Installation, dimensions variable. Van Abbemuseum, Eindhoven. Photo: Peter Cox.

p. 70 — Tania Bruguera, *Arte Útil*, 2009/2016, installation view. Van Abbemuseum, Eindhoven. Photo: Peter Cox. © ARS, New York / DACS, London 2022.

p. 70 — Agency, *Thing 001390 (Ten Dollar Bank Note)*, 2016. Courtesy of Agency.

p. 81 — Kader Attia screening an extract from *The Body's Legacies, Part 2: The Postcolonial Body* (2018), at the symposium "The White West," La Colonie, Paris, May 2018. Photo: Sven Lütticken. Courtesy of the artist.

p. 81 — Still from Kader Attia, *The Body's Legacies, Part 2: The Postcolonial Body*, 2018. Courtesy of the artist.

pp. 82–83 — "The Chimurenga Library," The Showroom, London, 2015, exhibition view. Curated by Chimurenga, the Otolith Collective, and the Showroom. Photo: Dan Weill Photography.

Chapter 2

p. 100 — *Coalbrookdale Illustrated Spring Catalogue* (Coalbrookdale, 1888), 13.

p. 103 — P. P. Caproni and Brother, *Catalogue of Plaster Cast Reproductions from Antique, Medieval and Modern Sculpture* (Boston, 1901), 120.

pp. 104–5 P. P. Caproni and Brother, *Catalogue of Plaster Cast Reproductions from Antique, Medieval and Modern Sculpture* (Boston, 1901), 11.

p. 112 Louise Lawler, *Storage*, 1984. Gelatin silver print, 38.7 × 58.9 cm. Courtesy of the artist and Metro Pictures.

p. 120 Edward J. Steichen, *Rodin—The Thinker*, 1902. Gelatin silver print, image: 36.2 × 43.8 cm; paper: 36.5 × 44 cm; matted: 55.9 × 66 cm. The Cleveland Museum of Art, Gift of Mr. and Mrs. Thomas A. Mann. Courtesy of the Cleveland Museum of Art. © The Estate of Edward Steichen / ARS, New York / DACS, London 2022.

p. 121 Arnoud Holleman and Gert Jan Kocken, *Broken Thinker*, 2016. http://www.brokenthinker.nl. Courtesy of the artists.

p. 128 Sean Snyder, *CCD Digital Image Sensor (5 Layers)*, 2009, detail. Courtesy of the artist.

p. 129 Plaster casts and two parts of Sean Snyder's *CCD Digital Image Sensor (5 Layers)* (2009), "The Imaginary Museum," Kunstverein München, 2012, exhibition view. Courtesy of Sean Snyder.

p. 130 Louise Lawler, *She Wasn't Always a Statue (A)*, 1996/1997. Gelatin silver print, 45.1 × 47 cm. Courtesy of the artist and Metro Pictures.

p. 131 Louise Lawler, *Hand on Her Back (traced)*, 1997/1998 /2013. Adhesive wall material, dimensions variable at any scale determined by exhibitor. Courtesy of the artist and Metro Pictures, New York.

p. 134 Sean Snyder, *0.99€*, 2015. Courtesy of the artist.

p. 137 "Nymph Preparing for the Bath." Three D Scans, https://threedscans.com/lincoln/nymph. Screenshot, 2022.

p. 139 Plaster cast at Villa Vassilieff, Paris, 2016. Photo: Sven Lütticken.

Chapter 3

pp. 154–55, 154 Stills from Zachary Formwalt, *An Unknown Quantity*, 2015. Single-channel HD video, sound, 39 min. Courtesy of the artist.

p. 155 Andrea Fraser, *Index*, 2011. Originally published in *Artforum* (Summer 2011), as part of Jacob Fabricius's project "24 Advertisements." Courtesy of the artist.

p. 160 Perspectival schema of the *Last Supper* of Dirk Bouts (Louvain, St. Peter, 1464–67), after G. Doehlemann. Illustration in Erwin Panofsky, *Perspective as Symbolic Form*, trans. Christopher S. Wood (New York: Zone Books, 1991), 61 (fig. 7).

p. 161 "The Last Zoom," 2020. Meme by unknown artist.

p. 164 John Ruskin's gang of road builders in North Hinksey, June 1874. Photo: Henry Taunt. Courtesy of Oxfordshire County Council – Oxfordshire History Centre.

pp. 178–79 See Red Women's Workshop, *Capitalism Also Depends on Domestic Labour*, 1975. © See Red Women's Workshop.

pp. 188–89 Kate Crawford and Vladen Joler, *Anatomy of an AI System*, 2018, detail. https://anatomyof.ai.

p. 190 Peter Nadin and Christopher D'Arcangelo, announcement of refurbishments, 1978. Courtesy of the estate of Christopher D'Arcangelo.

pp. 194–95, 196, 197 — Hans Haacke, *Seurat's "Les Poseuses" (Small Version), 1888–1975*, 1975, installation view and details. Fourteen panels and color reproduction of *Les Poseuses* by Georges Seurat in the museum frame; framed under glass, panels 70.5 × 60.5 cm each; reproduction 60.6 × 70.5 cm. Courtesy of the artist and Paula Cooper Gallery. © DACS 2022.

p. 200 — Andrea Fraser, *132 €*, 2014. Week 45 of "52 Weeks of Gulf Labor." Published as an advertisement in *Frankfurter Allgemeine Sonntagszeitung*, August 17, 2014. Courtesy of the artist.

p. 201 — Still from Nicole Teeny, *The Writer*, Boston, 2013. Video, 2 min. Performer: Katie Warzak. Courtesy of the artist.

p. 201 — Harun Farocki and Antje Ehmann, "Eine Einstellung zur Arbeit" ("Labour in a Single Shot"), Haus der Kulturen der Welt, Berlin, 2015, exhibition view. Photo: Aya Schamoni / HKW.

Chapter 4

p. 224 — Stills from an MP4 movie on Sean Snyder's (now defunct) website, https://mnemosynedrone.info. Courtesy of the artist.

pp. 226–27 — Riet Wijnen, *Sculpture Sixteen Conversations on Abstraction*, 2016. Courtesy of the artist.

p. 231 — César Domela, *Ruth*, 1928. Photo paper mounted on cardboard, 65 × 47 cm. 1983 print in *7 Photomontages 1928–1934* (Paris: Galerie de France; Genoa: Galleria Martini & Ronchetti, 1983). Kunstmuseum Den Haag. © ADAGP, Paris / DACS, London 2022.

p. 231 — AEG stamp, designed by Peter Behrens, ca. 1910.

p. 236 — Frame enlargements from Alexander Kluge, *Willi Tobler und der Untergang der 6. Flotte* (*Willi Tobler and the Decline of the 6th Fleet*), 1969–70.

p. 237 — Production of Alexander Kluge's science-fiction films at the Hochschule für Gestaltung Ulm, 1969–70.

p. 245 — The Elea 9003 computer installed at the Monte dei Paschi bank, early 1960s. Product design by Ettore Sottsass. Courtesy of Olivetti.

p. 251 — Advertisement for the Valentine typewriter. Product design by Ettore Sottsass. Courtesy of Olivetti.

p. 255 — Title page of Natascha Sadr Haghighian, *Dear Artfukts, Look at My Curve: A Report to an Academy*, 2013. Courtesy of the artist.

pp. 264–65 — Jonas Staal, "Steve Bannon: A Propaganda Retrospective," Het Nieuwe Instituut, Rotterdam, 2018, exhibition view. Photo: Nieuwe Beelden Makers. Courtesy of the artist.

Chapter 5

pp. 296–97 — Illustration in Heinz Haber, *The Walt Disney Story of Our Friend the Atom* (New York: Golden Press, 1956), 17.

pp. 300, 301 — Cloud chamber photographs in Gÿorgy Kepes, *The New Landscape in Art and Science* (Chicago: Paul Theobald, 1956), 200 and 201.

p. 308 — Cover of Denis de Rougemont, *Lettres sur la bombe atomique* (New York: Brentano's, 1946). Artwork by Matta.

pp. 314–15	Guy Debord and Asger Jorn, “Mutant” manifesto, in Jacqueline de Jong's *Situationist Times*, no. 3 (January 1963). Courtesy of Ellef Prestsæter, https://vandal.ist/thesituationisttimes/. Photo: Øivind Möller Bakken.
pp. 320–21	Yves Klein in the *Immaterial Pictorial Sensibility* room at Museum Haus Lange, Krefeld, Germany, January 1961. © Succession Yves Klein c/o ADAGP, Paris / DACS, London 2021. Photo © Charles Wilp / bpk, Berlin.
p. 322	Sigmar Polke, project for “Blockade '69,” Galerie René Block, Berlin, 1969. © The Estate of Sigmar Polke, Cologne / DACS 2022.
p. 323	Exhibition poster for Stanley Brouwn, “durch kosmische strahlen gehen,” Museum Abteiberg, Mönchengladbach, 1970.
pp. 326–27	Robert Barry, *Radiation Installation (Central Park)*, 1969. Courtesy of the artist and Galerie Greta Meert.
pp. 328–29	Susanne Kriemann, *Pechblende (Prologue)*, Prefix ICA, Toronto, 2016, exhibition view. Photo: Sven Lütticken.
pp. 330–31	Taryn Simon, *Black Square XVII*, Garage Museum of Contemporary Art, Moscow, 2015, installation view. © Garage Museum of Contemporary Art.
p. 340	Ei Arakawa and Green Tea Gallery (with Stefan Tcherepnin and Hanna Törnudd), *Yum Yum Vibe*, 2013. Performance at “Japan Syndrome — Amsterdam Version,” Rietveld Academie, Amsterdam. Photo: Malthe Stigaard.

Chapter 6

p. 358	Bik Van der Pol, *Birds Must Be Eliminated (Bird Shot)*, 2000. Installation view, Vrije Universiteit Amsterdam, 2005. Courtesy of the artists.
p. 358	Carsten Höller and Rosemarie Trockel, *Ein Haus für Schweine und Menschen* (*A House for Pigs and People*), documenta X, Kassel, 1997, exhibition view. Photo: Sven Lütticken. © DACS 2022.
pp. 372–73	Hans Haacke, *Rheinwasseraufbereitungsanlage* (*Rhine Water Purification Plant*), Haus Lange Museum, Krefeld, 1972, installation view. Glass and acrylic containers, pump, polluted Rhine water, tubing, filters, chemicals, goldfish, and drainage to garden, dimensions variable. Courtesy of the artist and Paula Cooper Gallery. © DACS 2022.
pp. 374, 375	Carsten Höller and Rosemarie Trockel, *Silberfischchenhaus* (*Silverfish House*), 1999, details. Liesegang® overhead projector, switch, acrylic glass, filter paper, sugar solution, silverfish, 150 × 62 × 54 cm. Courtesy of the artists and Sprüth Magers. © DACS 2022.
p. 378	Bik Van der Pol, *Are you really sure that a floor can't also be a ceiling?*, MACRO, Rome, 2010, exhibition view. Courtesy of the artists.
p. 381	“Umgebung des Seeigels,” and“Umwelt des Seeigels.” Illustrations in Jakob von Uexküll, *Streifzüge durch die Umwelten von Tieren und Menschen* (1934; Hamburg: Rowohlt, 1956), 32 (figs. 19a and 19b).
pp. 384, 385	Pierre Huyghe, *Umwelt*, “Influants,” Esther Schipper, Berlin, 2011, installation views. Ants and spiders on wall, dimensions variable. Courtesy of the artist and Esther Schipper, Berlin. © ADAGP, Paris / DACS, London 2022. Photo © Andrea Rossetti.

pp. 388, 389 — Bik Van der Pol, "library drawings" from *Catching Some Air*, 2000. Courtesy of the artists.

p. 392 — Roel van Duijn and car with roof garden, Amsterdam, October 1969. Photo: Ruud Hoff. © Hollandse Hoogte / Shutterstock.

pp. 396–97 — Agency, *Thing 001652 (Monkey's Selfies)*, Contour Biennale 8, Mechelen, 2017, installation view. Courtesy of Agency.

p. 398 — Agency, *Thing 000773 (Pseudomonas)*, 2013. Courtesy of Agency.

pp. 404–5 — Jonas Staal, *Interplanetary Species Society*, Reaktorhallen, Stockholm, Sweden, 2019. Public Art Agency Sweden. Photo: Jonas Staal. Courtesy of the artist.

ABOUT THE AUTHOR

Sven Lütticken is an art historian. He is associate professor at Leiden University's Academy of Creative and Performing Arts / PhDArts, and he coordinates the research master's track Critical Studies in Art and Culture at the Vrije Universiteit Amsterdam. He is the author of *Secret Publicity: Essays on Contemporary Art* (NAi Publishers, 2005), and *Idols of the Market: Modern Iconoclasm and the Fundamentalist Spectacle* (2009), *History in Motion: Time in the Age of the Moving Image* (2013), and *Cultural Revolution: Aesthetic Practice after Autonomy* (2017), all published by Sternberg Press.

COLOPHON

Sven Lütticken
Objections
Forms of Abstraction, Vol. 1

Published by Sternberg Press

Copyeditor	Sarah Stephenson
Proofreading	Zoë Harris
Image research	Zoë Harris
Design	Rogier Delfos
Printing	Tallinn Book Printers

ISBN 978-3-95679-530-5

Distribution	The MIT Press Art Data Les presses du réel Idea Books

Sternberg Press
71–75 Shelton Street
London WC2H 9JQ
www.sternberg-press.com

Sternberg Press